THE
LAND OF THE LAMAS

THE
LAND OF THE LAMAS

NOTES OF A JOURNEY THROUGH
CHINA, MONGOLIA AND TIBET

WITH MAPS AND ILLUSTRATIONS

BY
WILLIAM WOODVILLE ROCKHILL

GYAN

Published by

GYAN

Gyan Publishing House
5, Ansari Road
Daryaganj, New Delhi-110002
Phone: 011-47034999, 9811692060
E-mail: books@gyanbooks.com

Distribution Network
gyanbooks.com
India, USA, Canada, UK, Australia, France

ISBN : 978-81-212-2367-6 (PB)
First Published, 1891

2nd Impression 2021

Printed at: Gyan Press, Delhi.

The Land of the Lamas
Author: William Woodville Rockhill

THE LAND OF THE LAMAS

NOTES OF A JOURNEY THROUGH CHINA MONGOLIA AND TIBET

WITH MAPS AND ILLUSTRATIONS

BY

WILLIAM WOODVILLE ROCKHILL

NEW YORK
THE CENTURY CO.
1891

CHINESE PILGRIM ON THE ROAD TO LH'ASA.

PREFACE

IN the following pages I have endeavored to give the results obtained during a journey of several thousand miles through a very imperfectly known portion of the Chinese Empire. My object has been to supply facts concerning the country, of an historical, geographical, and ethnographical nature, and not to attempt to turn out a well-finished bit of literary work.

Besides the notes collected on my journey, I have been able to improve and complete my work in many cases by those made during a four years' residence in Peking, when I was in daily and intimate intercourse with natives from various parts of Tibet and the border-land of Kan-su. Chinese literature, so rich in geographical and anthropological lore, has also been of great service to me, having supplied me with many facts, and has enabled me to offer explanations of customs, names, etc., which, while they may not always turn out to be correct ones, cannot fail to be of value.

In transcribing native words, whether Chinese, Tibetan, or Mongol, I have used as far as possible the system of transcription of Chinese imagined by Sir Thomas Wade, in which the letters have pretty much the same value as in French. As regards Tibetan, in which language there are a number of sounds foreign to Chinese, I have thought fit to accent some of the vowels, but all, as in the Wade system, are to be pronounced as in French. Tibetan is not, as most Asiatic languages, pronounced as it is written, so I had either to transcribe the written characters, which would have afforded to those unacquainted with the language only absolutely unpronounceable words, or else to give the sounds as heard in the spoken language. I have selected the latter course; those who know Tibetan can easily find the native words thus transcribed, and those who have no knowledge of this language will be spared much trouble, and be able to pronounce the words with the softest of Tibetan accents, that of Lh'asa.

I have passed over as rapidly as possible my journey through China, for the country I traversed has been in great part studied before me by other travelers who have told better than I could possibly do, of its beauty or dreariness, of its resources, of the customs and legendary lore of the people.

The route map is a reduction from my survey on a quarter-inch scale, made with prismatic compass, hypsometer and aneroid; and while I claim no very great degree of exactitude for it, I used every care in its preparation, and I believe it will prove of some value in adding to our knowledge of the topography of the country I traversed and in correcting a few errors of the only two travelers who have, previous to my journey, been over parts of it, General Prjevalsky and Pundit Kishen Singh.

WASHINGTON, January 22, 1891.

CONTENTS

Supplementary Notes and Tables

ILLUSTRATIONS

MAPS.

THE LAND OF THE LAMAS

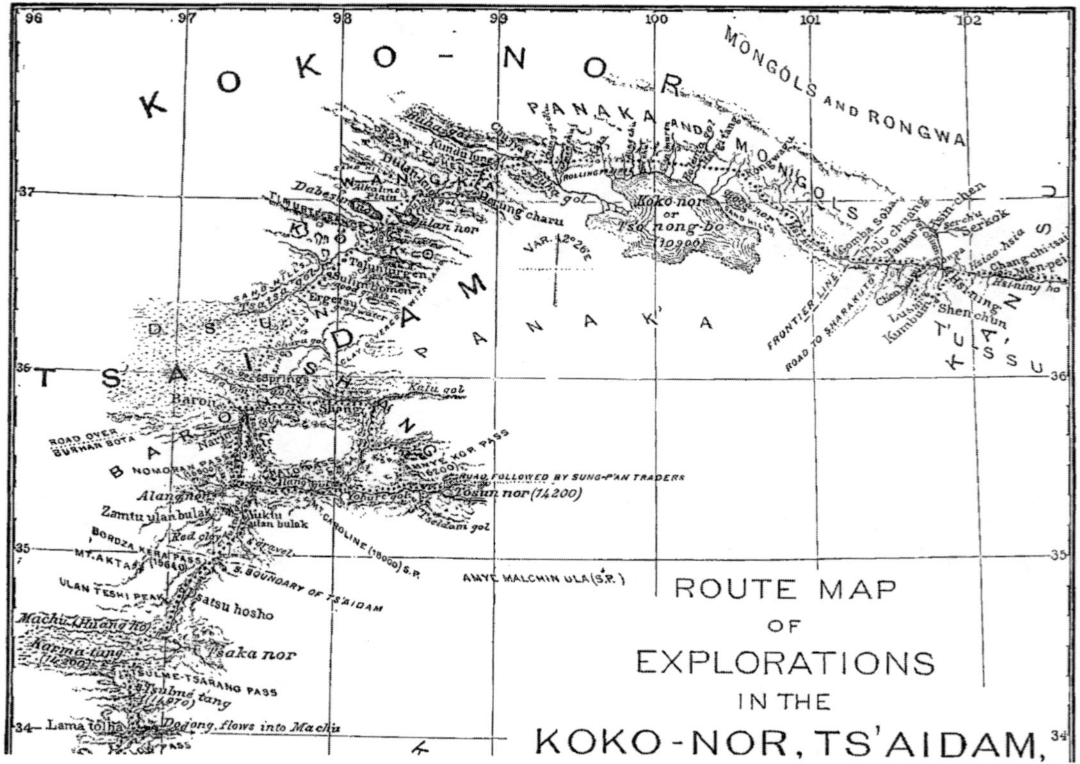
ROUTE MAP
OF
EXPLORATIONS
IN THE
KOKO-NOR, TS'AIDAM,
KOKO-NOR
MONGOLS AND RONGWA
PANAKA AND MONGOLS
TS'AIDAM
PANAKA
DSUN
BARONG
SHANG
KURLUK
T'U-SSU
Koko-nor
or
Tsa-nong-bo
(10900)
VAR. 12°26'E
FRONTIER LINE
ROAD TO SHARAKUTO
Hsi-ning
Shen-chun
Serkok
Kumbum
Dulan-kit
Dabesun
Tsaidam gol
Kalu gol
Alang nor
Tosun nor (14200)
ROAD FOLLOWED BY SUNG-P'AN TRADERS
ROAD OVER BURHAN BOTA
NOMORAN PASS
NIYE KOR PASS
S. BOUNDARY OF TS'AIDAM
ANYE MALCHIN ULA (S.P.)
ULAN TESHI PEAK
MT. AKTA
BORDZA KERA PASS
Zamtu ulan bulak
Machu (Huang ho)
Karma-tang (14200)
Tsaka nor
SULME-TSARANG PASS
Lama tolha
Dogong, flows into Machu
96
97
98
99
100
101
102
37
36
35
34

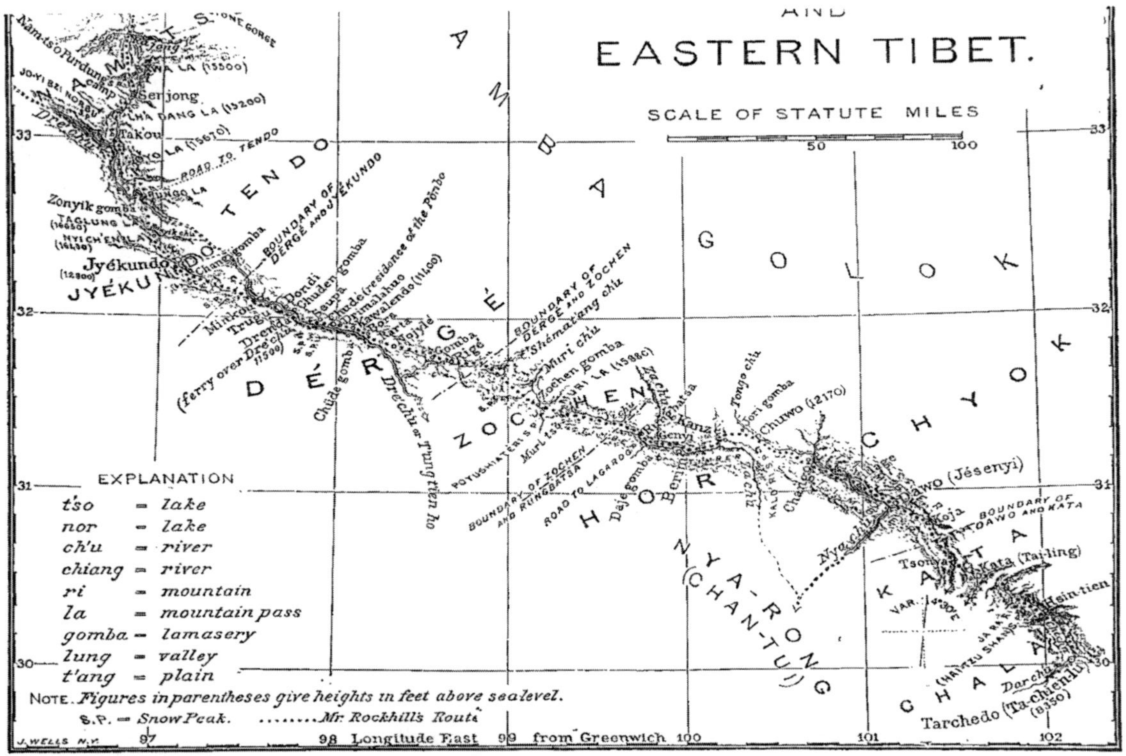
EASTERN TIBET.
SCALE OF STATUTE MILES
50
100
EXPLANATION
t'so = lake
nor = lake
ch'u = river
chiang = river
ri = mountain
la = mountain pass
gomba = lamasery
lung = valley
t'ang = plain
NOTE. Figures in parentheses give heights in feet above sea level.
S.P. = Snow Peak.
........Mr. Rockhill's Route
97
98 Longitude East
99 from Greenwich
100
101
102
33
32
31
30
A M B A
G O L O K
C H Y O K
H O R
N Y A - R O N G
(CHAN-TUI)
C H A L A
K A T A
D É R G É
Z O C H E N
T E N D O
JYÉKUNDO
Jyékundo
(12800)
ROAD TO TENDO
BOUNDARY OF DÉRGÉ AND JYÉKUNDO
BOUNDARY OF DÉRGÉ AND ZOCHEN
Dre ch'u or Tung t'ien ho
(ferry over Dre ch'u)
Chüde gomba
Zonyik gomba
Ser jong
LHA DANG LA (15200)
Takou
Kanzé
Chuwo (12170)
Dawo (Jésenyi)
BOUNDARY OF DAWO AND KATA
Kata (Tai-ling)
Nya ch'u
Tsonya
VAR. 1°30' E
Hsin-tien
Darchi ch'u
Tarchedo (Ta-chien-lu)
(8350)
BOUNDARY OF ZOCHEN AND RUNGBATSA
ROAD TO LAGARONG
Dajé gomba
Berim
Zach'u
Tongo ch'u
Jori gomba
Muri ch'u
Zochen gomba
MURI LA (15880)
Shémat'ang ch'u
Jyude
Nam-tso Purdung's camp
STONE GORGE
J. WELLS N.Y.

THE LAND OF THE LAMAS

I

PEKING, T'AI-YUAN, HSI-AN, LAN-CHOU FU

TIBET has been my life hobby. I began while at college to study the few works written by Europeans on this subject, and was later on led to learn Chinese as a means of gaining further information about the country and its inhabitants. In 1884 I was attached to the United States Legation at Peking, and it seemed then as if I might be able to carry out cherished schemes of exploration in Tibet if I could but learn the spoken language, a knowledge which, from the first, I held to be an absolute requisite of success. No foreigner could help me, for none spoke the language, and none of the natives whom I at first met would consent to teach me, being suspicious of the use I might make of my knowledge. I finally gained the friendship of an intelligent lama from Lh'asa, and with him for the next four years I studied Tibetan, giving also some time to the study of Chinese.

European travelers who had attempted to enter Tibet had usually done so from either India or western China. The frontiers along both these countries are thickly inhabited, or rather the only practicable roads through these border-lands pass by large towns and villages, and so those travelers had found themselves confronted on the very threshold with the one serious obstacle to ingress to the country, a suspicious people, who see in every stranger desirous of visiting their country a dangerous interloper, whose sole purpose is to steal the treasures with which they think their land is teeming, and a possible forerunner of invading armies.

To the north, Tibet is composed of high plateaux intersected by numerous chains of mountains running from east to west, a bleak, arid country, either desert or inhabited by a scattered population of nomads. To the south of these pastoral tribes, and then only in the larger valleys, live a sedentary people who cultivate the soil. Hence it appears that a traveler, coming from the north, can advance much farther into the country without having to fear serious opposition by the people than from any other side.

These considerations and the further fact that the only serious attempt to enter Tibet from the north, that of Fathers Huc and Gabet in 1845, had proved successful, made me choose this route as the one I would follow.

In the winter of 1888, having resigned my post of Secretary of Legation, I made preparations for my journey. The route selected was the highway, which, passing by Hsi-an Fu and Lan-chou Fu, leads to Hsi-ning Fu near the Koko-nor, and which from that point is known as the northern route to Lh'asa. My outfit was simple and inexpensive, for, dressing and living like a Chinaman, I was incumbered neither with clothes nor foreign stores, bedding, tubs, medicines, nor any of the other endless impedimenta which so many travelers consider absolute necessities.

The most rapid and on the whole the most convenient

way to travel in northern China is by cart; each will carry about 300 pounds of goods, and still leave room enough for a passenger and driver, and the tighter one is packed in one of these primitive conveyances the more comfortably will one ride, for, as these carts are innocent of springs or seats, the jogging when they are empty is

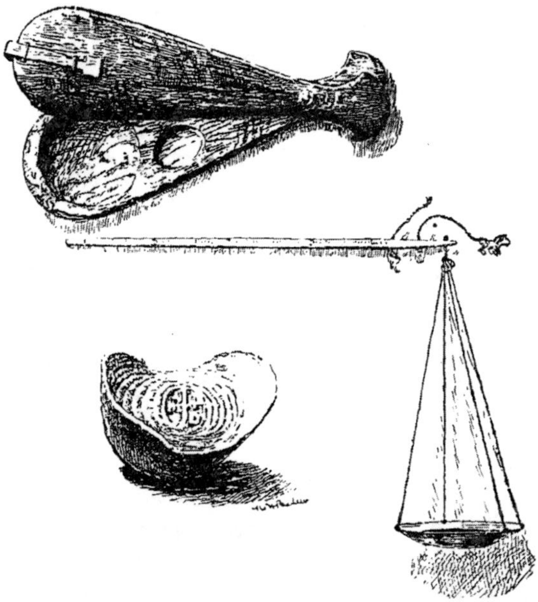

SILVER SCALES AND CASE, AND SHOE OF SYCEE.

dreadful. I made a contract with a cart firm to supply me with two carts, with two mules to each, to take me to Lan-chou Fu, the capital of the province of Kan-su, in thirty-four days. For every day over this they were to pay me Tls. 2,[1] I giving them the same amount for every day gained on the time agreed upon. This arrangement

1 A *tael* or ounce of silver is worth about $1.25. In Chinese it is called *liang*. The word *tael* is of Dutch or Malay origin. See Yule, "Glossary of Reference," p. 675. In Mongol the word *liang* becomes *lan*, a word used by Russians instead of *tael*.

worked admirably, and I reached my destination two days ahead of time. Early on the morning of December 17th, having donned the comfortable Chinese dress, and taken leave of the German Minister, whose guest I had been while in Peking, I left for a five weeks' jog through northern China, accompanied by one servant, a man called Liu Chung-shan, who had traveled with Lieutenant Younghusband through Chinese Turkestan to India a year or two previously.

It was late at night when we reached Tou-tien, a large, straggling village, composed of inns and eating-houses, where we stopped only for a few hours to feed the mules and rest, taking advantage of the bright moonlight to push on. I found it somewhat difficult at first to accustom myself to this mode of starting in the middle of the night, or rather as soon as the moon rose, but as it is a custom of the country, it is best to comply with it, otherwise one arrives too late at the inns to get either rooms or food.

Every one we passed in the night the drivers thought was a brigand, and, to judge from the number of watch-houses and patrolmen along the road, there seemed to be some reason for their fears. Even within the immediate vicinity of Peking, and notwithstanding the strenuous efforts of the high officials, highway robbery and brigandage break out afresh every winter. Poverty usually prompts the peasant to adopt this means of making both ends meet.

The road as far as Pao-ting Fu, the capital of the province of Chih-li, lay over the flat but wonderfully fertile plain which stretches across all the eastern and northern parts of the province, but which at this season of the year did not present a single feature of interest. Some twenty miles before reaching Pao-ting we passed through the town of An-su ("Peace and Tranquillity"), an appropriate name for a place which owes its local celebrity to the numerous "sing-song girlies" who go from one inn to the other singing songs which they accompany on the *san-hsien* (three-stringed banjo). An-su Hsien has not, however, a monopoly of this mode of entertaining the weary traveler, for all along my route through this province I found these "wild flowers," as the Chinese euphemistically call them, ugly, dirty, powdered, and rouged, and many of them not more than ten or twelve years old.

Pao-ting Fu,[1] though not large, is a densely populated city, and a very important business center, receiving great quantities of foreign goods from Tientsin, with which city it has good river communication. The streets are narrow and dirty, the shops small but well-stocked with every variety of merchandise. A number of foreign missionaries, both Catholic and Protestant, live here in extremely comfortable quarters, and do not appear to be overburdened with work. Leaving Pao-ting for T'ai-yuan Fu, the capital of the province of Shan-hsi, the road at first lay over a level, densely populated, and well-cultivated country, now bare in the extreme. Even the dead grass had been carefully raked up to supply fuel for the *k'ang*, for this, with sorghum stalks, roots, and dry twigs which they knock off the trees, is all the people use to heat their homes and cook their food, though coal is both cheap and plentiful in the hills near-by.

At Ching-feng-tien, a small village, we stopped for the night in a wonderfully clean inn. Throughout northern China the inns are all alike. They are built around the

[1] It is 110 miles S. S. W. of Peking, or 335 *li*. The *li* is usually estimated as a third of a statute mile. I have followed this estimate throughout this work.

four sides of a large central yard. The buildings opening on the street are the kitchen, restaurant and innkeeper's rooms; around the other sides of the court are numerous little

THE COURTYARD OF AN INN.

rooms for guests, those facing the *porte-cochère*, which passes through or beside the kitchen, being usually the best fitted up. On one side of the yard are long, open sheds for mules and horses. Each room (and this applies not only to inns but to all houses) is supplied with a *k'ang* or stove-bed, which in some respects is even an improvement on the bed wardrobes of our country, for not only is this *k'ang* a bed, but it is a hotbed. With a *k'ang*, a room is furnished; without it, it is uninhabitable. One end of every room is raised about two feet from the ground and covered with a thick coating of mud or tiles. In the interior is an empty space, at one end of which is built a chimney on the outer wall of the house; at the other is a hole through which fuel is put into this structure. When the fire is lit, this hole is closed and the fuel smolders until entirely consumed, imparting such a high degree of temperature to the whole *k'ang* that hardly any bed covering is necessary even in the coldest night of winter. But this is precisely what makes a heated *k'ang* so uncomfortable to one not used to it; roasting on the side next the *k'ang* and freezing on the side away from it, there is no position in which one can get comfortable all over. In Kan-su there is another variety of *k'ang* but the principle is the same.

The noise in a Chinese inn is deafening, and it never ceases day or night. Each guest yells from his door to the *huo-chi*, or servants, for everything he wants, the *huo-chi* shout back, the cook bawls out the names of the dishes as they are ready, the cart-drivers wrangle with the *chang-kuei-ti* (innkeeper), and the mules bray, and the pigs, of which there are always a half-dozen about, grunt and squeal, till one in sheer desperation joins in the general hubbub, and tries to shout it down.

At Fu-ch'eng-i, a small market town, with a likin station, which I reached on the second day out from Pao-ting, the plain of Chih-li comes to an end in this direction, and the loess country commences. A few miles to the west, at Ch'eng-ting Chou,[1] it imparted its yellow color to the whole country, and gradually increased in thickness as we approached the range of mountains which divides Chih-li from Shan-hsi, till at Huo-lu Hsien, where we stopped for breakfast, the road was in a cut about thirty feet deep. Passing Huo-lu, the road entered a rough broken country of limestone formation, and crossed several ranges of low hills. On the morning of the 23d of December, I reached the Great wall, and passed through the "northern heavenly gate" (*Pei-t'ien men*), altitude 2000 feet. This branch of the Great wall, which forms the boundary line between the provinces of Chih-li and Shan-hsi for several hundred miles, differs from that usually visited by tourists at Nan-k'ou, a little to the north of Peking, in that it is everywhere faced with stone, instead of brick, as at the latter place. While on the subject of the Great wall, I must note that there are two Great walls: one called the frontier wall (*Pien ch'eng*), extending from the gulf of Chih-li to Ch'ia-yü kuan, at the western extremity of Kan-su; the other, known as "the long wall" (*Ch'ang-ch'eng*) or "the myriad li wall" (*Wan-li ch'eng*), branches off from the first near its eastern end, and, describing an arc of a circle around the northwestern extremity of the province of Chih-li, follows the crest of the range dividing that province from Shan-hsi, for several hundred miles. These two walls were built at different times from the third century B. C. to the fourteenth century A. D., and to oppose various enemies, Turks, Mongols, or Manchus. In size, shape, and material they differ considerably. The

[1] A little to the west of this city flows the Hu-to ho which has its source in the Wu-t'ai district in Shan-hsi. This river frequently figures on our maps as P'u-t'ao ho "Grape river," but erroneously.

former is faced with brick until it reaches the eastern border of Shan-hsi, from which point to its western extremity it is of dirt; the latter is faced with brick or stone throughout its whole length, and is altogether a much more imposing structure.

This section of the country through which I was traveling is rich in mineral wealth, in coal and iron especially; as to agriculture it is largely dependent upon the rainfall, for irrigation is impossible as there is very little running water[1] and the peculiar cellular formation of the loess which sucks up moisture from the lower beds alone makes cultivation a possibility. Drought is inevitably followed by famine throughout this Shan-hsi loess region. In many places, to add to the size of their fields the peasants terrace the hillsides, and carefully cultivate every level bit of ground, on which they raise wheat, beans, and cabbages. Their houses are mostly of limestone, neatly cut in blocks, giving them a much more substantial appearance than is usual in Chinese buildings. Along the banks of the few streams were numbers of small flour-mills in which the nether stone revolved while the upper one was held in place by chains fastened to the side of the building.

The next town of any importance I passed through was Ping-ting Chou, a small place, but if *p'ai-lou* or "memorial arches" are only erected to commemorate virtuous acts, as I believe they are intended to be, it must be the most virtuous place in the empire. Every twenty or thirty feet throughout the whole length of the main street was a *p'ai-lou*, but as I saw no new ones, the people have, perhaps, abandoned virtue and walk now in the way of sin.

[1] Between Yü-shui and Hsi-ch'iao p'u, a distance of 140 *li*, I saw no running water. That obtained from wells was very brackish, and not abundant.

The town is on the edge of a plateau. The road to the base of this is both steep and rough; it is called the "Declivity of the southern heavenly gate" (*Nan-t'ien men p'o-t'i*), and its lower extremity is marked by a very fine stone arch.

The watershed between the basins of the Hu-to ho and the Fen ho,[1] the principal river of Shan-hsi, was reached on the T'u-hsü ling (altitude 4800 feet), and that night we stopped at the small village of Huang men, "the yellow gate," a most appropriate name, for it is the gate to the yellow loess country. We left there at 2 A. M., the moon shining brightly. Before us lay a broad expanse of bare, yellow hills made bright in the moonbeams; not a house, tree, or shrub to be seen anywhere, but precipitous rifts and chasms, many of them four or five hundred feet deep, intersecting the hills in every direction and casting great shadows across the landscape. Thus viewed at night, the scene was weird in the extreme.

Some twenty-five miles farther on, at Shih-lieh (or tieh), we had to stop to change the axles of the carts, as west of this point all vehicles are of a broader gauge than in Chih-li.

On the morning of the 26th I arrived at T'ai-yuan Fu, which, like all other large cities in northern China, is surrounded for miles with tombs and temples in every stage of dilapidation. The city, which is situated on the left bank of the Fen ho, is not large, not more than eight *li* by five, and the suburbs are insignificant, with none of the life and bustle usually met around large Chinese cities. In fact T'ai-yuan has not the commercial importance one would expect, although the size and neatness of its houses bear testimony to the well-known thriftiness of its people.

[1] Richthofen has transcribed the name of this river *Fuen*. This spelling has been adopted on most of the recent maps, both German and English, but *Fuen* is an impossible sound in Chinese.

As bankers the Shan-hsiites are unexcelled, and as merchants and traders they show both energy and enterprise combined with much honesty. In all the neighboring provinces, in Mongolia, Tibet, and Ssu-ch'uan, I found them, and everywhere their thrift and integrity were acknowledged by all.

Shan-hsi produces hardly anything for exportation save iron and salt, while it imports cotton stuffs, tea, tobacco, opium, wheat, and rice.[1] In the northern part of the province the people live on white potatoes and oats; farther south the food does not differ much from that of the population of Chih-li—wheat bread, vermicelli, cabbages, bean-curd, and now and then a little pork or mutton. The people are smaller than in Chih-li and readily distinguished by the most unobservant from the inhabitants of that province; they are a kind, obliging folk, with whom one may apprehend no trouble, and without any of the blustering and quarrelsomeness of their neighbors to the east.

On the 27th of December I was up by one in the morning, and soon ready for an early start, when, to my dismay, I found that my last maximum and minimum thermometer, which I had hung up in my doorway, had been stolen. I stormed, and threatened the innkeeper and all his men for over an hour, but I was unable to get it back. The problem of the best mode of safely carrying thermometers over the rough roads had much preoccupied me, but the question was rapidly settling itself; breakage and thieves were

[1] On the road between Pao-ting and T'ai-yuan I passed endless numbers of mules and donkeys carrying eastward cast-iron ware, wheel-tires, pig-iron, shovels, coal, coke, and lime; also hundreds of coolies carrying a very thin black earthenware, made at Ping-ting Chou. Baron von Richthofen, "Report on the Provinces of Honan and Shansi," p. 24, estimates the yearly production of iron in this province at about 160,000 tons.

relieving me of any further anxiety; I had now but three thermometers left.

The road from T'ai-yuan led almost due south for nine days' journey down the valley of the Fen ho to near its mouth, and then to the great bend of the Yellow River in front of T'ung-kuan.[1] Our road led through a number of large towns and villages; the country was well cultivated, the fields irrigated with the water of the Fen ho. A few miles south of Ping-yao Hsien[2] (212 *li* from T'ai-yuan) we passed under a beautiful memorial arch (*p'ai-lou*) made of limestone, most delicately chiseled and polished; it is one of the finest I have seen in China. Besides these arches, one passes continually in this province "road tablets" (*tao-pei*) erected to commemorate a mother's or father's eightieth birthday, official preferment, a kindness received, or what not. They are slabs of stone, eight or ten feet long and about three broad, set in small brick structures with ornamental tile roofing. In no other province of China have I seen such numbers of "road tablets." At one place, not far from Wen-hsi Hsien, I counted twenty in a row.

At Liang-t'u, about eighty miles south of T'ai-yuan, I noticed a fine, stone bridge of eight arches spanning the Fen ho. It is the only bridge over this river between T'ai-yuan and its mouth, but is no longer serviceable, its western extremity having been carried away by a freshet. Here we had to stop for some little time to let a convoy of criminals

[1] A high road leads from T'ai-yuan north to Tai-Chou, Ta-t'ung, and K'uei-hua Ch'eng, in Mongolia. Another, but not suitable for cart travel, goes west to Fen-Chou, Yung-ning, and thence across the Yellow River into Shen-hsi. It is but little traveled. The altitude of T'ai-yuan is approximately 3240 feet.

[2] Richthofen, *op. cit.*, p. 20, says of this town that it is foremost among commercial centers in the plain of T'ai-yuan, that it commands the road to Ta-t'ung and Mongolia, and also an important bridle-path to Huai ching Fu in Ho-nan. I found it a lively, dirty place, with wonderfully narrow streets, and well-stocked shops.

pass us. First came four mounted soldiers with pistols in their hands, followed by five open carts. On each was a heavy wooden cage about three feet square. Inside crouched

CAVE-DWELLINGS IN LOESS COUNTRY (FEN HO VALLEY).

a prisoner in red rags (a sign that he was condemned to death), with a heavy block of wood fastened to one foot, sticking out of the cage, and with iron chains around his neck and body. The long, tangled hair of these culprits fell around their dirty unshaven faces; they looked the picture of profoundest human degradation. Two of them had been brought in these cages all the way from Ili, in Turkestan, a journey of over four months, for no other purpose than to chop off their heads in their native province.

Although cave-dwellings dug in the loess were seen at intervals from near Huo-lu Hsien, they became numerous only in the valley of the Fen ho. Among the poorer people these cave-dwellings are simply holes dug in the vertical side of a loess cliff, a sufficient thickness of it being left in front to constitute a wall for the dwelling; in this a door and a window are cut. In the vicinity of Tai Chou in northern Shan-hsi I have seen some two stories high, but such are not usual. The better class of cave or cliff dwelling consists of a brick-lined, arched excavation about twenty-five feet long and twelve broad. The front is also of brick, and the floor is usually paved with tiles. Many of the houses in central Shan-hsi, which are not cave-dwellings, have been, nevertheless, built in the same style, consisting of several vaulted chambers covered by a flat roof on which is a foot or more of earth.

At Ling-shih Hsien, and for some miles to the south of it, the loess attains its greatest thickness, forming a range of hills which cuts the valley at right angles. The river flows through a gorge, and along its side is a bridle-path, but the highroad crosses over the hills by a pass famous in Chinese history, the Han-hou ling (alt. 4160 feet).[1] The road was very steep and narrow, and in the darkness of night we groped our way along the side of a deep gorge. Every hundred feet or so a recess had been cut in the cliff where a cart could stop while one going in an

[1] This pass is also called Kao-pi ling, Han-hsin ling, and Ling-shih ling.

opposite direction passed it; and, so as to tell each other of their position on the road, the carters and mule-drivers (and there was no end to them on either side of the mountain)[1] kept shouting all the time the weird cry peculiar to their occupation. We reached the top at dawn. A heavy iron-covered gate here closes the road, and a few inns are clustered around it where one can get a cup of tea, and some hot dumplings stuffed with hashed mutton and cabbage, one of the few really good dishes met with in northern China.

At Huo Chou we were once more in the valley bottom, and trundled on to Chao-ch'eng Hsien where we stopped for the night. The Chiang ho, an affluent of the Fen, flows by this place, and over it is a bridge which attracted my attention by its peculiar ornamentation. While built, like most stone bridges in northern China, with parapets on either side made of sandstone slabs about five feet long and three high set between pillars, these slabs, unlike any I had seen elsewhere, were covered with comic bas-reliefs in which the chief actors were monkeys. The tops of the pillars, which are usually sculptured to represent lions, were in this case cut into cubes, pyramids, cones, drums, heaps of fruit, monkeys, etc., each pillar having a different capital. Furthermore, at the north end of the bridge was a bronze or iron cow, about five feet long, resembling the famous bronze cow near the Summer Palace at Peking, although of inferior workmanship.

[1] Between T'ai-yuan and the Yellow River we continually passed long lines of carts, mule or donkey, carrying merchandise north. The principal goods were cotton, tobacco, brick-tea (for Mongolia), cotton stuffs, flour, etc. Richthofen estimated the quantity of flour carried north over the Han-hou ling at about 200 tons daily, and tobacco, he says, occupied nearly as conspicuous a place in this traffic.

Along this part of our route, game was wonderfully plentiful; hares, pheasants, and ducks could be bought for a few cents, and so tame and numerous were the pheasants we saw pecking corn in the fields beside the road that when we threw stones at them they only moved off a few feet and recommenced eating. Since leaving Peking, we had had the fine weather which invariably prevails in Chih-li during the winter months, but from T'ai-yuan it became overcast, and we had several severe snow-storms before reaching the Yellow River. This cloudy weather with occasional falls of snow continued during the rest of our journey through China, but we had very little windy weather, to my astonishment, for violent north-westerly winds blow at and around Peking nearly every day during this season of the year.

I next passed through P'ing-yang Fu, one of the most important prefectural cities in the southern portion of the province, but now in a ruined condition, which argues badly for its present prosperity.[1] Some thirty miles to the south of this city we left the river Fen, which here bends westward, and continued for three days (147 miles) in a southwesterly direction, passing numerous towns and villages, none of which deserve even a passing mention, and finally came to the bank of the Yellow River. The country during this part of the journey was an uninteresting plain; the only trees were persimmons[2] and

1 "The story is told, that several years ago, a band of rebels, coming from Honan, entered the city quite unexpectedly, but left again after a slight pillage. When they were at some distance, the mandarins, in order to give some substance to their projected report to the Emperor of having saved the city by martial defense, ordered some shots to be fired after them from the wall. The rebels, considering this an ungrateful treatment, turned back, and destroyed the city, killing a great many people." —Richthofen, *op. cit.*, p. 22.

2 Chester Holcombe, "Journal North China Branch, R. A. S.," New Series X, 64, speaking of this part of Shan-hsi, says, "large orchards of persimmon trees, grafted, are found, and not

jujubes. The mountains bordering the plains to the east, called Feng-tiao shan, were in this part more elevated and with barer and more serrated peaks than farther north, reaching their greatest height a little to the north-east of P'u Chou,[1] where they may have an altitude of about 3000 feet above the plain.

On the morning of January 5th, I came to the Yellow River, where, meeting the Hua shan range, it is deflected from its southerly course, makes a sharp bend eastward, and enters a mountainous country. The river was between 500 and 600 yards wide, a sluggish, muddy stream, then covered with floating ice about a foot thick. On the Shan-hsi side were only a few hovels in which lived the ferry-men, and near-by, on the top of a loess cliff, the ruins of an old fort; while on the right bank, which rose rapidly by a series of loess-covered hills to the dark, rocky heights of the Hua shan range, was the town of T'ung-kuan, one of the most important customs stations in the empire.

The Yellow River here is shallow, in the main channel only is it over four or five feet deep;[2] and, from the proximity of the houses on the Shan-hsi side to its bank, I conclude that it never rises much above the level at which I

infrequently the traveler meets with apparatus by which persimmon whiskey is distilled. . . . The product tastes not unlike a poor quality of Scotch whiskey."

1 Strategically speaking P'u Chou is of some importance, for it commands the roads leading to the two principal ferries across the Yellow River: the one, west of the city, called P'u Ch'ing kuan (or Tai-chin kuan acc. to Richthofen); the other, south of the city 80 *li*, T'ung-kuan. One hundred and twenty *li* south-southwest of the city is Kiai Chou, with the largest salt works in China. Richthofen has estimated that there is produced annually about 150,000 tons of salt from the marshes around it.

2 Holcombe, *op. cit.*, p. 65, says: "It was nowhere more than six feet deep, and on returning, three of the boatmen sprang into the water in midstream and waded ashore, carrying a line from the ferry-boat to prevent us from rapidly drifting down with the current. The water was just up to their hips." He crossed it in October.

saw it.[1] The common people around T'ung-kuan speak of this place as the "head of the Yellow River," for within a short distance from here its three principal affluents, the Wei, the Lo, and the Fen, empty into it.

I experienced not a little delay, and a very considerable loss of temper, before I could even get the ferrymen to consent to take us over to T'ung-kuan. After declaring for over two hours that there was too much ice on the river to attempt a passage, they finally accepted the terms I offered them, and agreed to try it, but four hours more were lost before we could get together the crew of seven or eight men. Three or four came, and after a while said that they must go and fetch the others who were smoking opium in their den; when the latter finally turned up, it was without the first who had staid to have their turn at the pipe, so that at last even the stolid peasants who were waiting like us to be ferried across lost patience, and seized the heavy sweeps, and with but half a crew we pushed off, the boat so loaded down with passengers and my carts and mules that the ice came up to the gunwale. While half a dozen men armed with poles and boat-hooks kept the blocks of ice from crushing down on us, the others worked the sweeps, with the usual amount of shouting and yelling indulged in by Chinese on such occasions, and in due time we reached the farther bank.

T'ung-kuan, though not a large place, is, and has been from olden times, a point of much strategic importance, as the trunk-roads between Eastern China and the West and Northwest meet here. Hence, also, its importance as

[1] T'ung-kuan is about 450 miles from the mouth of the Yellow River, and the river there is not over 1300 feet above sea-level. There is hardly sufficient slope for the waters to flow off rapidly in the lower part of the river, hence the terrible inundations which at short intervals sweep over Ho-nan and An-hui.

a customs station and likin barrier, for nearly all the traffic between Shan-hsi, Chih-li, Ho-nan, Kan-su, Shen-hsi and Ssù-ch'uan passes here, and the main route to Tibet, Burmah, India, and Turkestan lies through it. The town is surrounded by high walls with two truly monumental gates, and other walls run for some distance along the crest of the hills to the east of it.

At the inn where I stopped to breakfast I met the Nepalese tribute mission going Nepalwards. It had left Peking about a month before me, but had come by the Ho-nan route. The mission was in no hurry to get home as the chiefs and even the servants were in receipt of a daily allowance from the Chinese government as long as they were in the empire, and were transported, fed, and lodged free of all expense, nor did they have to pay any duties or octroi dues on their goods, either when going to Peking or when returning home. There were about forty persons in the mission, a number of them Chinese from the Tibetan border-land or from Lh'asa, these latter acting as interpreters for the Goorkhas, with whom they conversed in Tibetan. All tribute missions to the Court of Peking are treated with the same liberality as was this one, and as the members of such missions can bring to Peking a very large amount of goods to sell free of all charges, and carry back to the frontier of their own country an equally large quantity under the same favorable conditions, it is no wonder that the right to present tribute to the emperor is considered a valuable privilege, and is eagerly sought after by tribes and peoples living near the Chinese border.

The road between T'ung-kuan and Hsi-an Fu, the capital of the province of Shen-hsi, a distance of 110 miles, is a fine highway — for China — with a ditch on either side, rows of willow-trees here and there, and substantial stone bridges and culverts over the little streams which cross it. The basin of the Wei ho, in which this part of the province lies, has been for thousands of years one of the granaries of China. It was the color of its loess-covered soil, called "yellow earth" by the Chinese, that suggested the use of yellow as the color sacred to imperial majesty. Wheat and sorghum are the principal crops, but we saw also numerous paddy-fields where flocks of flamingoes were wading, and fruit-trees grew everywhere.

Hua Hsien, through which we passed the day after leaving T'ung-kuan, once a thriving town, now only a heap of ruins, has a bustling village outside its dilapidated walls. It was here that the late Mohammedan rebellion broke out, and direly has it suffered for its crime, for at present Hua Hsien's only claim to remembrance is the superior quality of its persimmons. I bought a large quantity of dried ones, and found them quite as good as represented, being, to my mind, far better than our best dried figs, and not unlike them in taste. For several months after a piece of bread and some dried persimmons constituted my daily lunch, and, when among the Mongols and Tibetans, I found them a highly prized gift.

Before reaching Wei-nan Hsien,[1] we passed over some of the loess hills at the base of the Hua shan range, and from their summits I got for the first time a view of the Wei River, a rather broad but apparently shallow stream, with a very sluggish current. Near the top of these hills was a little archway in the upper part of which was a small shrine dedicated to "the Lord of primordial Heaven" (*Yuan-t'ien Shang-ti.*) My knowledge of Chinese mythology is too crude to allow me to identify this deity, but

[1] Eighteen miles west of Hua Hsien.

his title is an uncommon one; I never heard it before or since.

Wei-nan Hsien was the largest and busiest place I had seen in Shen-hsi. A small stream flows to the west of it, and is spanned by a fine stone bridge with a very pompous name. The business part of the city is the suburbs. This is generally the case with Chinese towns in the north; merchants by transacting their business outside of the city proper escape the payment of octroi dues, and travelers can reach or leave the inns at any hour of the night, while if they lodged in the town they would have to await the opening of the gates at dawn.

We next passed through Lin-t'ung Hsien, famous in Chinese history as the resting-place of She Huang-ti, the great emperor of the Chin dynasty, who founded the empire, built the Great wall, burnt the Confucian books and the literati. His capital was at Hsi-an Fu (called in those days Ch'ang-an), and his tomb is in a hill, less than a mile to the southeast of Lin-t'ung, known as the Li shan. Ssu Ma-ch'ien, the Herodotus of China, says that "An army of more than 70,000 laborers, gathered from all parts of the empire, was employed in excavating the bowels of the earth at this spot, down to 'threefold depth'; and in the heart of the cavern thus formed palatial edifices were constructed, with positions duly allotted to each rank of the official hierarchy, and these buildings were filled with marvelous inventions, and rare treasures of every kind. Artificers were set to work to construct arbalists, ready strung with arrows, so set that they would be shot off and would transfix anyone who should penetrate within their reach. Rivers, lakes, and seas were imitated by means of quicksilver, caused to flow by mechanism in constant circulation. Above, the configuration of the heavens, and below, the outline of the countries of the earth were depicted. Lights were made with the fat of the 'man-fish' with the design of keeping them continually burning. Urh She (the young emperor) said: It behooves not that those of my father's female consorts who have borne no children should go forth into the world; and he required of them, hereupon, that they should follow the dead emperor to the tomb. The number of those who consequently went to death was very great. When the remains had been placed beneath ground, it chanced that some one said: The artificers who have made the enginery know all that has been done, and the secret of the treasure will be noised abroad. When the great ceremony was over, the central gate of the avenue of approach having already been closed, the lower gate was shut, and the artificers came out no more. Trees and hedges were planted over the spot to give it the appearance of an ordinary mountain."[1] All trace of this splendor has forever disappeared, and Lin-t'ung is only noted to-day for its hot springs, over which some former emperors have built handsome bathing pavilions open to the people. The water is sulphurous, and in the warmest springs has a temperature of 106° F.

A five hours' ride from Lin-t'ung brought us to Hsi-an Fu, the capital of the province of Shen-hsi, and the most important city in this part of China. The length, height, and solidity of its walls are exceeded only by those of Peking; and the life and movement within the city, its streets paved with flagstones, the imperial palace, and imposing temples and governmental buildings, complete the resemblance with the capital. The political and com-

[1] W. F. Mayers, "Journal North China Branch, Royal Asiatic Society," New Series XII, p. 14.

mercial importance of Hsi-an is attributable to its central position. Here converge the roads leading into Kan-su, Ssu-ch'uan, Ho-nan, Hu-peh, and Shan-hsi. The peculiarly mountainous nature of the country surrounding the Wei basin, the existence of only two practicable roads through the range on the south, the Tsung-ling shan, and two through the mountainous province of Kan-su on the west, all of which converge to this plain, and consequently to Hsi-an, have given the city from of old a very great importance, both strategical and commercial.[1] The enterprise and wealth of its merchants and traders, who have availed themselves of all the natural advantages of their city, is well-known in China. Throughout Kan-su and Ssu-ch'uan, in Mongolia, Turkestan and Tibet one meets *lao-shan* merchants and traders. At Ya-chou Fu, the center of the tea trade in western Ssu-ch'uan, most of the tea factories are owned by them, and at Lan-chou Fu, in Kan-su, more than half of the tobacco factories, the principal industry of that city, are in their hands.[2]

To Kan-su, with which province I was chiefly concerned, Hsi-an sends chinaware, cotton piece goods, silks, tea (Hu-nan brick tea), and some wheat, while it receives from it Lan-chou water-pipe tobacco (*shui-yen*), bean-oil, opium

[1] Chinese itineraries supply the following data:

From Hsi-an Fu to Ch'eng-tu (Ssu-ch'uan), 2300 *li* (766 miles).
From Hsi-an Fu to Lan-chou (Kan-su), 1470 *li* (390 miles).
From Hsi-an Fu to Hami (Turkestan), 4480 *li* (1493 miles).
From Hsi-an Fu to Kuldja (Turkestan), 8020 *li* (2673 miles).
From Hsi-an Fu to Yarkand (Turkestan), 9250 *li* (3083 miles).
From Hsi-an Fu to Peking, 1632 *li* (544 miles).

[2] For administrative purposes, Hsi-an is divided into two prefectures (*Hsien*), Ch'ang-an and Hsien-ning, the first name being that under which this city was known in the time of its greatest splendor.

A very handsome breed of smooth-haired greyhounds is found in a district about fifty miles north of Hsi-an. They are called *Hsi kou* or "Western dogs," and most likely were originally imported from Turkestan.

of a superior quality, musk, rhubarb, lambskins, hides, furs, and medicines.

At Hsi-an is centered the trade in turquoise beads, articles much valued among the Mongols and Tibetans. They are found in Ho-nan, and used in roughly rounded pieces as taken from the mine, or in small disks, all of them having a hole drilled through them. They are sold by weight, the average price being about five taels a catty, and no traveler passing through Hsi-an on his way to the Koko-nor, Mongolia, or Tibet should omit laying in a supply of them,[1] for with them he can buy better than with money all the necessaries of life such as butter, milk, cheese, etc., to be procnred among the people inhabiting those regions.

The Protestants have no missionaries at Hsi-an, but now and then some Bible colporteurs stop here for a few days, though, from what Chinese have told me, their books are neither eagerly bought nor carefully read, and I doubt very much if they do any good in this way, an opinion shared by many missionaries in China.[2] The Catholics have a church here, and there are about 30,000 Christians in the province; the bishop does not, however, live here, but at Kun-yuan fang.

Having completed a few purchases of chinaware, turquoise beads, tea, etc., and changed my carts for the larger ones used in western China, I left Hsi-an on the

[1] He should take in preference round beads; the flat ones are not so much prized, at least among Tibetans. Mongols prefer the greenish or off-color beads.

[2] See, for example, Rev. James Gilmour's "Among the Mongols," p. 193: "But it seems very doubtful, if, in many cases, much good is accomplished by placing the Bible in the hands of a heathen as a first step towards his enlightenment." Mr. Gilmour advocates, however, giving them tracts, but I believe that these are not more efficacious, especially as many I have seen in the hands of Chinese are purely polemical, attacking the Roman Catholic doctrine, more even than Buddhism and Taoism.

afternoon of the 10th of January, and pushed on as far as Hsien-yang on the left bank of the Wei ho, at the head of navigation on that river. The country was a flat, yellowish plain for miles around; away on the left was the dark line of the Tsung-ling mountains, closing the Wei valley to the south, while to the north the loess rose in gentle slopes towards the highlands of Kan-su. Crossing the Wei ho by a very rickety bridge put up every winter as soon as the river freezes, we entered the town, where the size and number of the shops, the life in the streets, and the crowds in every inn testified to the commercial activity of this locality.[1]

From Hsien-yang the road steadily ascended through a well-cultivated country over successive ranges of loess hills, the general direction of which is northeast and southwest; at Yung-shou Hsien,[2] 72 miles from Hsi-an, we had reached an altitude of 4950 feet, and a few miles beyond this little town we crossed the first range of mountains at an elevation of 5125 feet above sea level. On the evening of the 12th we reached Pin Chou,[3] or Hsin-ping Chou, in the valley of the Ch'ing ho, a large affluent of the Wei, into which river it empties a little to the west of Lin-t'ung. We saw but few villages on the way; the people either living in scattered farm-houses, or in cave-dwellings, passed unobserved. In the Ch'ing ho valley were quantities of fruit-trees, pear and jujube being especially numerous. The pears, though large, were

1 Kreitner, "Im Fernen Osten," p. 483, calls it Yen-yang, and Richthofen Han-yang. Its altitude is 2140 feet above sea level. Hsi-an is 1800, or, according to Colonel Mark Bell, 1700 feet.

2 Kreitner calls this place Yung-sso shien. Instead of passing by Ch'ien chou I took a short cut by way of T'ieh Fo ssu, some 15 *li* to the west of it, thus lessening the distance to Yung shou some 12 miles.

3 Kreitner calls this second pass Tu-ssai; the only name I heard given it was Liu-p'an shan, "six zigzag mountains," a very frequently used one in northern China. The altitude of Pin Chou is approximately 3140 feet.

coarse, and not to be compared with the "white pear" growing around Peking.

A few miles beyond Pin Chou we passed through a small village at the foot of a high sandstone cliff, far up in the face of which a number of little temples had been excavated; access is gained to them by ladders hanging down the rock. All around these temples little niches have been cut in the cliff, and in them the people light small lamps so numerous that the whole surface of the rock has become blackened by the smoke. This hill is called Hua-kuo shan, "the hill of flowers and fruits," from the beauty and excellence of the flowers and pears which grow on its flank.

About five miles farther on we came to the "Big Buddha temple" (*Ta Fo ssŭ*).[1] The valley is here bounded on its southwestern side by a bed of sandstone over a hundred feet thick. In the vertical face of the rock a number of cave-temples have been cut; only one, however, is still in repair. The chamber constituting the temple is circular, about fifty feet in diameter and sixty high, in shape imperfectly spherical, the top ending in a cone. The rock inside the chamber has only been partly removed, the greater portion of it having been sculptured into a colossal statue of the Buddha seated cross-legged on a lotus, with raised right hand and opened left, the conventional representation of the Buddha preaching. On either side of this figure, but a little in front of it, are two statues of demiurges. The statue of the Buddha is about forty-five feet high, the others, twenty; all three are thoroughly Chinese in shape and ornamentation, and are covered with a thick coating of paint and gold-foil. The temple is entered by an archway passing under a high, brick ter-

[1] Kreitner transcribes its name "Ta-fh-zh"!

race built against the rock; a large hole in the upper surface, prolonged through the rock into the cave, admits light into the sanctuary. The other temples to the right of this one are much smaller, some of them not over six feet in height and ten broad. Kreitner says that the principal image is the largest statue of the Buddha in China; this is a mistake, for there are a number larger, and even among stone statues this one cannot take the first place.[1] In 1887, while on a journey through eastern Mongolia and northern Shan-hsi, I had occasion to visit the famous Yung k'an temples about ten miles northwest of Ta-t'ung Fu on the road to K'uei-hua-ch'eng. The principal stone statue there is over sixty feet high and incomparably finer than that of the Ta Fo ssŭ.[2]

To the left of the temple a number of small chambers have been excavated in the rock, accessible only by steps cut in the stone. These rooms were probably originally used by the priests attached to the temples, but at present they are occupied by some of the villagers.

At T'ing k'ou,[3] some ten miles beyond this place, we left the valley bottom, and for the next hundred miles (as far as Ping-liang Fu) traveled over an open, level country, with small villages here and there, and solitary farmhouses, each surrounded by a high wall worthy of a fron-

1 The picture which Kreitner, *op. cit.*, p. 505, has of this temple does not give even a rough idea of its shape or of the statues.

2 The Yung k'an temples date from the Toba dynasty (A. D. 386-532). Probably the Ta Fo ssŭ temples were excavated at the same time, as the sovereigns of this dynasty are said to have made a number of such cave-temples. Richthofen, "Report on the Provinces of Honan and Shansi," p. 5, mentions a cave-temple a few miles south of Honan Fu, dating from the Wei dynasty (*i. e.*, Toba), and dedicated to the mother of Buddha.

3 At T'ing-k'ou the Hei shui flows into the Ch'ing ho. The latter river has its principal source southwest of Ping-liang Fu. It receives the Ma-lien ho not far to the east of Ch'ang-wu Hsien, which is forty *li* west of T'ing k'ou. Kreitner, *op. cit.*, p. 508, calls the Ch'ing ho at T'ing-k'ou the Ma-lien ho, but he is unquestionably wrong. See "Shui-tao ti kang," VI, 14.

tier guard-house. The average altitude of this section of country is over 4000 feet.

Seventy *li* west of T'ing k'ou, at the little village of Yao-tien[1] (altitude 4600 feet), we entered the province of Kan-su, half of the village belonging to that province, half to that of Shen-hsi. In the center of the village, on the Kan-su side, commence rows of willow-trees, ten feet apart, on either side of the road, and they are continued from here to Liang-chou Fu, in northwestern Kan-su. It is said that Tso Tsung-t'ang, the conqueror of Kashgaria and sometime governor-general of Kan-su, having heard that it was customary in western countries to have shade trees along the highways, had them planted. To him is also due the vigilant patrolling, still kept up by his successors, along this road. In no province of China have I met with so many patrol stations and soldiers as here. The men are well-dressed, armed with percussion rifles, and seem to discharge their duties fairly well. The troops stationed in Kan-su must be very numerous; in every town and village I saw large detachments of them. This province contains numerous troublesome elements, Mohammedans, border tribes, and large numbers of convicts. The country is, moreover, very thinly settled, and highway robbery and brigandage would soon become open rebellion if not kept under strict control.

I cannot conceive why Lieutenant Kreitner should speak of such a miserable place as Ping-liang Fu, where I arrived on the 16th of January, as a "ziemlich grosse Staubstadt" with 60,000 inhabitants; for, at the outside, it may have 10,000, and it is one of the poorest-looking cities I have seen in China, a country of dilapidated towns. The greater part of the land within the city walls has

[1] Kreitner, *op. cit.*, p. 508, calls this village Yan-ye.

been turned into vegetable gardens, and this is the only neat-looking bit of ground in the place. The Taot'ai's Yamen is half in ruins, and poverty, decay, and neglect are seen at every turn. Ping-liang is, however, an important market-town, and in the eastern suburbs are many well-stocked shops.[1]

To the west of Ping-liang we entered a narrow valley bordered by low hills of sandstone and shale, the ground covered with brush, with here and there a small farmhouse or two, around which pheasants were disputing with the domestic fowls the possession of stray grains of wheat on the threshing floors. We ascended imperceptibly till we reached Wa-ting kuan,[2] a small but important place built on a rocky ledge at the junction of the road to Ku-yuan Chou with the highway. From this point the road rapidly ascended, the latter part of it being very steep, although showing remarkable engineering skill in its construction, till we reached the top of another *Liu p'an shan* (altitude 9358 feet),[3] in a range trending northeast and southwest; and after a rapid descent over a good road we arrived at Lung-tē Hsien, as miserable a town as any I had yet seen.

The poverty of the people throughout all this part of Kan-su, is painfully visible. The villages are composed solely of dingy, mud hovels, not over twelve feet square,

1 A very bad road goes from Ping-liang to Han-chung in west Shen-hsi by way of Feng-hsiang Fu, from which place a good road leads to Hsi-an Fu.

2 Kreitner's Ooting-ye.

3 Colonel Bell, "Proc. Royal Geo. Society," XII, 66, gives its altitude as 8700 feet, and Kreitner, who calls it Lo pan san, 2606 meters. Nearly all the traffic seen on the road was going eastward and consisted of water-pipe tobacco. We passed daily about one hundred camel loads (266 pounds to a camel), and twenty-five carts, each carrying 1500 pounds. The range in which is this Liu p'an shan does not, as Colonel Bell thinks, constitute the watershed of the Yellow and Wei Rivers; for the K'u-shui ho, which flows by Ching-ning, 30 miles farther west, empties into the Wei. The watershed is crossed 3 miles to the west of T'ai-p'ing tien.

a *k'ang*, in which grass or dry powdered manure is burnt, taking up more than half of the room. On a long flat stove made of mud, in which a fire of grass is kept burning by means of a box-bellows, is a thin cast-iron pan, the only cooking utensil in the house; a quern or small hand-mill, a few earthenware pots, some bits of dirty felt and cotton complete the furniture of one of these dens, in which frequently eight or ten persons live huddled together. Around the mouth of the *k'ang* lie a few lank pigs, while half a dozen dirty, skinny children, clothed only in too short and much patched jackets, gambol about and romp in the mud with asthmatic fowls and mangy dogs. The food of the people is vermicelli, and cakes of wheat flour called *mo-kuci* or *mo-mo*, varying in size and thickness but never in their sodden indigestibility. Only at New Year they indulge their taste for meat, eating such quantities of pork, or mutton if they be Mohammedans, that they frequently sicken and die from the effects of their gormandizing. Their only pleasure, excepting this yearly feast, is opium smoking, nor can I fairly begrudge it to those who lead such lives, people who cannot possibly rise above their present level, who are without any of the comforts, to say nothing of the pleasures, of life. If it destroys their appetite for food, so much the better, for they will have stilled the gnawing pangs of hunger which otherwise they would feel every instant of their lives; and under the effects of the drug their imagination is excited, they talk, forget their woes, and enjoy themselves for a brief while. Men, women, and often young girls and boys indulge in opium smoking, except they be Mohammedans, who never touch it, using invariably the native drug (*t'u-yen*) which costs about 200 cash an ounce, and which does not have as deleterious an effect upon them as the foreign;

this is, fortunately, so expensive that it is absolutely beyond their reach. The Kan-su people are a gentle, kind-hearted set, ready to oblige, and honest withal; and, though they have, like all mankind, certain objectionable traits, among which procrastination is the most provoking, I hold them to be the pleasantest people in China.

After leaving Lung-tē we followed a stony gorge for about twenty miles, and came to the town of Hui-ning, where there is a large number of convicts. They roamed about the streets and in the inns, with heavy iron chains around their legs and iron collars on their necks; some of them, who had tried to escape, with logs of wood fastened to one leg. None seemed in the least ashamed of these ornaments, and all took their punishments with the usual Chinese stoicism.

On the way down the valley leading to this town, I had repeatedly asked passers-by the name of the stream which flowed through it, but had received no satisfactory answer. At the inn at Hui-ning it was my first question to the inn-keeper, and then I learnt that its name was nothing less than Ch'i-shih-ehr-tao chiao-pu-kan ho, "Seventy-two-arrived-with-feet-not-dry River." I must admit that I thought I was being hoaxed, but on consulting an excellent Chinese guide-book I found that it spoke of this river or rivulet as the Shih-tzu ho or "String-of-characters River." The name given me unquestionably meeting with all the requirements of length, I duly entered it on the list of rivers of China.

An-ting Hsien, through which we next passed, is in the center of a broad and fertile valley of loess formation. The population of the adjacent villages is smaller than one would expect, and much fallow soil is met with, but the people have a much more prosperous appearance than in the country farther east. Several important roads pass through this town,[1] and, were it not for the proximity of Lan-chou, An-ting would be a very important commercial center; the transit trade is considerable, and there is here a likin station whose receipts are very large.

Thirteen miles to the west of An-ting we crossed a low pass (altitude 7865 feet),[2] and entered the valley of the Hao-wei ho which flows into the Yellow River about ten miles to the east of Lan-chou. The soil grew stonier as we neared a range of granite mountains running north and south, which a few miles farther on deflects the Yellow River in its easterly course, and forces it to take a great bend to the north. Here and there in the lower part of the valley I saw some small paddy-fields and numerous little grist-mills, built, with absolute disregard of possible freshets, along the bank of the river. Most of the villages, however, and the greater portion of the cultivated land, were on the hillsides. Some two miles more, through a rocky gorge leading due north, and we came on the Yellow River, where, issuing out of a gorge of granite rocks, deep down in which it has worn a narrow channel, it bends suddenly to the north and flows swiftly on through a broad, open country till lost in the distance. The river was not over 175 yards wide in the gorge, swift and beautifully clear, but partly covered with huge blocks of ice which had got jammed in this narrow channel. The yellow color of its water in its lower course is due, in a measure, to the dust blown into it below Ning-hsia Fu, but principally to the loess silt continually brought down by the important affluents which flow into it near T'ung-

[1] A road goes to Kung Ch'ang Fu and thence to Hsi-an via Ch'in Chou, or to Han-chung via Li Hsien, Hsi ho, and Lüeh-yang.

[2] Kreitner calls this pass Tshe-da ling, and gives its altitude as 2200 meters (about 6820 feet). The Hao-wei ho is also called Ko-men ho.

kuan. Only occasionally in its upper course are its waters discolored and blackish, owing to rains in the vicinity of Ho Chou in western Kan-su. A few miles more through the loess which covers, to a great depth, the western slope of the range of mountains we had just crossed, and, passing through Tung-kuan p'u, we saw some six miles ahead of us the walls of Lan-chou Fu, and the high chimney of the now abandoned woolen factory; and an hour or two later I had reached the house of Mons. l'Abbé de Meester, of the Belgian Catholic Mission, in the southern suburb, who most hospitably received me and gave me a little pavilion in his neat compound.

Here my cart journey of 1350 miles was at an end, and I could once more stretch my limbs to their full length. What must have been the satisfaction felt by my carters also when the long drive was over, I can only imagine by my own. It was a source of endless speculation with me how these men kept themselves in condition. Whenever the road was at all rough they went on foot; they hardly ever slept at the inns where we stopped, as their teams occupied nearly all their time; cat-naps caught on the way seemed to satisfy them. Their food, moreover, was of a most unsubstantial nature, vermicelli, bread, and tea *à discrétion.* I changed my drivers only twice between Peking and Lan-chou Fu, but none of them, on arriving at the end of their long journey, seemed any the worse for their work.

II

LAN-CHOU FU, HSI-NING, KUMBUM, TANKAR

LAN-CHOU FU, the capital of the province of Kan-su, is situated on the right bank of the Yellow River in a broad loess valley, whose principal width is on the left bank, the hills from Tung-kuan p'u to Lan-chou forming an arc of a circle with about a three-mile radius, its western extremity in front of the city and opposite a spur of the southern hills. Though not very extensive, it is densely populated (70,000 to 80,000 inhabitants),[1] a majority of the people being Mohammedans. To the west of the Chinese is the Manchu city, which is but sparsely inhabited, the greater part being given up to governmental uses. There are no suburbs of any importance, except on the south side, where stands the closed woolen factory erected by Tso Ts'ung-tang, besides a number of tobacco factories and a few houses. The walls are kept in excellent repair, and cannon of foreign make are mounted on them. On a hill which commands the city to the west is an entrenched camp, but most of the garrison, 3000 men, are stationed in the Manchu city.

A great deal of tobacco is grown around Lan-chou, and the preparation of it is the principal industry of this place. A large proportion of this business is in the hands of Shen-

[1] Kreitner, *op. cit.*, p. 54, gives the population as half a million, and Colonel Bell, *op. cit.*, p. 68, says it is reported to contain 40,000 houses. He does not mention, however, whether they are all inhabited.

hsi people who, besides natural enterprise, have capital, two requisites for success in trade sadly lacking in Kan-su. The Lan-chou tobacco plant is not large, but has a fine, broad leaf with very small fibres. In the preparation of the famous water-pipe tobacco (*shui yen*) the leaves are not plucked until they have been thoroughly frosted, by which means, it is said, the tobacco acquires its peculiarly bright, reddish color. The first operation in the factories, of which there are some fifty, is to chop the leaves and pour a quantity of linseed oil over them. When the mass has become thoroughly saturated, it is made into blocks about four feet square, and put under a press, whereby most of the oil is expressed. The block is then planed into fine shreds, like Turkish tobacco, and very slightly compressed in small moulds. When these cakes have dried a little, they are ready for the market.[1] Two varieties of tobacco, differing only in price, are made by this process; a third and superior one, called frequently "green tobacco," is made by plucking the leaf before it gets frosted, and drying it so that it will retain the green color. To intensify this color, a small quantity of sulphate of copper (*lu-shih mo-tzŭ*) is mixed in when the linseed oil is poured over the tobacco. The rest of the process of manufacture of this variety is similar to that of the other kinds.

This industry, the annual value of which can not exceed half a million of dollars, is, as remarked, the only impor-

1 Each cake weighs two ounces (*liang*). The first quality is called *po-t'iao yen* (*ching yen* at Shanghai), the second is *huang yen* "yellow tobacco," the third *mien yen* "powdered tobacco." The three varieties are exported in cases, each weighing 120 catties (156 pounds), worth at Lan-chou from Tls. 9 to Tls. 13 a case, according to quality. Lan-chou annually exports 20,000 cases of *po-t'iao* and 30,000 of *huang yen* and *mien yen*. Between Lan-chou and Peking, or Shanghai, from Tls. 7 to Tls. 8 *likin* is levied on each case. Richthofen, *op. cit.*, p. 40, says it sells at Hsi-an for Tls. 26 a picul (133 pounds).

tant one of this city. The tea trade in the province is a government monopoly (*kuan shang*), and only Hu-nan brick tea can be bought in it, although a small quantity from other localities is surreptitiously introduced, generally by the officials themselves, and is cheaper than the brick tea. Tso T'sung-tang, when governor-general, endeavored to add to the industries of this province the manufacture of woolen goods, and thus utilize the immense quantities of wool to be had at a nominal price from the Mongols and Tibetans. He had built, at great expense, the factory previously referred to, and equipped it with the most improved European machinery, but carelessness and rascality brought his venture to a premature and disastrous end.

The Russians are so far the only foreigners who have attempted to trade in Kan-su. For many years they have had shops in Mongolia and Chinese Turkestan, and recently an enterprising firm opened houses in five of the principal cities of western Kan-su,[1] but the provincial authorities and the native mercantile classes have made their venture abortive, and when I was in the province all these stores, save the principal one at Lan-chou, were closed. The Chinese had, very naturally, insisted on the Russians paying the same imposts as native merchants, since they were not in localities privileged by treaties. This did not leave the latter a sufficient margin to be able to carry on business, and they had temporarily closed, with the hope, however, of soon being able to reopen their shops, as their minister at Peking was in negotiations with the Tsung-li Yamen to have them accorded the same advantages as if doing business at open ports.[2] Some years

[1] At Su-chou, Kan-chou, Liang-chou, Hsi-ning, and Lan-chou.

[2] Their shops in Lan-chou contained red, blue, and violet broadcloths, chintzes, brassware, rugs, hardware, cotton piece-goods, matches, looking-glasses, and a variety of other odds and ends suitable to Mongols and

may, however, elapse, unless other complications come to the aid of Russia, before the Chinese make such an important concession. Nevertheless, it appears highly improbable that the Russians will be able to "drive British goods from Kan-su," as Colonel Bell seems to fear, for their cheapest and shortest route for receiving or shipping merchandise is by way of Hankow, the route taken by nearly all foreign goods, whether British, American, or German, destined to Hsi-an or Kan-su.

The country around Lan-chou is not highly cultivated, nor is it even very productive, the rainfall being insufficient, and the amount of snow usually small. The winter weather, I was told by old residents, is fine, and not very cold, slightly misty, with light westerly and northwesterly winds. These climatic conditions extend to the whole valley of the Yellow River, west of Lan-chou, and to that of the Hsi-ning River, until near Tankar; but north and south of Lan-chou, towards Liang-chou, and especially Kan-chou,[1] the rainfall is much heavier, the summer heat greater, and the winters correspondingly warmer. What has been said of the climate of the Yellow River valley does not, of course, apply to the higher country in the mountainous region adjoining it; there snow and rain fall in great quantities.

The people in Lan-chou, and in all the cities of western Kan-su, live on vermicelli, cabbage, potatoes, and mutton. Rice is but little used by them on account of its price,

Tibetans. The sales were not important, not exceeding Tls. 1000 a month. One of the principal difficulties to contend with was the absence of any article, save rhubarb and musk, suitable for exportation, and the agent was remitting nearly all the money received in checks to Hankow.

[1] Mineral oil is found on the surface of the water in certain wells near Kan-chou. It is used to lubricate cart-wheels. Samples have been sent to Shanghai and analyzed; the oil is said to have great illuminating power. Kerosene is brought in small quantities only to Kan-su where it is sold for medicinal purposes at forty cash a catty.

which is sufficiently high to exclude it from their daily food. A fine quality is grown at Kan-chou, but that is the only locality in the province where it will thrive, and the crop is not large. Mutton throughout Kan-su is wonderfully cheap, 400 or 500 cash (80 cents to $1.00) being the usual price for a fine sheep. The bread, made in a variety of shapes, is vastly superior to that of any other part of China, and is nearly as white and light as ours.

Lan-chou Fu, until about four years ago, was the residence of the governor-general of Kan-su and Chinese Turkestan. Recently, Turkestan (*Hsin chiang*, or "the New Dominion") was put under a governor (*Tao-t'ai*); and the governor-general administers from Lan-chou both Kan-su and Shen-hsi, his presence being much more needed in the disaffected province of Kan-su than in the purely Chinese one of Shen-hsi.[1] The most interesting portion of the population of Kan-su are the Mohammedans, who, from what information I have been able to gather, form about one-fourth of the whole.[2] Their number was greatly reduced by the terrible butcheries during the late rebellion (in the little town of Tankar, for example, with a present population of not over 10,000, some 10,000 Moham-

[1] Lan-chou Fu is strategically an important place, for it commands the road to Turkestan and the best, though at present the least traveled, one to Tibet. From here a good cart-road leads to Ili-Kuldja in ninety days, to Kobdo in forty, to Sa-chou in twenty-two, and from that point to Hotien and Kashgar. It is also near Ho-chou, the chief Mohammedan center in the province, and a hotbed of rebellion. Distances are:

Lan-chou to Liang-chou,	630 *li*	(210 miles).
Lan-chou to Hsi-ning,	435 *li*	(145 miles).
Lan-chou to Ho-chou,	320 *li*	(107 miles).
Lan-chou to Ning-hsia,	940 *li*	(314 miles).
Lan-chou to Lh'asa,	- 4270 *li*	(1423 miles).

[2] No census has been made of Kan-su since 1858. Mr. P. S. Popoff, in his paper on the population of China, gives that of Kan-su in 1879 as 5,411,188, no very exaggerated estimate I feel convinced, though his authority for this number is not a very trustworthy one.

medans were put to death), and in several localities they are still obliged to comply with so many vexatious regulations, that large numbers are prevented from returning to their former homes.

The Kan-su Mohammedans generally are far from conversant with the tenets of their faith, and confine themselves to the observance of a few rules of life, such as abstaining from the use of pork, and also of other meats if the animals were killed by unbelievers, from opium, and wine, but are not particular as to the last rule.[1] They are taught by the *Ahons* to read and write Arabic, but I never met one among them, not even an Ahon, who would have been considered a passable Arabic scholar. Whenever they quoted to me passages of the Koran, it was in Chinese, and I was told that it was in this language they studied it. Some among them recite the daily prayers, and make the prescribed ablutions, but these are few in number, and are much admired by their co-religionists.

Mohammedans here are divided into two sects, known as "white-capped Hui-hui," and "black-capped Hui-hui." One of the questions which separate them is the hour at which fast can be broken during the Ramadan.[2] The black-capped Hui-hui are more frequently called *Salar*, and are much the more devout and fanatical. They live in the vicinity of Ho-chou,[3] in and around

[1] They also cut their mustaches *en brosse*, and frequently shave a small portion beneath the nose. They are Chinese enough to comply with the custom of letting their beards grow only after the age of forty.

[2] Another point which divides them is that the white-capped burn incense, as do the ordinary Chinese; and the Salar condemn this, as paganish. The usual way by which one finds out to which sect a Mohammedan belongs is by asking him if he burns incense.

[3] Ho-chou has a population of about 30,000, nearly entirely Mohammedan. There are twenty-four mosques in the city, and its schools are very highly spoken of by all believers. This city

Hsün-hua t'ing, their chief town being known as Salar pakun (or paken). The first teacher of the schism followed by them was a man called Ma Ming-hsin, who lived in the middle of the last century, but the Salar themselves, who are of Turkish extraction, have been settled in western Kan-su for at least four centuries. The Salar, and many of the Mohammedans of the other sect, have distinctly un-Chinese features, aquiline noses, long, oval faces, and large eyes, peculiarities easily accounted for by an infusion of Turkish stock with the Chinese, of which we should find, if proof were necessary, ample and conclusive testimony in Chinese histories and ethnological works.[1]

The Salar have retained their original language, and still speak it with such purity that it is perfectly intelligible to the traders from Hotien and Kashgar who come to

is a source of constant anxiety to the provincial government on account of the latent spirit of revolt in its people. Scarcely a year passes without some revolt in or around it, and a large garrison has to be kept there.

[1] Colonel Yule, "Marco Polo," 2d edit., II, 23, quoting a Russian work, has it that the word Salar is used to designate Ho-chou, but this is not absolutely accurate. Prjevalsky, "Mongolia," II, 149, makes the following complicated statement: "The Kara-tangutans outnumber the Mongols in Koko-nor, but their chief habitations are near the sources of the Yellow River where they are called Salirs; they profess the Mohammedan religion, and have rebelled against China." I will only remark here that the Salar have absolutely no connection with the so-called Kara-tangutans, who are Tibetans. In a note by Archimandrite Palladius, in the same work (II, 70), he attempts to show a connection between the Salar and a colony of Mohammedans who settled in western Kan-su in the last century, but the "Ming shih" (History of the Ming dynasty) already makes mention of the Salar, remnants of various Turkish tribes (*Hsi-ch'iang*) who had settled in the districts of Ho-chou, Huang-chou, T'ao-chou, and Min-chou, and who were a source of endless trouble to the empire. See Wei Yüan, "Sheng-wu chi," VII, 35, also "Huang ch'ing shih kung t'u," V, 7. The Russian traveler, Potanin, found the Salar living in twenty-four villages, near Hsün-hua t'ing on the south bank of the Yellow River. See "Proc. Roy. Geo. Soc.," IX, 234. The Annals of the Ming dynasty ("Ming-shih," Ch. 330) say that An-ting wei, 1500 *li* southwest of Kan-chou, was in old times known as *Sa-li Wei-wu-chr*. These Sari Uigurs are mentioned by Du Plan Carpin (p. 651), as *Sari* Huiur. Can *Sala* be the same as *Sari?*

Hsi-ning and Ho-chou.[1] Occasionally an *Ahon* from Turkestan, or even more remote regions, comes to Kan-su; thus about three years ago one came from Tarpatia (*i. e.* Turkey), visited all the towns and villages of the western part of the province, and was everywhere received with the greatest kindness.[2]

Chinese New-year was so near at hand when I reached Lan-chou that I had to defer my departure for Hsi-ning until the festivities were over. The delay caused me no regret, for the time passed quickly with my kind host and in visits to the manager of the Russian store, Mr. Vassinieff who had passed the greater part of his life among the Mongols, at Kobdo and Uliasutai, and with whom, although we had to carry on our conversation in Chinese, I enjoyed myself immensely.

Finally New-year, with its fire-crackers and visiting, was over, and, having hired three mules to carry my luggage and bought a pony for myself, I left on the third of the first moon (February 3d) for Lusar, a small village about twenty miles south of Hsi-ning, where I hoped to be able to organize a little caravan, and strike out through the Koko-nor steppe towards Tibet.

It was most delightful to feel one's self free in movement and in the saddle—no longer cramped up in a small cart—and the ride to Hsin ch'eng,[3] a village some thirty

1 Chinese Mohammedans speak of their faith as *Kei chiao*, or *hsiao chiao*, and of themselves as *Hui-hui* or *Kei-chiao jen*. *Hsiao chiao* or "little doctrine," is used as opposed to *ta-chiao* or "great doctrine" the common form of Chinese belief. *Hui-hui*, in olden times *Hui-hu*, was used to designate the Uigurs, or all Turkish tribes.

2 A Mohammedan of Tankar once gave me the following curious description of Turkey. It is, he said, called Rum, and is under the just and mild rule of the Padishah. The country enjoys great happiness and prosperity, thieving and murder are unknown within its borders, and perfect honesty and justice distinguish its officials!

3 Hsin ch'eng ("new town") is quite a large market town, advantageously situated at the junction of the roads to Ho-chou, Hsi-ning, P'ing-fan, and Liang-chou; the road to

miles west of Lan-chou and on the Yellow River, was a most agreeable one, especially as Abbé de Meester accompanied me that far. The bottom of the valley was stony, and, in most places, unfit for culture, or even for habitation. The land on the hillsides was tilled, however, and irrigation ditches carried the river water all over it. The water is raised by immense wheels, generally fifty to sixty feet in diameter; they belong to villages, and in a few cases to individuals, who, for a small consideration, sell the water to the peasants. The price is calculated by the quantity which flows from the wheel while a given length of joss-stick burns. The principal crops grown in this part of the Yellow River valley are wheat, tobacco, a poor quality of cotton, beans, cabbages of enormous size, red peppers, and potatoes. The villages we passed were neither numerous nor large, though several showed by the extensive ruins which surrounded them that, probably, they had been, before the rebellion, thriving little towns.

At Hsin-ch'eng a branch of the Great wall crosses the Yellow River, and follows the right bank for some miles southward; it is like every part of the wall I have seen west of Chih-li, which as said before is made of earth, without any brickwork, and it has a ditch along its front. Some nine miles farther, in a southerly direction, through a gorge of red sandstone formation, we came to the mouth of the Hsi-ning ho,[1] where in a little ferry-boat we crossed the Yellow River.

the last two places going up the valley of the Hsiao-ssŭ ho. This river bears also the names of Ni-shui ho and P'ing-fan ho, and on some European maps it has, for some unknown reason, beeu even given a Mongol name, Charing gol. Forty-four *li* east of Hsin ch'eng there is a Ku ch'eng, or "old town."

[1] Usually called Hsi ho. It also bears in Chinese geographies the name of Huang ho. The Yellow River, where the Hsi ho empties into it, is not over 100 yards wide and is quite shallow. On the rocks along its banks I saw no water-marks more than ten feet above the surface of the stream.

A line drawn north and south and passing by this point would divide the purely Chinese region of Kan-su from that in which there is a large foreign element. In this western section the Chinese occupy the large towns and principal valleys, while the non-Chinese tribes are relegated to the smaller and more elevated valleys, near the two great chains of mountains which traverse the country from east to west.

Ho tui-tzŭ, where we stopped the first night after crossing the Yellow River, is a small village near the left bank of the Hsi ho. I was obliged to remain here a day while I sent a man, over the mountains to the south of us, to the San ch'uan (Huc's "Trois Vallons"), with a letter to a lama of that place. While at Lan-chou a Mongol in the service of Mr. Vassinieff gave me a letter to this man, telling me that he would be a good one to secure as a companion on my travels, as he had accompanied Potanin for two years, and knew the country around the Koko-nor. Finding it would take me too much out of my way to go to San ch'uan myself, I sent him the letter with a note asking him to meet me at Lusar.

Our earliest knowledge of the San-ch'uan is through Huc, who says that its people are called *Dschiahour*, but this is a mistake as this name applies only to people of Tibetan race, and the San-ch'uan is peopled with Mongols, whose early home was probably in the Ordos territory, to the north of Shen-hsi. Their features are distinctly Mongol and so is their language, though they make use of many Chinese and Tibetan words and expressions. They all speak Chinese and wear the Chinese dress, except on festive occasions when the women don the Mongol costume. My experience of the San-ch'uan Mongols does not bear out Huc's statement concerning their quarrelsome, bloodthirsty nature; I found them quite as timid as the other tribes of their race. Huc evidently misunderstood his informant who must have told him that the Jya Hor,[1] meaning the Tibetans along the Kan-su border, were a truculent, bloodthirsty, bullying lot, and he, thinking the name applied to the San-ch'uan Mongols, gave them all the martial virtues they long to have, but sadly lack.

There are no Chinese living in the San-ch'uan, and the population does not exceed three hundred families. These people are devout Buddhists, and have several small lamaseries. They derive large profits from the sale of the mules they raise, which are much prized throughout western

[1] See Huc, "Souvenirs d'un Voyage," II, 36. *Dschiahour* is a Tibetan expression composed of two words *Rgya*, "China," and *Hor*, a Tibetan tribal name; it is pronounced *Jya-Hor*. There are two other regions inhabited by Horba: one in eastern Tibet, called *Horsé k'a-nga*, or *Hor-chyok;* another north of the Nam t'so in western Tibet, known as *Nub-Hor* or "western Horba." The San-Ch'uan Mongols are included by the Chinese among the *T'u-ssŭ*, or Aboriginal agricultural tribes, of Kan-su, and frequently figure in Chinese works as "Chi T'u-ssŭ," and "Yen T'u-ssŭ," or "Chi Yen tsai kou T'u-ssŭ." The "Illustrated Account of the Tributaries of the Empire" ("Huang ch'ing chih kung t'u"), published in the latter part of the eighteenth century, mentions a number of *Mongol* tribes living in the southern portion of the Nien-pei district, the section of country now occupied by the San-ch'uan Mongols. The same work (V, 55) mentions a tribe, called Tung-kou, living in the same district (*Hsien*), whose chieftains bear the family name of Li, and who descend from Li K'o-yung, a Shat'o Turk and famous warrior of the T'ang period. (See W. F. Mayers, "Chinese Reader's Manual," p. 117.) Potanin, "Proceedings Roy. Geo. Soc.," IX, 234, speaking of the Amdo Mongols (Prjevalsky's Taldy or Daldy), says "they are governed by elders, whose office is hereditary, and who trace their descent from a half historical, half legendary, prince, Li Ching-wang. . . . Some of the Amdos profess Islam, others retain Lamaism." These Mongols were found by Potanin and Prjevalsky in the upper Ta-t'ung valley, and consequently within the territory under the rule of the Mongol prince styled Mori Wang (Prjevalsky's Murwang). The only Mohammedan Mongols I heard of were called Tolmuk or Tolmukgun. They were said to live north of Tankar (probably meaning the Ta-t'ung valley), and numbered some 300 or 400 families. The Chinese Tung-kou, Potanin's Amdo Mongols, Prjevalsky's Taldy, Doldy, or Daldy, and my Tolmukgun are probably one and the same tribe. It is a bare possibility that the title of the Mongol prince referred to above, viz., *Mori*, may be connected with the family name of

Kan-su. San-ch'uan is also of interest from the fact that Huc's servant Santan Chemda still lives there. I spoke to the old man's nephew about him, and Abbé de Meester knew him well. He is still hale and hearty, a lover of good cheer and gambling, and a lukewarm Christian.

The mode of culture in the lower part of the Hsi-ho valley shows that rain and snow suffice to supply the requisite amount of moisture only when proper precautions are taken.[1] All the fields are covered with pebbles so as to protect the soil from the direct rays of the sun and the action of the wind. By this means small crops of wheat, beans, peas and other vegetables are raised. However, the greater part of the valley is fallow, though bearing marks of former cultivation.

the first chief of the Tung-kou, Li K'o-yung. At all events, it appears likely that the name Daldy or Taldy has reference to that name, and that it represents the Chinese *Ta Li-tzŭ.* It is certainly not a Mongol ethnic appellation. Prjevalsky, "Reise in Tibet," p. 185, says, "the Daldy or Doldy live to the north of Sining and are called Karlun by the Tangutans, and Tunschen by the Chinese. . . . The Mongols call them Zagan Mongol or White Mongols." In connection with this statement it is interesting to read in the history of the T'ang dynasty, that "in the sixth year of Hsing-yuan (A. D. 790), the T'ufan took our Pei-t'ing (Urumtsi) vice-royalty. . . . There were 60,000 tents of the Shat'o people adjacent to Pei-t'ing, which were also subject to the Huiho, and the Huiho (Uigurs) never ceased from plundering them, so that they were reduced to great distress. The Kolu people and the White-robed T'u-chüeh (Turks) were on friendly terms of intercourse with the Huiho, and yet had to complain of their robberies, and, consequently, when the T'ufan sent them valuable presents to bribe them, they gave in their allegiance." These Kolu, whose name is also written Kolohu, were a Turkish tribe situated northeast of Pei-t'ing (near the modern Urumtsi). They are generally known as Karluks. The White-robed T'u-chüeh were the ten hordes of the Western Turks. See S. W. Bushell, "The Early History of Tibet," in "Jour. Roy. Asiat. Soc.," N. S., XII, 504. The Tung-kou of the "Huang ch'ing chih kung t'u" are very probably the Kolu of the "T'ang shu," and the name may be rendered "Eastern (*Tung*) Kolu" (or Kou-lu).

1 As the Hsi-ho in its lower course flows between high walls of loess, and is fifty to seventy-five feet below the bottom of the valley, irrigation is impossible. The river is a small stream about twenty-five yards wide, shallow, clear, and swift. The ranges of hills on either side of it are of red argillaceous limestone and sandstone, on top of which is a thick bed of loess. The southern range is the higher of the two, probably averaging 800 to 1000 feet above the river.

Some three miles beyond Hsiang-t'ang,[1] at the mouth of the Ta-t'ung ho (pronounced Tei-t'ung), we entered a narrow gorge through a range of high mountains of limestone and quartz formation, which here intersects the valley. The road is cut in the rock, in places two hundred or three hundred feet above the river, for a distance of about twelve miles; and this presents the only serious obstacle to cart travel between Lan-chou and Hsi-ning. Here I saw large parties of gold-washers, but their profits are, I was told, very small. It is a common saying among the people, that when a man has tried in vain to make a livelihood by every conceivable method, he finally takes to gold-washing.

From the western extremity of this gorge,[2] where is Lao-ya ch'eng (or p'u), Huc's "Village of the old duck," to Hsi-ning, a distance of some forty-eight miles, the valley is nearly everywhere in a high state of culture; villages and scattered farm-houses are seen on all sides, rows of willow-trees border the fields, which are irrigated from the river, and a general appearance of thrift is noticeable.

Nien-po was the only city we passed between Lan-chou and Hsi-ning; it is a small one without suburbs, but carries on an important business with the tribes in the adjacent mountains, especially during the fairs which are held several times a year, when large numbers of mules are sold.[3] From here to Lusar I journeyed in com-

[1] Potanin, *op. cit.*, p. 234, says that Li Ko-yung's tomb is at Hsiang-t'ang (Shang dang). On some of our maps this place is called Santza.

[2] It is called Lao-ya hsia or "the gorge of Lao-ya p'u."

[3] I cannot imagine how Huc managed to take two days to travel from Lao-ya p'u to Nien-po, a distance of 17 miles over an excellent road. He must have stopped the first night at Kao-miao-tzŭ (or t'ang), 7 miles west of Lao-ya p'u. Huc calls Nien-po Ning-pei Hien, but the name is locally pronounced Nien-pei. On our maps, however, it figures as Nan po!

pany with a large party of Khalkha Mongols[1] from Urga, near the Russian frontier. Their tribe is the richest in the empire, and numbers of this people may be seen during the winter months at all the great lamaist sanctuaries in northern China, Mongolia, or Tibet, where they nearly always bring presents of considerable value, horses, camels, silver, satins, etc.

Not far to the west of the village of Ch'ang-ch'i-tsai we passed in front of a high sandstone cliff, against the face of which a small temple painted in gaudy colors has been built. It is known as "the White Horse Temple" (*Pai ma ssŭ*), and the following legend is told concerning its erection : Long ago a herd of horses were grazing on the top of this cliff, and among them a mare with a blind white colt. For some prank the mare reprimanded him, when, not recognizing his parent's voice, he kicked her. Hardly had he done so than his sight was restored; he saw his wickedness, and, filled with shame, threw himself from the cliff, and was dashed to pieces on the rocks below. To commemorate this act of self-destruction in vindication of the claims of filial devotion, the White Horse Temple was built on the spot where the colt met with his death.

When about eleven miles from Hsi-ning we passed through the "little gorge" (*Hsiao hsia*), first crossing the river by a substantial bridge of heavy logs, constructed somewhat on the cantilever system. At the ends of the bridge are cribs of logs, held in place by heavy stones around and overlapping them. Each successive tier projects farther over the stream than the one immediately under it, and when about twenty-five feet above the river the cribs reach to within fifty feet of each other. The intervening space is spanned by three long logs, and small

1 Their name is pronounced Halha.

ones, split, form the floor. The structure, though simple, can resist the strongest flood. Such bridges are common throughout the Kan-su border-land and the west of China generally.[1] The road through this gorge presented absolutely no difficulty, and, though a little rough, it was soon passed, for it was not over a quarter of a mile long. Abbé Huc, probably from memory, thus describes his passage through it: "Un jour avant d'arriver à Si-Ning Fu, nous eûmes une route extrêmement pénible, très dangereuse, et qui nous invita souvent à nous recommander à la protection de la divine Providence. Nous marchions à travers d'énormes rochers et le long d'un profond torrent dont les eaux tumultueuses bondissaient à nos pieds. Le gouffre était toujours béant devant nous; il eut suffi d'un faux pas pour y rouler; nous tremblions surtout pour les chameaux, si maladroits et si lourds quand il faut marcher sur un chemin scabreux. Enfin, grâce à la bonté de Dieu, nous arrivâmes sans accident à Si-Ning."[2]

From here I could see in the distance the walls of Hsi-ning, and shortly afterward I entered the town, and put up in a large inn in the eastern suburb.

Hsi-ning Fu is commercially and strategically the most important town in western Kan-su; from here diverge roads going north, south, east, and west, through broad, well-settled valleys, leading into the heart of the country inhabited by the foreign or aboriginal tribes of this border-land. The western one is the road to the Koko-nor steppe and Tibet; the southern to Kuei-tê, on the Yellow River, and thence to Sung-p'an t'ing in northwestern Ssu-ch'uan, while the northern traverses a thickly settled and

1 They are met with throughout the Himalaya, and in Norway or Sweden. See W. Simpson, "Architecture in the Himalaya," in "Trans. Roy. Inst. Brit. Arch." Session 1882-83, pp. 72, 73, and fig. 92.

2 Huc, "Souvenirs d'un Voyage dans la Tartarie," etc., II, 53.

highly cultivated country, and passes through Mobashen, one of the most important trading posts of the section. The eastern road is the one I followed to reach the city.[1]

Marco Polo speaks of this place as Sin-ju, and it is frequently referred to by mediæval writers as Seling, by which name it is still known to Mongols and Tibetans. This pronunciation seems to show that Hsi-ning was first made known to Tibetans through the people of Ssu-ch'uan, who pronounce the character *ning* as *ling*, a sound never given it at present in any part of Kan-su.[2]

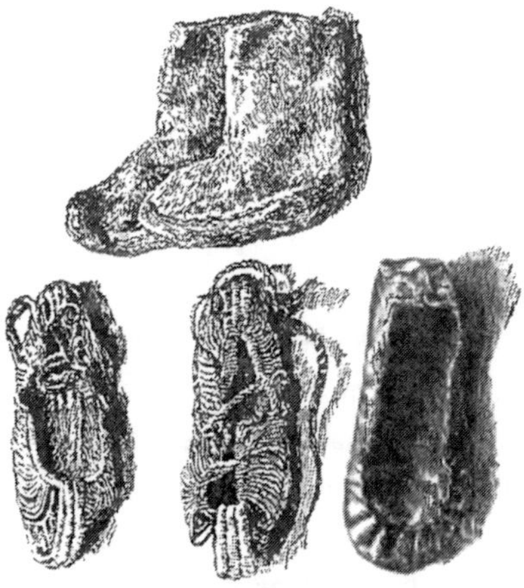

WOOLEN SOCKS, HEMP SANDALS, AND LEATHER MOCCASINS WORN BY CHINESE OF WESTERN KAN-SU.

The city is not over three-quarters of a mile from east to west, and a third of a mile from north to south; and at least half of the space inside its walls is taken up by official buildings. The sole suburb is

1 The Chinese say that Hsi-ning is situated at the mouth of four valleys, considering the valley of the Hsi ho, to the east and west of the city, as two distinct ones. These valleys are called Pei-ch'uan, Tung-ch'uan, Nan-ch'uan and Hsi-ch'uan: "North River," "East River," "South River," and "West River." *Ch'uan* also means "valley."

2 In Polo's time Hsi-ning was Hsi-ning Chou. The latter word is pronounced *ju* by the Mongols. At present Tibetans call this town Seling K'ar or Kuar, and the Mongols, Seling K'utun, *K'ar* and *K'utun* meaning "fortified city." Rob. Shaw, "Visits to High Tartary," p. 38, refers to it as Zilm or Zirm, and in "Report on the Trans-Himalayan Explorations . . . during 1865–67," p. 26, it is called Jiling. Orazio della Penna, "Breve Notizia del Regno del Tibet," writes the name of this place, Scilin, Scilingh and Silin.

on the eastern side and is half a mile long, but has only one important street, in which are a great number of inns, eating-houses, butcheries, bakeries, and other stores. The population of Hsi-ning is probably between 30,000 and 40,000, a large proportion of which is Mohammedan. There is a garrison of 3000 men, and also a considerable floating population.

Although the trade carried on here is unquestionably large, it does not amount to any great sum annually, as the merchants and traders of the place are sadly in need of capital. I was told by one of the responsible merchants that there were not over two or three houses that realized an annual profit of Tls. 1000, and that Tls. 50 or 100 was about all the average shopkeeper could reasonably expect.[1]

While many of the people of Hsi-ning show by their features traces of their foreign lineage, a number of their customs point even more clearly to the same fact. Here, for the first time, I saw women wearing a dark blue or black veil across the lower part of the face when on the street, in fact a decent Mohammedan woman would not

[1] Bean oil (*ching yu*) is the principal export. It is worth Tls. 2. 3 a picul, and sells at Lan-Chou for Tls. 3. 5. It is usually carried down in summer on rafts (*fa-tzŭ*) made of inflated ox-hides, on which some planks are tied. They frequently descend the Yellow River as far as Ning-hsia Fu. The oil is carried in tubs or goatskins. The hides composing the raft are sold at the end of the journey. Wool, musk, rhubarb, lambskins, furs, gold, and salt (from the Ts'aidam) are exported, but in small quantities, except lambskins, in which there is a large trade. Cotton piece-goods, mostly native, iron and copper ware, woolen stuffs, silks, saddles and harness, guns, boots, hats, felt, flour, vermicelli (*kua-mien*), Hami raisins, chinaware, tobacco, and a number of other articles of minor value are the principal goods sold. Native white cotton-cloth (*lao pu*) sells for Tls. 0. 5. 3 to Tls. 0. 6. 0 a piece measuring 36 to 40 Chinese feet; blue cotton-cloth, Tls. 0. 7. 0 a piece. Foreign cotton piece-goods are disliked, for they are not as strong as native. They sell for Tls. 2 to Tls. 2. 5. 0 a piece. Russian red leather (*bulgari* in Tibetan), foreign paper, pens, and penholders are in demand. The last two articles are much prized by the lamas, who prefer them to the Chinese goods; engrossing pens are the only kind they will buy.

venture out without one. Sending a guest repeated presents of food, drinking wine with him from one cup, leading his horse on his arrival and departure, holding the stirrup, and assisting him into the saddle, are all customs foreign to the Chinese, as far as my observation goes.

There exists at Hsi-ning, and also at a number of other localities along the Kan-su frontier, a set of men known as *Hsi-chia* or *Hsieh-chia*, and divided into Mongol and Tibetan ones. In the localities where they reside they act as commercial agents for the Mongols and Tibetans, with whose languages they are thoroughly conversant, as all of them pass a certain number of years among the peoples with whom their families have business relations. Their duties are hereditary, and secure to them much influence among the tribes and no inconsiderable profit. I had in my service, while at Lusar, a Fan Hsieh-chia or Tibetan Hsieh-chia, and found his knowledge of the habits, language, and people most extensive and accurate.[1]

Hsi-ning, besides being the *chef-lieu* of a prefecture (*Fu*) and an important military post, is the residence of the imperial controller-general of the Koko-nor, or Seling Amban[2] as he is called by Tibetans and Mongols.

1 *Hsieh-chia*, may mean "rest home" or "rest family." In this connection the passage in Huc's work (II, 54) where he speaks of the "Maisons de Repos" is of interest. It is very possible that originally, and even down to Huc's time, the Hsieh-chia kept inns where Tibetans and Mongols could put up free of all charge, the commissions received by the keepers of these establishments on all the purchases of their guests more than compensating them for what their board cost, but such is no longer the custom, at least with all the Hsieh-chia who came under my notice. *Cf.* what is said, *infra*, of the *Kutso* of Tibetan princes; these two classes are very similar, as far as duties and privileges are concerned.

2 *Amban* is a Manchu word equivalent to the Chinese *Ta-ch'en* "minister of state." There is also an Amban residing at Lh'asa, and an assistant Amban at Shigatsé in Ulterior Tibet. The official title of the Seling Amban is Ch'ing-hai pan shih-wu ta-ch'en, that of the Lh'asa Amban is Chu Ts'ang Ta-ch'en or "minister-resident in Tibet."

He is always a Manchu of high rank and represents the emperor in all matters relating to the administration of, or ceremonial relations with, the non-Chinese section of the population of this part of the empire. The Koko-nor, the Ts'aidam, and all northeastern Tibet as far as the upper course of the Yang-tzŭ, are more or less within his jurisdiction.

The staff of the Amban comprises a number of secretaries and clerks (*Pih-t'ieh-she*), and a corps of thirty-two agents or *T'ung-shih;* on the latter devolve the principal duties of his office. They carry the orders of their head to the different chieftains, arbitrate quarrels between tribes, collect the money tribute, and are practically the only representatives of the Chinese government known among the remoter tribes. These *Tungsé*, as they are called by Tibetans and Mongols, have, from the very nature of their duties, innumerable opportunities for making money out of the people, of "eating them," as Tibetans call it. So, though their pay is only a yearly allowance of Tls. 24 for the keep of a horse, they realize hundreds and sometimes thousands of taels on each journey they make. Their principal source of profit is the *ula.*[1] When any official starts on a journey outside of China proper he receives from the officer who has control of the country through which he is to travel an order on the tribes for a certain number of men, saddle and pack animals, food, etc., to be supplied him at specified stations; this is known as an *ula* order (*yi piao*). The numbers of men and animals, and quantities of food are generally much in excess of the

[1] I do not know the origin of the word *ula*, which is used throughout Mongolia and Tibet. It is curious to note, however, that it was used in India in mediæval times. Thus I find in Ibn Batuta's Journeys (Defrémery's trans., III, 95), "Quant à la poste aux chevaux (dans l'Inde) on l'appelle *oulák*."

real wants of the party to whom the order is given, so the chief of it usually makes the people at each *ula* station pay him a certain sum of money instead of the supplies, etc., to which he is entitled, taking only what is absolutely necessary for him. If, however, he takes all the pack animals, it is because he is carrying merchandise with him to sell at enormous profit, having no freight to pay on it. When one considers that the journeys of these Tungsé frequently last a year, it is easy to realize that their profits make up amply for the smallness of their pay.[1]

I must mention another source of profit of these officials as it helps us to form an idea of the Chinese administrative methods outside the borders of Kan-su. All Chinese wishing to trade among the Mongols and Tibetans across the frontier must apply to the Amban for a pass (*piao*), for which they pay Tls. 2 for every man they intend taking with them. As this pass is good for only forty days, it almost invariably expires before they can return home, and they become liable to heavy fines and even confiscation of their goods. The T'ung-shih do their best to detect any traders they suspect of not having their passes in order, and the latter are obliged, if caught, to give the former presents, frequently of considerable value, for overlooking the irregularity.

This system of forty-day passes has had another effect; it has practically killed legitimate trade between the Kan-su people and the Tibetans and Mongols, and has

[1] The highest officials going to or coming from Lh'asa are not above these practices, which weigh terribly on the people, and in many cases drive them to revolt. See Nain Singh's remarks in "Report on the Trans-Himalayan Explorations . . . during 1865–67," p. 87, and also the "Hsi-chao t'u lüeh," written by a former Chinese Amban of Lh'asa. He shows by numerous examples how the country has been depopulated by excessive demands of *ula*.

encouraged a large contraband trade carried on from Sung-p'an t'ing in northwestern Ssu-ch'uan. Thus, nearly all the tea used outside the Kan-su border is from Ch'iung-chou, and is brought by these Sung-p'an traders, who are known as Sharba.[1]

The Amban himself hardly ever crosses the frontier. He occasionally visits the great sanctuaries and lamaseries situated within easy reach of Hsi-ning, and once a year he receives the Mongol princes at Tankar. He then distributes to them in the name of the emperor, and in quantities fixed by regulations, satin, embroidered pouches, knives, etc., and exhorts them to obedience. The chieftains do obeisance, kotowing in the direction of Peking, in a hall reserved for such functions, and also partake of a banquet. Every three years these chiefs go to Peking, to carry tribute to the emperor and renew their oaths of allegiance. The former ceremony is known as the "little tribute," the latter as the "great tribute."[2]

The Amban, when I was in Hsi-ning, was Se-leng-o, who had previously been at Lh'asa in the same capacity,

[1] This word is probably Tibetan, and means "Easterners." Sung-p'an t'ing, in northwest Ssu-ch'uan, has been visited by only one European, Captain Wm. Gill, in 1877. The principal products sold there were skins, musk (sold for three times its weight in silver), deer horns, rhubarb and medicines. Gill was misled by his innkeeper, who told him it took three months to go from Sung-p'an to the Koko-nor. Twenty-five to twenty-eight days are usually employed on this journey. See "River of Golden Sands," I, 376 *et seq.* The "Sung-p'an Sifan," given in Lacouperie's "Languages of China before the Chinese," p. 97, is very good Tibetan very badly transcribed. The same may be said of nine-tenths of the words in the so-called Meniak vocabularies of Lacouperie, Hodgson, and Baber, and of Francis Garnier's Mosso phrase, "Voy. d'Expl. en Indo-Chine," I, 520, where *Khe tché ma seu* is only *Kä-cha ma she*, a common Tibetan expression for "I don't understand."

[2] From a memorial by the Amban, published in the "Peking Gazette" of Nov. 4, 1888, it appears that he makes sacrifices to the spirits of the Koko-nor, in the presence of the Mongol chieftains at a place called Tsahan tolha ("White head," probably thus called from a snow peak nearby) to the north of the lake. On such occasions he also distributes presents in the name of the emperor. I never heard of this ceremony when in the country.

and who is noted among all his subordinates as one of the most close-fisted officials that have ever filled the office.

In the inns at Hsi-ning one finds little comfort; most of the space is taken up by stables for horses and mules, yards for camels, godowns for wool and oil, and what remains is used by small shopkeepers, or agents of Shen-hsi or eastern houses buying goods for exportation. The rooms are frequently without k'angs, having only copper fire-pans in which they burn bricks made of coal and chopped straw. On the broad, flat rim of the fire-pan stands usually a pot of tea and milk. When there is a k'ang, it is often only a wooden box without any chimney or firing-hole; the planks on top are removed when it is necessary to light it, and, dry powdered manure having been spread inside it, a few live coals are put in, and the planks replaced. The fire smoulders till all the manure is consumed, and the heat thus created is considerable.

I had not been in my inn half an hour before two or three policemen made their appearance, and told me that I must send my name to the magistrate, let him know whence I came, where I was going, what was my business, etc., none of which did I care in the least to tell, especially where I was going.[1] I consequently made up my mind not to remain longer in town than the morrow, and to go at once to Lusar where I knew there were no inquisitive officials. I was most anxious to keep out of the way of Se-leng-o, whom I knew to be strongly opposed to foreigners, and likely to put an extinguisher on my plans of travel in Tibet, if he got any inkling of them.

[1] In Chinese towns all innkeepers are obliged to have registers in which are entered the names, etc., of all their guests. This is sent every day to the police magistrate, and by him all arrivals and departures are reported to the magistrate or prefect.

The next morning at daylight, having donned a big Mongol gown and fur cap, and with clean-shaved head and face, I left with the Khalkhas I had met near Nien-pei, and rode to Lusar. Passing through the cemetery outside of the city, and crossing the hills, we soon found ourselves in the valley of the Nan-ch'uan. Hardly had we lost sight of Hsi-ning than we seemed to have suddenly left China and its people far behind, so great were the changes that everywhere met us. No longer were all the passers-by blue-gowned and long-queued Chinese, but people of different languages, and various costumes. There were Mongols, mounted on camels or horses, and clothed in sheepskin gowns and big fur caps, or else in yellow or red lama robes — the women hardly distinguishable from the men, save those who, from coquetry, had put on their green satin gowns and silver head and neck ornaments, to produce a sensation on entering Lusar or Kum-bum. There were parties of pilgrims, tramping along in single file, and dressed in white woolen gowns pulled up to the knee, each one with a little load, held by a light wooden framework, fastened to his back. They belonged to some of the Tibetan tribes living in the valleys to the north of Hsi-ning. Many other queer-looking people we passed that morning, of whom I will speak later.

Our road led us towards a high, black line of nude and jagged peaks, rising like a wall across the southern extremity of the valley, and called on our maps South Koko-nor range, through a well-cultivated country dotted with numerous villages, inhabited by Chinese, and T'u-ssŭ, agricultural tribes of mixed Chinese, Tibetan and Turkish descent. When about fifteen miles up the Nan-ch'uan, we turned to the southwest, and, crossing the low hills which here border it, we looked down into a vale of loess formation, lying at our feet, and saw a straggling village built on the side of a hill, at whose base two small streams met. Here was a grove of slender poplar sap-

KUMBUM (T'A-ERH-SSŬ).

lings, black with flocks of croaking ravens and small, yellow-billed crows; and shaggy, grunting yak, camels with gurgling moans, and little, rough ponies, led by their wild-looking masters, were drinking in the stream. On the flat roofs of the village houses were men and women, gossiping, spinning yarn, or spreading out manure to dry. This was Lusar. I looked to the left and there were the golden roofs and spires of the temples of Kumbum, with walls of green and red; and over the hillside roundabout, long, irregular lines of low, flat-roofed houses, partly hid behind clean, whitewashed walls, the homes of the 3000 odd lamas who live at this great sanctuary of the Tibetan and Mongol faith. On the hill-slope, between the village and the lamasery, was the fair-ground, where a motley crowd was moving to and fro, where droves of yak and strings of camels were continually passing; and scattered about in the distance were the traveling tents of those who preferred their ordinary dwellings to the small, dingy rooms for rent in the lamasery or at Lusar.

We rode through the crowded street of the village, and entering a little inn, secured four small rooms, opening on a courtyard, for the modest sum of 4000 cash a month, fire and light included.

Lusar, which is now a village of perhaps 800 inhabitants, about half of whom are Mohammedans, has become important only within the last forty years. Before that, Shen-ch'un, in the valley of the Nan-ch'uan, a little above where we left it, did all the business now transacted here. This accounts for the fact that Huc makes no mention of this village in his narrative. Beside the Chinese population, there is quite a large number of T'u-ssŭ, one of whom holds official rank, but has no jurisdiction over the Chinese, who are amenable only to their own officials at Hsi-ning.

The day after my arrival was the 12th of the first moon, when the Chinese in every village and town of the empire celebrate the dragon festival. Lusar had its share of the feast, and I went to see the fun. The street of the little village was filled with a gaily dressed and motley crowd, all pressing on towards the small Chinese temple (*Han jen ssŭ*), at the foot of the hill, where the theatrical representation was to begin. It was no more nor less amusing than such plays usually are in China, but the spectators more than compensated by the originality and brightness of their costumes for any lack of interest in the show. Among the audience were representatives of all the Tibetan tribes near the Koko-nor, parties of T'u-ssŭ, Mongols, and traders from eastern and central Tibet, hosts of bare-headed lamas, and beggars in picturesque rags, while peddlers with hot dumplings or confectionery, and children and dogs pushed through the laughing and noisy crowd.

The Tibetans, both men and women, wore high-collared gowns of sheepskin or undyed cloth, reaching barely to the knee, and hanging very full about the waist. On their shaved heads the men had little pointed red caps trimmed with lamb-skin, big clumsy foxskin hats, or else dark-red turbans. The gowns of the "swells" were of garnet-colored cloth, trimmed along the bottom and on the collar with leopard, otter, or tiger skin, and those of the fashionable women, with broad bands of red black and green stuff around the hem. Most of the men had a large circular silver ring, set with turquoise and coral beads, in the left ear; and the women wore heavy silver pendants, also set with coral beads, in

HAT WORN BY KOKO-NOR TIBETANS AND MONGOLS. TOP RED, RIM BLUE.

SILVER CHARM-BOX. (MADE AT LH'ASA.)

both of theirs. But the principal distinction in the dress of the women consisted in their fashion of wearing the hair. It was plaited in innumerable little tresses from the crown of the head, and hung down over their shoulders and back like a cloak. Three broad bands of red satin or cloth, to which were attached embossed silver plates, or cowry shells, pieces of chank-shell,[1] turquoise, coral, or glass beads, were fastened to the hair, two depending from that which fell to the shoulders, one from that which fell to the waist.[2] Nearly all, men and women, wore copper or silver charm-boxes (*gawo*) around their necks, from which also hung their prayer-beads.

The T'u-ssŭ, or agricultural aborigines, were dressed very much like the Chinese, their gowns being a little shorter and fuller; most of their women had red handkerchiefs tied around their heads, and wore violet silk gowns of Chinese pattern.

[1] It is curious to find the true cowry (*Cypræa moneta*), and the chank-shell (*Turbinella rapa*), in such a remote locality. They are probably imported from India through Lh'asa, as are also the amber disks worn by the K'amba women in northeastern K'amdo.

[2] See illustration, p. 70.

But the wildest figures among them all were the Hung mao-tzŭ,[1] the K'amba of eastern Tibet, with long, matted hair cut in a fringe over the eyes, dirty sheepskin gowns pulled up above the knee, and boots with rawhide soles and red or variegated cloth tops fastened below the knee with a broad garter. In their belts were long, straight swords, and hanging around their necks were charm-boxes and prayer-beads. The day was warm, and they had slipped their right arms out of their gowns, which hung loosely on the left shoulders, and their hands rested defiantly on the hilts of their swords.

The Mongols of the Koko-nor and Ts'aidam have adopted nearly in its entirety the dress of their Tibetan neighbors, hoping thereby, like the ass in the lion's skin, to be taken for those swashbucklers. Young girls dress their hair in Tibetan fashion, but married women retain their national mode and wear two heavy tresses, falling on either side of the face, and encased in black embroidered satin.

There were also at the play Tibetans from Lh'asa and Ulterior Tibet, tall men with swarthy complexions, and many of them with angular features. They wore the Chinese queue, and dark violet gowns, trimmed with leopard skin; and their speech was softer than that of their eastern compatriots.

Lamas in red cloth, with bare right arms, and shawls thrown over their shaven pates to shade them from the sun, were everywhere, in the shops or on the street, walking about in company with friends and relatives, many of whom had come a month's journey to see them and attend the fair.

[1] Huc translates this expression by "longues chevelures," but it means "red-capped men." The sheepskin or *pulo* gown is usually their sole garment; shirts and breeches are worn only by the wealthiest or by "les élégants."

Nor were the shops in the little village without interest. In one there was for sale bells, trumpets, little copper bowls in which butter is burnt, and all the other innumerable things used in the temples; next to it was a shop where heavy leather boots, made for the Tibetan and Mongol trade, buckskin boots, and red cloth shoes for lamas, and many other styles to meet the different tastes were offered for sale.

For three or four hours I wandered about, no one paying any special attention to me; some took me for a Mongol, others for a Turk, and a few for a foreigner (*Olossu*). All the questions I asked were answered politely, and not an ungracious remark was made to, or, as far as I could hear, about me. I certainly should not have fared half so well in any Chinese town I have ever seen; but the Chinese showed themselves most kind during my sojourn of a month and a half at Lusar, confirming the excellent opinion I had already formed of the Kan-su people. Most of them were conversant with Mongol and Tibetan, and had traveled extensively among the border-tribes, so I had an excellent opportunity of acquiring a knowledge of those peoples, and of finding good men to accompany me westward.

Though the streets of Lusar were gay and full of life, it was within the temple grounds, about a quarter of a mile off, that the principal attractions of the fair centered. Following the crowd which was going in that direction to trade, and, *en passant*, to do a little praying at the temple, I walked over the hillside covered with open-air restaurants, butchers' and bakers' stalls, dealers in hides and peltries, peep-shows, in which, I am sorry to say, European obscene pictures were the cynosure, gambling tables, and all the endless variety of trades and peoples met with at such fairs in China. Passing under a big white *ch'ürten*[1] which served as gate to the lamasery, we found ourselves in a broad street, at the end of which was a building with red and green walls, and near it a row of eight small *ch'ürten*. To our right the white-walled lamas' houses covered the hillside, and behind them we could just see the tops of the golden spires of the chief temple. On either side of the road traders and peddlers had spread out their wares, all the gaudy trinkets and odds and ends capable of captivating the crowd, prayer-beads, mirrors, images of the gods, knives, buttons, silks, cotton piece-goods, tea, Tibetan cloth, incense sticks, salt, sulphur, wooden bowls, and other articles too numerous to mention; but among them foreign goods were represented only by a few boxes of vile matches, Russian leather, some Japanese photographs, buttons, and needles.

Around a man selling medicines the people crowded, every one anxious to lay in a stock of drugs, and especially plasters, of which Tibetans and Mongols are extraordinarily fond, and which they delight to stick on their bodies, no matter what their complaint may be. Here I noticed some T'u-ssŭ women from near Tankar, wearing long green gowns trimmed with red; two broad bands of red satin or cloth edged with black, on which were sewn disks of chank-shells, passed over their shoulders and crossed in the back. They wore the gray turned-up felt hat and heavy leather boots in common use among these tribes, and dressed their hair like the married Mongol women.

Suddenly the crowd scattered to the right and left,

[1] This word means "offering holder." Great numbers are built in the vicinity of lamaseries, and serve to point out the roads leading to them. They are also something like the stations in the Catholic "Path of the Cross," as pilgrims, when journeying to a shrine, perform prostrations before each *ch'ürten* met on the way thither. (See illustration, p. 64.)

the lamas running for places of hiding, with cries of *Gékor lama, Gékor lama!* and we saw striding towards us six or eight lamas with a black stripe painted across

GÉKOR AND BLACK LAMAS IN THE KUMBUM FAIR.

their foreheads and another around their right arms—black lamas (*hei ho-shang*) the people call them—armed with heavy whips, with which they belabored any one who came within their reach. Behind them walked a stately lama in robes of finest cloth, with head clean-shaved. He was a Gékor, a lama censor or provost, whose duty it is to see that the rules of the lamasery are strictly obeyed, and who, in conjunction with two colleagues, appointed like him by the abbot for a term of three years, tries all lamas for whatever breach of the rules or crime they may have committed. This one had heard of the peep-shows, Punch and Judy shows, gambling tables and other prohibited amusements on the fair-grounds, and was on his way with his lictors to put an end to the scandal. I followed in his wake and saw the peep-show knocked down, Punch and Judy laid mangled beside it, the owners whipped and put to flight, and the majesty of ecclesiastical law and morality duly vindicated.

Returning to the temple grounds, we passed in front of some of the houses of lama officials, which differed notably from those inhabited by the common herd. They had high, pink walls, with little windows near the flat roofs, which projected slightly over the walls. The casements of these windows were broader at the top than at the bottom, as are in fact all windows in Tibetan temples; in them is neither glass nor paper, but heavy planks close them on the inside. Through the open doors of these houses I could see that they were two-storied, a narrow veranda running in front of the upper story which alone was inhabited, the ground floors serving as stables and storehouses. Passing before the large courtyard of the gold-roofed temple, I entered it by a little door on the left where there was a row of large prayer-wheels, or rather barrels, painted red, each of which I set in motion as I walked by. Below me, in the courtyard, and standing on a broad plank walk, a number of lamas were prostrating themselves before the holy images inside the temple.

There were three of these; in the center was Gautama Buddha, on his left Dipankara Buddha, and on his right Tsong-k'apa, or Jé rinpoch'é, as he is generally called. These images were about six feet high, and of gilt bronze. As the temple was not open to the public, and there was but little light filtering in, I could not distinguish anything else within it. The general style of architecture is Chinese, the same red pillars and sculptured woodwork gaudily painted as met with in all Buddhist temples in northern China. The roof, or rather roofs—for there are two superposed, the lower one projecting considerably beyond the upper—are of tiles heavily plated with gold. The upper roof is supported by a row of low, red lacquered pillars, and windows underneath it admit light into the sanctuary. In the main wall, which is painted red, there are no windows; all the light comes from above.

To the right of this "gold-roofed temple" (*chin-t'ing t'ang*)[1] is the Jé k'ang, the temple of Jé rinpoch'é. This also has two superposed roofs, but of green tiles, and the wall is covered to about ten feet from the ground with tiles of the same color, the rest of it being painted red. A narrow walk leads around the temple, on either side of which are rows of prayer-wheels. In front, inclosed by a low wooden paling, is one of the sacred "white sandalwood trees" (*tsandan karpo*), but not the most sacred one, which is in a special inclosure. The image of Tsong-k'apa is on a throne about ten feet high; it is not over three feet high, and is, I was told, of pure gold. In front of it is an altar where burn innumerable butter-lamps amidst offerings of fruit, confectionery, bowls of water, etc. From the ceiling hung ceremonial scarfs (*k'atag*) fifty feet

[1] This temple is called by lamas the Jo k'ang or "Home of the Lord (Buddha)." See p. 105, note 2.

long, and smaller ones were being continually hung on the arms of the god by an attendant lama to whom the worshippers handed them.

After looking through the temple we walked around it on the outside, keeping it on our right hand, a mode of showing respect for sacred things observed in all lamaist countries. My Chinese servant, who accompanied me in my walk, nearly got into trouble here, for, not knowing the importance attached to the proper performance of this observance, he started off to the right with the building on his left. He had not gone two steps, however, before he was pulled up and turned back in the right way, by a number of lamas and visitors, with some forcible remarks about his improper conduct in holy places.[1]

Although I did not see the convent treasure-house and the "white sandal-wood tree" until later, I will describe them here. In a small yard inclosed within high walls stand three trees about twenty-five to thirty feet high, a low wall keeping the soil around their roots. These are the famous trees of Kumbum, or rather tree, for to the central one only is great reverence shown, as on its leaves appear outline images of Tsong-k'apa. The trees are probably, as conjectured by Kreitner,[2] lilacs (*Philadelphus coronarius*); the present ones are a second growth,

1 The main distinction, at least in the eyes of the common people, between the old pre-Buddhist sect of the Bönbos and the Buddhists is that the former walk around sacred buildings keeping them on their left, a way considered unlucky by the lamas. The Romans in their ceremonies circumambulated temples keeping them to their right; the Druids observed the contrary. To walk around the lucky way was called *Deasil* by the Gaels; and the contrary way or unlucky way, *withershins* or *widdersinnis* by the lowland Scotch. See Jamieson's "Scottish Dict.," *s. v.* Widdersinnis; R. A. Armstrong "Gaelic Dict.," p. 184.

2 Kreitner, "Im Fernen Osten," p. 708. I was told that in spring these trees have large clusters of violet flowers, but if they are lilacs I am astonished that the Chinese do not speak of them as such, for that shrub is well known in Kan-su and throughout northern China. (See Prjevalsky, "Mongolia," II, 79.)

the old stumps being still visible. There were unfortunately no leaves on the tree when I saw it; and on the bark, which in many places was curled up like birch or cherry bark, I could distinguish no impress of any sort, although Huc says that images (of Tibetan letters, not images of the god) were visible on it. The lamas sell the leaves, but those I bought were so much broken that nothing could be seen on them. I have it, however, from Mohammedans that on the green leaf these outline images are clearly discernible. It is noteworthy that whereas Huc found letters of the Tibetan alphabet on the leaves of this famous tree, there are now seen only images of Tsong-k'apa (or the Buddha?). It would be interesting to learn the cause of this change.[1]

Next to this inclosure is the treasure-house. On the panels of the gates opening into the yard of this building are painted human skins, the hands, feet, and heads hanging to them and reeking with blood. On the walls of the yard, and protected by a broad roof, are pictures of some of the guardian deities (*Ch'ü-jong*) in their hideous trappings of snakes, human skins, skulls, and bones, wallowing in blood and surrounded by flames, escorted by imps more ghastly than they, with heads of bulls, hogs, dogs, or eagles. The building is small and very dark, so I could with great difficulty distinguish the curious things with

Tibetans call all sweet-smelling wood *tsandan* (*i. e.*, sandal-wood). Sir Joseph Hooker, "Himalayan Journals," I, 298, says that the Lepshas and Bhoteas call the funereal cypress *tsandan*. The Kumbum tsandan karpo is certainly not a cypress, however.

1 When Lieutenant Kreitner visited this place (1879), the images on the leaves were as at the present time. See "Im Fernen Osten," p. 707. The Arab traveler, Ibn Batuta, saw in the fourteenth century at Deh Fattan on the Malabar coast, in the court-yard of a mosque, a tree called "the tree of testimony." Every year there was a leaf on it on which was written "by the pen of divine power" the formula: "There is no God but God; and Mohammed is the envoy of God." The inhabitants used it to cure disease. See Ibn Batutah, "Defrémery's Transl.," IV, 85.

which it is filled. Bowls of silver, ewers of gold, images of the gods in gold, silver, and bronze, pictures, beautifully illuminated manuscripts, carpets, satin hangings, cloisonné vases and incense-burners, enough for a museum! One big silver bowl was pointed out to me with a bullet hole through it, made in the late Mohammedan rebellion, when the lamasery was attacked, and the lamas with gun and sword defended their temples and treasures, and were killed by hundreds on the steps of the sanctuary, or beside their burning houses. But Kumbum fared better than most of the lamaseries of the country, for the Mohammedans spared the temples and the sandal-wood trees, not even taking the gold tiles from the roof, a most extraordinary piece of sentimentalism on their part, or rather a miraculous interposition of the gods to preserve their holy place.

On the 15th of the first moon (Feb. 14th), the Hsi-ning Amban and the high Chinese authorities of this part of the province came to see the butter bas-reliefs to be shown in the temple courtyard that evening. The road by which they were to come was lined for more than half a mile by lamas squatting on the ground, while the abbot and the other convent officials, all on foot, stood a little way off awaiting their arrival. Finally the plaintive notes of the Chinese bugle were heard, and the Amban and his suite came in view, the great man borne in a green sedan-chair, a yellow umbrella, the sign of his dignity of ambassador, carried before him. He passed down the long line of lamas, his well-mounted escort carrying bright-colored pennants on the ends of their lances, some blowing bugles whose notes were echoed back by the deep-sounding convent conch-shells and long trumpets shaped like Alpine horns.

When it had grown dark I again walked to the gold-roofed temple, for the great sight of the festival, the butter bas-reliefs. Outside the southern wall of the temple were

THE BUTTER BAS-RELIEFS OF THE 15TH OF THE FIRST MOON AT KUMBUM.

the two principal bas-reliefs under a high scaffolding, from which hung innumerable banners painted with images of gods and saints, while here and there were gaudy Chinese lanterns with pictured sides. The bas-reliefs were about twenty feet long and ten feet high, supported by a framework and lit up by rows of little butter-lamps. The subjects were religious, representing in the usual lamaist style, gods, scenes in the various heavenly abodes, or the different hells. The central figure in each was about three feet high, and in the background were long processions, battles, etc., each figure — and there were hundreds — not over eight inches in height. Every detail was most carefully worked out in these great slabs of butter, and painted in the florid but painstaking style of lamaist illumination. Around these tableaux had been wrought elaborate frameworks of flowers, birds, Buddhist emblems, from amidst which a squirrel was peeping, or about which a dragon was twisting its long, scaly body. Along the walk which led around the temple were seven smaller bas-reliefs, about eight feet long and four feet high, representing scenes similar to those in the larger ones, and worthy of the greatest praise, not only on account of the labor bestowed on them, but for their real artistic merit.[1]

It takes about three months' labor to finish one of these bas-reliefs, for which the only reward awaiting the makers is the praise of their fellow-lamas, and a small sum of money given as prize to the designers of the best piece of work. Every year there are new designs, and new artists who bring their experience and skill to add to the beauty of the display, for this feast is held in all lamaseries, though in none, not even in those of Lh'asa, is it so beautiful as at Kumbum. Those lamas who are experts in modeling

[1] In one of the temples of Potala at Lh'asa there are impresses in butter of the hand and foot of Tsong-k'apa. "These impresses," says the Wei Ts'ang t'u chih, "have remained unobliterated since his time; they are worshipped, and large copper bowls filled with butter burn before them."

butter travel about from lamasery to lamasery, the fame of their skill frequently preceding them, and are sure of a hearty welcome, food, and lodgings wherever they choose to stay.

The next morning the bas-reliefs had disappeared, the lamasery had resumed its habitual quiet, and the people were returning to their homes in the mountain or on the steppe.

Chinese authors divide the aboriginal or foreign tribes inhabiting the Kan-su border-land into two principal classes, agricultural and nomadic.[1] I find mentioned in Chinese works thirty-four different tribes belonging to one or other of these classes; but though it is very probable that in most of the T'u-fan there is a certain admixture of Tibetan blood—in some cases a very strong one—they cannot any longer be classed among Tibetan tribes like the Fan-tzŭ composing the second class.[2]

I had no opportunity of collecting much information concerning the T'u-fan, but, from the few I met and whose language I heard, I have become convinced of their mixed descent. Their language is primarily Tibetan but with a very large proportion of Chinese, Turkish, and Mongol words and expressions. Their dress I have previously described; their dwellings and mode of cultivating the soil will be mentioned further on.

The Fan-tzŭ are essentially nomads, and of pure Tibetan stock. They call themselves Bopa (written Bodpa, and

[1] To the first they give the name of *T'u-jen*, "agriculturalists," *T'u-fan*, "agricultural barbarians," or *Fan min*, "barbarian people"; to the second that of *Sheng Fan*, "wild barbarians," *Hsi Fan*, "western barbarians," or more commonly *Fan-tzŭ*, "barbarians." To some among the wildest of this latter class they also apply the name of *Hei Fan-tzŭ*, or "black barbarians."

[2] The Mongols are not counted as either Fan-tzŭ or T'u-fan. They are nearly invariably called *Ta-tzŭ*, a

usually pronounced as if written Peuba), the generic name for all Tibetans. The Mongols call them *Tangutu*, or *Kara Tangutu*, "black Tibetans," an expression which has reference either to their savagery, or to the black tents in which they live.[1] The section of country within the Kan-su border inhabited by Tibetans is known to them as Amdo, hence the name they give themselves, *Amdo-wa;* and those who inhabit the more fertile valleys take the name of *Rong-wa.*[2] To the west of the Amdowa, living in the steppe or the mountains around the Koko-nor, are the *Panak'a* or *Panak'a sum*, "the three Pana tribes," who, save in their more complete independence, differ in nothing from their neighbors. The Amdowa are organized into a large number of bands, under hereditary chiefs responsible to the Amban at Hsi-ning for the good behavior of

word which I have heard explained in different ways, some referring its origin to the queues worn by the Mongols, others to their mode of bowing, and still others giving it as an abridged form of the older *Ta-ta-ehr* or *Ta-ta-tzŭ*, from which came our word Tatar. On the thirty-four border tribes of Kan-su, see Appendix.

1 Orazio della Penna, in Markham's "Tibet," p. 309, says that Tangut means "dwellers in houses." H. H. Howorth, "History of Hia or Tangut," p. 4, considers this word a Turki transcription of Chinese *Tang-hsiang*, the name of the early ancestors of the founders of the Hsia dynasty, and of the same stock as the people now living in northeastern Tibet. I find in the "Hsi-Ts'ang fu," p. 2, as follows: "The T'ang-ku-te are descendants of the T'ang-ku-küeh. The origin of the word *Ku-küeh* is the following: In olden times this people lived in the Altai Mountains of the Western regions. They were expert smiths and fashioned iron helmets commonly known as *Ku-küeh*, and from this is derived the name of the country. At present the Tanguts and the other Koko-nor Fan-tzŭ wear caps shaped like iron pots, high and with narrow rims, a red fringe hanging down over them; it looks like a helmet and is proof of the correctness of the etymology given above." (See illustration, p. 59.) From this it appears that the word Tangutan was not originally applied to a Tibetan people. Prjevalsky has, very wrongly to my mind, introduced the word Tangutan to designate these Koko-nor Tibetans, and this term should be discarded, except as a generic term for all Tibetans, in which sense it is in frequent use by Chinese authors. I will use throughout this work the term Koko-nor Tibetans to designate the Amdowa and Panak'a collectively. Prjevalsky, "Reise in Tibet," p. 196, mentions two subdivisions of the Amdowa, called Rongwa and Dscha-choo (ho), but the latter name is only Huc's Dschahours. See page 44, *note*.

2 *Rong* means in Tibetan "cultivable valley."

their people and the payment of the tribute money or poll-tax. The Amban confers on them Chinese official rank, a button, and a title. These Amdowa have not, as far as I could learn, any supreme chief. Not so the Panak'a, who, though like them divided into numerous bands, have two head chiefs, one living south of lake Koko-nor, the other to the north of it. This latter, the only one about whom I got certain information, is styled Konsa lama, and the office is hereditary in the family of the present incumbent, whose name is Arabtan. He is also, nominally, under the orders of the Amban, and has a blue button.[1] The chief to the south of the lake, whose name and style I did not learn, is practically independent of the Chinese, not even supplying the few T'ung-shih who venture into his country with any *ula* unless paid in full for it.

Physically the Koko-nor Tibetans are of slight build—I never saw a fat person among them—and about five feet four inches high, the women quite as tall as, and very frequently taller than, the men. The head is round, the forehead high but narrow, the nose more prominent than in the Chinese, the eyes frequently large and nearly horizontal, the ears closer to the head than in the Mongols, but still large, the cheek-bones prominent, the teeth regular and strong. Their muscles are not well developed, except the pectoral ones; the hands and feet are large. They have but little hair on the face and body, and they carefully pull out with tweezers all their beard. They are gay, loving "wein, weib, und gesang," intelligent, and trustworthy when once their word is engaged. However, they are quick-tempered, domineering, and

[1] He receives his appointment from the Amban. All such native officials are called *Ch'in-chai kuan*, "ambassadorial officials."

greedy. Both men and women drink to excess whenever they can, as do all Tibetans, and when under the influence of liquor are very quarrelsome. They are shrewd and enterprising traders, and able to hold their own even with the Chinese, to whom they sell large quantities of lambskins, wool, yak-hides, musk, furs (principally lynx and fox skins), rhubarb and deer-horns (*lu jung*). They transact their business at fairs held at the different temples and at Tankar, Kuei-tê, and Mobashen, and but rarely go to Hsi-ning. They are considered rich by their Chinese and Mongol neighbors, but the wealthiest among them, the Konsa lama Arabtan, does not own more than $20,000 worth of sheep, horses, and cattle, their only form of wealth.[1] They have but very few camels, as they are essentially mountaineers, using principally yak or *dzo*[2] (a cross between a domestic cow and a yak) as beasts of burden; moreover, the hair of these animals, which on the belly and legs is nearly a foot long, supplies the material of which they make their tents. Both the Tibetans and the Mongols often use the yak as a saddle animal. A wooden ring is passed through the cartilage of the nose, and a string is attached to it by which the animal is guided and fastened to the ground at night.

The Tibetan tents are rectangular, with a flat roof; some of them are not more than ten or twelve feet long, but I have seen many fifty feet long by thirty feet broad. A space about two feet wide is left open along the center of the top, to admit light and let smoke escape. Under it is a ridge-pole supported at each end by vertical posts;

1 Ponies are worth from Tls. 10 to 50, yak Tls. 6, sheep Tl. 1, wool Tls. 2 a *picul* (133 lbs.), lambskins Tl. 0. 0. 7, musk Tls. 2 an ounce, rhubarb Tls. 4 to 6 a picul.

2 *Dzo* are called *pien-niu* by the Chinese; they are smaller than the yak, but the cows are better milkers.

these are the only posts used for holding up the tent. The roof is stretched by cords which are fastened outside to the sides and corners, and which, passing over short poles

INTERIOR OF A TIBETAN TENT.

some distance from the tent, are pegged to the ground; the lower edge of the tent is held down by iron pins. Huc[1] most felicitously compares these tents to huge black spiders

[1] Huc, *op. cit.*, II, 159. See also illustration, p. 119.

with long thin legs, their bodies resting upon the ground. Sometimes, to keep off the wind and snow they build a low wall of mud and stones, or else of dry dung, around the outside of the tent, or, when large enough, inside of it; but they do not frequently resort to this expedient in the Koko-nor section, where there is but little snow.

In the center of the tent is a long, narrow stove made of mud and stones, with a fireplace in one end and a flue passing along its whole length, so that several pots may be kept boiling at the same time. These stoves, in which only manure is burnt, have sufficient draft to render the use of bellows needless, and are altogether a most ingenious contrivance. Around the walls of the tent are piled up skin bags, in which the occupants keep their food, saddles, felts, and innumerable odds and ends, of which only the owner knows the use and value. A small stone mortar for pounding tea, a hand-mill or quern for grinding parched barley, one or two copper kettles and a brass ladle complete the furniture of the abodes of both rich and poor. The inmates sleep on bits of felt laid on the ground, using their clothes as covering; they consequently sleep naked. In the spring, all the new-born lambs and kids are hobbled to long ropes on one side of the tents, and add but little to the attractiveness of these always dirty dwellings.

Hanging from one tent-rope to another may generally be seen, waving in the wind, festoons of little pieces of cotton on which are stamped the images of gods or some prayers or incantations to keep away demons of disease, and all impending evils. They are called *lung ta*, "wind horses," are sold by the lamas, and are in use all over Tibet and Mongolia; when traveling, a man will frequently have a large one attached to the fork of his gun.

The Tibetan's gun is his most valued possession. It is a matchlock with a long fork which pivots around a screw through the stock. The barrel and all the iron

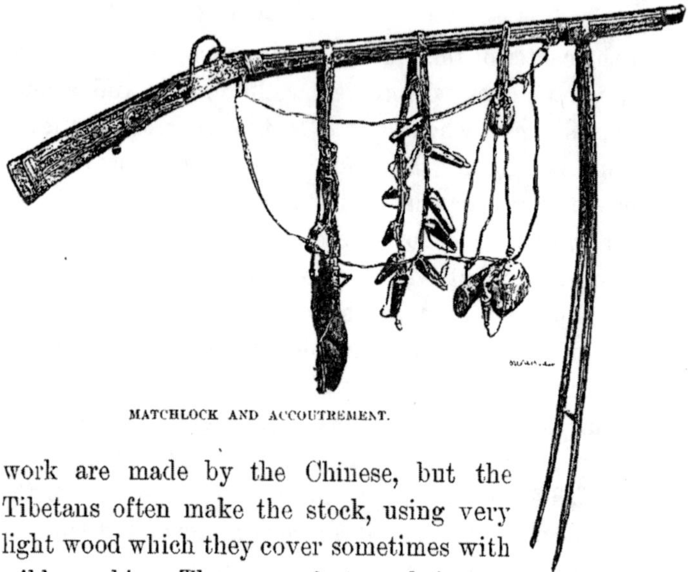

MATCHLOCK AND ACCOUTREMENT.

work are made by the Chinese, but the Tibetans often make the stock, using very light wood which they cover sometimes with wild-ass skin. They manufacture their own powder and slow-matches, and buy from the Chinese the lead[1] for their bullets. They use no wads in loading, and the bullets are much smaller than the caliber of the guns. They can make very good shooting with them at the average range of about 100 yards, but I never saw them hit a moving object, although some of them said they could. These Koko-nor Tibetans do not attach as much value to swords as do the people of eastern Tibet (K'amdo), and usually carry only common ones of Chinese make, with wooden scabbards.

[1] In the Ts'aidam and Tibet, lead is often sold for its weight in silver.

The food of the Koko-nor Tibetans, and also of the eastern Tibetans, consists principally of tea and parched barley or *tsamba*. To this Spartan diet they occasionally add vermicelli (*kua-mien*), sour milk (*djo*), granulated cheese (*ch'ura*), *choma* (*Potentilla anserina*)[1] or boiled mutton. The tea, previously reduced to powder, is put in the kettle when the water is hot and is left to boil for about five minutes, a little salt or soda being added. Then it is placed before the inmates of the tent, squatting in a circle.[2] Each one draws from the bosom of his gown a little wooden bowl, also used on very rare occasions as a washbowl, and fills it. Taking with his fingers a chunk of butter from a sheep's paunch filled with it, which has also been set before them, he lets it melt in his bowl, drinking some of the tea and blowing the melted butter to one side; and then adds a handful of tsamba from the small ornamented bag in which it is kept. He deftly works with his right hand the tea, butter, and tsamba into a ball of brown dough which he eats, drinking as much tea as is necessary to wash down the sodden lump. When ch'ura is eaten it is allowed to soften in the cup, and is afterward worked up with the tsamba and butter. Such is the daily food of this people and also of the Mongols. There are naturally no regular meals; the kettle is always kept full, and each one eats when hungry. When one has eaten sour-milk or anything which soils the bowl, it is customary to lick this clean, and, without further ado,

1 Prjevalsky, "Mongolia," II, 81. See also Huc, *op. cit.*, II, 168; and H. H. Howorth, "History of the Mongols," I, 524, where it is called *zuuna*. The Chinese call it *yao-miao-ken* or *jen shou kuo*, "fruit of respect and longevity," from its being sent to friends, with wishes for their welfare, by persons returning from the countries where it grows. In Kan-su the Chinese call it *choma* or *chüeh-ma*. It is found in many parts of Chinese Turkestan but chiefly in eastern Tibet.

2 The women eat at the same time as the men but not seated with them.

put it back in the gown. If any mutton is to be eaten it is boiled in the teakettle, and each one picks out a piece from the pot and eats it literally "*sur le pouce*," using his sheath-knife to remove every particle of meat from the bone, which is always cracked if it contains marrow; and, if a shoulder-blade, is put away for fortune-telling. Both Tibetans and Mongols are most particular in removing all the meat from a bone, and the Tibetans even have a saying to the effect that one may judge of the way a man will manage important business by seeing him pick a bone.[1] The greasy hands are wiped over the face, or the boots if they require grease rather than the skin.

The preponderance of testimony tends to prove that monogamy is the rule, and polygamy the exception, among the Koko-nor Tibetans. I believe this is the case among all nomadic Tibetans. Wives are bought from the parents by a go-between, and a man is frequently obliged to give as much as 300 sheep, 10 horses, and 10 yak for a fine-looking girl; so the parents of two or three pretty and clever girls are sure of making their fortune. On marrying, and then only, does a man leave his parents' tent and start one for himself, although he may previously have had horses and cattle of his own. Families are small; two or three children are the most I have ever seen in any of their tents.

This people sets little store on chastity in women, married or unmarried, as the existence of the following custom proves. In lamaseries in Amdo, there is held at different times a feast known to the Chinese as *t'iao mao hui*, "the hat-choosing festival." During the two or three days

[1] In the fourteenth century John du Plan Carpin, in his "Historia Mongolorum," edit. Soc. de Geog. de Paris, p. 640, says of the Mongols, "Apud eos magnum peccatum est si aliquid de potu vel de cibo perire aliquo modo permittatur: undè ossa, nisi priùs extrahatur medulla, dare canibus non permittunt."

the feast lasts a man may carry off the cap of any girl or woman he meets in the temple grounds who pleases him, and she is obliged to come at night and redeem the pledge. Chinese are not admitted to play at this game of forfeits, or allowed any of the privileges of this *fête d'amour.*

The old are but little respected, and it often occurs that a son kills his father when he has become a burden to him. The present Kousa lama is said to have disposed of his father for this reason. It also frequently happens that when a person is dying a relative or friend asks him, "Will you come back, or will you not?" If he replies that he will, they pull a leather bag over his head and smother him; if he says he will not, he is let die in peace. The probable explanation of this custom is a fear that the spirit of the dead will haunt its former abode.

The remains of the dead are exposed on the hillsides in spots selected by lamas; if the body is rapidly devoured by wild beasts and birds of prey, the righteousness of the deceased is held to be evident, but if it remains a long time undevoured, his wickedness is proved.

With the exception of the yak-hair cloth used for making tents, and a coarse kind of woolen stuff out of which summer gowns and bags are made, the Koko-nor Tibetans manufacture nothing. They are expert tanners and always make their own sheepskin gowns, the men doing the sewing. They use cream for softening the skins, and any stone of suitable shape as a scraper. All their ironware is made by itinerant Chinese smiths who visit their encampments. Their saddles, knives, swords, matchlocks, kettles, ladles, and wooden bowls are made for them by the Chinese according to certain patterns chosen by them.

The Koko-nor ponies are celebrated all over Mongolia and northern China, as much on account of their speed as for their wonderful endurance. While I do not believe that they are faster than the eastern Mongol horses, their powers of endurance are certainly wonderful. They average, probably, thirteen hands high, and are mostly light gray or black. The Tibetans never feed them, even when traveling, nor at that time are the saddles ever removed from their backs. When horses have been ridden too hard and are greatly fatigued, they doctor them with dried meat powdered, or else tea-leaves mixed with tsamba and butter. When on a journey, they hobble and side-line them during the day, and at night attach them by one foot to a rope made fast to the ground with pegs, and only a few feet away from their camp-fire. These horses are never shod on the hind feet, and but seldom even on the fore feet.

The most influential and wealthy portion of the Koko-nor Tibetans is the lama class, which has greatly increased in numbers in Amdo,[1] on account of the reputed holiness of

[1] It is extremely difficult to form even a very rough estimate of the population of this part of the Chinese empire, as the only basis we have is the number of lamas inhabiting the lamaseries of Amdo, which is estimated by persons in a position to be well informed at from 25,000 to 30,000, about two-thirds being Koko-nor Tibetans, the other third Koko-nor and Ts'aidam Mongols, eastern Mongols, and Tibetans. It is safe to reckon that one male out of every three becomes a lama; consequently the population of Koko-nor Tibetans is approximately 30,000 males, or about 50,000, including the females, who are probably less numerous than the males. It must be borne in mind that outside of the border there are no lamaseries; they are all within the agricultural regions where supplies are easily procured. The largest lamasery is Lh'abrang, four days south of Kuei-tê, with about 5000 lamas. Kumbum, which, prior to the Mohammedan rebellion, had over 7000 lamas, has now only 3000. There are twenty-two other lamaseries in Amdo, with from 200 to 1000 lamas each. The above estimate of the Tibetan population on the border of Kan-su covers the whole of Kan-su and the north and south Koko-nor, the Golok, of course, excepted. The "Hsi-yü k'ao ku lu," Bk. 16, says that a census of the non-Chinese tribes under the supervision of the Hsi-ning Amban, made in 1725, gave 50,020 persons. This includes Tibetan tribes living in K'amdo which I have excluded.

this country, where the founder of the most popular form of lamaism, known to the Chinese as the "Yellow Church," and to Tibetans as *Gélu*, or "Virtuous School," was born in the latter part of the fourteenth century. In 1360 at a place or district called Tsong, or Tsong-k'a,[1] not far from the lamasery of Kumbum, an Amdo woman named Shing-zä a-ch'ü bore her husband, Lu-bum-gé, a child whom they called Tsong-k'a-pa after his birthplace. At the age of seven his mother shaved his head, and consecrated him to the church. From his hair, which she threw on the ground, the famous "white sandal-wood tree" sprung forth. On becoming a novice he received the name of Lo-zang draba, "Fame of good sense," but in after ages he became known as Jé rinpoch'é, "The precious lord." At the age of sixteen he commenced his theological studies, but a year later, by his teacher's advice, he went to Lh'asa, then, as now, the chief seat of Buddhist learning,[2] and studied in the monasteries of the various sects all branches taught, excelling in each, and gaining many friends and adherents to his theories, especially those concerning the organization and discipline of the clergy, who had become dissolute, and obnoxious to the people and government. Sivaitic and Shamanistic forms of worship and superstitions antagonistic to the Buddhist faith and to the doctrines preached by the expounders of the Mahāyāna school had also been introduced, and a reform appeared to be demanded.

1 The little Tibetan work from which I have taken these biographical notes says that this locality also bore the name of Do-mang Tsang-k'a.

2 It is said that he was presented to the "King of the Doctrine (*Ch'ügi jya-bo, Dharmarāja*) who resided in the Bri-kung (Brébung?) lamasery. This dignitary was probably the head of the church of Tibet, and a follower of the Kadamba school. It is possible that Friar Oderic referred to this lama when speaking of *lo Abassi*. This last name is possibly an inaccurate transcription of a Tibetan title, Lo-zang shé (rab), for example, a common one among lamas of high degree.

Encouraged and protected by the King of Tibet, Tsong-k'apa founded the *Gélu* denomination, and a few miles out-

Tsong-k'apa, born at Kumbum.
The Talé-lama of Lh'asa. Pan-ch'en Rinpoch'é of Trashil'unpo.

THE INCARNATE GODS OF TIBET. (FROM A TIBETAN PAINTING.)

side of Lh'asa he erected what is known as Gadän gomba, or "the happy lamasery." His followers were called *Gélupa* or *Gadänba*, the first name being now universally used.

The new sect rapidly gained adherents throughout Tibet and Mongolia, and it is probable that at an early date a lamasery was founded near the birthplace of Tsong-k'apa. The name given it was Kumbum, "Hundred thousand images," possibly on account of the pictured leaves of the "white sandal-wood tree." The Chinese have always called it T'a-erh-ssŭ, "the convent of the Dagoba," under which name we first find it mentioned by Friar Orazio della Penna in the early part of the eighteenth century.[1] Its fame and riches rapidly grew, and under the fostering care of the emperors of the reigning dynasty in China, who have sedulously protected the lamas, it soon became one of the most important lamaseries in the empire.[2]

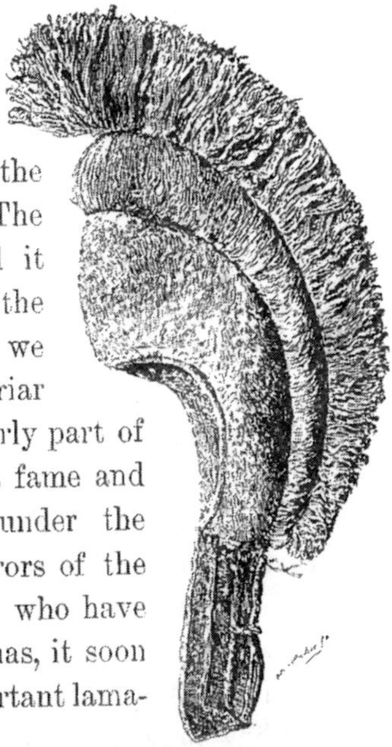

YELLOW HAT WORN BY LAMAS IN CHURCH CEREMONIES.

In 1708 the newly incarnate Talé lama Lozang kalzang Jyats'o resided at Kumbum until the Chinese army had put down the rebellion in Tibet, and conducted him back to Lh'asa, by which means the Chinese obtained their first permanent foothold in that country.[3]

I do not propose to examine into the organization of the lamaist church throughout Tibet, nor will I renew the

1 "Tarsy, paese del regno d'Amdoa, resta lontano una buona giornata da Scilin, o Scilingh." "Notizia del Regno del Thibet," p. 29, in Klaproth's edit. On p. 21, he calls it Kungbung.

2 The most revered lamasery in China is that at Wu-t'ai shan in Shanhsi which is said to have been founded in the first century, A. D.

3 The Pan-ch'en Rinpoch'é Paldän Yéshé stayed four months at Kum-

vexed question of the origin of the points of similitude in this hierarchy and that of the Church of Rome. However, a few remarks are necessary concerning the organization of the lamaseries of Amdo. They nearly all belong to the Gélupa sect, which is, as previously mentioned, called by the Chinese "yellow-capped sect," its followers wearing yellow hats in church ceremonies, to distinguish them from the followers of the old church, who have red ones.[1] At the present time, dark red clothes are almost universally worn, except by the lamas of high degree, the reason for this change being that red does not soil as rapidly as yellow, and, moreover, there is no yellow to be had in Tibetan cloth (Chinese, *pulo*), the stuff of which lamas' clothes are made.

Some of the principal lamaseries receive annual subsidies from the emperor; and in these all the lamas entered on the registers (*t'o*), comprising only those whose instruction enables them to take part in the church ceremonies, receive an allowance of flour and grain, not enough, however, to feed them during the year. The gifts of the laity, of families and friends, the pay they receive for reading prayers for laymen, or rich lamas who prefer to perform their religious duties vicariously, and numerous other perquisites add very considerably to their revenues. The houses in which the lamas live belong to them, and those who have large ones increase their means by renting a part of them to visitors or to other lamas. Another important source of revenue is money-lending, which is practised extensively by the lamas in Amdo, and, in fact, in all other countries where they are

bum during the winter of 1779–80 when on his way to Peking. See Turner, "Embassy to Court of the Teshoo lama," p. 459, where he calls it Coomboo Goombaw (Kumbum gomba).

[1] In Tibetan the first sect is sometimes called *Dja-sér*, "Yellow Cap"; the second *Dja-mar*, "Red cap." The convent of Sérkok, north of Hsi-ning, is a Kadamba one, but this is a reformed sect nearly identical with the Gélupa.

found; the usual rate of interest is two per cent. a month.

In Amdo the lamaseries do not own as much property as they do in Tibet, but many of the lamas are quite wealthy; they are enterprising traders, and make frequent journeys to Peking, Urga, Lh'asa, or Hsi-an Fu, where they purchase all the articles most readily sold in their country.

At the head of every lamasery is an abbot (*k'anpo*), who is either sent from a large lamasery to fill this office or, in a few cases, is chosen by the lamas. Under him are a certain number of officers, of whom some act as magistrates and provosts or censors, others attend to the temporal affairs of the convent, and still others superintend the ceremonies.[1] In a few of the larger lamaseries there is an official appointed by the Amban who assists the lama officials (*seng kuan*) in enforcing discipline, but whose principal duty consists in observing the spirit animating the convent, whether it is friendly or hostile to the Chinese government, and keeping the Amban duly posted. This official is styled Erh lao-yeh, or "the second gentleman," by the Chinese.

The rules of the larger lamaseries are very strict, and, while crimes can usually be compounded by the payment of fines, the misdemeanors of the lower-class lamas are punished by whipping, solitary confinement, or expulsion. The ecclesiastical authorities have, even within the limits of China, power of life and death over the lamas of their convents; the civil authorities can not, or rather do not choose to, assail these prerogatives, and generally submit

[1] The *Jassak* and *Gékor lamas* act as provosts; the *Nyérpa* attends to the finances, supplies, etc.; the *Dronyér* looks after guests; the *Wudzépa* orders and conducts the ceremonies. The Jassak, Gékor, and Wudzépa are appointed by the K'anpo for a term of years.

without demur to the decisions of the ecclesiastical courts.

In nearly all the large convents there are certain dignitaries who do not take part in the administration nor in most of the ceremonies, but who, by their presence and superior sanctity, add to the fame of the establishments, and thus cause the laity to increase their offerings marvelously. There are forty-eight of these living saints, or rather incarnations of former saints, in Amdo, the Koko-nor, and the Ts'aidam. Over thirty of them are from Kumbum, while only a very few are born in central Tibet. They are divided into three classes, according to their greater or lesser degree of holiness; the most holy of all resides in the great lamasery of Kuei-tē, and, strange as it must appear, there is none at Kumbum.[1]

They are supposed to be in constant prayer for the welfare of the locality where they reside; and are frequently consulted by the laity as to the success of any undertaking, for as fortune-tellers they are supposed to be "equaled by few, excelled by none."

The Wu-dzé-pa is, as previously said, the director of church ceremonies and of the choirs. In this connection, the system of musical notation used in the convents to teach the lamas to chant is worthy of notice. The books, called *yang-yig*, "hymn or song books," contain a kind of descriptive score, consisting of a wavy line showing when and for what space of time the voice should rise or fall. Where the conch-shell should be sounded or the drum beaten is shown by the figure of a

[1] Saints of the highest class are styled *Kushok*. Kushok Tashu rinpoch'é is the first — he resides at Kuei-tē; Kushok Duwa is the second, Kushok Ch'ubchen the third. Those of the second class are styled *Alaksan*; those of the third *Sér-gi chyong-wa*. In Mongol they are called *Hutuketu*, *Chabéron*, and *Gégén*—their generic name is *hubilhan*, "incarnations"; in Tibetan they are known as *tru-ku*, and in Amdo as *Karwa*.

PSALM-BOOK (YANG-YIG) WITH DESCRIPTIVE SCORE.

shell or a drumstick. This system of notation is specially interesting from the fact that it is, as far as I am aware, the only one found in eastern or central Asia;

the Chinese have none, nor have I heard of any in Korea or Japan.[1]

The other objects used in church ceremonies are the small hand-drum (*damaru*), frequently made of children's skulls covered with snake-skin, the bell (*dril-bu*), and the *dorjé* (the Indian *vajra* or Indra's thunderbolt). Other instruments used on occasions are the trumpet, often a human thigh-bone with a whip-lash of skin, the *purbu*, or triangular nail, which plays an important rôle in exorcisms, the holy-water vase (*bumba*), the spherical mirror (*mé-long*) over which holy water is poured, the skull libation-bowl, and a variety of minor things too numerous to mention.[2]

LIBATION-BOWL—BOWL MADE OF SKULL, BASE AND COVER OF GILDED BRONZE.

The non-official lamas are divided into two classes. The first are those who have simply shaved their heads, taken the five minor vows, put on the red gown, and made their home in a lamasery; these are usually called *Draba*.

[1] Father Orazio della Penna was the first to record this peculiar musical notation. See "Breve Notizia del Regno del Tibet," p. 72 of Klaproth's edition.

[2] All images of gods have yellow gowns in which they are wrapped; the holy-water vase is never used without its skirt. The books have likewise their clothing (*nabzé*), without which it is held improper to leave them when not in actual use. See illustrations, pp. 103 and 106.

They do all such work as printing books, looking after the horses and cattle, gathering cattle dung, cooking, sweeping the temples, and trimming the lamps. The second class are those who have studied the sacred books, and have been ordained *gélong*,[1] taking on them vows of chastity, poverty, abstinence from tobacco, liquor, gaming, etc. From their number all the lama officials are chosen. Among the Tibetans and Mongols of the Koko-nor lamas are addressed as *Aka*, the title *Lama* (Sanskrit *guru*) being reserved for those of high degree and of known saintliness.

The *Draba* are not even bound to celibacy in this part of the empire; at certain seasons of the year they can obtain leave of absence and return to their families; but they must not show themselves in the company of their wives within the convent. Among the Mongol lamas from the Ts'aidam and the Koko-nor, nearly all are married, the *Gélong*, of course, excepted.

I have frequently been questioned as to the morality of the lamas of Mongolia and Tibet, and I can only answer that, while I do not believe that the standard attained by those persons would be considered very high by us, there are large numbers of them and even of the laity who observe their moral laws, and there are undoubtedly not a few men among the *Gélong* who strictly adhere to the vows of chastity, poverty, truthfulness, and all the other obligations they have taken upon themselves in entering the order.

[1] Huc, *op. cit.*, II, 283, speaks of a "confrérie des *élans*, instituée par le Bandchan Remboutchi." This *confrérie* is simply the body of the priesthood (*gélong-élan*). The Pan-ch'en rinpoch'é ordains lamas *gélong*, and ordination by him is the highest honor a gélong can aspire to. It is he who ordains the Talé-lama when he reaches the prescribed age, which in his case is, I believe, fifteen. With the word *aka* compare the Manchu *eke*, "elder brother."

Shortly after my arrival at Lusar, I was joined by the San-ch'uan lama, to whom I had sent a note when on my way to Hsi-ning. He was called Tsairang lama, and was a man of about fifty, with features rather resembling the Tibetan than the Mongol type. He had been with Potanin for two years, during which time he had accompanied him around the Koko-nor and to Kan-chou. He showed himself from the first most anxious concerning an authorization from the Chinese government to travel outside the border, which he insisted I must procure, as it would entitle me to an escort, without which traveling westward was impossible. When I told him that I had decided not to ask the Amban for either pass or escort, and, in short, that my method was to keep out of the way of officials except when absolutely forced to ask their assistance, he was but little disposed to join my party. Another consideration which must have influenced him to determine finally not to accompany me was that he would not be able to squeeze me to any great extent, certainly not so much as it seems he had squeezed Potanin, with whom according to one of my men he said he had made more in two years than he could have made in ten years of legitimate business.

It was this Tsairang lama that began the stories I was to hear so often repeated of the terrors encountered in meeting the Tibetans, of their wonderful marksmanship with their long guns, and of their audacity in attacking and pillaging caravans. To the stories of dangers from them were added others relating to the horrors of the country itself, winds that cut one's skin, water that destroyed one's stomach, pestilential emanations that poisoned men and beasts, sandy wastes, no grass, and not a living soul to be seen for days and days. However, he remained with me, for four or five days, and I heard from him much of what I have noted previously concerning the people of the San-ch'uan.

As soon as the festivities at Kumbum were at an end, I set to work getting together all the things necessary for a journey in the desert, and never in my life was my patience so sorely tried as during the six weeks which followed. The most insignificant purchase took days to complete; the people were lavish in promises, good-natured, smiling, but never accomplished anything. I required two small cotton tents, and, not being able to buy them ready-made, I had to get them sewed for me. It took three weeks before the hair-ropes, the blue and white cotton, the poles, pins, etc., were got together, and my tents were not ready till five weeks after ordering them. Horses and camels were also necessary, and, though I did not experience much trouble in buying serviceable ponies, I had to scour the whole country before I found five poor camels. The Mongols of the Koko-nor have but few, and hold good ones at enormous prices, reaching frequently to forty or fifty taels, while the Tibetans but rarely make use of them, preferring yak and ponies, and in this they show their good sense, as I was soon to learn to my cost.

My life at Lusar was monotonous in the extreme. At dawn an old lama, who lived in a watch-tower on the top of the hill overlooking the village, heralded in the day by blowing on a conch-shell. After seeing to the ponies, and killing as much time as possible over my breakfast, I strolled about from shop to shop talking and asking questions about the strange peoples and countries the shopkeepers had visited, or else I took a walk over to Kumbum to see some lama. When the sun had risen above the high hills which surround the village, I climbed on to the broad, flat roof of my dwelling where the tent-makers were at work, and basked in the sun. The weather was generally delightful, the nights never very cold, and in the daytime the thermometer frequently stood at 60° F. in the sun. Now and then a little snow fell, but it melted in the first warm rays of the sun, and vanished in heavy mists which rolled up the mountain side. The only really cold weather was when the sky became cloudy, and I learned that this was always the case. The wind seldom blew, and before the middle of March all the fields had been plowed, and sown with grain.[1]

[1] In the south Koko-nor range, some eight or nine miles south of Lusar, are the three peaks of the Lh'a-mo ri, visible from Hsi-ning, and easily recognized by the blackness of the rocks (porphyry) composing these needles. As one looks towards Kumbum from Lusar, a high, rounded peak is seen far to the east-southeast behind the lamasery. It is called by the people of Lusar, Amyé Stilia, and is said to have hidden within it great store of turquoises of which men cannot get possession.

There are fourteen mountains in and around Amdo which have the word *amyé*, "forefather," prefixed to their names, each one holding concealed within it some precious substance, and all revered, and, to a certain extent, worshiped by Chinese, Tibetans and Mongols. The "Hsi-yü t'ung wen chih," B. XV, gives their names as follows:

1. Amyé malchin musun.
2. Amyé gan-kar.
3. Amyé bayan-kara.
4. Amyé wu-djan t'ou-po.
5. Amyé ék'yi.
6. Amyé dung-zug.
7. Amyé ser-ch'en.
8. Amyé na-ri t'on-po.
9. Amyé murun.
10. Amyé bayan tson-dru.
11. Amyé bar-wa dan.
12. Amyé dar-jyé.
13. Amyé nich'ugun.
14. Amyé k'uk'en kurban.

The names of Nos. 1, 5, 9, 10, 13, and 14 are Mongol; those of the others are Tibetan. No. 1 is the most sacred; it was pointed out to me from a hill beside the Tosun nor, about fifty miles east-northeast — a rounded mountain with snow several thousand feet down its side. The Amyé Stilia does not figure in the above list, which does not agree with that of Prjevalsky, "Mongolia," II, 76. His Kumbum damar is probably my Lh'a-mo ri. In the German translation of the narrative of Prjevalsky's third journey, "Reise in Tibet und am oberen Lauf des Gelben Flusses," Amne-matschin and Ama (*sic*) ssurtu figure on the map as names of mountain ranges; and in Petermann's "Geographische Mittheilungen" (Tafel I, 1885), I find nothing less horrible than Amnimanchenponra Gebirge!

While on this subject I must call attention to the present condition of our maps of China and Central Asia, where specimens of five or six systems of transcription figure side by side on the same maps. To mention only those occurring on English and German maps of the country I traveled, Kui-tē figures as Culdui, Nien-po becomes Nan-po, Taukar is

During my stay at Lusar I had no end of trouble resulting from the rascality and violent temper of the servant I had brought with me from Peking. This man seemed to have resolved to make it so uncomfortable for any one who showed an inclination to join me in any capacity, that he should have to give up all idea of doing so. He was afraid of some new man supplanting him in his functions of disbursing officer, which brought him now and then some considerable squeezes. I myself usually paid all persons I had employed or from whom I had bought anything, but Chinese in the service of foreigners have a wonderful knack in eluding every measure their masters may take to prevent them from levying commissions on salesmen or others.

There is a story told of the head boy of a wealthy foreigner who led an expedition through China about ten years ago, which illustrates aptly the rascality of these servants, and the usual weakness of the masters who nearly always allow them to go scot-free, rather than take the trouble to have them punished. This traveler had had a large escort furnished him by the authorities of all cities through which he had passed, and had always, when changing them, handed to his steward a sum of money to reward them, besides paying all their expenses while traveling. When discussing

Donkir, Hsi-ning is Silin, and Sa chou is Saitu (the Mongols always call it Saju). Then we have innumerable errors resulting from two or three modes of transcribing the same character, errors easily corrected by referring to Playfair's "Cities and Towns of China," or similar works. We find *Da*-t'ung ho and *Ta*-*t'*ung Fu, Si-*nan* Fu and Chi-*ngan* Fu, Ping-fan *Sian* and Hua *Hsien*, Ko-ko-nor and *Kuku* k'ut'un. Again we use the native word for river, pass, or fortress, etc., and follow it with an English translation, as if the original was part of the name, *e. g.:* Pai-*ho* river; Nan *k'ou* pass; Dungbura *k'utul* pass; Di *ch'u* river, etc., *ho* meaning river, and so on. Such errors would not be tolerated on maps of Europe, America, or Africa; why disfigure those of this section of Asia with them?

with the magistrate at Ta-chien-lu the question of getting an escort for a projected journey through Tibet, he said that he intended not only paying all expenses, as he had always done, but rewarding the men composing the escort. The magistrate looked surprised at the statement that the illustrious traveler had always paid his escort and their expenses during the eighteen months his journey in China had lasted, and declared that these men had had all their expenses paid by the authorities, and that not one of them had ever received a cash from him. With but little trouble it was found that the boy had quietly pocketed all the money given him for the escort, amounting to several thousand taels. He confessed, but the master, for some reason, was satisfied with dismissing him, and he returned to Shanghai, where he now occupies a prominent and even honored place among the merchants of that city.

This one of mine was, unfortunately for him, too fond of his wine, and often told me things about his exploits which he had better have kept to himself. Of one piece of sharp practice, perpetrated while serving Lieutenant Younghusband, he was especially proud. He said that, when leaving K'uei-hua ch'eng for Hami, he himself had bought the carts and mules which his master had hired, and had given for them much less than Younghusband had to pay as hire. This was his start in business, and by the time he reached India (six months later), he had stolen over three hundred ounces of silver. Although this confession put me on my guard at an early stage of my journey, he was able to make over Tls. 50 on the hire of the carts from Peking to Lan-chou Fu alone.

I was in despair about securing men to accompany me in my wanderings; weeks had passed, and I seemed no nearer getting my party ready than when I arrived; so I thought I should ask the keeper of the inn at Hsi-ning, where I had stopped, and who had then been most polite to me, and had since paid me several visits at Lusar, to help me to find two or three reliable men, one of whom I hoped would be a lama. He sent me in a few days, two Mohammedans, with whom I was greatly pleased: one, a man of about forty-five, who had passed his life as muleteer between Kan-su and Ssŭ-ch'uan; the other, a young Hsieh-chia, who had lived some three years with the Panak'a to the north of the Koko-nor. But the third man, the lama, was not so easily found. I went to Hsi-ning myself, and talked it over with Ma chang-kuei-ti, and he finally remembered a friend of his, the steward of one of the large lamaseries to the northward, who, he thought, would probably know of some one willing to go with me. I asked him the name of this lamasery. "Kuo-mang ssŭ," he said; "in Tibetan it is called Sérkok gomba."[1] "Why, then you are speaking of Bu lama," I exclaimed. "He is an old friend of mine; it was with him, when he was in Peking some five years ago, that I commenced studying Tibetan. I will go and see him myself, and, from what I know of him and from what you tell me of his influential position, I think I may be able to secure the services of a good man."

The following day I left, accompanied by one of my men, for Bu lama's home. Our road led us along the Pei-ch'uan[2] some twenty-five miles, till we passed the village of Hsin-chen (or ch'eng), near which a wall crosses the

1 This lamasery is probably the "Altyn gomba" of Prjevalsky and Kreitner.

2 The river which flows in this valley is called Pei-ho or Pei-ch'uan, but Prjevalsky gives it a Mongol name, Buguk gol; he might just as well have given it a Russian one, for no Mongols live along it, except near its head.

valley. This Pei-ch'uan valley was half a mile broad, and everywhere under cultivation; villages were numerous, but many of them in ruins, sad mementos of the rebellion. Fruit-trees grew around, and fine poplars lined the road in many places. Altogether, the country on the Pei-ch'uan compared favorably with the best along the Hsi-ning river. The population in the main valley is entirely Chinese, but in the lower portions of the numerous smaller ones which open into it, T'u-ssŭ live, while nomadic Amdowa or Rongwa inhabit the highlands at their heads.

A short distance beyond Hsin-chen we turned to the east[1] and entered a side valley down which flowed a fine brook, the Sér ch'u, or "golden stream," which we ascended some ten miles, passing numerous T'u-ssŭ farms and villages, till we finally saw the spires of the Sérkok gomba temples, rising behind a wall better suited to a fortress than to the abode of peaceful monks, for it had flanking towers and loopholes on every side. The T'u-ssŭ farm-houses were each surrounded by a solid, loopholed wall, and near every one was a small grist-mill. The only peculiarly Tibetan feature about these T'u-ssŭ houses was the use of poles with printed prayers on bits of cotton hanging from them, the "wind horses" referred to previously.

The people were busy in the fields, cutting the sod and piling it in heaps to which they set fire. When all roots and grass had been consumed they threw this top-dressing of powdered loess and ashes over the soil, which usually received no other fertilizer. The fields tilled the previous year were not plowed; only those on which a sod had

[1] The road up the main valley leads to Mobashen (Prjevalsky's "Mu-ba-chin-ta"), which is about fifteen miles above Hsin-chen.

formed were worked, but ground is so abundant here that even with this system of culture much remains fallow.

Entering the heavy gates of the lamasery we inquired for the house of Bu lama, or Stanzin ch'ü-p'el as he is called in religion, and were led to the finest one in the convent, where I received a most hearty welcome not only from the lama, but from all his household who had been with him at Peking. His dwelling consisted of four pavilions, two of them two-storied, opening on a central courtyard where there was a broad, stone altar with juniper boughs piled on it. The houses were in Chinese style, but with smooth board floors and extremely clean; the copper fire-pans and kettles shone like gold, and the lama and every inmate of his house had dusting-cloths in their hands so frequently that I soon felt thoroughly uncomfortable. The upper story of one of the buildings was used as a private chapel; its walls were lined with images of the gods, and Bu lama's special patron saints were set in little niches. Here the lama went through a long series of prostrations every day, but the more complicated ceremonies of his religion he got performed vicariously — he himself was not a gélong, but merely a lay brother, though the richest man in the lamasery. One pavilion was allotted to me, and the lama's *chef*—he had an excellent Chinese one—soon served me a meal such as I had not eaten since leaving Peking. On the walls of the room were many pictures he had brought back from his voyages, and a photograph of himself, his friend Pal-dän zanbo, and me, taken some years before at Peking; and in a prominent place among his curios was a tin trumpet my little daughter had once given him.

We talked till a late hour about my family and my plans, and, having got the lama's promise of assistance,

I fell asleep on the soft Ning-hsia rugs which covered the k'ang, in the comforting belief that my days of trouble were near an end.

The next day was the 25th of the moon, and a busy one, for lamas were to come at an early hour and read prayers during the whole day.[1] Everyone was up by daylight, cleaning and scrubbing the already immaculate rooms and cooking food for the expected guests. Bu lama had no book-learning; he had devoted his time to the temporal affairs of his lamasery, and did not know how to chant the litanies, read the sacred books in measure, or perform the duties of a gélong, but, being a wealthy man, he had the most devout lamas in the convent meet at his house twice a month to read prayers for him, when he entertained them with the best the place afforded. At about seven o'clock five old lamas made their appearance, wrapped in the long, sleeveless cloaks of red with high stiff collars worn in church ceremonies; and, having removed their boots, they took their seats on the k'ang. Spreading their books out before them, they commenced chanting, one of them leading the ceremony and at certain stages ringing a bell or sounding a drum which he held in his right hand, while he shook a dorjé held in the left, or else clapping his hands or snapping his fingers; then the other lamas did likewise. Every half-hour or so they stopped for a while to drink buttered tea, and at noon an Homeric meal of dumplings, boiled mutton, soup, bread, etc., was served them, which Bu lama and I helped to consume.[2]

1 The 1st, 8th, 15th, and 25th of each moon are holy days among the lamas, and are called *dus-bzang* (pronounced *dubzang*), "good time, lucky day." The 1st and 15th are celebrated by church ceremonies; the 8th and 25th are observed by the lamas reading services in their houses, or in holding services at the homes of the wealthy ones among them.

2 During the first part of the service, attendants burnt juniper boughs

HAND-DRUM (DAMARU). BODY MADE OF TWO SKULLS.

Three of the lamas had resided for some years at Lh'asa, and, having learnt from Bu lama that I took a profound interest in their religion, they advised me to go there. They insisted that there were no difficulties to encounter on the journey when once the Ts'aidam had been reached, for they, like all the people hereabout,

on the altar in the courtyard, and threw on them meal, milk, wine, and tea. Then they arranged along its edge plates of fruit, nuts, cakes, rolls of bread, butter, etc., which remained there during the day.

thought their countrymen around the Koko-nor the most barbarous of men and the most to be feared. They asked me many questions concerning India, and Russia, which they called the Buriat Kingdom.

Prjevalsky and Szechenyi had visited their convent, but, as these travelers did not speak Tibetan, they had had no intercourse with them. The lamasery, they said, had been destroyed during the Mohammedan rebellion and was not now as vast and beautiful as it used to be, but the great sanctity of the living Buddha, who made his residence here, brought many pilgrims and rich presents. There are about 700 lamas at Sérkok, nearly all of them Tibetans, and it is held to be one of the finest lamaseries north of Hsi-ning. Bu lama told them that I had translated into my native tongue some of the sacred books (parts of the Kandjur), and he showed them a copy of my translation of the confessional service, which I had given him at Peking. They took the book, raised it to their foreheads in sign of respect, and declared that I was a great *pundib.* Then they asked endless questions concerning the state of Buddhism in foreign lands. They were astonished that it no longer existed in India, and that the church of Ceylon was so like the ancient Buddhist one. When told of our esoteric Buddhists, the Mahatmâs, and of the wonderful doctrines they claimed to have obtained from Tibet, they were immensely amused. They declared that though in ancient times there were, doubtless, saints and sages who could perform some of the miracles now claimed by the Esoterists, none were living at the present day; and they looked upon this new school as rankly heretical, and as something approaching an imposition on our credulity.

After a while the lamas resumed their recitation, and I

went with Bu lama to visit the temples. As they differed in their interior arrangement from those I had seen at Kumbum, I will describe them briefly. We first visited the hall where readings of the sacred books take place. It was about 150 feet by 75 feet; the light came from above, as in all temples; the ceiling rested on two rows of pillars covered with handsome Ning-hsia rugs. On the farther side, and facing the entrance, was a low platform about six feet square, covered with rugs and cushions; here the abbot or the lama conducting the reading takes his seat. The whole hall was filled with rows of cushions, before which were low, narrow stands on which to place the books. There were no ornaments or images in this hall,[1] but the walls were divided into panels about twelve feet square, and in each of these was painted on cotton some god or scene from the life of the Buddha Shakyamuni, all of them highly interesting and very quaint. Adjoining this hall was a small building, a tea-kitchen (*ja k'ang*), in which were huge copper caldrons to boil tea, set in a stove of masonry, and along the wall were perhaps a hundred copper beakers in which it is served to the lamas.

THE GODDESS DROL-MA. (IMAGE COVERED WITH GARMENT OF YELLOW SATIN.)

[1] The second story, however, was filled with images of every size, and made of silver, bronze, wood, or clay. They were arranged along the walls. There were no altars before most of them, and only very small ones before the rest. Nearly all temples have their image rooms on the second floor.

These readings of the sacred books by the whole congregation of lamas are performed at the expense of wealthy laymen who are supposed to acquire as much merit by having the 108 volumes constituting the Tibetan canon read for them as if they themselves had done it. The 40,000 to 45,000 loose leaves of these volumes are divided among the lamas seated in front of the low tables in the hall, and they all set to work to chant or read through the piles assigned them as fast as they possibly can, interrupting their work now and then to drink tea, also provided by the person for whose benefit they are reading. As each lama can read about forty leaves a day, the whole canon is soon gone through. It also often happens that some person offers the monks of a convent an entertainment of tea, or buttered tea, or tea with butter and milk, in which case it is served in the lecture hall; these general teas are called *mang ja*.[1]

Near this hall was the chief temple of the lamasery, the Jo k'ang, in which were three large bronze images of the Buddha Shakyamuni, copies of the three made of him during his life. The gold-roofed temple of Kumbum is also a Jo k'ang, but the image of the Lord (Jo) there preserved is said to be an original. In front of the temple was a great courtyard, and on the outer side of its front wall were painted large pictures of the chief sanctuaries of the

[1] Many lamas earn their living by reading the sacred books for some person's benefit. One, who was my teacher for three years, used to read the 108 volumes of the Kandjur in about six months for a sum of fifty ounces of silver. Chinese Buddhist monks (*Ho-shang*) do not, as far as I am aware, have these recitations of the scriptures.

This custom of dividing up a sacred work and having it read by a number of persons appears to have been known to the Mohammedans, for I find in Ibn Batuta's "Travels" the following: "In the *zâuiah* of Cairo, after the morning prayer, copies of the Koran divided in sections are brought. Each fakir takes one and so they make a reading of all the Koran." "Travels of Ibn Batuta," Defrémery's transl., I, 72.

Buddhist faith,[1] and rows of prayer-barrels were placed at either extremity of it.

Before the images of the Jo[2] innumerable butter lamps were burning, and Bu asked me if I would not like to offer a few to the god. I said it would give me much pleasure, and turning to the lama who filled the lamps I gave him a little piece of silver, worth perhaps fifty cents, and asked him to bring me some. The mode of offering a lamp consists in lighting it, holding it up with both hands before the image, and then placing it on the altar. I had quite forgotten how cheap everything, even church worship, was in Amdo, and was horrified when I noticed that the lama had prepared for me perhaps seventy-five lamps to light, but I was obliged to light them all, and I was declared a most devout and worthy person by all the old women worshiping outside the portals of the temple. Offering ceremonial scarfs (*k'atag*) and lighting lamps are two easy methods of complying with local customs in Buddhist countries, where visits to temples for purposes of idle curiosity are very much disliked, and in many places forbidden. I have always observed these customs whenever I thought it necessary.

After visiting a few more buildings, of minor interest, we turned homeward.[3] On passing through the yard of

1 There were represented, Potala (Lh'asa), Trashil'unpo, Dorjé-dzin (Vadjraséna where the Buddha attained enlightenment, at Gaya in India), O-mi shan (*Jya-nag lang-ch'é*) in Ssŭ-ch'uan, Wu-t'ai-shan (*Ri-vo tsé-nga*) in Shan-hsi, P'u-t'o shan (*Lh'o chyok Potala*) in Chih-chiang, Ch'iu-hua shan (*Shar chyok sai-nying po*), and Peking (*Jya-nag Peiching*). The lake of Tali Fu (*Tali ts'o*) and the *Doké la* in the Tsarong are also famous pilgrimages, but no pictures of them were to be seen here.

2 The three original Jo images are kept, one in the Jo k'ang at Lh'asa, another in the Chan-t'an ssŭ (Sandal-wood temple) at Peking, the third at Kumbum. To these, lamas give also the name of *Kusum* (*Kāyatraya* in Sanskrit); and by a curious perversion of the Mahāyānist doctrine of the *Kāyatraya*, they say that the Lh'asa Jo is the Dharma-kāya, the Peking Jo is the Sambhoga-kāya, and the Kumbum Jo is the Nirmana-kāya.

3 A curious feature in the exterior decoration of the walls of most Tib-

HOLY-WATER VASE. (WITH COVER OF YELLOW, RED, AND BLUE SILK.)

one of the temples we met a lama whom I had known in Peking, and who, now one of the temple's attendants, was carrying a vase of holy water. Bu lama poured a little in his hand and drank it, probably to cure some

etan temples is the insertion, near the top, of panels of brushwood placed perpendicularly to the plane of the wall, the surface carefully trimmed so that at a distance they look like bits of rough stuccoing, probably the effect desired. Turner, "Embassy to the Court of Teshoo Lama," p. 293, tries to find some explanation of this curious style of decoration.

bodily pain, at least so I interpreted his action, for I have often seen uneducated Catholics use holy water in this way.

On reaching the house we found awaiting me the man Bu had chosen to be my guide on my travels. His looks pleased me very much, and he agreed to join me in a few days at Lusar. Nothing more detaining me at Sérkok gomba, I took leave of my friends, carrying with me several sheep's paunches filled with butter and a variety of other presents given me by the different people I had met, who also made me promise to come again and stay some time with them, when we should visit all the surrounding country.

I went back to Lusar in high spirits, and commenced making my final arrangements, but what was my disappointment a few days later when one of my men, whom I had sent to Sérkok gomba with a pony for the lama to ride back on, brought me word from him that he could not go, but that Bu lama was sending me another man, one whom I had known at Peking. A day or two later this man came, but one of the first things he told me was that Bu lama said I must not attempt to go to Lh'asa (I had never said a word to him about going there); that, though I should find no difficulty in reaching that city, I and all my men should certainly be put to death as soon as our presence there was found out, for the people would demand our execution, and the Amban would not be able to defend us. All this was very disagreeable; it was said in the presence of my men, and, as this lama had lived at Lh'asa for some five years, they naturally believed he spoke truth, and it was a crushing blow after what I had been telling them about the absence of danger. There was nothing for it but to reargue the question at once, and to attempt at all events to make a start; after that, to try every means to inspire them with confidence in themselves and in me. This, and the hope of a considerable cumshaw if they followed me to the end of my wanderings would, I believed, finally make them stay by me wherever I went. It would require too much space, and would moreover be tedious, to tell of all the attempts made by first one person, then another, to deter me from journeying westward; of the irresolute conduct of my men, who one day said they would not risk their lives on such a fool's errand as I proposed, and the next day swore they would go wherever I asked them. The little store of patience I had nearly gave out. It was then the early part of March, and I had not yet been able to purchase a single camel nor even to hire one. So I decided upon moving to Tankar about thirty-five miles to the west of Lusar, where I was assured that everything necessary for camp life, besides ponies and camels, could be easily and cheaply purchased.

About this time there came to Lusar a Khalkha Mongol, a living Buddha, from Parin, called the Cheunjin lama. He had been to Kiakhta, to Peking, Tientsin, and other places where foreigners lived, and had met me at Peking. He was now on his way to Lh'asa, and was waiting for the arrival of a large party of Mongols from the Ta-t'ung valley (Mori wang Mongols), with whom he was to travel. He asked me to join his party, and I should have been delighted to have done so, for, barring accidents and Chinese intervention, I should most likely have been able to reach Lh'asa, but his departure was not fixed; it might take place, he said, in May or June, or perhaps even later, at all events it would not before two or three months. This would not answer for me; my money-bag was not sufficiently filled to permit me to wait so long, and, much to my regret, I had to give up the idea of traveling with him.

To go to Tankar we took a good bridle-path down a valley which brought us to the Hsi-ning river at Tou-pa, a small town about a mile to the east of Ch'en-hai p'u. These two localities were important commercial centers before the rebellion, but are now partly ruined, and much of the trade has left them for Lusar and Lasa, the latter a small town in a valley to the north of Tou-pa. A short distance to the west of Ch'en-hai p'u[1] we entered a rocky gorge which extended all the way to Tankar, some fifteen miles.

Tankar (*Tan-ka-erh*)[2] is a sub-prefecture (*t'ing*), and the most westerly frontier town in this part of Kan-su. It commands the two roads to the Koko-nor: one going by Sharakuto to the south, and known as the Nan-k'ou, "South Pass"; the other up the valley of the Hsi-ning river, called the Chung k'ou, "Middle Pass." Its population of Chinese and Tibetans is not over 10,000, exclusive of a garrison of a nominal force of 200 men under a colonel (*Hsieh-t'ai*). During the rebellion of the Mohammedans it suffered greatly, and it is said that nearly 10,000 of them were killed by the imperial troops when it fell into their hands. Since then no Mohammedan has been allowed to reside in, or even to enter the city, unless a well-known and responsible inhabitant has become his security. The troublous times of the rebellion, and the rigorous meas-

1 This village is called Kuo-ja by Tibetans and Mongols. At the mouth of the gorge is another village called Tsamalun.

2 Huc calls it Tang-keou-eul, and Prjevalsky calls it Tonkir or Donkir. Tibetans and Mongols name it Dung kor, or Tung kor. The name is not Chinese; it may be *t'ang-mk'ar* "fort (commanding) the steppe." if it is a Tibetan name, of which I am not sure. Sharakuto is seventy *li* south of it.

ures in force since its suppression, have greatly affected the trade of this place, the Tibetans have found another market at Ta-chien-lu, and, although business is now improving, it is a far less important trading point than it was in the days before the war.

Though there is quite a large suburb on the east side of the city, all the trade is carried on within the walls, the Tibetans living in a number of caravansaries, where reside their commercial agents or vakils (*tsong-pön*, or *kar-pön*), who act as agents for them in their transactions, and are, to a certain extent, responsible for the people of their respective localities while at Tankar. The principal imports from Lh'asa and Ulterior Tibet are *tr'uk*, or woolen cloth of various colors and qualities, incense sticks, saffron from Kashmeer (*K'a-ch'é shakama*),[1] Buddhist books, brown sugar (*buram*), and dried dates (*kazur-pani*) from India, cowries, disks of chank-shells and of amber for ornaments, some furs, and a few other articles of no great value. The traders export articles of much greater value, comprising mules and horses, satins, silks, gold brocades, chinaware, etc., but with the exception of the horses, mules, and chinaware, very little is bought at Tankar, which is rather a depôt than a purchasing center. They go to Hsi-an Fu and Peking to make their more

[1] This variety of saffron is said to be the best. There is another called *kur-kum*. Among the most valuable articles brought to China by Tibetans, but more frequently by the Nepalese, are conch-shells with whorls turning to the right, called in Tibetan *yä-chyil dung-kar*. They sell for four or five hundred taels, are classed among jewels, and are used in lamaseries as trumpets. The Chinese also value them greatly. There is, or at least was, not long ago, a white whelk belonging to the emperor deposited with the Tartar general at Fu chow, to which great respect was shown, as the spirits of the storm were said to live inside it. On great occasions it was taken to sea, to insure good weather. See "Journal North China Branch, Roy. Asiat. Soc.," III, 120. At Lh'asa a white conch-shell is treasured. They say that when it is sounded there can be seen a faint semblance of the glory radiating from Shenrézig (Kuan-yin P'u-sa). See "Hsi-ts'ang t'u k'ao," V, 19.

important purchases, and for the sale of much of their more expensive goods, such as books and furs. I have every reason to believe that the annual value of the Tibetan trade passing through Tankar is not over Tls. 150,000. The people of eastern Tibet (K'amba) visit here only in small numbers and have but little to sell—some musk, hides, lambskins, and *choma;* their purchases are of still less importance. The Ts'aidam Mongols are in about the same case; they bring to Tankar large quantities of salt, but it is of an inferior quality, very dirty, and, though the only salt used in the western portion of Kan-su, is sold at a very low price. Hides and a little wool complete the list of their imports. The Koko-nor Tibetans bring here a great deal of wool of good quality, and they could supply much larger quantities if there was a better market for it. When I was at Tankar I saw a Tientsin agent of a foreign firm,[1] with some $12,000, buying wool for Tls. 1.8 a picul, or about a dollar a hundredweight.

SILVER COIN (*Tenga*), OF CHINESE TURKESTAN.

A few traders from Ho-tien (Khoten) and Kashgar visit Tankar annually, usually in autumn, bringing Khoten rugs, Hami raisins, dried melons, and a few other articles of no great value. They are spoken of as *Hei Fan-tzŭ*, "Black barbarians," or more commonly, *Ch'an-t'ou jen*, "Turbaned people."[2]

[1] The *hang* name was *Hsin t'ai hsing*, "The new great prosperous." I forget its English name. The wool was sent by camel to Ning-hsia Fu, thence by boat on the Yellow River to Pao-t'u, and thence by camel to Tung Chou, *via* K'uei-hua ch'eng and Kalgan. It costs about Tls. 7 to deliver a picul at Tientsin; transit passes (*lien-piao*) being used, of course, for they obviate the necessity of paying likin dues *en route*.

[2] This term is used in western China to designate all turbaned Mohammedans. The "Huang-ch'ing chih-kung-t'u" mentions a tribe of Ch'an-t'ou of western extraction (*Hsi-yü*) which came to Kan-su in the

Though the local trade of Tankar must be of much more value than its foreign, I found it, taken altogether, disappointingly small, the reason being, in all likelihood, want of capital and general depression produced by the recent unsettled condition of the country.

In the preceding remarks no reference has been made to the tea trade of Tankar, which one would expect to be very important, but which, for reasons previously given (p. 53), is quite small. Besides supplying the Tibetans and Mongols in the vicinity with tea, it is doubtful that any is exported from this locality.[1] The Sharba of Sung-p'an supply the Koko-nor and Ts'aidam at lower rates than the Kan-su traders can, and, their sojourn outside of China not being limited by any pass, they are free to go where they please and stay there as long as they see fit. Although tea (from Ch'iung-chou) is the chief article of trade of the Sharba, they also sell leather boots, cotton goods, hardware (principally padlocks), tobacco, and copper kettles, taking in exchange lamb-skins, musk, hides of wild and tame yak, wild-ass skins, and furs.

One day an old Tibetan trader from Shigatsé, from whom I had bought two camels, came to see me and we had a long and interesting conversation. He had made the journey between Lh'asa and Tankar four times, and

Hung-wu period of the Ming (A. D. 1366–1399), and settled near Tankar. Tibetans and Ts'aidam Mongols use the word *K'a-ch'é*, originally applied only to Kashmiris, to designate all and any people of Mohammedan type or wearing turbans, just as the Chinese use Ch'an-t'ou.

1 Abbé Desgodins, "Le Thibet," 2d edit., p. 349, thinks that about 800,000 lbs. of tea goes to Lh'asa from Hsi-ning or Tankar annually; careful inquiry leads me to believe that hardly any leaves that place. All Tibetan tea is Ssŭ-ch'uan tea, and passes through Ta-chien-lu or Sung-p'an. Sung-p'an t'ing is called Sung-sin k'ar by Tibetans and Mongols. The Ch'iung-chou tea is made into packages weighing fifty catties, and sells in the Ts'aidam for about Tls. 10 of silver each package.

had moreover been to Peking, Tientsin, Urga, and Manchuria. He greatly admired the honesty of foreigners in money transactions. One day, while at Urga, he had occasion to get a check cashed at a Russian house, and, though he could not make himself understood by the clerk to whom he presented it, its full value was paid him in good silver. Such honesty, he declared, could never be found in either China or Tibet. Referring to the journey to Lh'asa, he said that it would be a comparatively easy matter for me to traverse Tibet, going round Lh'asa but not entering that city. The people greatly feared firearms, and if they heard that I had any with me they would certainly not let me enter the country, and so I should be careful to keep them well concealed. He considered it necessary, however, to have a pass, if not the Amban's, at least one from the chief of the north Koko-nor Panak'a, the Konsa lama, for it was respected throughout Tibet, and had the advantage of costing much less than the former.

He told me, as he was about to leave, that he and the other traders at Tankar were going to have a *Ku-rim* or guilt-offering ceremony the next day, and he asked me to be present. A little pyramid made of tsamba, butter, and sugar (known as a *torma*), about a foot high and set in a small wooden framework, was placed on a scaffolding in a room of their caravansary, and the officiating lamas were seated near-by. While these read the service prescribed for the ceremony, all those for whose benefit it was being performed passed under the scaffolding, thus diverting from their heads any impending disease or evil. Then one of the lamas took the offering, and, followed by all the others, and the traders in their finest dresses and fully armed with guns and swords, marched out of the

A GUILT-OFFERING AT TANKAR.

town, and went to a place where a pile of dry brushwood had been prepared. Fire was put to the fuel, and, as the flames leapt up, the offering was cast into them; thus was consumed all the future bad luck of the trespassers, and they celebrated its destruction with much firing of guns, blowing of horns, and mumbling of prayers. When all had been burnt, the procession reformed, the traders, with drawn swords, in single file on either side of the lamas, and with much waving of weapons, and singing of songs in deep bass voices supposed to be terrifying, they returned to their homes.

After a week spent at Tankar my preparations for the journey westward were about complete, when suddenly the lama from Sérkok gomba announced that he must go home, that he would not accompany me even as far as the Ts'aidam. I had become so wearied of arguing with first this one, then that one, about the practicability of the journey, that I did not attempt to make him change his mind, but told him to leave at once. I wrote a letter to Bu lama, complaining of the conduct of this man, and reproaching himself for sending an old friend such a white-livered wretch, and despatched it by one of my men. As soon as the messenger had left I saddled my horse, left all my traps with the innkeeper and rode off to Lusar, to bring back what I had left there, and make a start for the Koko-nor at once, hoping to pick up a man or two on the road, or possibly in the *ts'ao-ti*[1] itself.

On arriving at Lusar I found a young man waitiug there to see me whom I had met several times previously and whose bright face and obliging ways had most favorably impressed me. He said he came to offer me his

1 The Chinese use this name to designate the Koko-nor and Ts'aidam. In Ssŭ-ch'uan it is used as a generic term for all eastern Tibet.

services to go wherever I chose and do whatever I bid. He could speak both Mongol and Tibetan, and had been to the Ts'aidam. The bargain was soon made, and Yi Hsien-sheng[1] became, from that moment until I left him at Shanghai, my right-hand man. The next day my messenger to Sérkok gomba returned, leading a magnificent Tibetan mastiff, which I remembered having greatly admired in Bu lama's house, also carrying a big ball of butter, cakes of brown sugar, katag, etc., sent me as peace-offerings, and accompanied by a letter apologizing for the conduct of the lama, and informing me that he had received a sound thrashing and had been locked up.

I staid at Lusar only about a week, making my final arrangements before starting. During that time an old lama from Réwang gomba, some five days' journey south of Lusar, stopped at my inn on his way home from Lh'asa. He described most graphically the journey of the caravan he had joined, through the desert of northern Tibet, and the attacks made on it by small parties of brigands (*Golok*). Several times, he said, his party had met hairy savages, with long, tangled locks falling around them like cloaks, naked, speechless beings, hardly human, who threw stones at the travelers, but who, having no arms, could do but little harm. This story of hairy savages I had often heard from Tibetans, while at Peking, and I was interested at hearing it again. From many things that happened later, on my journey, I am convinced that this story has its origin in travelers seeing bears standing erect. In northern Tibet these brutes are numerous

[1] *Hsien-sheng*, "Teacher, Sir," is used in western Kan-su as an honorific term, applied to all persons who have received any education, no matter how elementary.

and large, and people who are in constant dread of meeting brigands take the bears, seen probably at a distance, for them; this notion is further strengthened by the sight of their tracks, which, especially those of the hind paws, have some resemblance to those made by men with naked feet.

The old lama also mentioned that the new incarnation of the Pan-ch'en rinpoch'é of Trashil'unpo had recently been found in Poyul, and that the present Talé-lama was aged thirteen.

On the 22d of March, everything being ready, I said good-bye to Lusar, and returned to Tankar. About five inches of snow had fallen during the night, so it was very late when we reached that town. The camels, of which I now owned five poor ones, gave us any amount of trouble, and two of them showed such unmistakable signs of distress that I feared I should have to stop some days at Tankar to buy others. As it was, one day was passed there, waiting the arrival of a man, who had asked to go home to take leave of his parents, but on the 24th we were ready for the start. Just as the little caravan was leaving the innyard one of my men walked up to me and said he could not go with me, he was to be married in three months, and consequently must stay at home. He brought me another man to take his place, a native of Kuei-tê, who spoke Mongol and Tibetan, and he trusted I would accept the substitute. I had no time even to tell him what I thought of him, but I welcomed the new arrival, and with a few words of farewell to the kind people of the inn I gave the signal to start.

III

KOKO-NOR AND TS'AIDAM

ABOUT fifteen miles west of Tankar, villages and Chinese were left behind and we found ourselves among the nomads. Our road lay towards the source of the Hsi-ning river, near Lake Koko-nor. The first day out we made but little progress, being obliged to stop continually to readjust the loads on the camels, so that we reached only late in the day a lamasery called Gomba Soba, some eighteen miles from Tankar. The lamas were very kind, bringing us fuel and water, looking after our cattle, and helping to put up the tents. But notwithstanding this, my men were very nervous, and as it grew dark they started at the least noise, and when the dogs barked became terribly excited. Finally my Tientsin servant could stand it no longer; he rushed out of the tent, and commenced discharging his revolver, to drive away the lurking thieves with which his imagination peopled the vicinity. This was more than I could bear; I gave him a lecture and disarmed him, much to his disgust, for, although he did not know how to use effectually a revolver, he was very proud of having one at his belt.

The next day we continued our route. As we went on, the valley grew wider, and the adjacent hills lower and less abrupt. The ground was well covered with grass, and the water from numerous springs trickled down the hillsides, or formed bits of bog through which we with difficulty picked our way. The few camps we saw

TIBETAN CAMP NEAR THE BAGA-NOR.

were some of them Mongol, others Tibetan, but the former seemed to predominate.[1] They are a very poor

[1] These Mongols are known as Tung-korwa or Tankar Mongols. These, together with the Tolmukgun and Mori Wang clans, all of them under the rule of Mori Wang, form the Eastern Koko-nor Mongols, and number perhaps 800 to 1000 tents.

people, their flocks of sheep and goats generally not exceeding a hundred for each tent, while five or six ponies, and as many camels, complete their worldly possessions. They live in constant dread of their Tibetan neighbors, who rob and bully them in the most shameful way. Their flocks are herded by the women, who use slings to "round them up" when scattered, throwing stones or dried dung with wonderful precision to considerable distances. The Tibetans also have this custom, but with them the women never perform these duties, as, living in more remote and exposed localities where there is danger from marauders, it is necessary that the men should tend the flocks.

On the afternoon of the third day after leaving Tankar, we reached the water-shed between the Hsi-ho and the Koko-nor, and, from the top of a low pass (altitude, 12,248 feet), we got our first view of the great lake, a glistening sheet of ice, stretching as far as the eye could reach to the west and bounded to the south by a range of high, bleak mountains with snow-tipped peaks. We camped that night a few miles to the north of a little lake formed of a small bay cut off from the great lake by drifting sands; it is known as the "little lake" (Baga-nor, or Ts'o ch'ung).[1]

The Koko-nor, or "Azure lake," is some 230 miles in circumference and its altitude is about 10,900 feet above sea level.[2] On its northern and western sides are steppes and ranges of low hills; to the south a steep,

[1] The Chinese call it *Hai erh-tzŭ*, "the lakelet," literally, "son of the lake."

[2] The name is written *Kuke* (last syllable as French *queue*), "blue," and *noor*, "lake." The Tibetan name is *Ts'o ngon-po*, also meaning blue lake. The Chinese have given it different names at different times, such as *Hsien hai* or *Hsien shui*, "Bright or fairy lake," *Yun-ku yen ch'ih*, *Ling hai*, *Pei huo ch'iang hai*, *Hsi hai* and *Ch'ing hai*. The last two names are the only ones used at present: the former means "Western lake"; the lat-

high, and rugged range of mountains reaches its very shore. The country to the north and west of the lake, the only part with which I am at all familiar, is a fine grazing land, traversed by a number of large streams, two of which merit the name of river; and here nomads find excellent camping grounds in the swales and hollows where there is shelter from the violent west and north-west winds, called by the Chinese "black winds," which blow almost continually in this bleak region.

We saw but very few camps of either Mongols or Tibetans while in the basin of this lake, but, as the season was not advanced, it is probable that a large part of the population was still in winter quarters, in sheltered and remote nooks in the hills. Furthermore, the Tibetans do not like the plains, they are essentially a hill people; and so it is possible that they do not live in any great numbers near the lake. However, many deserted camps seemed to show that the former supposition was more correct.

The next day we crossed the Baléma gol; its bed of coarse gravel was nearly half a mile broad. I saw quite a number of herds of wild asses and antelopes (*Procapra picticaudata*), also hares, sand grouse, and sheldrakes; buzzards and a very large species of hawk were also plentiful, and the ground in many places was riddled with the burrows of a species of lagomys.

The trail until we passed the Baléma gol was very plain, but from that river it grew rapidly more and more indistinct, and I felt anxious to secure a guide as soon as possible, especially as our camels were not strong enough

ter "Azure lake." Chinese authors give its circumference at from 700 to 1000 *li*. Prjevalsky, "Reise in Tibet," p. 177, says it is 266 kilometers in circumference and 106 kilometers in its greatest length. Its water is salty and it is, as far as we know, not very deep.

to make long marches in search of water. I tried at several Tibetan camps to get a man to accompany us, but the people asked more for their services than I was willing to give, so we pushed on across the Ulan muren[1] to the northwest corner of the lake, to a place known as Dré ch'u, from the little stream which flows by it. Here was a small Tibetan encampment, and as soon as we had pitched our tents I sent a man to ask some of the people living in it to come talk with me, and by the same occasion to buy some butter and sour milk. After awhile two old men came, and I asked them if they would guide me to Dulan-kuo, some three days thence. By a long talk and an exhibition of the goods I was to pay them with, we finally struck a bargain; I was to give them four pairs of boots and an ounce of silver. I had been advised before leaving Tankar to take with me a supply of boots such as are made there for Mongols and Tibetans, and had bought thirty pairs for Tls. 10. They proved of the greatest convenience, and secured for me the service of men who perhaps would not have consented to leave their homes if I had offered to pay them in silver or any other commodity. In the Koko-nor and Ts'aidam boots are a regular unit of value; sheep, hides, barley, furs, etc., are valued at so many pairs of boots, and when these are not in demand, tea, k'atag, pulo, or cotton takes their place.[2]

TRADE LEATHER BOOT, AND MONGOL GARTER.

[1] The Ulan muren gol, Prjevalsky's Ulan Koshung, was the largest river I saw flowing into the lake. Its bed was about two miles wide, and covered with boulders of red and purple sandstone and coarse gravel.

[2] In the Ts'aidam a pair of boots (worth about 35 cents at Tankar)

While we were near the Koko-nor the weather was so very hazy that I only rarely got a view of the lake, but while camped on the Dré ch'u it cleared up a little and I was shown a dark spot far to the south which was said to be a rocky island inhabited by a few lamas. When the ice is thick these recluses visit the mainland and collect provisions enough to last them until the following winter, for, there being no boats on the lake, they are cut off for half the year from the outer world. This rocky island, it is said, fills the orifice through which the waters of the lake rushed out when they came by a subterranean passage from Lh'asa to the Koko-nor country. It was brought there by a god who had taken the shape of a great bird, and by this timely expedient had saved the country from being entirely submerged.[1] The Chinese call it Lung ch'ü tao, "Dragon colts' island." Every year in olden times when the lake was covered with ice the people who lived on its shores turned loose on the island a number of tame mares. When the spring came, they caught them again, and with each mare was a colt, and these were called "dragon colts." When, in the Sui dynasty (A. D. 589–618), the T'u-k'u-hun conquered the country, they were most anxious to perpetuate this breed of horses, but, though they turned loose 2000 wild mares in the valleys and gorges of the island, they could procure no colts and the breed became extinct.[2]

Leaving the Koko-nor our road lay due west through a

buys two ewes, a yak hide, four wild-ass skins, or eight pecks of barley. A *wu-chai shou-pa* (a variety of *k'atag*) worth Tls. 0.2.3 at Tankar is the price of five ewes in the same region.

[1] For this legend see Huc, "Souvenirs d'un Voyage," II, 192 *et seq.*, and Prjevalsky, "Mongolia," II, 141. It was told me several times by lamas in substantially the same terms as those in which they give it.

[2] See "Fang yü chi yao wen-chien," Shan-hsi, p. 12. Cf. what the great Buddhist pilgrim Hsüan Chuang says of the dragon colts of Ch'ü-chih (Kuche). "Ta T'ang Hsi-yü Chi," Bk. I. Timkowski, "Travels," II, 270, calls this island Kuisun tologoi. There are, I believe,

region of low hills of sandstone and shale, traversed at long intervals by little streams flowing down to the lake, till we

CAMPING IN THE KOKO-NOR.

reached the Buha gol, the most important river in the Koko-

two other smaller ones in the lake. "The Hsi-yü t'ung wen chih" calls the island Kuyisu tolohai. The legend concerning the dragon colts was first given in the history of the T'ang dynasty (T'ang-shu), Bk. 231, History of the T'u-k'u-hun.

nor basin. It first became known to us through Huc, who called it Pouhain gol, but, as the name means "Wild Yak River," Buha gol is the only correct transcription of the Mongol words. The valley through which it flows is five or six miles wide, and in many places the soil is wet and spongy, but in immediate proximity to the river it is composed of sand and gravel, in which grows profusely a shrub called *barku* by the Mongols, and *sa-liu* by the Chinese. Huc has left us in his "Souvenirs" (II, 202) a most graphic, though possibly embellished, account of the danger and trouble he and his caravan experienced when crossing this river. The bed was about three-quarters of a mile in width where I came on it, but the stream was not more than forty feet wide and two feet deep. It is, however, very probable that forty-five years ago the bed was much broader, as the sand and gravel on the left bank show, and that at the season when Huc crossed the river (end of October) there was much more water in it than when I saw it. I was told by several traders at Lusar and Tankar that the passage of this river was frequently attended with much difficulty; one of them even assured me that he had once been detained three days, trying to get his caravan of yak across the rotten ice. The preceding remarks are due to the good name of Abbé Huc, whose veracity in this very matter has been impeached by Colonel Prjevalsky, and who has been attacked so violently that more than one person has doubted whether he and Gabet ever set foot in Tibet, to say nothing of Lh'asa. Unquestionably it was from memory, several years after the events had occurred, that Huc wrote his work, and while he never, as far as I know, invents, he frequently embellishes, as, for example, in the account cited previously of his passage through the Hsiao hsia (the gorge near Hsi-ning).[1] However, his notes on the people, their manners and customs, are, invaluable, and, while many of his explanations of terms and habits are not exact, they are the very ones generally received by the people of the country to which they relate. Altogether his work cannot be too highly praised, and if it had been properly edited and accompanied by explanatory notes, accusations such as Colonel Prjevalsky has made against him could never have found acceptance with the public.

The South Koko-nor range forms the water-shed between the valleys of the Buha gol and Dulan gol, on which is Dulan-kuo, the capital (a very great name for a very little place, but I find none better) of the Mongol Prince of the Koko-nor (*Ch'ing-hai Wang*). The mountains in this part of the range are called Dagar té-chen; they are about fifteen hundred feet high, and on their southern flank are covered in many places with stunted cedar and juniper trees. Although the ascent was gradual and the ground free from stones, two of the camels gave out on the way and caused us such delay that we were three days in reaching Dulan-kuo, some twenty-five miles distant. The top of the pass over the range is marked by a huge pile of stones, from amidst which protrudes a quantity of brushwood with rags of every size and description hanging from it. Such monuments are called in both Mongol and Chinese *obo*,[2] and they are formed in the course of years by travelers who throw

1 See p. 50. I am glad to find the following in Colonel Mark Bell's "The Great Central Asia Trade Route," Proc. Roy. Geog. Soc., XII, 69. "Prjevalsky has, I think, too hastily thrown discredit on the works of this talented Jesuit [Lazarist], to the pertinency of whose remarks, and to the accuracy of whose observations, whenever and wherever I have been able to test them, I desire to pay tribute."

2 *Obo* is a Mongolized Tibetan word, *do bong*, "pile of stones," or *do bum*, "ten myriad stones." They are found all over Mongolia and Tibet. In many countries shepherds put up small ones as guides to take their flocks to water, or to go to camp.

down stones on the highest point of the pass, to thank the gods for the assistance they have vouchsafed them in guiding them on their way to the summit. They may have been set up originally as landmarks to point out the road from afar, and afterward have become objects of worship; or perhaps, as each passer-by contributed his stone to such useful cairns, they have grown gradually to their present size, which is frequently very considerable.

On the south side of the mountain we met a small party of lamas and Amdowa, returning home from Lh'asa. They told us that they had been three months on the way, and that, though there had been only about forty men in their caravan, they had not been attacked nor had any accidents befallen them. They were very apprehensive about traveling through the Koko-nor, and much surprised at our good luck in not having been plundered. They talked a great deal about the war between the Lh'asa people and the *Ying-gi-li*, as they called the British, and said that Tibet was in a state of great excitement. The lamas had recruited numbers of men from Ch'amdo in eastern Tibet, and had sent them to the front, telling them that they had nothing to fear from the British guns, for they themselves would be at hand [in a safe place], and would recite incantations to render them invulnerable. In the first fight

Among the ancient Peruvians "when a traveler reached the summit of a pass he never forgot to throw a stone, or sometimes his beloved pellet of cocoa, on a heap by the roadside, as a thank-offering to God, exclaiming, '*Apachicta muchani!*' 'I worship, or give thanks, at this heap.'" C. R. Markham in "Narrative and Critical History of America," I, 251. In Fiji any one who meets a god must afterward, on passing the same place, throw thereon a few leaves or blades of grass, to show that he keeps the event in mind. Thos. Williams, "Fiji and Fijians," p. 197 and p. 202. Cf. also "The Century Magazine," December, 1890, p. 185. *Obo* are found in Korea and Japan, but not in China. The pass referred to in the text is, perhaps, the *Tsahan obo k'utul*, mentioned in Chinese itineraries of this part of the empire.

a number of these Ch'amdo warriors had been killed, or wounded, and the survivors had then and there started back for their homes, and left the lamas to fight their own battles as best they could.

About fifteen miles from the summit of the pass we came to a little brackish lake, the Tsahan nor, or "White lake," and a few miles farther on we reached the Dulan gol, a small but clear and rapid stream. The mountains were more steep and rugged on this side, and porphyry, which was so prominent a feature in their composition on the northern slope, was now replaced by granite and conglomerate.

We reached Dulan-kuo, "The hot place,"[1] on the 4th of April. It is a small village of little mud huts, used as storehouses, each inclosed within adobe walls. In the yards the Mongols live in their tents, and they enjoy all the pleasure of nomadic life, with some of the security of a town. The only building in it which deserves the name of house is an insignificant wooden one built by Chinese carpenters for the prince. A small lamasery, in which live a Gégén (a minor incarnation) and about twenty lamas, is close to it, but the prince's officers live in tents in his spacious courtyard. The house was a piece of extravagance on the part of this potentate, as he hardly ever stops in it, and so was the Peking cart, now falling to pieces under a shed. The Wang lives in a tent some miles away in a side valley, but when I was in his country

[1] Huc, *op. cit.*, II, 211, speaks of a ruined lamasery on the Toulain gol, but there does not appear to have been any village in his time, nor does he mention any in the Ts'aidam. This proves the truthfulness of my informants when they told me that all the villages in the Ts'aidam had been built within the last forty years as a means of resisting the sudden attacks of the Panak'a. Prjevalsky, "Mongolia," II, 160, calls this place Dulan *Kit*, and explains the word *kit* by "church." I never heard it called by this name, and believe he was misinformed.

he was absent at Peking, where he had been called to assist at the marriage of the emperor.

The Prince of Koko-nor is the highest dignitary among the Mongols in this part of the empire, his ancestor having been made a *Chin-wang* by the emperor of China, in 1697.[1] His clan, called Wang k'a or the "Royal Clan," does not number more than two hundred families, and every member of it is very poor. The Prince is naturally the richest, but his steward assured me that his master owned only about 1000 sheep, 40 camels, and from 40 to 50 horses. Any one among them who owns 200 or 300 sheep, 8 or 9 camels, and a few horses is considered well to do, and as his wants are few and satisfied at little expense he really is. They all wear their sheepskin gowns, or felt summer ones, till ragged and tattered; their felt tents, when new, cost only about ten ounces of silver; their saddles, harness, guns, swords, cooking utensils and other necessaries can be bought for ten to fifteen ounces more. They cultivate the soil sufficiently to raise what barley is needed to make tsamba; their goats, sheep, or half-breed yak supply them with milk to make butter; and the skins of lambs, those of the few sheep they eat, and the wool they can shear or pull from them, pay the Sharba for all the tea they require. Their

MONGOL CHARM BOX MADE OF WOOD. (IMAGE IN INTERIOR STAMPED IN CLAY.)

1 See H. H. Howorth, "History of the Mongols," I, 525. He says the Ch'ing-hai Wang descends from Dalai Kung Daichi, second son of Gushi Khan the conqueror of Tibet. Prior to 1697 this Prince of Koko-nor was a vassal of the Talé lama.

only luxury is tobacco, which they use as snuff; men and women indulge this habit to excess. They grind the dry leaf into powder and then mix with it a quantity of dung ashes, so as to take away some of its strength. This mixture, which they prefer to the most highly perfumed Chinese snuff, they carry in a horn, in shape like a powder-horn, and continually inhale quantities of it, pouring it on the thumb-nail of the left hand. Sour-milk (*tarak*) and distilled mare's milk (*arreki*)[1] are two other luxuries they sometimes indulge in, but they are not as fond of drink as the Tibetans, and are rarely seen intoxicated.

Huc and, after him, Prjevalsky[2] have described the Ts'aidan Mongols as morose and melancholic, speaking little—in fact, hardly better than animals. I was glad to find all those I met quite different from what the accounts of these travelers had caused me to expect. Not only they showed themselves ready to do anything for me, but they exerted themselves to make my stay agreeable, inviting me to their tents to eat, singing choruses for me, or playing on a rough kind of banjo they manufacture themselves. Most of them spoke Tibetan, so I could converse with them freely; and I found them quite as lively as any other tribes of their race I have met. I have never seen vivacious, loquacious nomads—I do not

1 William of Rubruk, *op. cit.*, 305, speaks of *caracosmos*, "hoc est clarum lac jumenti." See also Yule's "Marco Polo," I, 250, but he does not mention *arrcki*, which is distilled from *kumiz*. I never saw these Mongols use the latter beverage.

2 Huc, *op. cit.*, II, 212: "La teinte morose et mélancolique de ces tristes contrées semble avoir influé sur le caractère de ses habitants, qui ont tous l'air d'avoir le spleen. Ils parlent trespeu . . ." Prjevalsky, "Mongolia, II, 149: "Their eyes are dull and heavy, and their disposition morose and melancholic." And in the account of his third journey, "Reise in Tibet," 8, he remarks of them that they are "lazy, false, dishonest, and stupid, but not devoid of a certain cunning."

believe there are any—and the Mongols have the faults and virtues of their race and form of civilization. They are certainly honest; neither in the Ts'aidam nor in eastern Mongolia have I found them false and knavish, as Prjevalsky asserts he did; on the contrary their honesty is proverbial, and so is their guilelessness and gullibility, as every Chinese who has traded with them can testify.

While at Dulan-kuo I required some sewing done, so two sisters, the wives of the head man of the place, and his assistant came to my tent to do it. The work was to line with sheepskin a pulo gown; to do this they

TS'É-PA-MÉ (AMITABHA).—(GILT BRONZE CAST AT DOLON-NOR.)

had to take it to pieces. When all was done, except sewing on the collar, the two women went home and put on their finest clothes, then came back and gave the gown the finishing touches. They told me that this was one of their customs when making a gown for any of their chieftains, and they wished to show me the same respect they would to him. As soon as the gown was finished I was asked to put it on, and then accompany them to their tent, where they had prepared a little entertainment for me. On the farther side of the tent, and facing the door, was a low altar and the household gods; the seat of honor was to the right of this. Having drank tea and eaten tsamba, a little bottle of wine was produced with a piece of butter on top of it; the butter was put on the altar, and a cup of wine poured out and handed to me. After dipping my forefinger in it and scattering a little towards the four cardinal points, I drank some and then handed the cup to my host, who raised it to his forehead without drinking any, and passed it to the next person on his left, and so around the tent. When the cup had come back to me, I was told to drink all the wine in it. Such is, they said, the custom among them, when they have a distinguished guest.

The owner of the tent was a physician, and while I was with him a young girl came in and asked for some medicine for what I diagnosed as rheumatic fever. Feeling her pulse on both wrists at the same time, and looking her in the face intently the while, he asked one or two questions, and then brought out a number of small leather bags with medicines he had brought from Lh'asa. He measured out doses of some of these powders with a small silver spoon, and gave them to her, accepting nothing for the consultation or remedies given. These Mongols are very fond of medicines, and use exclusively Tibetan ones, which are generally vegetable substances. One they often spoke to me about, as the most valuable in the Tibetan pharmacopœia, was elephant's milk. They said that it was brought to Lh'asa from India, and sold there at a very high price; they were much surprised to learn that I had never heard of its curative properties. I had with me a bottle of Eno's fruit salts, and the next day, when this lama came to see me, I mixed some with water. The effervescence completely mystified him; the strength of this unknown drug must be very great, he thought, and for a while elephant's milk was completely overshadowed.

I was much worried the day after my arrival at Dulan-kuo on learning that a T'ung-shih from the Yamen of the Amban had just come in with quite a large party of Chinese and Tibetans. I feared that he had been sent to intercept me, or to make my progress into Tibet so difficult by arousing the suspicions of the people along the road it was supposed I wished to follow, that they would forbid my coming. I at once told one of my men to call on him, ask if he had had a prosperous journey, and beg him to come driuk tea with me as soon as he was rested. Later in the day he came to my tent, and made himself most agreeable. He said he was going to eastern Tibet to collect the tax due the imperial government by the natives, and, having finished this work, he would go on to Ta-chien-lu. I told him that after visiting the Ts'aidam, I proposed going to Sa-chou, and then to Khoten and Kashgar. Speaking of going to Lh'asa, he told me that a number of his colleagues in the Yamen had at one time or the other been there by the northern route (the one going over the Burhan-bota, south of Baron Ts'aidam), and that, though none of them had had large parties, generally but twenty to twenty-five men, they had been able to resist all attacks of brigands and to reach their destination without much trouble or heavy loss of live stock. The journey from Tankar to Lh'asa usually took from sixty to seventy days. As from Dulan-kuo to south Ts'aidam we had to follow the same road we decided to travel together. I was the more ready to do this as it would give me opportunities of finding out whether he had any orders concerning me, and by cultivating his friendship get him perhaps to use his very considerable influence with the Mongols and Tibetans to my benefit. Some presents I sent him and his men soon after our first interview promptly gained me his good-will, and I was able in the course of the following fortnight to so ingratiate myself with him that he eventually rendered me two very important services, in fact, had he not acted as he did, it is doubtful whether I would have been able to traverse eastern Tibet.

The four days I remained at Dulan-kuo did not do my camels much good. The grazing around the village was very poor, and there were such flocks of magpies tormenting the poor beasts that they did not have a moment's peace. I had to wrap them in felt sheets and hire a boy to protect them from the attacks of these pests, yet with all our care they fared but badly and I was obliged to get three extra ones to carry the greater part of the loads as far as Baron Ts'aidam, where I hoped to get rid of these troublesome beasts. I also hired two men to accompany me to the latter place, one the steward of the prince, the other a Mongolized Chinaman,[1] both of them clever and well-informed men who gave me much valuable assistance and information.

On April 8th we left the hospitable little village, the caravan now quite imposing, some twenty men and twenty

[1] It is no uncommon thing in the Koko-nor region to meet Chinese naturalized among the Tibetans or Mongols. They dress and live exactly as their new fellow-countrymen do, save that they do not marry. The very loose matrimonial relations prevailing among these peoples do not find favor with the Chinese.

to thirty camels and packhorses. A few miles below Dulan-kuo we debouched from the valley, and then crossed a plain, some ten miles broad. In this are two small salt lakes: to the east, the Dulan-nor which receives the stream that flows by Dulan-kuo; and to the west, the Dabesun-nor[1] which receives the Kachu-osu from the south and another stream from the west. The northern part of this plain is cultivated wherever possible and irrigation ditches carry water over it, but the sand is rapidly covering the fertile land, and the Mongols will soon be obliged to till the remoter side valleys. The southern part of the plain is an alkaline shaking-bog in which the foot sinks at every step, where quicksands are numerous and travel possible only along some very narrow and scarcely discernible trails. The mountains which border it to the south, the Timurté,[2] constitute the northern water-shed of the Ts'aidam basin, which is from 600 to 800 feet lower than the Koko-nor and Dulan-nor basins. The political boundary between the territory of the Ch'ing-hai Wang and the neighboring Ts'aidam prince, the Beileh of Koko, is, however, to the north of the range and passes through the two lakes just mentioned. In the hill country to the east live Tibetans (Panak'a) belonging to the south Koko-nor tribe.

After crossing these mountains we entered the desert of Koko Beileh. The sand has been blown against the Timurté till it forms a line of hills in places as high as the mountains themselves. Here and there on the level grows a low brush called *haramagu*,[3] of which camels are

1 Their approximate altitude is 10,600 feet above sea level, that of Dulan-kuo about 11,100.

2 The north side of these mountains is dolerite; the central and south parts, pudding-stone. Their highest peaks are not over 1200 feet above the plain. A few junipers and cedars grow on their northern slope.

3 In Chinese *Pei-tzŭ*. Prjevalsky, "Mongolia," II, 167, calls it *karmyk* (*Nitraria schoberi*), and A. D. Carey, "Proc. Roy. Geog. Soc.," IX, 745, gives its name as *harmo*.

very fond, and whose red berries the Mongols sometimes cook and eat. Bands of wild asses and antelopes alone exist in this part of the country, which is too barren for even the Mongols. Through it flows the Tsatsa gol, which is lost finally in the great central marsh of the Ts'aidam.

The name Ts'aidam appears to be Tibetan, *ts'ai*, "salty," *dam*, "plain," a very appropriate name, as salt is the chief if not sole product of this forsaken land. I am mistaken; it is not the sole product, for the Ts'aidam breeds mosquitoes so numerous and bloodthirsty that Mongols and cattle have to flee before them every year, and seek shelter in the adjacent mountains. Again, the name Ts'aidam is explained by a Mongol word[1] *tsayidam*, meaning "broad, wide expanse of country"—also a fit appellation for this plain, some six hundred miles from east to west, and a hundred to a hundred and fifty miles from north to south. The Chinese call it *Wu Ts'aidam*, or "the five Ts'aidam," from the country being divided into five principalities, called Korluk, Koko, Taichiner, Dsun, and Baron,[2] over each of which is a chief or *Dsassak*. Koko has two dignitaries, one with the title of *Beileh*, the other with that of *Beiseh*, conferred on them by the Chinese emperors.

The population of the Ts'aidam is estimated at from 1000 to 4000 tents, or from 4000 to 16,000 persons. Taichiner is said to be the most populous part of the country and also the most extensive, while Baron[3] is the smallest, but possibly not the poorest, though the people live

[1] I give this word as Mongol on the authority of a Chinese polyglot geographical dictionary, "Hsi-yü t'ung wen chih," but I am not prepared to vouch for its correctness.

[2] Baron (written *baragon* according to I. J. Schmidt's "Mongol. Wörterbuch") means "right side, or south"; Dsun (*dsegön*), "left-hand side, or east."

[3] Prjevalsky, "Reise in Tibet," 87, gives the population as from 1000 to 2000 tents. The T'ung shih with whom I traveled, the steward of the Prince of Koko-nor, and later on the steward of the Dsassak of Baron

in what we would consider abject poverty. Wherever the Ts'aidam Mongols are in proximity to Tibetans they have villages like Dulan-kuo, but in the Taichiner and the northwestern part of the country they have not been obliged to adopt so extensively this mode of defense.

East of Baron and in the Ts'aidam basin is another small state which, though it does not politically form a part of the Ts'aidam, belongs to it geographically. It is called Shang, and was detached from the Ts'aidam by the Mongol princes and presented to the Talé lama, probably when, in 1697, they transferred their allegiance from his government to that of Peking. It has a population, of Mongols, of about 300 tents. I will have occasion later to refer at length to this principality.

We traveled for four days in a southwesterly direction through this desert country, in one place sandy, in another boggy, stopping on the bank of some little stream or near a brackish pool where grew a coarse spear-grass. The heat during the day was oppressive, the nights very cold;[1] the alkaline dust raised by the shuffling feet of the camels stuck to our skins, which soon were cracked and bleeding. On the Shara gol we found a small encampment, and on the Tso gol another; they were the only ones we saw between Dulan-kuo and the village of Baron, which we reached on the 14th of April. Near a place called Ergetsu on the Tsatsa gol we had to leave the direct road to Baron, which is practicable only in winter, when the

Ts'aidam agree on the following figures:

Taichiner,	1000	families (*wa-ka*).
Korluk,	1000	"
Koko,	1000	"
Baron,	300	"
Dsun,	1000	"
Total	4300	families (*wa-ka*).

To these must be added some 500 lamas. I think, however, this estimate is too high by, perhaps, 1500 families.

1 April 11th, 5.30 A. M., 22° F.; 2 P. M., 81° in the shade; 6 P. M., 39°. April 15th, 6 A. M., 32°; 1 P. M., 81° in the shade; 8 P. M., 33°.

ground is frozen and hard, and to take a circuitous one, which brought us on to the Bayan gol nearly twenty miles east of that village. This river, the largest of the Ts'ai-

VILLAGE OF BARON TS'AIDAM.

dam, was over two hundred yards wide where we crossed it, a shallow and turgid stream, flowing on a bed of soft red mud, through which we experienced considerable difficulty in getting our horses and camels. It takes its rise in two lakes on the farther side of the high range which bounds the Ts'aidam to the south, and after flowing through Shang, where it is called Yohuré or Yohan gol, passes a little to the north of the village of Baron, and, like all other rivers in this country, is finally lost in the great central marsh.

From what I had been told at Dulan-kuo and by the Mongols who were with me, I was prepared to find the village of Baron a lively trading post, with Tibetans and Chinese, and an abundance of all ordinary supplies. But instead of that, I now saw a miserable little place, partly in ruins, in the midst of the marsh, the water so near the surface that it oozed out when we drove our tent-pins into the ground. A few old women and half a dozen men, some miserable dogs with about fifty sheep and goats were to be seen; the rest of the people had fled on hearing that a Hsi-ning T'ung-shih was coming, so as not to be impressed on the hated ula service. This did not save them, however, for the T'ung-shih sent Mongols to hunt them up, and claim the service and supplies they owed him, or their equivalent in marketable goods.

This village of Baron[1] is not over eight miles from the foot of the great mountain chain which marks the border of the high Tibetan table-land, but such a mist hung over the country that I only once got a sight of it, when directly to the south of the village I saw the mouth of the valley leading to the Nomoran and Hato passes, and a little to the west that going to the Burhan bota, the road to Lh'asa.[2]

1 Altitude, 9880 feet. Prjevalsky does not give the altitude of this locality, but for Dsün, about 20 miles west of it, he gives 8839 and 9200 feet; the latter figure is probably sufficiently correct.

2 On our maps this range figures under a variety of names, none of

It was a great disappointment to find this village so destitute and forlorn, with neither provisions for ourselves nor feed or even grass for our stock. There was not the remotest chance of finding any one here to travel with me, nothing, in fact, to justify the name of "trading post" given it on the few maps where it figures. The T'ung-shih was obliged to stay here some time while his men scoured the country for the ula, but waiting would have done me no good, and I resolved to go to the village of Shang, some thirty miles to the east, a place represented to me as in a land flowing with milk and butter. Though disillusioned now as to the resources of the Ts'aidam, I felt convinced that Shang could not be worse than the place I was in, and would probably be better.

The road to Shang skirted the foot of the mountains, up the dry bed of the Kor gol, and in the latter part along the bank of the Bayan or Yohuré. Between the two villages I did not pass a single tent, but if we had entered the mountains I should probably have seen quite a number. The weather had become cold, and a heavy snow fell during the whole day; and we experienced similar sudden and wide changes in temperature all the time we were in this country. Shang turned out a most agreeable disappointment; I found it a good-sized village of perhaps a hundred houses, in a broad valley surrounded by

which are known in the country. The name Kuen-lun is given it generally, but early Chinese geographers applied this one to another range, in all probability the north Koko-nor or Nan shan. Prjevalsky calls it Burh'an Buddha range and on other maps it is called Angirtakshia, both incorrect expressions. Burhan Buddha is properly *Burhan bota* (as pointed out by Huc, *op. cit.*, II, 215), and means "the Buddha's kettle." Angirtakshia is the name of a pass, as is Nomoran, Hato, Burhan bota. Prjevalsky, who gave names to so many peaks, lakes, and localities which had well-known native ones, missed a fine chance here. The range has no name. Why not give it his, as he was the first scientific European traveler who crossed it? or that of the much maligned Huc, if it must have one?

high mountains, the plain covered with grass wherever it was not under cultivation. We entered a big courtyard on which some half-dozen little hovels opened, and took refuge from the driving snow in one of them, while the guide, carrying a few small presents and a k'atag, went to the house of the governor, told him of our arrival, and asked for a place to put up in. Shortly after a number of men appeared, bearing the framework and covering of a large Mongol tent which they soon had erected in the yard. The governor sent me word that there was no comfortable house empty, and that I would be more at my ease in a tent. He sent me by the person who brought the message a jug of buttered tea, some tsamba, granulated cheese (*chura*), butter, etc. The messenger also said that the *K'anpo* (for the governor bore this title) trusted that if I had any trading to do, I would give him the preference. It is curious to notice how all the chieftains among the Mongols and Tibetans monopolize trade in their respective localities. Their people buy from and sell to them, and they thus make up largely for the fact that their offices are not salaried. A Mongol is afraid to trade a horse or a camel to any one if he knows his chief has one to sell, or, if he does venture to sell it, he most likely gives part of the price received to his chief, so that he may pardon him the liberty he has taken in infringing on what is almost a recognized right.

Shang, or Shang chia as the Chinese call it, is, as previously mentioned, a fief of the Talé lama, given him by the Mongol chieftains of the Ts'aidam. It is governed for him by an Abbot (*K'anpo*) from the great lamasery of Trashil'unpo, who is changed every five or six years. The population, which is estimated at 300 families, is entirely Mongol, but the Abbot usually has around him a certain number of Tibetans. The present incumbent has a steward and a cook, both of them Tibetans, who act also as his ministers and counselors. His minister for foreign affairs is an old Mongol who lived for some years at Lh'asa, and afterwards at Hsi-ning and Peking, whose knowledge of Chinese and Tibetan qualifies him for this exalted position. The Amban at Hsi-ning has no authority over Shang, and, not being near the high road to Tibet, its people usually escape having to supply the ula.

I found here some five or six Chinese traders from Lasa, near Tou-pa. They were in a state of great trepidation, for they had heard that I was a Hsi-ning T'ung-shih, and they were about to hide in the mountains until I had left. Their trading passes had long since expired, and they feared lest they should be obliged to pay a big squeeze to have the irregularity condoned. The previous year one of them had been caught, and had had to give the T'ung-shih several horses and some twenty pieces of cloth and cotton.[1]

As they found that I was not the personage whom they dreaded, we became good friends, and several of them were of great use to me during the remainder of my stay in the Ts'aidam. They told me of the many tricks traders had to practise in dealing with both the Mongols and the Tibetans, using short weights, bad silver, lime in their flour, low grades of goods, etc. The natives had, they said, become so used to adulterated goods, of which larger

[1] The chief man in this trading party, in which some eight or ten men were employed, told me that if he cleared fifty strings of cash (Tls. 35) a year, he was doing very well. He hired camels to Tankar for seven pairs of boots a head (about Tls. 2); each camel carried sixteen yak hides, worth Tls. 0.7.0 each at Tankar. He bought skins of the wild yak and wild ass, sheep, goat, and lamb, and a few furs, mostly lynx, for which he gave boots, vermicelli, wheat flour, shirtings, needles, thread, etc.

quantities were given than could be if they were of good quality, that they would not now accept the better kinds; hence, *nolens volens*, all traders had to be dishonest.

Among the inhabitants of Shang, and also of Baron and Dsun, I saw a number of eastern Mongols, who had certainly not "gone west" to make their fortunes. Many of them were recognizable by their lighter complexions, but especially by their softer speech. The Tibetans call them *Mar Sok.* I was generally taken for one of them. Among Mongols and Tibetans large noses and ears are considered beautiful, and I remember once upon asking a Tibetan how he thought I should look if dressed in his costume, he answered me that I would make a fine-looking Tibetan, as I had big ears and a big nose.

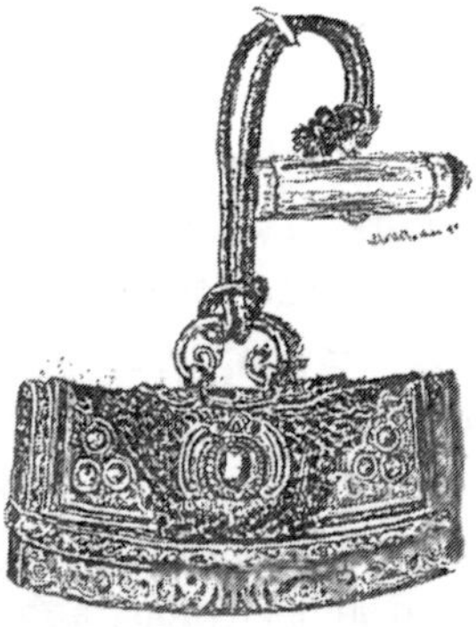

MONGOL STEEL AND TINDER BOX. (MOUNTING IN SILVER, CORAL BEADS.)

The Mongols are neither dutiful nor respectful to parents or old people. Several old men came to me complaining bitterly of their present destitute condition, while their sons and daughters were living in the midst of plenty. It is no uncommon thing for them to turn their aged parents out of the tent and force them to live literally on the dunghill, with only a bit of ragged felt to protect them from the inclemency of the weather, and some bad tea and mouldy tsamba to keep life in them. There is no redress to be had from their rulers; it is an established, if not an honored, custom.

While at Shang I took particular pains to learn something concerning the marriage laws among this people; for, when at Dulan-kuo, I had been assured by several intelligent men that polyandry was found among them, that a woman had frequently two or three husbands, sometimes more. At Shang they said that, though such was undoubtedly the case in Baron, Dsun, and other sections of the country, it was not allowed by the Abbot at Shang, who insisted on a woman having only one husband. When he absented himself, his wife was given in safe-keeping to a married couple who were responsible for her good behavior and sure delivery to the husband on his return. However, a certain kind of temporary marriage is tolerated. All the Tibetans and traders who come here to reside for any length of time, take to themselves Mongol wives; on the departure of the "husband" the children stay with the mother, and she is usually well provided for, the man giving her the house they lived in, and some cattle, if he owned any. In other parts of the Ts'aidam the so-called polyandrous marriages are not only temporary, but are contracted for a much shorter time than at Shang, say a week, a fortnight, or a year, but the good and virtuous abbots have, without interfering very materially with a long-standing Mongol custom, removed some of the opprobrium which is attached to the promiscuity that obtains in the neighboring country. It is but fair to remark that the feast called the "cap-choosing festival," referred to previously, is celebrated with great splendor at Shang.

Hoping that the Abbot might prove willing to assist me in organizing my caravan, I sent him some handsome presents, and he asked me to come and dine with him. I found him a dirty-looking man of about fifty, in much soiled red pulo clothes, seated on a pile of rugs and cushions in a corner of his kitchen. He asked me and my attendants to sit on some rugs, facing him, and as soon as we were seated, we without ceremony handed our wooden bowls to the cook, who filled them with buttered tea. After conversing for a while about our travels, ages, etc., some wooden platters with pieces of boiled mutton piled on them were set before us. Having done ample justice to this plain but wholesome dish, our bowls were filled with boiled rice and choma, well buttered and sugared. Having disposed of this and licked our bowls clean, they were then filled with vermicelli and hashed mutton—this was given us on account of our Chinese tastes—and the feast finished with a large jug of barley wine (*nä ch'ang*), a rather pleasant drink, something like Chinese samshu and water.

After dinner I broached the subject of going to Lh'asa, but the Abbot said at once he could do nothing to help me; his people never traveled that way, except in large caravans, and there was no one now who would venture to go with me unless I had a larger party than he believed I had. Then the story of the dangers encountered on the road was repeated once more to me, with some slight variations and embellishments, and I was told of the terrible fate which had overtaken the Russian Amban (Prjevalsky), who had tried a few years previously to traverse eastern Tibet. He had been attacked by the wild Golok, or had been poisoned by pestilential emanations, for he had never been seen again in the Ts'aidam. The Abbot advised me finally, for he said he was desirous to have me reach my journey's end peacefully,[1] to go see the Dsassak of Baron Ts'aidam; all caravans going to and coming from Tibet

[1] I had told him that my home was to the west of India, and that I could reach it only by traversing Tibet, which country I had previously visited. He said that he was aware, without my mentioning even the fact, that I had lived for some time in Tibet, for how else could I have learned to speak the language, especially that of Lh'asa.

passed through his country, his people frequently went to Lh'asa, and there, better than anywhere else, I would be able to get men to go with me. He also said that he had been told that I intended following up to its sources the river which flowed by Shang. This, he assured me, was a very perilous journey, as these sources were in a desert country south of the mountains, traversed only now and then by Sung-p'an traders and parties of Tibetan brigands. When I got up to leave, the K'anpo handed me a piece of fine red pulo, some cakes of brown sugar (brought from India, through Tibet), and a few other things, apologizing for the scantiness of his gifts, for which the remoteness and poverty of the country were his excuse. He renewed the offer, made me previously through his steward, to do "at the best and lowest terms" any trading I might wish, and I bowed myself out.

Although the Mongols are not devoid of politeness, they have no terms to express thanks, and but few even for saluting each other. When a present is made to any one he will raise it with both hands to his forehead, but he cannot find an appropriate word to say. When saluting each other the polite mode is to hold out both hands, palms uppermost, and, bending the body slightly, say, *amur sambéné*.[1] When addressing a person of superior rank they use the word *abreu*, corresponding approximately to our "sir," and, when speaking to people of high degree, the word *noyen*. In all social relations the most perfect equality reigns among them. The poorest man in a tribe drops into his chieftain's tent, gets his bowl filled

[1] Swearing is practically unknown among Mongols and Tibetans. The only strong expression, and one not often heard, among the Koko-nor and Ts'aidam people is *ah lama*, *kon-ch'ok ch'en-po*. Protestant missionaries in Lahul have translated our word "God" by *kon-ch'ok*, but it has never had that meaning in Tibetan.

with tea, and takes snuff out of his chief's horn, as he would with any other member of the tribe. The chief will not give him a seat of honor near him — he leaves him

WIND PRAYER-WHEELS.

squatting on the ground near the door — but with this exception he treats him quite as well as he would his most honored guest. The chief may often be met in the tent of the lowest of his subjects, drinking or smoking with him, trying to trade ponies or get him to engage in some business venture on part profit.

The Ts'aidam Mongols are very devout Buddhists, more so in fact than the Koko-nor Tibetans, and I trust that the outward visible signs of their piety are proofs of their inward spiritual grace. Whereas, among the Koko-nor Tibetans the laity do not bother themselves about praying, thinking that they pay the lamas quite enough to do all that is necessary for their good, the Mongols are continually mumbling prayers, twirling prayer-wheels, or perhaps doing both at the same time. One guide I had never laid down to sleep without saying his prayers and making three prostrations. At Shang nearly every house had on the end of a pole, stuck on the roof, a couple of small prayer-wheels kept in motion by the wind, which was caught by a simple arrangement of wooden cups fixed on the ends of horizontal sticks and looking like our anemometers. Their beads, while primarily devised to score prayers on, have become convenient counting machines; they are also used for fortune-telling, and are always ornamental when worn around the neck. There are but few lamas living in the Ts'aidam, probably not more than 300 or 400, and they are in constant demand for reading prayers in the tents of the illiterate "black people." "Beating the drum" it is usually called in Tibetan, and this name gives a fair idea of the ceremony. I used to see every day some lama riding off to a distant tent, a large flat drum tied to his back, his gown filled out with book, bell, trumpet, and all the other necessary instruments for church service. In the evening he came back with a sheep's paunch full of butter, the price of his drumming and reading, added to the contents of his capacious gown, or else some tsamba, mutton, or yak meat. The old men and women about Shang nearly drove me wild repeating *Om mani pémé hum*, the famous six-syllable prayer, the great invocation to Shenrézig, the lord who watches over the world.[1] There were always a half-dozen of them hanging around my tent, hoping to get medicine for some one of their many ailments, and they never stopped mumbling the charm, every now and then drawing in a long breath and imparting fresh energy to their tones. They got from me a little vaseline or Eno's fruit salts, either of which, I assured them, was a sovereign remedy for any disease, and they went away rejoicing, to come back the next day asking for more.

Now that I was at the foot of the great Tibetan plateau,

[1] For the history of the origin of this famous formula, see Appendix, *infrà*.

my men's nervousness increased visibly, for on every side they heard the most ghastly tales of the effects of the *yen-chang* on travelers. The T'ung-shih had told them that on one of his expeditions into the country two of his men had been killed by it, and they imagined themselves dying in the desert, and devoured by eagles, bears, and wolves. The giddiness, shortness of breath, nausea, and other distressing symptoms due to the rarefied air at high altitudes, are attributed by the Chinese and all the people of central Asia to pestilential emanations, or poisonous vapors, coming out of the soil.[1] When one has been over the great plateau, he quite comprehends why this explanation, which at first seems far-fetched, is accepted by peoples without any scientific training, for, strange as it undoubtedly appears, it is not in the most elevated localities that the effects of the rarefied air are most painfully felt by either men or beasts; hence, doubtless, the failure to connect the *chang-ch'i* with the altitude.

After my dinner with the Abbot of Shang, his secretary for foreign affairs and the other dignitaries of his court, his cook and steward told my men so much of the horrors of Tibetan travel that they actually got the "fantods," and came to me with long, ashen faces, and said they wanted to go home. I asked them to defer their departure until I left the Ts'aidam, and in the meanwhile to accompany me

[1] Huc, *op. cit.*, II, 214, describes graphically the effects of *yen-chang*, but in the words a Chinaman would use. See also Prjevalsky, "Mongolia," III, 78. In Kan-su it is called *yen-chang*, in Ssŭ-ch'uan *chang-ch'i*, both expressions meaning "pestilential vapor." Tibetans call it *la-du* (*la-dug*), "pass poison." This people attribute it in some cases to great quantities of rhubarb which grow on the mountain sides, and say that in those places it is most virulent in summer. Eating garlic, or even smoking tobacco, is held to be an antidote. Animals affected by it are also given garlic. Dr. Bellew, when traveling to Kashgar over the Karakorum pass, found great relief by taking frequent doses of chlorate of potash. See "Kashmir and Kashghar," 164.

to the south side of the mountains, to explore the sources of the Bayan gol. Not only was I desirous to complete the survey of this part of the country, which had not been visited by Prjevalsky, but I knew that I should certainly have to cross passes where there would be an abundance of *yen-chang*, and I thought the experience would give my men a little pluck and shake their belief in the mortal effects of the dreaded poison. To this they agreed, and we made ready for the trip, which I decided to make as rough as I possibly could, by taking barely enough food, and no tent; and they, themselves, unintentionally added considerably to our discomfort by forgetting the tea-bag.

Still another reason prompted me to undertake this trip. One evening, a Mongol told me of a journey he had once made to the lakes in company of a Chinese trader who wished to buy rhubarb from the Tibetans that annually visit their shores. They had seen innumerable herds of wild yak, wild asses, antelopes, and *géresun bamburshé*.[1] This expression means literally "wild men"; and the speaker insisted that such they were, covered with long hair, standing erect, and making tracks like men's, but he did not believe they could speak. Then, taking a ball of tsamba he modeled a *géresun bamburshé*, which was a very good likeness of a bear. To make the identi-

[1] Prjevalsky had in 1871 an experience very similar to mine. He calls the animal *kung guressu*, *i. e.*, "man beast." This is a hybrid word: *kung* is probably Chinese, *hsiung*, "bear"; and *guressu* is Mongol, *géresun*, "wild." Legends concerning wild men in central Asia were current in the middle ages. King Haithon of Armenia, in the narrative of his journey to the courts of Batu and Mangu Khans in A. D. 1254–1255, speaks of naked wild men inhabiting the desert southeast of the present Urumtsi. See Bretschneider, "Notice of the Med. Geo., etc., of Central Asia," p. 299. Plano Carpini, "Historia Mongolorum," p. 648, refers to savages without the power of speech, unable to rise of themselves if thrown down, etc., living south of Omyl (or Cummyl, *i. e.* Hami), in the same region.

fication perfect, he said that the Chinaman cried out, when he saw one, "*Hsiung, hsiung*," "Bear, bear"; in Tibetan, he added, it is called *dré-mon*. The Mongols do not class the bear among ordinary animals; he is to them "the missing link," partaking of man in his appearance, but of beasts in his appetites. The bear takes the place of the "king of beasts"[1] among them and the Tibetans, for they hold him the most terrible of animals when attacked, and a confirmed man-eater! This is certainly the primeval savage of eastern Tibet, the unwitting hero of the many tales I had heard of paleolithic man in that country.[2]

As a specimen of the barefaced way in which these Mongols are bullied by their Tibetan neighbors, the following anecdotes may prove of interest. A day or two before I left Shang, a Mongol came to me for help to regain a horse which was unjustly detained from him by a Tibetan living about thirty miles away. He had lent it him to carry home some provisions, but when he asked for it, the rascal coolly said that he knew nothing about it, that he had never borrowed it. The simple Mongol thought that if I would but lend him the red tassel which hung from my horse's

1 The following names of animals found in the Koko-nor and adjacent countries may be of interest. It is curious that the Chinese call the wild ass "wild horse" (*yeh ma*), for every one of them admits that it is an ass, and should be called *yeh lo-tzŭ*. One was taken very young to Hsi-ning and every effort made to tame it, but ineffectually.

Name.	*Mongol.*	*Tibetan.*
Ovis Poli	M., Kuldza F., Argali	Kuldza. Argali.
Antelope Hodgsoni	Orungo.	
Wild ass	Holu or Hulan	Kyang.
Yak	M., Buha F., Imeh	Dung yak. Mdu.
Musk deer	Kuderi	La.
Deer	M., Bura. F., Bura muril.	
Antelope Procapra picticaudata	Tsérin	Go.

2 There is no doubt, however, that intelligent and educated Chinese, well acquainted with the appearance, habits, etc., of bears, believe there are primitive savages in the mountains of eastern Tibet.

throat-latch, and he should show it to the Tibetan as a proof that I ordered him to give up the beast, he would undoubtedly do so. I replied that, while I doubted the power of my *ch'i-hsün* to get back his property, I would lend it him; so, twisting around it a little wool on which I put some wax, impressed with my seal, I handed it to him, and he left in high spirits.[1] The poor fellow came back the next day with the tassel but without the horse, and said that he could do nothing more to get possession of it, for the Abbot said he had no power to help him.

A few years ago a band of about a hundred Tibetans made a raid on Shang, seized a lot of stock and goods and made a rush for the mountains, near the Tosun-nor. Some Chinese traders who were there at once resolved to follow them. They got about fifteen Mongols to accompany them; caught up with the Tibetans; killed several, and repossessed themselves of all the raided property. Although this should have shown the Mongols that by united and prompt action they could resist and even conquer their old enemies, it did not have that effect, and they have not since then withstood the Tibetans, who, not discouraged by this defeat, have kept on spoiling them.

While at Shang I traded off my camels to the Abbot for ponies, and, for the first time in my life, I got the better of a man in a trade, and then only unintentionally: the day after I had turned over my camels, the seemingly best one died. I had been obliged to abandon another camel in the desert, near the Shara gol, but I found some traders at Tsu-hu who were confiding enough to give me a pony for that one, which they thought they could find

[1] These tassels are used only by military officers in China, and by all officials in Mongolia and Tibet. The mode of delegating authority referred to is in constant use in these countries.

on their way north. Later on I was told that they had found it, but dead; however, they came out even in the trade, for the pony they gave me played me the trick of dying before I reached the source of the Yellow River.

On the 24th of April I left with my two youngest and most promising men for the source of the Bayan gol, sending the other two and all the packhorses to Baron dsassak by the direct road with orders to await me there. We took as a guide one of the Chinese traders, who said he had twice been to the Tosun-nor, and knew the country

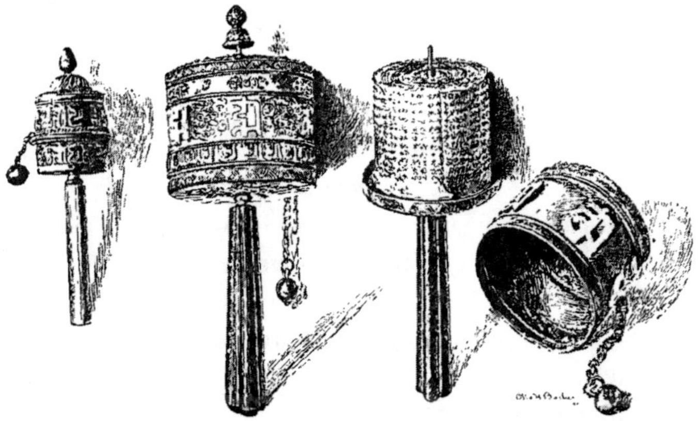

COPPER AND SILVER PRAYER-WHEELS.

well. Riding up the bank of the river, which to the east of Shang flows in a narrow valley between high and steep mountains, we passed a number of small tents, near which parties of men and women were plowing and irrigating their fields, prior to sowing them with barley. Some thirty miles up the river, where a small stream, the Katu gol, flows into it from the east,[1] the valley turned suddenly south.

Here we met the only party of Mongols we saw during

1 On most of our maps the Katu gol is made to flow out of the Tosun-nor, which is placed in the same latitude as Shang and the lower course of the Bayan gol. The Katu gol is not over twenty miles long, and does not flow out of a lake.

the trip. They were coming down from the lakes, driving yak, loaded with meat and skins they had got on a ten days' hunt. As soon as they saw us, they drove their cattle up a little ravine, and, lighting the matches of their guns, prepared to give us a warm reception, taking us, from our dress, for Tibetans. One of my men ran forward, shouting to them in Mongo that we were from Shang; and soon we were, if not in each other's arms, at least smoking each other's pipes, which ought to signify our being on quite as friendly terms. These men said that when two parties meet in this wild country they always get their guns ready, as it was highly improbable that the stronger party would pass the other without trying to rob it. This proved to be really the custom, as I had afterwards frequent proof; several times I had considerable difficulty in preventing my men taking pot-shots at small parties we saw approaching, for no better reason than that they were possible enemies.

Following up the river southward until about half-way through the range, the guide insisted on turning up a side ravine, and after a few miles we commenced climbing the flank of a steep mountain whose peak was covered with deep snow. Here, for the first time, we saw yak; they were pasturing on a declivity at the farther side of the valley, and the place higher up was so thickly covered with their droppings that it looked like an old barn-yard. The ground, as we advanced, was covered with broken rocks, shale, and slate. Innumerable streams flowing from the melting snow converted the soil into soft mud through which we had to wade, holding to our horses' tails, for they were soon too blown to carry us. Then we got in the snow, and towards nightfall we reached the top of the pass, only to hear from the guide the doleful tidings that he had made a mistake, that we were off the right trail and must go back and cross another *col* which we could see a little way on our right. No time was to be lost. We started at once, plunging through the snow-drifts, in which we sank nearly to our armpits; a piercing wind blowing in our faces inspired us with fresh courage to reach a place of shelter. After an hour's hard work we stood on top of the other pass, the Amyé-k'or (altitude, 16,220 feet).[1] We floundered down its steep side, and, having once more got below the snow-line, threw ourselves on some rocks, and, fireless and supperless, waited for the dawn. This was roughing it with a vengeance, and I believed that if my men stood a week of this kind of work they would be ready not only to brave the wilds of Tibet but to find life there luxurious.

Just as soon as there was light enough, we pushed on southward, and after a few hours of rough descent through a narrow gorge we came out again on the Yohuré gol, a clear stream, some fifty feet broad and three feet deep, flowing in a westerly direction through a fine valley. Only later I found that it was the same river I had followed through Shang, for it is so muddy in the lower part of its course that I could not recognize it in the clear mountain stream I now saw.

While making tea and drying our clothes, I saw a herd of yak coming down to the river to drink, and I thought I should try and get a shot at one, so, picking up a Winchester carbine, I crept towards them. When within about 600 feet of the herd I found a good position behind a rock, and taking careful aim at the biggest bull I could single out I blazed away, but apparently without doing

1 My guide said this pass was called the During ula, but I was assured later on by a man thoroughly acquainted with the country that it was the Amyé-k'or and one of the most difficult passes in the range.

any damage to the great, black monster, who only ran a short distance towards me and then made for the river. When I attempted to reload my gun I found the magazine empty, and remembering Prjevalsky's remark that "wild-yak shooting is as dangerous as it is exciting, for a wounded beast, especially an old bull, will often attack his pursuer,"[1] I concluded that I did not care as much about this sport as I had thought, and so sneaked back to camp by a circuitous road out of sight of the herd. An hour or so afterwards, when passing by the spot with my men on our way to the Tosun-nor, what was my astonishment to find my yak lying dead with a hole through and through him, and the pleasurable sensation I then felt at the result of my single shot effaced all memory of my previous funk. The men, who were all Mohammedans, would not take any of the meat, and so I had to content myself with the tail as a trophy, and left the body for the wolves and vultures, which had cleaned every bone when we passed again next day.

The only stream which empties into the Yohuré is the Tseldum — about eight miles above the point where we entered the valley. Six miles farther east is the western extremity of the Tosun-nor, "Butter Lake." I had not time to go around the lake, but as I learned that the trip would take several days I judged that the circumference was forty to fifty miles. Its altitude above sea level is approximately 14,200 feet. The South Koko-nor Panak'a camp along its banks in summer, when the grazing is very fine, and rhubarb and musk-deer are abundant; the Sharba of Sung-p'an pass by it, going to or returning from the Ts'aidam; at all other times the country is uninhabited.

The mountains along the upper course of the Yohuré

[1] "Mongolia," II, 193.

are much less precipitous than those along the lower, and are covered with loess and grass to their summits. A few rocky peaks and needles are occasionally seen; the highest, and apparently the culminating point of the range along the left bank of the river, is a little west of where it receives the Alang gol.[1] This peak, or rather *massif*, terminates in three needles with snow several thousand feet down their sides; and I estimated its altitude at between 17,000 and 18,000 feet. I have called it Mt. Caroline. The country was everywhere literally alive with game; yak and wild asses were particularly plentiful, but *orungo* and *tsérin* antelopes, wild goats, bears, wolves, hares, ducks, geese, sheldrakes (*huang ya*), sand-grouse, and partridges also were met in vast numbers.

Wild-ass shooting proved a difficult sport, these handsome animals having wonderfully acute sight and hearing, and when at all frightened running at tremendous speed for great distances and generally up the mountain sides. They were so numerous, however, between the mouth of the Alang gol and Lake Alang, that without much fatigue I got some good shooting; but, when not very badly wounded, they usually managed to get away, one, whose front leg I had broken, giving me a chase even of several miles before I could get another shot at it. Each band of ten or twelve is led by a stallion; and when in motion they go in single file, with heads erect and tails outstretched. These asses but rarely bray, and the few times I heard their voice it resembled more a bark than what their tame congeners treat us to; it was neither as powerful nor as prolonged as theirs. At night

1 This river figures on some of our maps as Bai gol, but I did not hear this name given it. Bai is probably an inaccurate transcription of Bayan.

they herd close together, and in a circle, with heads towards the center, their heels ready for any wolf or other enemy that may venture to attack them. They are not over ten and a half to eleven and a half hands high, the body is short, the head rather large and coarse, the tail short and thinly covered with hair. The neck, belly, and legs are white; the rest of the body is fawn-color, running into deep brown along the back. Between the Tosun-nor and the Alang-nor, a distance of from seventy to eighty miles, we saw at least a thousand; in some places we had even to keep our horses very closely hobbled to prevent them from joining the great herds which surrounded our camps.

Two days and a half of hard riding took us from the Tosun-nor to the sister lake west of it, called the Alang-nor. The stream which flows out of this little lake passes through a bog of red clay several miles in length, and carries down with it such a quantity of mud that the limpid waters of the Yohuré below their confluence are deeply dyed. The drainage from the hills south of the Alang gol, which are mostly of the same clay, also brings a large amount of silt to the stream. The lake is not over eight miles in its greatest breadth, and has probably no large feeder, at least for the greater part of the year. Its name is variously given, *Alang*, *Alag*, *Ari*, or *Areki.*[1] In Shang it is usually called Areki-nor; in Baron Ts'aidam, Alang-nor.

After visiting the lake we turned our faces northward, and, entering the mountains, took the trail to the Nomoran pass, on the farther side of which was the

1 *Alang* means, I was told, *anus*. *Alag* is explained in the "Hsi-yü-t'ung wen chih" by "variegated," and *Areki* is said by the same authority to be *hayariki*, "coarse gravel," referring to the bed of the lake, probably. The altitude of this lake is approximately 13,800 feet.

camp of the chief of Baron Ts'aidam. The road presented no difficulty on the south side, save near the top of the pass, where we found a mass of broken slate and shale covering the ground, as on the Amyé k'or. Snow had fallen during the two preceding days, and we had some trouble in getting through it, especially on the north side of the summit, where it covered the rocks and completely hid the road.[1] We were again overtaken by darkness in the mountains, and had to stop on a narrow ledge of rocks, at the base of which we could hear a torrent roaring, and there pass most wretchedly another sleepless and supperless night. When daylight came we found we were only some five hundred yards from the valley, where grass, fuel, and water were abundant.

The same day we reached the camp of the Dsassak, in a little valley near the Nomoran gol, called Narim, and found our men and horses comfortably settled, the beasts luxuriating on the fine, long grass which covered the hillsides.[2]

The Dsassak lived in two small tents differing nowise from those of his people. He was a stout man of twenty-eight, and had succeeded his father a few years previously when the latter, having lost his sight, abdicated in his favor. He said he had met me two years before at Peking, and mentioned some trifling circumstance which recalled our meeting to my mind, and so we were at once "old

1 I made the altitude of this pass to be 16,521 feet; Prjevalsky gives it as 16,100.

2 As it appears we completely missed the trail on descending this important pass, I am not in a position to say much of its advantages or disadvantages. It is one of those most frequented by travelers to eastern Tibet, and in old days to Lh'asa; and its name, which means "easy, comfortable," would tend to prove that it is preferable to that on its east, called Hato k'utul or "Stony Pass," which I found the better one. The roads over these two passes meet on the north side of the Bordza kéra Pass. This Nomoran gol must not be confounded with a stream of the same name mentioned by Prjevalsky, "Reise in Tibet," 115, which is much farther west.

friends," although I had not perhaps exchanged ten words with him in my life. He spoke neither Chinese nor Tibetan, but an energetic-looking man of about forty,

INTERIOR OF MONGOL TENT.

who was squatting on the ground near him, translated my Tibetan into Mongol for him. This man was his steward Dowé, of whom I had heard at the village of Baron, where every one feared him on account of his determined character, and radical methods of enforcing his master's commands. Two or three years previously the Dsassak had called upon the people of that village for a certain number of horses and pieces of pulo. They had been neither willing nor able to comply with his demands, so Dowé, as a punishment, pulled down half the village, and forbade them to rebuild it; hence the miserable appearance of that place.

The Dsassak declared himself quite ready to help me, though he seemed rather embarrassed when he heard that I did not have a pass from the Amban, but only a "dragon pass" (*lung piao*) from Peking, for which Mongols and Tibetans entertain but slight respect, as they cannot read it and verify its contents. I asked him if he would let me hire some of his people to go with me into Tibet, and sell or hire me pack-animals. Dowé, the steward, at once volunteered to go wherever I chose; he had been three times to Lh'asa, once to Bat'ang, and on another occasion through the Golok country to Sung-p'an in Ssŭ-ch'uan. His experience and well-known courage and ability made him a most valuable acquisition, and I held out such golden promises to him that he at once entered into all my plans and tried to further them as best he could. In a day or two I found insuperable difficulties in the way of my going to Lh'asa. The Dsassak insisted that no party of less than twenty men could undertake the journey, which takes about fifty days. The only man, besides Dowé, who was willing to go wanted forty taels of silver, no unreasonable amount, as he would be absent five or six months; but at this rate my small funds would not hold out, they would all be spent even before I left the Ts'aidam. Pack-animals would also be required, there being no provisions procurable between the Ts'aidam and Nagch'uk'a (eleven days from Lh'asa). As there was great likelihood of part of my horses dying on the way, I should have to hire ten or fifteen more and pay big prices for them. Do what I could I saw no way of undertaking the journey. My Chinese, while not positively refusing to accompany me if there was a sufficiently large party, would not listen to any proposition from me of risking it as we were then organized. The Dsassak—I must do him the justice to say—never put any obstacle in my way; he let me do as I chose, only asking me to protect his men as best I could, and keep out of unnecessary danger.

I had thought long previously that, if prevented from going to Lh'asa, I should, as an alternative course, try to cross eastern Tibet, and to make my way to Ch'amdo and thence to Assam, or, if that route was closed, to Ta-chien-lu. So I suggested to Dowé to go with me as far as the first Tibetan town south of the Dré ch'u (upper Yang-tzŭ Kiang), which would not require such a large outlay on my part, as we should have to carry provisions for only a fortnight. The T'ung-shih I had traveled with between Dulankuo and Baron had recently gone over this route, and I hoped to be able to catch up with him and get him to help me through. In fact, our friendship and the probability of securing his valuable assistance, if he found me so far advanced in the country that I could be got out of it only by being escorted to Bat'ang or Ta-chien-lu, led me to believe that I should be quite successful in my attempt to make this journey in which Prjevalsky had failed only a few years before, although much better provided with men, horses, and money than I was.

When I again saw the Dsassak I mentioned this new plan of travel to him. He declared that it was absolutely unfeasible; that I should never be able to cross the Dré ch'u. Some five years previously, he said, the Olossu Amban (Prjevalsky) had passed through Baron Ts'aidam, and, with about eighteen Russian soldiers, tried to traverse eastern Tibet (K'amdo), and reach Bat'ang. All had gone well till they reached the river and attempted a passage. Then the lamas who lived on the farther shore had, by their prayers and incantations, raised the wind and the waves and made the river impassable. On his way back to the Ts'aidam he had been attacked by the Golok and had lost all his baggage and several camels. Nobody could cross this terrible river without permission from the lamas; only very few persons ever traveled that way, and the country traversed before reaching Jyékundo, the first Tibetan town met with, was fraught with danger. Still Dowé was willing to guide me, and said that he could get another man to join the party, so that we would be seven all told, and could probably reach Jyékundo. His readiness to undertake the journey was all I asked, and we were soon busy making preparations, buying butter, meal, and mutton, shoeing horses, and making saddle-pads for the pack-animals.

The Dsassak sent me every day a large jug of arreki, a decidedly better drink than the Tibetan nä ch'ang, and considerably stronger. I told him that in our country it was supposed to be due to the use the Mongols made of this drink, or rather of fermented mare's milk, that phthisis was unknown among them. He said that consumption was far from being an unknown disease in his country, that people frequently died of it, even those who were confirmed tipplers.

I always found waiting for me in his tent, his only luxury; this was curds (*tarak*). Daily, an old woman prepared a huge kettleful, the already curdled yak or goat milk being put on the fire and stirred well while boiling. It was a most agreeable dish, especially when slightly sweetened, and is as much used by the Tibetans (who call it *djo*) as by the Mongols.

In the chief's tent I invariably found a lama reading in a low, monotonous chant some big Tibetan volume, and he, without interrupting his lecture, managed to lend an ear to our conversation. It is customary with rich laymen to have every day of the year lamas reading the sacred books for their benefit. Near the Dsassak lived a saintly lama, a Gégén, and with him were some half-dozen monks, the chief's prebendaries, each of whom received a yearly stipend of four pairs of boots and two ewes. Their duty was to keep up a continuous reading of the Kandjur, with monthly or fortnightly special services, and occasional exorcisms and other hocus-pocus.

Dowé advised me to pay a visit to this living Buddha, as he was such an enlightened saint and so great and veridic a fortune-teller that it would be well to consult him as to the success of my undertaking. Taking a few presents and the handsomest k'atag I had, I went to his tent, accompanied by two Chinese, Dowé and another Mongol, who was to join the party. The saint was a good-looking boy of nineteen, from eastern Tibet, dressed in yellow satin garments, with a fringe of horsehair shading his eyes while he read in a big book placed on a low table before him. The Mongols knelt and he blessed them by touching their bare heads with his hand; then, seating ourselves on cushions at either side, I told him my object. He took a little gold box which was set with coral and turquoise beads, and which contained dice, and after holding it to his forehead and muttering a short prayer, he shook it and looked at the dice. Next, he took a small volume, and, referring to a page, probably that whose number corresponded to that on the dice, he conned it for a while, and then delivered himself of this portentous prediction: "You are desirous of going to K'amdo; it is a difficult country to reach; the road thither is beset with dangers. You will reach the bank of the Dré ch'u, but you may fall in with Golok, or some other mishap may overtake you or your animals. As to crossing the river, that is a very difficult and uncertain matter; you may accomplish it, or you may not. But as to going through all eastern Tibet, that is absolutely beyond my ken; I can say nothing about it. At all events be careful, be careful (*séms ch'ung, séms ch'ung*)." When he had finished, I turned around to see the effect of this remarkably equivocal oracle on the Mongols, and was pleased to find their faces radiant; they considered that it foreboded good luck for the trip. They had a "Captain Cuttle" faith in this Tibetan "Jack Bunsby."

The lama then became the inquisitive boy he was, and wanted explanations concerning the presents I had given him, which comprised a razor, a concave and convex looking-glass, and a piece of Pears' soap. He was much puzzled with the last article, whose use was unknown to him; so I had to give him a lecture on soap in general, and on Pears' in particular, which, I explained to him, was used by our crowned heads and goddesses of music, hence a fit present for a saint of his standing. This won his heart, and, before I left, he said he would pray for the success of my undertaking; but that he advised me strongly to let everyone I met in Tibet know I was one of the T'ung-shihs from the Hsi-ning Amban's yamen, as they were the only persons who could travel without let or hindrance in that wild and lawless country.

SILVER CHATELAINE, KNIFE, SEAL, AND SEALING-WAX.

The favorable prophecy of the Buddha Lab jyal-sę́-ré,[1] did not prevent Dowé from having a grand prayer-meeting in his tent prior to our departure, which was fixed for the 5th of May. Two lamas pounded on the drum all day, and stuffed themselves with his choicest viands; they burnt sheep's shoulder-blades, and examined the cracks made in them by the fire. The fates were decidedly in favor of the undertaking; and Dowé finally announced that, my luck having stood the crucial test of divination by sheep's shoulder-blades, he was ready to start.

My disappointment at not being able to go towards Lh'asa was a little relieved by the Dsassak assuring me that a large party of Russians, seventy-five, had reached there during the preceding winter. He said he had been advised of it by a band of pilgrims who had recently returned from Lh'asa. The chief, he said, was an old man with a long white [blonde?] beard. I then believed it was Prjevalsky's expedition, for, though I had been told at Peking of the General's death, I had been informed that his party, under the leadership of his lieutenant, had continued its advance. I am now at a loss to understand to what expedition he referred, but that the story he told me had become widely spread throughout

[1] Lab gomba, not far from Tumbumdo, in eastern Tibet, has given the Ts'aidam a number of saints of great holiness. This one, although only a Gégén, is said to be worthy of being a Hutuketu, but Baron Ts'aidam can not afford such a luxury, which would require the payment of a large sum to the Peking Colonial Office.

the southern Ts'aidam and northeastern Tibet there can be no doubt, for it was repeated to me again, with hardly any variations, by the chief of the Nam-ts'o tribe near the Dré-ch'u.

Considerable snow had fallen during our stay at Narim, so Dowé decided on crossing the range by the Hato Pass,[1] which is generally freer from it than the Nomoran. The trail lay up the Iké gol which meets the Nomoran gol below Narim to form the Tsahan gol flowing to the east of the village of Baron. *Hato* means "stony," and the last part of the road before reaching the summit justified the name given this pass, but, taken altogether, the road was infinitely easier than those over the two other passes in the range which I had previously crossed. The descent on the south side was extremely steep, but short, and we soon found ourselves again in the valley of the Alang gol, near one of my former camps.

1 Approximate altitude 15,290 feet.

IV

SOURCES OF THE YELLOW RIVER. NORTHEASTERN TIBET. THE NAM-TS'O TRIBE

JAMBYANG (MANJUSHRI). (GILT BRONZE, MADE AT LH'ASA.)

MY caravan, as finally organized on leaving Baron dsassak, comprised two Mongols and four Chinese, seventeen ponies, and two Tibetan mastiffs worth in point of courage four more Chinese. Only six out of the whole lot of horses were strong and in good condition. Those I had got in the Ts'aidam were miserable-looking animals, as in fact are all ponies from that country; sway-backed, with such long hoofs that on rocky ground they were continually stumbling; a sorry lot indeed to start with on a long journey, but the best that could be had. We carried about five hundredweight of barley, a big leather bag of tsamba, forty pounds of butter, and ninety pounds of mutton.

Crossing the Alang gol, some ten miles east of the lake, we made for the mouth of a gorge in the southern range, through which flowed a small stream, the Yuktu gol, and camped near its southern end at a place known as the Yuktu ulan bulak, "the red springs of the Yuktu." This point marks the extreme limit of the summer wanderings of the Tibetan K'amba when on their gold-washing expeditions. On two or three occasions parties of Chinese have come to wash gold in this locality, but the chief of Baron Ts'aidam, in whose territory it is, has invariably forbidden them from continuing their search, the reason assigned being that they were not provided with a permit from the Amban at Hsi-ning, but with only a trading pass. The Mongols themselves never wash gold; they say they do not know how. The method followed by the Tibetans is extremely simple; they use a little cradle dug out of a log of wood, about three feet long and a little less than a foot wide, into which they throw the sand with their hands. The gold obtained is mixed with much dirt, but is readily sold to Chinese traders in Tibet for from twelve to thirteen times its weight in silver, or I should rather say, in rupees.

The country between the range to the south of the Alang-nor and the source of the Yellow River, some sixty miles in width, has an average altitude of about 14,500 feet, and is traversed by a succession of low hills of sand, gravel, and clay. I saw no mountains of any importance along the route except Mt. Akta and a few contiguous peaks, all of them with a slight covering of snow, and some twenty miles to our west. It appears that a branch of the Yellow River comes out of the southern flank of this little range. The country over which we journeyed was barren in the extreme, with hardly any vegetation and no running water; nearly forsaken even by yak and asses, of which latter we saw only a very few. The weather, as we advanced, became worse and worse; squalls of snow and hail, with north to northwesterly winds, succeeded each other with such rapidity that we had not time to dry our clothes during the few moments of sunshine. Then at this high altitude our horses quickly showed signs of great fatigue; even the dogs, following wearily behind, had frequently to lie down and rest. We felt no brighter than the animals; our clothes seemed to weigh tons, our guns loaded us down, and walking, even on the level, was such a violent effort that perspiration poured down our faces.

On May 9th, after camping at Dsatsu hosho, where we found enough water in a hole to make our tea, but not enough for the poor horses, we followed the dry bed of a stream along the foot of some low hills, till at last we came to where the water surged up from its underground bed and flowed on towards the Yellow River. The divide between the Ts'aidam and the Yellow River is some fourteen miles north of this place, a low line of loose gravel hills (altitude, 15,650 feet). The pass over it is called Bordza kéra k'utul, and marks the boundary between Tibet and the Ts'aidam. The branch of the Yellow River, which we first saw when about ten miles to the west of Lake Ts'aring, flowed in a broad valley of sand and bright quartzite gravel over a mile in width, the stream itself not more than fifty feet wide, very shallow, and quite slow.

As we drew near the river I was riding ahead of my party when I saw in a little pool a big brown bear eating a dead yak. I made signs to my men to bring me a gun, but when the one who brought it saw that I was going to shoot at a bear, he turned heel and ran, and none of the rest of the party would approach. This time, fortunately, the magazine of my Winchester was full, and two or three shots put an end to the "wild man." But even when he was dead I could not get the Mongols to come close, so deep-set was their repulsion and dread of the "man-eater." This bear

SHOOTING A BEAR NEAR KARMA-T'ANG.

belonged to the species called *Lagomyiarius* by Prjevalsky; he was over seven feet long and weighed probably between 600 and 700 pounds. Bears are very numerous around the Yellow River, where they do not keep to the hillsides, but are frequently met with on the plains. Holes about five feet deep and as many broad, dug by them, were continually passed; the Mongols said that these were their dens, but it is more than probable that they were dug by them when hunting for their favorite food, the lagomys.

South of this branch of the Yellow River are low hills, beyond which is a swamp about ten miles broad and twenty miles long, and through which two streams flow, emptying into Lake Ts'aring. This is known as Karma-t'ang, "the plain of stars." Every year in the seventh moon, sacrifices to the river god are made in the name of the emperor on the north bank of the main branch of the Yellow River. They consist of a white horse and seven or eight white sheep. Every third year an official is deputed by the Amban at Hsi-ning for this purpose; the other years it is the duty of the Dsassak of Baron Ts'aidam to offer the sacrifices. I was assured that the Chinese deputy does not usually offer them, but pockets their value; and I have serious doubts about the Dsassak's honesty in the matter, as he is allowed only ten ounces of silver by the Amban to purchase the horse and sheep, and make the journey. But though all these shortcomings are probably well known to all concerned, this does not prevent the Amban sending a despatch to the emperor, saying: "The worship of the source of the Yellow River at Odontala and the two snow-clad mountains of the Alang-nor and Amyé Malchin was duly performed in the prescribed form, the litanies being recited with devotional care, etc., etc.[1]

Along the foot of the hills to the south of Karma-t'ang

[1] "Peking Gazette," Sept. 15, 1885. I heard nothing of sacrifices to mountains near the Alang-nor, nor to the Amyé Malchin. I gather from Chinese geographical works that the latter mountain is identified with the sacred mountain Chi (or Ki) to which the Emperor Yü is said to have sacrificed in days of old. See Legge, "Shu-King," p. 71, in "Sacred Books of the East," III.

runs the trail followed by the wild tribes of the Golok K'amba, when journeying to and from Lh'asa, or when on their way to attack some caravan bound for that city. My guide was most anxious to push on as rapidly as possible to avoid an encounter, and would not hear of visiting the lake, which we could partly distinguish a few miles to the east. Not much was to be gained by doing so, as Colonel Prjevalsky had reached it in 1884, so I did not insist on leaving the trail.[1] Crossing Karma-t'ang the oppressive, even painful, effects of the rarefied atmosphere were more manifest than at any other stage of the journey. If the men only had been thus affected, I should have attributed it in a degree to indigestion of mutton and tsamba, but the horses and even the dogs seemed to suffer quite as much as we did.[2]

1 The Yellow River in its upper course is called Soloma by the Mongols and Ma ch'u (written *Rma ch'u*) by the Tibetans. It is also called Altan gol, "Gold River," by the Mongols, but this name is not given it near its source. The Yellow River proper may be said to commence where it issues out of Lake Noring, the most easterly of the two near Karma-t'ang. Into it and Lake Ts'aring flow a number of important streams from the great marshes of Karma-t'ang, Tsulmé-t'ang, and Do jong, which bring down much more water to these reservoirs of the Yellow River than the northern or main branch. Lakes Ts'aring and Noring are also called Ts'aka-nor and Tsaga-nor, and Jarang and Norang. The name Ts'aring is said to be Tibetan *ts'a*, "salt," and *ring*, "long"; Noring is *ngon*, "blue," and *ring*, "long." Jarang, Norang, are probably corrupt pronunciations of these words. *Ts'aka* also means "salty"; Tsaga I am unable to explain. Prjevalsky saw fit "by right of discovery" to christen the Ts'o Ts'aring "Expedition Lake," and the Ts'o Noring he called "Lake Russia." Ts'o Noring was known as the Ala-nor in the Yuan period. See "Shui-tao t'i-k'ang," V. Karma-t'ang (written *Skar-ma t'ang*) is called *Odontala* by the Mongols and *Hsing-su hai* by the Chinese, meaning "starry plain or starry lake." In the thirteenth century it was known as *Odon nor*, "starry lake."

The old highroad from Hsi-ning to Lh'asa, the route of which I had so far generally followed, turned westward after crossing Karma-t'ang and kept that direction to the ferry, or rather crossing-place, over the Dré ch'u, called Dré ch'u rabden. This point figures on Chinese itineraries as Kojisai. The "Hsi-ning Fu hsin chih" says that at certain seasons of the year the river can be forded at this latter point. It adds that it is 1710 *li* from Hsi-ning, by the road *via* Karma-t'ang.

2 The approximate altitude of Karma-t'ang is between 14,000 and 14,200 feet. At Tsulmé-t'ang, another plain to the south of it (altitude, 14,900

The country and climate changed considerably, to the south of the Yellow River. The hills became more imposing and several ranges of considerable height came in view; the ground was exceedingly rough, everywhere covered with little hummocks bristling with stiff grass, around which were small pools of water, or else boggy soil white with alkaline efflorescences. Among these we had to twist and turn our horses, which often stumbled over them, or put their feet in the deep holes. Walking was extremely fatiguing under the circumstances, and when camping not a level bit of ground could be found on which to lie down. All this country must be a vast marsh in the rainy season.

Storms became more frequent and severe as we approached the watershed of the Dré ch'u;[1] we had great difficulty in finding any dry dung for fuel, and the wind and cold were so piercing that the horses refused to graze, and stood huddled together in some sheltered nook, depending entirely on the quart or two of barley we could feed them daily. It was interesting to watch them feeding when the weather was clear; they had a habit of pushing away with their lips the soil, or snow, which covered the new grass, and when they got a day's rest they could by this means get a "square meal," but it happened so rarely that before we reached the Dré ch'u eight had to be abandoned to their fate and the mercy of wolves and bears. As to ourselves, night brought us but

feet) we were infinitely more oppressed than on top of the range dividing the two plains (altitude, 15,600 feet), where we stopped for about two hours.

[1] From April 16th, when I reached Shang, to May 25th, when I left Jyékundo, thirty-nine days in all, snow fell on twenty-two and rain on two. Wind blew on thirty days, the severest being, naturally, north and northwest. Snow was but rarely accompanied by strong wind. On May 15th, at an altitude of 14,800 feet, snow and sleet fell with violent southwest wind. West to southwest winds usually brought snow.

little rest or enjoyment, for we could not lie down, a horizontal position being quite painful, so we had to sleep propped up with our saddles, and then only by snatches. The continual wind, snow, and sleet had cut and burnt our skins, and our eyes, though protected by the horsehair screens worn in these countries, were sore and burning.

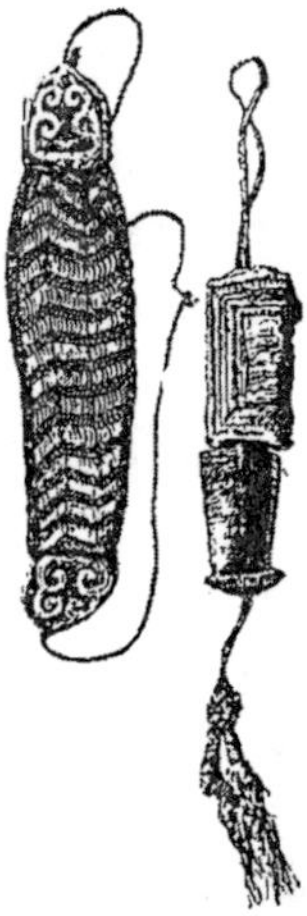

EYE-SHADE AND CASE.

It was near Karma-t'ang, I was told later on by a K'amba, that Prjevalsky had a brush with the Golok when returning from the Dré ch'u. The Tibetans' version of this affair is that about 300 Golok attacked the Russians, but were repulsed, two of their number and some ponies being killed, and the Russians losing some camels. The explorer gives a thrilling account of this feat of arms in his letter to the Czarewitch, dated August 8, 1884:[1] "They rushed to the attack with yells. The hoofs of their steeds sounded hollow on the damp soil, their long spears bristled and glistened, their long cloth robes and black, floating locks streamed behind them in the wind. Like a cloud, this savage, bloodthirsty horde dashed upon us," etc. This is certainly a most graphic description and close enough to the truth, but later: "The first volley did not stop the enemy; they continued to gallop towards us, their commander crying, 'Charge! charge! *God is with us! He will help us!*'" Is it possible that the heathen chief used such expressions? Was he a Mohammedan, or Nihilist in disguise? The latter supposition is probable, as Prjevalsky, who had no interpreter or guide at that time, could not otherwise have understood him. But the climax is reached

[1] See "Proc. Roy. Geog. Soc.," 1885, p. 171.

and Huc, who has had so much to suffer at the hands of this great traveler, is outdone when we are told that the Golok, repulsed by the rapid volleys of the Russians, turned and hid behind the nearest rocks, "opening fire upon us with their flint-locks at 300 yards." The best matchlocks (not flint-locks) ever manufactured for, or owned by, Tibetans would not carry 150 yards, and the average not over as many feet. The general and his party were safe!

The only incident which broke the daily monotony of our life in this desert was when, having finished eating our evening meal, the Mongol Dowé pulled out of his saddle-bag a sheep's shoulder-blade, and, after reciting a short prayer over it,[1] put it in the embers. Here it remained till thoroughly charred, when it was carefully removed, and we all crowded around to hear what was in store for us on the morrow. He examined closely the cracks made in the bone by the fire: the longitudinal ones represented our journey, the transversal ones what was to befall us; one side of the bone was reserved for our animals, one for ourselves. Then by the color of the bone, he foretold the weather; in fact, there was nothing hidden from him. Fortunately, luck appeared to be with us, and the signs were always favorable, but augured disasters for the horses.[2] When the supply of shoulder-blades was ex-

1 Or, as William of Rubruk says, "thinking over the subject about which he wished to consult the bone." And this is probably the correct explanation, for prayer, as we understand it, is not a Buddhist custom. *Mön lam*, which we often translate by "prayer," means an asseveration, an aspiration, a resolve, but more frequently a wish. The Tibetans at Ta-chien-lu, noticing that Captain Wm. Gill never bought native food, but always had plenty to eat, and, never having heard of tinned provisions, said that he held up his bowl to heaven whenever he was hungry, and wished (*Mön lam jyab*) for whatever kind of food he wanted, and the bowl was at once filled with it by divine agency.

2 This mode of divination, which anthropologists have called scapulimancy or omoplatoscopy, is also used by the K'amba, who are reckoned very expert in divinatory science. It has existed in Asia from the oldest times, and is the usual method among all Mongol tribes. It was and

hausted, Dowé was still able to obtain a hazy view into the future by divining with his prayer-beads, but this method was not held in much esteem by him, and he resorted to it only to learn if we should find a horse that had strayed, or as to other such unimportant questions.

South of Karma-t'ang we came to another plain, like it covered with pools of water, and with several small lakes, and traversed by a rivulet which flowed into one or the other of the two big lakes to the north. This second plain is called Tsulmé-t'ang by Tibetans, and Oron utu kedeu by the Mongols.[1] The hills around this plain, and also Karma-t'ang, were literally black with yak; they could be seen by thousands, and so little molested by man have they been, that we rode up to within two hundred yards of them without causing them any fear. However, after leaving the Yellow River we saw no more wild asses or antelopes — only bears, yak, wolves, lagomys, and sheldrakes — but all love of shooting had left me; I had quite enough to do with surveying the route, and watching the men and horses.

Crossing another low range of hills to the south of Tsulmé-t'ang we entered the basin of the Do-jong.[2] Here

perhaps still is resorted to in Japan, where the shoulder-blade of a goat is used. Attila, before the battle of Châlons, thus learnt of his impending defeat. William de Rubruk, in his "Itinerarium," p. 318, has an interesting note on this custom. See Appendix, *infrà*. Cf. also Lubbock, "Origin of Civilization," p. 238; Étienne Quatremère, "Histoire des Mongoles de la Perse," p. 267, and E. B. Tylor, "Primitive Culture," I, 124.

1 On the map compiled by G. W. E. Atkinson from Pundit A—K—'s survey, in Petermann's "Geographische Mittheilungen," 1885, Tafel 1, it is called Singma thing. The pass over the hills which divide it from Karma-t'ang is called *Tsulmé charang* in Tibetan, and *Oron utu hamer* in Mongol. Altitude is 15,640 feet.

2 These hills are called on our maps Lamatolha range, but this name, meaning in Mongol "Lama's head," applies only to a small mound of red clay and gravel in the Do-jong valley. Do-jong is called Dogen gol in Mongol; and this stream is unquestionably an affluent of the Yellow River. Prjevalsky, on the map accompanying the narrative of his fourth journey, agrees with me on this point. On former maps it is called Dug bulak or Bug bulak, and is made out to be the

we saw the first signs of human habitations, low walls made of cattle dung, used by the Tibetans to inclose their tents and make pens for their sheep and goats. But the season was not enough advanced for the people to have left the more sheltered valleys farther south for these bleak uplands, and though we strained our eyes to find a black tent we could discover none. Dowé so far had guided us well, but he now announced that it was so long since he had been over the route he had forgotten it somewhat. There could be no doubt about the general direction; we must go south, and so we continued slowly onward, the men obliged to walk nearly all the time to relieve their horses, or enable them to share the loads of the pack-animals, now too heavy for these exhausted beasts.

On May 13th we crossed the water-shed between the Yellow River and the Yang-tzŭ,[1] and entered the valley of the Ra-jong, a much larger and less forsaken one than any we had yet seen. Signs of recent occupation by Tibetans were numerous, and Dowé assured me that, besides the excellence of the summer pasturage in this valley, the natives were attracted here by the quantities of gold found in the sands and gravels of the streams. To the south the valley was closed in by a long, high range of mountains, the first really imposing one we had met. The river flowed through a red sandstone gorge in its western extremity, the summits rising nearly vertically above it two or three thousand feet. Clouds hung over their sides so thickly that our guide could no longer find his landmarks, and his perplexity and mine were very

head-water of the Ja ch'u or Za ch'u. Dug bulak means "source of the Dug or Dogen"; and as A—K— struck the river where I did, *i. e.*, near its source, he was naturally informed that it was Dug bulak, "the source of the Do-jong."

[1] Where we crossed the water-shed it was about 15.450 ft. above sea level. The Ra-jong is 800 to 900 feet lower.

great, for to add to our trouble the provisions were nearly exhausted; what I had estimated sufficient for more than a fortnight had been devoured in ten days. Any one who has traveled with Asiatics or Africans knows the enormous quantities of food these people can stow away, and their great improvidence; and so, in this case, nearly a hundred pounds of mutton, forty pounds of butter, and a large bag of tsamba had been disposed of in a few days, and we were reduced to eating mutton tallow with our tea and tsamba. A small bag of rice, and another of choma, which I fortunately discovered in my Tientsin boy's kit, where he had secreted them for his future and private delectation, helped us to stave off the pangs of hunger.

We crossed the valley and commenced the ascent of the range to the south, but were able to go only a few miles, all the horses but two giving out long before we reached the summit; violent squalls of snow and hail overtook us, so, after abandoning a large part of our luggage on the mountain side, we finally gave up in despair, and finding some springs with a deserted camp near-by, we decided to rest for a day or two, and send Dowé ahead to explore, and, if possible, reach a Tibetan camp and secure assistance.

NOR-BU JYABO (GOD OF RICHES). GILT BRONZE, MADE AT LH'ASA.

The next day he returned with two wild-looking fellows, and four yak. These men consented to take us as far as the camp of their chief, Nam-ts'o Pur-dung, for eight china cups (worth about twenty cents), but would not make any bargain to go farther before getting his consent. They said that in the Ra-jong valley and all the surrounding country rain and snow were nearly incessant, and certainly our experience bore out their statement.

The summit of the pass[1] (altitude, 15,500 feet) was crossed the next morning, and a half-hour's very precipitous descent brought us into the valley of Mar-jya kou, which trends in a southerly direction, and is the winter camping-ground of the Nam-ts'o tribe of K'amba, who during the summer months move into the Ra-jong valley which we had just left. A large, clear stream flows down it and into the Dré ch'u, some forty miles farther south. We found the vegetation quite advanced, the ground covered with the little fern-like *Potentilla* and a variety of pink and white flowers, and along the banks of the river the grass sufficiently high to afford good grazing — a most pleasing change from the bleak, brown desert we had been in for the last fortnight.

Some nine miles down the valley we came to the camp of our guides, where we stopped for the night. We were sadly in want of food, but these people said they had so little for themselves that they could not afford to sell us any tsamba or butter, and we had to get along as best we could on a few handfuls of beans and rice we discovered in the bottom of one of our saddle-bags.

They told us that there lived in a tent near-by a very famous fortune-teller, and advised me to consult him as to what was to befall me on my journey. This news greatly delighted Dowé, for his supply of sheep's shoulder-blades had given out, and for the last few days he had not been able to have his daily peep into the future. The man was called, and soon made his appearance. A dirty sheepskin gown, and boots with red cloth tops, above which showed

[1] Called *Ra-wa la*. *Ra-wa* means "queue" in K'amba Tibetan. In the Lh'asa dialect *tra-ta* is used, instead, to designate this appendage.

his bare legs, composed his dress, but what struck me most were his features and hair — a thin aquiline nose, large eyes, and a tangled mass of curly locks hanging over his shoulders and half-hiding his face. He looked like a European in disguise, rather than an Asiatic. Later on I found this type quite common in eastern Tibet, among the men especially, but I have never noticed it among persons from the central or western part. Having been asked to tell my fortune, he took out of his gown a little book, with a string attached to each leaf, and, having twisted the strings together, he handed it to me to "draw" one. Then he read the writing on the page I had chosen, and, referring to another larger book, he said that, if I wanted to reach my destination, I must travel quickly, not lose a minute anywhere, for that was my only chance of success. This was timely and sound advice at all events, and I trusted I should be able to follow it.

The people of this part of Tibet enjoy great celebrity as fortune-tellers not only throughout their own country, but also in Kan-su and Mongolia, and I have frequently heard the most astonishing tales of their wonderful clairvoyance.[1]

One of the men who had guided us to this camp was a most accomplished villain, if his own stories could be believed, and his looks certainly were worthy of a cut-throat. He said that all Chinese were thieving rascals, and he was proud to say he had killed several himself; that it would afford him pleasure to add some of my party to the list of his victims, if his chief Nam-ts'o Pur-dung so ordered it. My men looked aghast, for all this was said in

[1] I find it mentioned in Chinese histories that the sorcerers of the Uigurs were called *Kam*. Can they have been K'amba? We know that the Mongol emperors of China had Tibetan magicians at their court.

the most matter-of-fact and placid way while drinking tea with us. The rest of the men in this camp were not so bloodthirsty, and, taking me for a Chinese official, their only fear was that I would "eat them" by demanding food and pack-animals of them without offering pay, and great was their relief when assured that I always paid for everything I got.

The next day we moved down the valley to a place called Sér-jong, a few miles from the chief's camp, and it was with considerable anxiety that I awaited the return of Dowé, whom I had sent to him with presents, and a request to sell me food, for on my reception here depended the future of my whole journey. With horses no longer fit to travel, without food, without a guide, I could go no farther if he refused me help. After a while my man returned and said the chief was coming to visit me; and he soon made his appearance, accompanied by two of his sons and a number of servants. Nam-ts'o Pur-dung was a fine-looking man of fifty, with clear-cut features and an expression of much dignity. Unlike the generality of his countrymen, who let their hair hang loosely over their shoulders, his head was shaved. His sheepskin gown was trimmed with a broad border of otter fur, and on his head was a blue cloth cap with sable trimmings. The servants wore cotton-covered hats with broad rims and very high but narrow crowns, exaggerated Korean hats — commonly worn in this country as in the Koko-nor and Ts'aidam during summer. The Déba brought me a bag of tsamba, another of chura, and some butter; and said that the next day he would send me two sheep. This very kind reception astonished us, but it was soon explained. About a fortnight before, he told us, he had seen a T'ung-shih from Hsi-ning on his way south, who had said it was possible that an official from Peking would pass this way, and had asked him, as a personal favor, to do all he could to assist him. This was a truly agreeable surprise and proved that the protestations of friendship on the part of my late fellow-traveler had been sincere. His assistance was most timely, as the chief added that, but for the T'ung-shih's request, he would have done nothing for me.

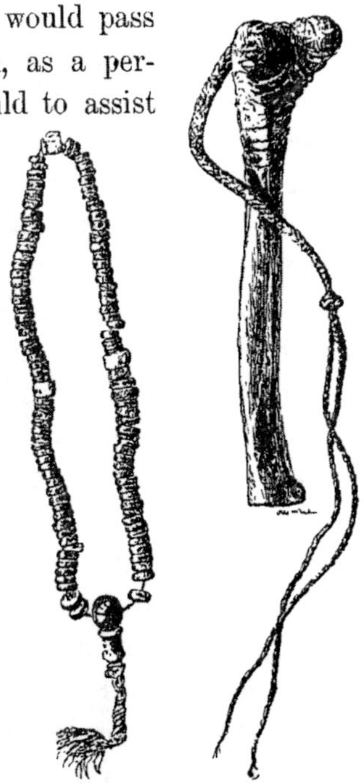

ROSARY MADE OF DISKS CUT FROM HUMAN SKULLS. HORN USED IN EXORCISMS, MADE OF HUMAN TIBIA; LEASH OF HUMAN SKIN.

He and his party stayed with me till the next day, amusing themselves with my guns, the old chief making some very good shots. When he tired of this, he took out a small book of prayers, or rather invocations to deities and mystic sentences, and read it for a half-hour or so, checking off each reading on his rosary by means of a little silver clamp set with coral. Before going to sleep, and again the next morning, he burnt opposite the tent a quantity of juniper spines and made an oblation of tea — religious rites sedulously observed by all respectable people in eastern Tibet. I accompanied him the next day to his tent, which I found differed from those of his people only in that it was larger, some fifty feet long and forty feet broad. The general *ameublement* was in all points similar to that of the Koko-nor Tibetan tents. His wife, a buxom woman of thirty-five, wearing a crown of large amber disks in each of which was set a coral bead, and with similar ornaments sewed on black satin bands holding together the innumerable plaits of her hair, presided over a long line of copper kettles, from which she dealt out milk and tea that male and female slaves placed with a bag of tsamba and a box of butter before each new-comer. She was the Déba's second wife, and by her he had a son and a daughter; the first wife was dead, and had left him five sons. The chief's most valued belongings were a very common Lefaucheux revolver he had bought from a Chinese, and a few fowls brought from Ssŭ-ch'uan as curiosities, and the only ones I saw in this part of the country.

He agreed to hire me a number of yak to carry my luggage to Jyékundo, the first town south of the Dré ch'u, and exchanged three or four fresh ponies for my worst ones. Besides a few presents of no great value which I gave him before leaving, I promised to send him a revolver and a hundred cartridges on arriving at Jyékundo. This prize delighted him; he said that his peace was being continually disturbed by the Golok and the Dérgé people, who made razzias on his lands, but now he would be able to sleep quietly, for when they learnt, as he would take care they should, that he had a "six-shooter," they would be more wary how they troubled him. I asked him what was his name, for Nam-ts'o Pur-dung was only a nickname which meant the "Hammerer of Nam-ts'o"; but he said that no one might know it, it was a profound secret, and his enemies feared him the more on account of this mystery which hung about his personality.

The exposed and difficult position which this borderer holds, and the little store he can put on the assistance of the Chinese government are exemplified by the following which took place in 1884, and of which he briefly spoke to me during my stay with him.

In the winter of 1883, the chiefs of Nam-ts'o, Tendo, etc., made representation to the Amban at Hsi-ning that of late years they had been the victims of tyrannical oppression and extortionate levies from Dérgé, as well as of constant raids upon their territories by the Golok, in addition to which Déba jong (*i. e.*, Lh'asa)[1] forced them to pay an annual subsidy in tea and silver in aid of its military expenditure. They requested that an officer be sent from Hsi-ning to deal with these irregularities.

A pi-tieh-shih, or government clerk, a major, twenty Chinese soldiers, and fifty Mongols were accordingly despatched, and the story of their exploits is told as follows in the report made to the emperor by the Amban Li Shên:

"They reached the territory of the Nam-ts'o tribe on the Yü-shu frontier, on the 2d of August, 1884, having traveled with all due expedition, and were visited by the *Po-ch'ang*[2] and others of the tribe, who stated that the King of Dérgé had sent his controller with 3000 men to occupy a place called Tendo,[3] from whence he was going very shortly to make an attack upon the Nam-ts'o tribe; and the pi-tieh-shih and the major were requested to tell them what they should do.

"The pi-tieh-shih and the major thereupon issued a

1 The kingdom of Lh'asa is thus called throughout Tibet. The expression Lh'asa dé, used by some European authors, I never heard while in the country. *Dé* (*sdé*) means "a district, a canton."

2 Nam-ts'o Pur-dung's Chinese rank is *Po-ch'ang*, "head of a hundred." Tibetans call him *Deba*; and, when addressing him, *Pönbo*, "Official."

3 Called by Chinese, Cheng-to. It is the capital of a district southeast of Nam-ts'o some 40 miles. It was visited by A—— K——, who calls it Tendhu. It is an important trading center, and has over 200 houses besides a lamasery with several hundred inmates, but Chinese traders do not visit it.

summons which they sent to the controller of Dérgé, calling upon him to appear before them, and await the action they might take. In reply the said controller sent a written representation in the following words: 'The Nam-ts'o demand blackmail from our people, and, unless the Déba of Nam-ts'o is rigorously treated within the space of three days, my men are so numerous that it will be impossible to keep them back.'

"The pi-tieh-shih and major then consented to Nam-ts'o Pur-dung being sent for and examined with a view to dealing with him, but the controller declined to be present at the inquiry; and on the 11th of September, at the end of upwards of a month's delay, Nam-ts'o Pur-dung sent a man to say that the Dérgé people had brought up two brass howitzers, and their troops were contemplating an immediate advance, so he earnestly prayed for assistance.

"The major then went to Tendo, with an escort of fifty sabers, to demand an explanation of the reason for these unauthorized and criminal hostilities, whereupon the controller, having no explanation to give, recalled his troops and remained in observation.

"At this juncture, one Lu Ming-yang, a lieutenant stationed at Kanzé,[1] reached the place (*i. e.*, the capital of Dérgé), in the progress of a tour of inspection, and the pi-tieh-shih wrote officially to him requesting him, as he was on the spot, to help to establish peace. In due course, the lieutenant replied that he had laid the contents of the pi-tieh-shih's despatch before the high authorities of Ssŭ-ch'uan, and expected an answer in about sixty days,[2] when he would proceed to take action.

1 He was still commander at Kanzé when I passed through that place. His detachment comprised about twenty unarmed infantry soldiers.

2 The *hsieh-tai*, or "colonel," stationed at Ta-chien-lu controls the actions of the officers posted in eastern Tibet. Lu could easily have

"Matters remained *in statu quo* until the 10th of February, 1885, when the lieutenant informed the pi-tieh-shih and major that he had been ordered to summon the controller of Dérgé before him. The pi-tieh-shih then hurried off to Bat'ang, which he reached on the 20th of February,[1] to assist in the inquiry, and had an interview with the lieutenant. The controller of Dérgé, however, never put in an appearance, and, after waiting many days for him, the pi-tieh-shih returned to the place from whence he came, Lieutenant Lu also taking his departure."[2]

This narrative is interesting for many reasons, but principally as illustrating the condition of the country and the little deference shown to the Chinese government by the most powerful state of eastern Tibet. I shall have occasion farther on to speak of the endeavors being continually made by the Lh'asa people to annex this part of the country or at least to make it their tributary. Here I will only call attention to the fact that in the foregoing story of events in Nam-ts'o in 1884–85 we see some thirty or forty Chinese living on the Tibetans for a year during which time they make considerable sums out of them by the ula, accomplishing nothing, snubbed by the Dérgé people, and leaving the chiefs of Nam-ts'o and Tendo exposed to the revenge of their enemies for having called in the assistance of the hated Chinese.

The tribes of pastoral Tibetans living north of the Dré ch'u, from its sources to Jyékundo or even farther

heard from him in twenty days, but, as he could do nothing in the matter, he only wanted to "save face" by procrastinating.

[1] The pi-tieh-shih probably left Jyékundo and reached Bat'ang by passing through Dérgé dron-cher. The time usually taken to perform this journey is ten or eleven days.

[2] See "Peking Gazette," Sept. 15, 1885.

east, were organized by the Chinese government in 1732 into thirty-nine hundreds ruled by hereditary chieftains or *Déba*, and under the control of the Hsi-ning Amban, or, in case of tribes located near the Ssŭ-ch'uan border, under that of the governor-general of that province. These tribes were to pay to the emperor an annual tribute of one horse for every hundred; and had also to supply to all Chinese officials and tribute missions traveling through their country horses, yak, guides, and food, in other words the ula, from the Dré ch'u to Dolon batur in the Ts'aidam. The horse tribute was soon after commuted for a poll-tax of $\frac{8}{100}$ of an ounce of silver each family, and this arrangement has been adhered to down to the present day.[1] These clans or tribes are known as *K'amba*,[2] a name which in reality applies to all inhabitants of *K'ams*, or *K'amdo*, as the eastern portion of Tibet is called, but in common parlance, except when reference is made to those northern tribes, that name is replaced by a host of special ones particular to the people of the different districts, such as Horba, Dérgéwa, Lit'angwa, etc.

The most interesting, but unfortunately the least known, of these tribes of northern Tibet are the *Golok*, who inhabit a large district extending from near the border of

[1] See "Hsi-Ts'ang t'u k'ao," V, 20.

[2] Prjevalsky in the letter to the Czarewitch cited already (p. 175), speaking of the Nam-ts'o K'amba, says: "Here wander with their flocks of goats and sheep the Mongols of the tribe of Kam." I cannot conceive how he could have made such a mistake, as there is absolutely nothing Mongol about this people, who are good representatives of old Tibetan civilization, possibly descendants of the Tang-hsiang of the sixth century of our era. Hooker, "Himalayan Journals," I, 127, has the following interesting remark: "The northern part of the Lepchas country is inhabited by Sikkim Bhoteas (or Kumpa), a mixed race calling themselves Kumpa Rong or Kumpa Lepchas; but they are emigrants from Tibet, having come with the first rajah of Sikkim. Their province is northeast of Lhassa." Kumpa K'amba and Kumpa Rong (or Rongwa) mean "agricultural K'amba," or "K'amba living in an agricultural district."

northwestern Ssŭ-ch'uan to the sources of the Yellow River. The few representatives of these tribes I met differed from the rest of the population of eastern Tibet only in their language, which, although undoubtedly Tibetan, is hardly comprehensible to any one who has not made a special study of it. There are said to be over a thousand tents (or about 5000 souls) in these Golok tribes, chief among whom is the A-chü Golok, whose head is known as A-chü jyabo.[1] Many of the people live in caves in the hills, and all of them are dependent on either the Sung-p'an traders, or the neighboring Tibetan tribes, for the barley and metal work they use. They sometimes visit Tankar, but the greater part of their trading is done at the lamasery of Lh'a-brang, at Kuei-té, or at Sung-p'an, where they carry musk, hides, furs, and some gold dust. Trading is, however, the least important of their vocations; pillaging caravans and making forays on the agricultural Tibetans supply them, without much trouble, with the few articles necessary to their existence. Some lamas live among them, in tents, but most of those of their people who enter the order reside at Lh'a-brang or Dajé gomba in the Horba country.

All the pastoral tribes, called in Tibetan *Drupa* or *Drukpa*,[2] are ruled by chiefs called *Déba*, who have no other officials under them. They have, as far as my observation goes, very little authority; in case of war they lead their men, and in time of peace they see that the pasture lands of their tribes are not encroached upon; they levy the various taxes for China, for Lh'asa, or Dérgé, as the case may be, and sometimes arbitrate quarrels among their

[1] The "Huang-ch'ing chih-kung-t'u," VI, mentions six tribes of Golok, three of whom it calls A-shu (A-ch'ü) Golok. See also Huc, "Souvenirs d'un Voyage dans la Tartarie," II, 231.

[2] Written, *Hbrog-pa*.

clansmen, but generally the people settle such matters between themselves.

Besides these strictly nomadic tribes, there is in every part of Tibet a large proportion of the population living in tents, and also known as Drupa; however, their organization is not, I have been told, a tribal one, but partakes of that prevailing in the section of country they inhabit, and, therefore, it will be treated later on when reference is made to the more civilized parts of eastern Tibet.

The Drupa are strictly pastoral, having herds of yak and horses, and flocks of sheep and goats. Dogs and a few cats, but no domestic fowls, are found among them. The Tibetan mastiff is rarely seen in eastern Tibet, but mongrels in which a slight strain of mastiff blood is discernible are constantly met, and make most admirable watch-dogs. These people rely on their agricultural neighbors for barley, and the only vegetable food they eat is choma, which grows abundantly all over the country. Their customs are nearly identical with those of the Koko-nor Tibetans; like them they marry only one wife, whom they purchase from her parents; like them also they get rid of their dead by exposure on the hillsides.

The K'amba are exceptionally fine horsemen, much more graceful than even the Mongols. Their saddles are also much better than those used by the latter people, the finest coming from Dérgé and Lit'ang. Like the Arabs they ride with such short stirrups that the thighs are horizontal, and use a large ringed snaffle-bit.

After spending the better part of a day with Nam-ts'o Pur-dung, I returned to my camp, where shortly afterward the guide he had promised me arrived, and also seven yak to carry the loads of my horses. Next morning we left for Jyékundo. Following the Mar-jya kou valley for a few miles, we came to the first houses we had seen in the country, small stone dwellings built against the hill-side, with several stories reached by notched logs set against the outer walls. Here the road branched into two: the longer but better one following the stream,[1] the other, steeper but shorter, leading up a valley on the left and over the Lh'a-dang la, a pass about 2000 feet high. A little way down the other side of this, we again came on the river; and here, at an altitude of about 13,800 feet, cultivation commenced, but the soil was so stony that the crops must be extremely small. Barley is the only grain raised; it is, I believe, of a peculiar loose-husk species, at least the better kind is. When preparing it for tsamba it is parched in a copper pan, and the husks are easily detached by winnowing. When the common kind of barley is used, the meal is very poor; the husks remain in it, and when mixed with tea it looks and tastes like a bran mash.

We stopped for the night in a small village called Ta-kou, about four miles north of the Dré ch'u, at which river the district of Nam-ts'o ends in this direction. The house we occupied belonged to the Déba, and is for the exclusive use of officials traveling along the road. Similar official inns are found along all the principal roads in Tibet; they are called *jya-tsu k'ang* by the natives, and *kung kuan* by the Chinese. Each of them has a few servants, generally two, the one a hostler (*ta yo*), the other an indoor help (*teu yo*, "upper servant") who supplies guests with tea, fuel, water, etc. These persons

[1] A mile or so below this point there are hot springs, and near-by a few houses. On the sketch-map prepared from the report of Pundit A— K— ("Proc. Roy. Geog. Soc.," VII, 136) there figures at this point a town called Niamcho. I could hear of no place with such a name. Nam-ts'o is the name of the whole district, and probably means, "Heavenly lake." A large lake to the north of Lh'asa bears the same name (in Mongol, Tengri-nor).

are usually women, and their duties are far from being sinecures when a large party is stopping in the house under their care. Tibetan villages are almost invariably built on rocky ledges, high above the streams, and where they do not cover any arable soil, so scarce throughout the country. The women are obliged to bring all the water, in barrels carried on their backs, from the streams below. A rawhide strap is passed across the breast, and around the barrel, whose bottom rests on the thick folds of the gown, which hang around the waist. In many localities the village is at least a quarter of a mile away, and the women are constantly employed at this hard work, which it is beneath the dignity of a man to perform.

The houses at Ta-kou, and all those I saw farther on, were built of stone, usually limestone or some shaly rock, the surface sometimes covered with a coating of mud or plaster. A large gateway with heavy double doors led into a courtyard, around which were the buildings and sheds. These houses also were two-storied, a notched log of wood set against the wall serving as a ladder to reach the upper one. The roof of the first floor serves as a gallery to the second story. It is made of mud, resting on heavy rafters. Holes are left in it by which the smoke escapes from the rooms on the first floor; and, in the case of interior rooms, these holes are the only apertures by which light is admitted. When there are any windows, they are simply openings about three feet square in the walls, without any means of keeping out the wind and cold, except in the finest houses, where heavy boards sliding in grooves are used to close them. There is absolutely no furniture; sometimes a log of wood roughly squared is found near the hearth; this is used to place one's cup on, but as a general thing even this primitive table is lacking. Some houses contain furnaces, on which the kettles boil over a dung fire; in others, there are large, open hearths, in the center of each of which are three stones to rest the pot on. The simplicity of the nomad is found in all the appointments of the agricultural Tibetan's home. In many houses there are not more than two or three four-walled rooms, all the rest of the building consisting of covered galleries opening on the courtyard. These have the great advantage of being better lighted and more airy than rooms, yet hardly colder; they are also freer

1. BRASS TEA-POTS (DÉRGÉ MAKE). 2. WOODEN BOWL, CHINA BOWL AND CASE. 3. BRICK OF TEA. 4. COPPER POT (KOKO-NOR). 5. COPPER KETTLE (TRASHIL'UNPO). 6. TSAMBA BAG. 7. WOODEN BUTTER-BOX. 8. TEA CHURN. 9. TEA STRAINER.

from vermin, with which one is fearfully tormented everywhere in Tibet, fleas especially swarming. The ground floor of all these houses is used as a horse-stable, as is often the case in mountainous and cold countries, Switzerland for example; and every house is provided with well-arranged latrines. It is probable, that the heat from the horses, which is sufficient to raise the temperature of the room over their stable, suggested the idea of having them under the dwelling-room. It is a curious fact which shows how little progress this people have made in the arts of civilization, that they appear to be unable to build but the roughest kind of houses and only those where there is little woodwork. Ssŭ-ch'uanese carpenters and brickmakers do nearly all the building in eastern Tibet, and also fell the timber necessary for the work. I met large numbers of them on the road to Kanzé, traveling to remote localities, to build temples and bridges, to make plows and pack-saddles, and do other kinds of labor in their respective trades.

The only tools I ever saw in the hands of Tibetans were a primitive sort of adze and occasionally the little Chinese axe. It is not surprising, therefore, to find among them very few household utensils made of wood. The tea-churn (*do-mong*) is a log split in two, hollowed out, and circled with willow twigs, and is of home manufacture, but their wooden cups and platters are turned by Chinese, as are also the wooden beads used in rosaries and known as *poti shing*. Basketwork is but rarely seen in this country; tea-strainers (*ja tsa*) of bamboo, and also of Chinese manufacture, were the only wickerware objects that I met with. However, the eastern Tibetans are expert potters, making two kinds of ware, one a light, glossy black, the other of reddish color and heavier. They use the Chinese potter's wheel, and the art has undoubtedly been introduced among them by that people, and in recent times. The forms of the tea-pots and bowls made by them reproduce those affected for these utensils when made of metal, and their decoration shows the combined influence of China and India.

V

PASSAGE OF THE DRÉ CH'U (THE RIVER OF GOLDEN SANDS)—JYÉKUNDO, DÉRGÉ, THE HORBA STATES, GIRONG

TA-KOU marks approximately the point on my journey where I left the border-land of northeastern Tibet[1] and entered a generally thickly peopled region occupied alternately by agricultural and pastoral tribes, and extending without interruption to Ta-chien-lu, the frontier town of western Ssŭ-ch'uan, where I left the country.

About four miles below Ta-kou we came on the Dré ch'u, the upper Yang-tzŭ chiang,[2] a beautifully blue river about a hundred and fifty yards wide and twenty feet deep, flowing swiftly between high, bare mountains of a reddish color. This was the terrible torrent of which

[1] On the sketch map illustrating A—— K——'s journey in Tibet, in "Proc. Roy. Geog. Soc.," VII, 136, Mogonzen, Rablu, and Gaba are mentioned as names of districts touching Nam-ts'o. None of these names was recognized by any of the natives I questioned about them.

[2] Marco Polo speaks of this river as the *Brius*, and Orazio della Penna calls it *Biciu*, both words representing the Tibetan *Dré ch'u*. This last name has been frequently translated "Cow yak river," but this is certainly not its meaning, as cow yak is *dri-mo*, never pronounced *dré*, and unintelligible without the suffix *mo*. *Dré* may mean either mule, dirty, or rice, but as I have never seen the word written, I cannot decide on any of these terms, all of which have exactly the same pronunciation. The Mongols call it *Murus osu*, and in books this is sometimes changed to *Murui osu*, "Tortuous river." The Chinese call it *T'ung-t'ien ho*, "River of all Heaven." The name *Chin-sha chiang*, "River of golden sands," is never applied to it in this part of its course, but is used for it from Bat'ang to Sui Fu, or thereabouts. Yang-tzŭ kiang (or chiang) is the name we give this great stream, but this appellation is unknown in China, where it is called *Ta chiang*, "Great river," or *Ta kuan chiang*, "Great official river."

I had heard so much, and which Mongols and Chinese agreed in considering the most formidable obstacle on this road. We were not to cross it at this point, however, and after following its bank for about half a mile, we entered a narrow valley trending southeast, and began the ascent of the Oyo la, an extremely steep and difficult pass, especially on its south side. We had to abandon three of the horses, on the way up; the hard work and scanty provender they had had since leaving the Ts'aidam had reduced them to skeletons. The mountain was almost entirely composed of shaly rocks which cropped out in nearly vertical layers, making walking over them extremely disagreeable.[1] The southern slope was at an angle of perhaps 30°, and covered with a mass of disintegrated stone and clay, through which we slid till we reached a grassy ledge some thousand feet from the summit, where we were glad to camp.

The next day we completed the descent, and, after following up for some miles a little affluent of the Dré ch'u flowing westward, we ascended by a very easy gradient the Rungo la (altitude, 15,800 feet), covered to a height of about 13,000 feet above sea level with a scrubby growth of brush, and from its top again saw the Dré ch'u twisting and turning among mountains from 2000 to 3000 feet high. The descent from this pass was even more precipitous than that of the day before, the ground under us a mass of broken-up and disintegrated mica-schist and slate.

There were three or four villages near the river, but though the guide tried in several houses to get some one to launch one of the numerous skin coracles we saw drying on the housetops, and ferry us across, none would do so. We then started up the river, hoping to find the

[1] The altitude of this pass is approximately 15,650 feet above sea level.

people more obliging at the next village. We had not proceeded more than a mile when we ran into a large party of horsemen coming our way. They were armed to the teeth with guns, lances, bows and arrows, and swords, some of them carrying two of these. Among them were several chiefs, and they lost no time in asserting their right to be obeyed, by saying that we should not cross the river, which marked the point beyond which no Chinese had the right to go unless authorized so to do by themselves or the chief at Tendo. They ordered us to accompany them to that town, which was only a day's ride to the east, and there see the Chinese T'ung-shih and the Déba and all the other chiefs of the country, who had assembled to settle some long-standing dispute about a boundary line. Although I would have been delighted to see my late fellow-traveler and all the dignitaries of the country, I conceived that it would not be prudent to venture there, that it would be putting my head in the lion's mouth; so, telling them that we would follow them, but slowly, as our horses were very tired, we let them ride on ahead, and, as soon as they were out of sight, turned down the river, and after a few miles of very rough riding we stood by the Dré ch'u at the ferry near the village of Dré-kou.

As we descended the steep mountain we could see a wee boat crossing and recrossing, looking no larger than a wash-tub and not unlike it in shape. The river was about a hundred and seventy-five yards wide, swift and deep, and we all felt rather nervous at the idea of having to make our worn-out horses swim this mill-race, and trust ourselves and all our belongings to such a fragile boat. But it had to be done, and done quickly, before any one could send orders not to ferry us across; night was falling rapidly, and masses of black cloud were gathering in the valley above us and a storm seemed imminent. In a trice we had unloaded the yak,

CROSSING THE DRÉ CH'U NEAR DRÉ-KOU.

unsaddled the horses, and with much shouting and pelting with stones driven them all into the river. The swift current carried them down about a quarter of a mile, but, accustomed probably to this kind of work, they reserved their strength till swept out of the main channel, and then, facing the current, they swam quickly to the bank, the yak, to my surprise, getting across much more rapidly than the horses. Our turn came next. The coracle is composed of yak-hides stretched over a few bent twigs, is about five feet long and four feet broad, and shaped like half of a walnut shell. So frail is it that one must be most careful not to put one's foot on the hide, but only on the ribs, for the least direct pressure on the skin makes the seams give way. A man stands in the bow and paddles or steers with a short oar, crossing the river diagonally, and then carrying his boat on his back up-stream so as to come back to his starting-point when swept across again. When four men and half our outfit were across, the storm came sweeping down the gorge, and the boatman declined to cross again with such a wind blowing, for his boat would surely be capsized. It was dark by this time, and rain commenced to fall in torrents; we huddled together under a ledge of rock and prepared to pass the night as comfortably as possible. Our kettle, tea, and tsamba had fortunately remained on our side of the river, and a villager having kindly brought us a bag of dry dung and a bellows, we were able to prepare our usual frugal evening meal.

The mode of salutation among the people in this section of the country is novel. They hold out both hands, palms uppermost, bow with raised shoulders, stick out their tongue, and then say *Oji, oji.* When desirous of showing respect to a person, or expressing thankfulness, they stick out their tongue and say *Ka-dri* (*bkah-hdrin*).[1]

[1] In central Tibet the salutation consists in sticking out the tongue, pulling the right ear, and rubbing the left hip, making a slight bow at the same time. The Chinese mode of bowing tends, however, to supersede this national one, which is now confined to the common people.

After a miserable night during which rain and snow fell continually, we were carried over to our companions, and were able to congratulate ourselves on the ease with which we had crossed the terrible river.[1] The horses were, however, very much fatigued by their swim, and we did not advance over six miles that day. Passing by the Zonyik ch'ürten, whose red walls and gilt spire make it a landmark, and then by the lamasery built near it, we again left the Dré ch'u, now flowing in a general southeasterly direction, and entered a fearfully stony gorge. Passing several small villages, we soon found the snow so deep that we could advance no farther, so descending below the snow line we camped and waited for the morrow, when we hoped to be able to make a trail across the mountains. The people in the villages appeared very poor, and so small was their supply of barley that we had to pay about ten cents a cupful, and could then buy only enough to give three or four horses one small feed. It is no uncommon thing here to find the poor people using chips of wood to infuse in water instead of tea, and pea-flour is a common substitute for tsamba.

The following day we managed, after much hard work through the deep, soft snow, to reach the summit of the Zonyik la (altitude, 16,300 feet), and the still higher and steeper Tagluug la (altitude, 16,650 feet), just beyond it. The sky was clear, so the radiation of the sun on the

Throughout Tibet to say a thing is very good they hold up the thumb with the fingers closed, and say *Angé tumbo ré*, "It is the thumb," *i. e.*, it is the first. Second class is expressed by holding up the index with the remark *Angé nyiba ré;* and so on down to the little finger, which means that it is the poorest of all, *T'a-ma ré*, "It is the last."

[1] The altitude of the river at this point I found to be 12,650 feet above sea level. This agrees well with previous observations. Prjevalsky, some twenty miles west of this point, makes its altitude 13,100 feet; and A—— K——, at Tuden gomba (Ch'üdé gomba?), some thirty miles lower down, 11,975 feet.

snow caused us much discomfort, though we wore the horsehair eye-shades used in the country,[1] and by the time we made camp in the Ranyik Valley, three of us were nearly blind. The descent from the Taglung la, the highest pass crossed on the whole journey, was comparatively easy, though the valley for the first few miles was covered with small angular stones, over which the jaded horses stumbled and slid. Near the head of the Zonyik Valley we saw a herd of some twelve argali, but the snow was so deep, and any exertion so exhausting, that I did not even attempt to get a shot at them. These were the only specimens of this kind of sheep I saw in Tibet proper, although I was told that they were common in the wilder gorges along the Dré ch'u.

Leaving the Ranyik lung-ba, where it took a south-easterly direction, we climbed the next day the Nyi-ch'en la (altitude, 16,450 feet), on which we found a great deal of snow, and, a few miles on its south side, entered the valley in which is Jyékundo. When about two miles south of the pass, we stopped near some tents to eat our midday meal. We had hardly lit our fire, when a man and a woman came to us, and offered me a little bucketful of sour milk, some fresh butter and cheese. This pleased my men immensely; they said it augured well for the reception we would receive at Jyékundo, for nothing, they hold, is a better omen, than to receive a present on arriving at or nearing the journey's end. In this connection I am reminded of another popular superstition of Tibet. If a person on going out, meets another carrying an empty pail or bowl, he will turn back, for it is a bad sign; but if the first person he meets, carrying anything, has his bowl or bucket full, it is a sign of good luck and very often

[1] See illustration, p. 175.

he will give the bearer a k'atag or a small present. In the same order of ideas may be classed this people's custom of always putting something in a vase, bowl, or pitcher when making a present of it, for to give it empty would be unlucky.[1]

Some six or eight miles below these tents we saw, after rounding a rather sharp bend in the road, the brightly colored walls of the lamasery of Jyékundo, crowning a high, steep hill, at the foot of which was an irregular mass of flat-roofed, mud-plastered houses, composing the town, and looking like old brick kilns.[2] Behind the lamasery rose precipitous mountains of dark slaty rocks, with here and there stunted juniper and cedar trees growing in the clefts; and farther away a long line of snow-clad peaks, an eastern continuation of the range I had recently crossed. Below the village the river flowed swiftly by, through a grassy bottom, where herds of yak and ponies were grazing; and women were trudging backward and forward between the river and the town, carrying barrels of water on their backs. Altogether it was a pretty place, and I looked forward to a week or two of rest in it with great pleasure, but was doomed to disappointment.

We took up our lodgings in the courtyard of a house belonging to a young woman to whom an admiring T'ungshih had given it, and tried to make ourselves as comfortable as possible under a broad shed which covered one side of it. Hardly had we started the fire to boil our tea than the yard was filled with people eager to see what goods

1 When selling grain or flour, the vender puts back a little in the measure, so as "not to cut the root of trade" (*tsa ché ma-nyon*).

2 Captain Turner, I find, made this comparison as far back as 1783. See "Embassy to the Court of the Teshoo lama," p. 215: "The peasant's home is of a mean construction, and resembles a brick kiln, in shape and size, more exactly than anything to which I can compare it."

we had for sale, for, learning that we were not traveling on official business, they concluded that we must be traders. My people told them that I was a T'ung-shih on my way to Ssŭ-ch'uan, but the fact of my traveling without ula puzzled them not a little; this was something they had not been accustomed to, an official traveling at his own expense and paying for all he required! Fortunately none of them had ever seen a foreigner, so, though my features were not like those of the men with me, they never imagined that I was anything else than a Chinese, but one from some remote part of the empire with which they were not acquainted. My men did their best to keep them in this opinion, feeling that on my safety depended their own. Fortunately, also, there were in the town some ten or eleven Chinese traders from Ta-chien-lu, and also one of the party of my fellow-traveler in the Ts'aidam, Fu T'ung-shih, and they exerted themselves to their utmost to dispel the suspicions of the people and lamas, and to further my plans. As soon as they found out that I was not an official who could or would squeeze them, they came promptly to see me, and having arranged a uniform story to tell the people, went and spread it about the town. The Hsi-ning Chinaman said he had known me for years, and that if any discourtesy was shown me it would certainly bring them trouble.

SILVER RING (JYÉKUNDO WORK).

As far as the people were concerned, this was enough; they soon became very friendly and were eager to do anything I desired. We luckily bought from some of the natives enough tsamba and butter to last for a day or two, and also hay for our horses; for on the morrow the courtyard was empty, and one of my new friends came and told us that the chief, or Pönbo, of the district, who was also the abbot of the lamasery, suspecting me of being a spy from the fact that I was not provided with the pass from the Hsi-ning Amban which all travelers from China carry with them, had issued orders forbidding any one trading with me. Whoever disobeyed was to be severely beaten, or, if a lama, his nose and ears were to be slit, and a reward of ten bricks of tea was to be given to the informer. As a reason for these orders, the Pönbo said that it had been revealed to him by his books on divination that I was a man deeply versed in magic art, with the power of bringing back to me, within three days, any money or goods paid by me to others, to my own great profit and their manifest loss. Hence these measures were necessary for the people's protection. This taboo was to be in vigor until he could return from Tendo, for which town he started at once to consult with other chiefs on his future action. This gave me eight days of respite in which to decide on some plan for continuing my journey southward, for in less time than that he could not possibly return.

Jyékundo (altitude 12,930 feet) is at the confluence of two small streams whose united waters empty into the Dré ch'u not many miles to the east of the town. The larger of these two streams comes from the south, and is called the Pach'i ch'u; the name of the other, which flows from the west, I did not learn. The town contains about one hundred families (400 persons),[1] some three hundred lamas, and a floating population of several hundred in which are a number of Chinese and fifteen Mongols with their wives.

[1] The number of children in Tibetan families rarely exceeds two. That of Nam-ts'o Pur-dung, in which there were six, was considered abnormally large.

A few miles south of the town is another lamasery, Changi gomba, with some 300 inmates, and in the little valleys in the vicinity there are, perhaps, from fifty to seventy-five tents and scattered houses, all of which may be counted in with this town, which is the *chef-lieu* of a semi-independent district.[1]

The importance of Jyékundo from a strategic and commercial point of view is considerable, as fairly good roads (for Tibet) radiate from it all over the country.[2] Commercially considered it is a distributing point for the Chinese trade in the northeastern part of K'amdo, and is the only town in that region where Chinese merchants are allowed to reside. The trade of this place, though large for the country, is not valuable; yak hides, lambskins, musk, gold dust, a few deer horns (*lu jung*, in Chinese), and a little wool are the principal exports to China. Only a small part of the tea trade is in the hands of the Chinese, nearly every native that owns a bunch of yak engaging in it more or less. To judge from the stock in

1 The Mongols referred to on p. 205 are sent to Jyékundo by order of the Hsi-ning Amban to learn Tibetan, act as an escort to Chinese officials, and look after the ula from the Ts'aidam. They remain here for three years, and have official rank. There are two from Dsün Ts'aidam, two from Koko Beileh, three from Taichiner, one from Amé dsassak, two from Tolmukgun (Mohammedans), one each from Erké Beileh, Wangka, Mori wang, and Dungkorwa (Tankar).

2 The most important road starting from this point is that leading to Ta-chien-lu in Ssŭ-ch'uan, which I followed. Another leads across the steppes on the west to Nag ch'u-k'a, where it meets the "northern route" (*chang lam*) from Hsi-ning, and thence reaches Lh'asa in nine days. Another leads to Ch'amdo, in about ten days. Still another passes by Tumbumdo and Tendo, and going through the Golok country comes to Sung-p'an t'ing in northwestern Ssŭ-ch'uan. The capital of Dérgé is reached from Jyékundo in six days, and from that town Bat'ang is only eight days farther south.

A—— K—— gives the name of this town as Kegedo, but no one recognized this. It is sometimes called Jyék'or, but the name is probably written *Rgyas rgyun mdo*, pronounced Jyä-gun-do. The termination *do*, meaning "confluence, a pair," is frequently pronounced *da* in eastern Tibet, and possibly *go*, as in Lagargo. *Kou*, another frequent termination in names of places, appears to mean "stream or valley."

trade of the Chinese at Jyékundo, the wants of the people are few and inexpensive; lastings, shirtings, flour, tea, vinegar, red leather, tòbacco, and chinaware are the principal goods sold or exchanged by them for the products enumerated.

The copperware and saddlery used in the country are manufactured at the capital of Dérgé (Dérgé dron-cher), or at Lit'ang, and the few pieces of ironware required come from Ta-chien-lu. Traders from Lh'asa visit Jyékundo every year when on their way to Ta-chien-lu, and supply it and the whole of eastern Tibet with cloth (*truk*), out of which the gowns of the wealthier class and all lamas' clothes are made.

The Chinese traders are mostly Shen-hsi men from near Hsi-an Fu. They are known in western China as *lao-shan*, and are by far the most enterprising of their class in northern and western China. They are authorized to

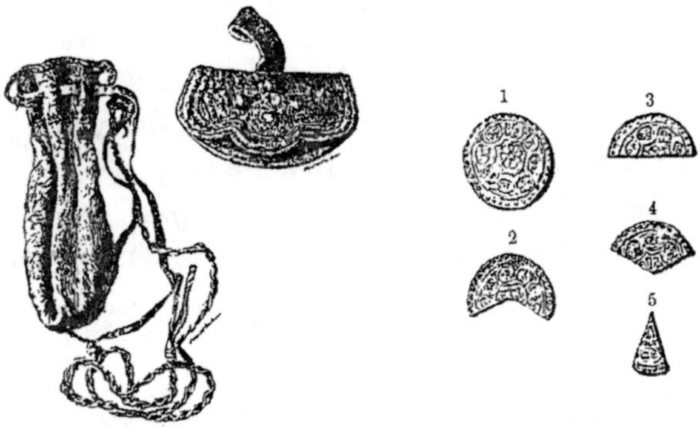

LEATHER MONEY BAG AND POUCH. SILVER COINAGE OF LH'ASA AND SUBDIVISIONS (TWO-FIFTHS OF ORIGINAL SIZE): 1. TRANKA. 2. DJO-GANG. 3. CHI-CHYÉ. 4. KARMA-NGA. 5. K'A-GANG.

trade in Tibet by the authorities of Ssŭ-ch'uan, who grant them yearly permits, a system unfortunately not known to the Kan-su officials, who by their forty days' permits have stifled all trade between their people and Tibetans and Mongols. These Chinese are mostly agents of Ta-chien-lu houses, and reside permanently at Jyékundo, several of them at the time of my visit having been there for the last five years. The profits of the trade are, they assured me, considerable, but the uncertain tempers and general untrustworthiness of the natives, who from one moment to another change from best of friends to bitterest foes, make their sojourn among them a most uncomfortable one.

From this point on my journey until I reached Ta-chien-lu, Chinese silver bullion was not received; only Indian rupees were current. When a smaller piece of money was needed, which did not frequently occur, at least in my case, rupees were chopped in half or quartered. I had considerable difficulty in inducing the *lao-shan* traders to exchange forty or fifty taels of silver for coin, as they assured me it was absolutely of no use to them unless they found some one wanting it to make ornaments. My gold, purchased at Peking for Tls. 20 an ounce, was here at such an extremely low price, Tls. 13 or 12.5 an ounce, that I had to keep it.[1]

Gold-washing is one of the commonest occupations throughout the country, as every stream seems to contain

[1] In eastern Tibet rupees are called either by their Chinese name, *yang-ch'ien*, *i. e.*, "foreign coin," or *p'iling gomo* with exactly the same meaning, go-mo (*sgor-mo*) signifying "a flat disk"— not "woman's face," as E. C. Baber was told (see "Travels and Researches in West China," p. 198). A rupee is valued by the Chinese at Tl. 0.3.2 or 0.3.1. The *tranka* of Lh'asa, worth Tl. 0.1.5, known as *gadän tranka* from the name of the mint at Gadän gomba, is not current in eastern Tibet except at a heavy discount. When counting money, Tibetans dispose it in piles of five coins each, but I could not learn what unit five rupees represented.

As to the price of goods in this locality, musk sold for twenty rupees a cod of about an ounce weight, tea (*shing-ja*, *i. e.*, wood tea — more wood than tea) one rupee a brick of about five pounds, wheat flour twenty-seven rupees a Chinese bushel (*t'ou*), tsamba or barley three quarts (a *sheng*) for a rupee, gold dust forty to forty-five rupees an ounce, sheep three to four rupees a

in its sands particles of the precious metal; and, though the quantity collected by any individual washer is undoubtedly small, the total amount procured annually cannot fail to be of great value. When passing at Zonyik ch'ürten, on the Dré ch'u, I saw a man trudging along with a gold-washer's cradle on his back, and, entering into conversation with him, learnt that he was going home after four days' work on the bank of the river. He told me that he had been fairly successful, so I asked him to show me his gold. He opened the needle-case hanging by his side, and, taking out a little cotton rag, exhibited about ten cents' worth of gold dust mixed with a considerable quantity of hornblende.

Mining is not allowed in Tibet, as there exists a deep-rooted superstition, carefully fostered by the lamas, that if nuggets of gold are removed from the earth no more gold will be found in the river gravels, the nuggets being the roots or plants whereof the gold dust is the grains or flowers.[1]

head, horses seventy-five to a hundred rupees, Chinese blue or white cotton a fathom for one rupee. The only foreign goods for sale were shirtings and lastings (the latter known to the Tibetans as *yü-ling*, their Chinese name). Tibetans measure by *t'o*, or span; *tru*, or cubit (from the elbow to the end of the middle finger), and *domba*, a fathom (both arms stretched to full length). A piece of native cloth has usually nine *domba* in it. Their scales are the ordinary Chinese steelyard, for which they use the Chinese name *cha-tzŭ*. For dry measures they have one corresponding approximately to the Chinese *sheng* and called *bo*; a *bo* full of anything is, however, called *k'ä* (*k'al*).

1 A Chinese description of Lit'ang, "Li-t'ang chih lüeh," p. 18, says: "All the streams and hills in the Li-t'ang district contain gold dust [literally, bran gold and sand gold], but the lamas will not allow the people to collect it, fearing lest the vitalizing fluids of the earth (*t'i-ch'i*) be perniciously affected thereby." William de Rubruk, *op. cit.*, p. 289, evidently refers to this superstition when he says: "Isti (Tebet) [*sic*] habent multum de auro in terra sua, unde qui indiget auro fodit donec reperiat, et accipit quando indiget, residuum recondens in terra. Quia si reponeret in thesauro vel in area, credit quod Deus auferret ei aliud quod est in terra." See also Appendix, on the origin of precious metals in Tibet, as described in native works. The Chinese have very similar ideas about mining or digging in the earth.

14

The occupations of the people of Jyékundo, and of all the other towns and villages I visited in this country, are few, simple, and as a general rule not very irksome. The

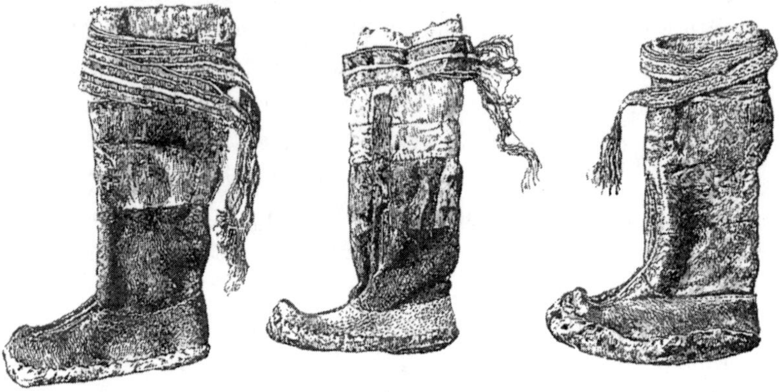

TIBETAN BOOTS AND GARTERS.

women weave a narrow woolen stuff called *la-wa*, the finer qualities being used undyed to make summer gowns, and the coarser to make bags; they also manufacture boots, the soles of raw hide, the vamps of leather or coarse cotton, the tops of colored pulo, usually red and green for women, and red or variegated for men. But "packing" water up from the river, spreading out and drying yak dung for fuel, parching and grinding tsamba, and sewing clothes, are their every-day occupations. The pursuits of the men are confined to distant journeys on their own accounts or simply as yak-drivers, to hunting musk-deer, and washing gold — in which latter the women participate. A very few men are smiths, making silver or gold ornaments,[1] repairing guns, kettles, saddles, etc.; but the best silversmiths are found in the lamaseries, where they make vessels for

[1] The chatelaine in the cut on p. 166 was made at this place. The iron seal in the same cut is a very fine piece of Dérgé workmanship.

church service, images of gods, etc. There, also, may be found wonderful illuminators and copyists, and men able to do any kind of work, tailoring, printing, sculpturing, and doctoring.

It is not too much to say that more than half of the time of nearly every man in the country is spent away from his home, and this renders the custom of one woman marrying several brothers less objectionable than it would be in a richer country where the conditions of life are different. Polyandry is perhaps the most striking antithesis between the pastoral and the agricultural Tibetans. Chinese authors have ascribed its origin to the superior physical and mental faculties of the women, an explanation which would hardly meet with the approval of anthropologists, however correct may be the premises from which they start.

From what natives have told me and from my personal observations, which show that polyandry exists only in agricultural districts, I am able to offer a plausible and probably accurate explanation of the prevalence of this curious custom. The tillable lands are of small extent and are all under cultivation, so it is extremely difficult for any one to add to his fields, which as a general rule produce only enough to support one small family. If at the death of the head of the family the property was divided among the sons, there would not be enough to supply the wants of all of them if each had a wife and family. Moreover, the paternal abode would not accommodate them. The secular experience of the whole human race showing that several families cannot live in peace and concord under the same roof, the only solution of the problem in this case was for the sons of a family to take one wife among them, by which means their ancestral estate remained undivided, and they also saved considerable money.[1]

Among the nomads, where existence is not dependent on the produce of the soil, where herds of yak and flocks of sheep and goats are ever increasing and supply all their owner's wants, this necessity of preserving the family property undivided can never have existed. Hence we find polyandry unknown among them; monogamy, and perhaps a very few cases of polygamy, is the rule where they are found.

Families are generally small in Tibet, three or four children, but more generally two. One or more children in every family enter the church, and as there are very few nuns (at least in eastern Tibet), the numbers of women and men are probably about equal. So while polyandrous marriages are frequently met with, they are not, I believe, by any means as numerous as we have been led to suppose. In Dérgé, the most thoroughly agricultural region in K'amdo, polyandry is the most prevalent, but there, as in other regions, polygamy is also met with among the richer classes. If it be furthermore remembered that temporary marriages are recognized throughout Tibet, whether contracted for six months, a month, or perhaps a week, and that these unions are not held immoral, we may safely assert that, as regards their marriage relations, this people are little removed from promiscuity, which is but "indefinite polyandry joined with indefinite polygamy."[2]

The offspring from these polyandrous marriages treat

[1] This explanation of polyandry is not offered as elucidating its origin, but rather its continuance in the country. Its remote origin is, I believe, rightly ascribed as an advance on the primitive unregulated state of savage tribes. See Herbert Spencer, "Principles of Sociology," II, 645.

[2] Herbert Spencer, *op. cit.*, II, 642.

as father whomever their mother teaches them to recognize by that name; the other husbands are the children's "uncles."[1] Family names are unknown in Tibet, and children are spoken of as of such and such a woman; hardly ever is the father's name mentioned.

Whatever be the marriage customs prevailing in a locality the wife is procured by purchase, as among the tribes of the Koko-nor, and as soon as the woman has entered the home of her husband she assumes control of nearly all his affairs; no buying or selling is done except by her or with her consent and approval. She is the recognized head of the house. This preëminent position of women in Tibetan society has been from of old one of the peculiarities of this race, of which parts have frequently been governed by women, as evidenced by the history of the state of eastern Tibet, called *Nü Kuo* by Chinese historians, where a queen always ruled, the male population being only warriors and tillers of the soil.[2] At the present day the large principality of Po-mo, near Sung-p'an t'ing, is governed by a queen.[3] Tibetan polyg-

1 It is interesting to note that while the Tibetan language is comparatively rich in words expressing father, mother, brothers, in relation to age or to sisters, uncles, and aunts, it has only one for "nephew or niece" — and this is also used for grandson and granddaughter — and none to express "cousin." The word *pön* (*spun*), "brothers, or brothers and sisters," is sometimes used to express this relationship.

2 See Appendix, *infrà*.

3 Many learned and worthy lamas whom I have questioned on the subject of polyandry have assured me that it is a sinful practice, solely attributable to the very lax morality of the people, and by no means a recognized institution. This opinion was also that of the early Christian missionaries in the country. Thus Georgi, "Alphabetum Tibetanum," p. 458 (quoting probably Father Andrada), says of it: "Ab hoc turpitudinis genere alieni sunt viri nobiles, et cives honesti." Orazio della Penna, "Breve Notizia del Regno del Tibet," p. 71, speaks as follows: "E circa li maritaggi tra le persone non molto comode vi è un pessimo abuso, non però ordinato della legge, ma introdotto dall' abuso, che quanti fratelli sono in una casa pigliano una sol moglie per tutti, attribuendosi la prole aquello, di cui la donna asserisce di aver conceputo, ma questo ordinariamente non succede tra persone nobili e comode, quali prendano una moglie sola, e talun grande più d'una, ma di raro." Female

amy is, as previously remarked, confined to the wealthier class and principally the chiefs, and has been introduced by intercourse with China and India.[1]

Before dropping the question of Tibetan women, I must note one of their most peculiar and objectionable habits, that of smearing their faces with a thick black paste, composed of grease and cutch, called *teu-ja*.[2] They say they use it as salve to protect their skins from the dry wind which would chap them and make them rough. The lamas tell another story: they say that Démo Rinpoch'é, who lived in the latter part of the eighteenth century, and who is one of the greatest of their latter-day saints, ordered all the women of Lh'asa to disfigure themselves thus whenever they showed themselves in public.

infanticide is not practised in Tibet except among the women married to Chinese. Marriage being by purchase, parents are interested in bringing up all their girls; probably many die in infancy, on account of the severity of the climate, want of care in bodily cleanliness, and lack of medical attention. I saw hardly any girls aged eighteen who were not married. E. C. Baber, "Travels and Researches in Western China," 97, speaks as follows on Tibetan polyandry: "Polygamy obtains in valleys, while polyandry prevails in the uplands. In the valley-farms, I am told, the work is light and suitable for women, but the rough life and hard fare of a shepherd on pastures 13,000 feet or more above sea level is too severe for the sex. This explanation has been given me by a European of great experience and long residence in these countries, whose personal conviction, though adverse to marriage in his own case, is strictly monogamous; nevertheless, he feels compelled to admit that the two systems, working side by side, mutually compensate the evils of each, and that both are reasonable under the circumstances, and probably requisite. The subject raises many curious and by no means frivolous questions, but I cannot help thinking it singular that the conduct of courtship and matrimony should be regulated by the barometrical pressure." Andrew Wilson, "Abode of Snow," p. 193, says that a Moravian missionary settled on the borders of Tibet defended the system, not as a good thing in the abstract, or one to be tolerated among Christians, but as good for the heathen in so sterile a country, where an increasing population would provoke eternal warfare or eternal want. Samuel Turner, "Embassy to the Court of the Teshoo Lama," p. 349, gives some curious reasons for polyandry in Tibet, which custom he thinks has not been unfavorable on the manners of the people.

1 King Srong-tsan gambo, who reigned in the seventh century A. D. at Lh'asa, married two wives, a Chinese and a Nepalese, and it is a matter of history that his household was not a peaceful one.

2 A Tibetan pronunciation of the Chinese *erh-ch'a*, "cutch."

This drastic measure was necessitated by the daily increasing disorders among the monks, whose composure was being continually upset by the sight of the pretty faces of the women, and who forgot the rule of their order which prescribed that when walking abroad they must keep their eyes fixed on the ground and look neither to the right nor the left, and had not eyes enough to look at the rosy-cheeked, bright-eyed maidens they met. The women obeyed the order, and soon the paste became as much the fashion as is the veil in other countries.[1]

Chinese writers of authority have stated that for every family in Tibet there were three lamas,[2] and I do not believe that this is an exaggerated estimate. From Jyé-kundo to Ta-chien-lu, a distance of about 600 miles, I passed forty lamaseries, in the smallest of which there were 100 monks, and in five of them from 2000 to 4000. Although the greater part of K'amdo is not under their direct rule, they are everywhere the *de facto* masters of the country.[3] In their hands is nearly all the wealth of the land, acquired by trading, donations, money-lending, and bequests. Their landed property is frequently

1 See Huc, *op. cit.*, II, 258. Klaproth, in his "Déscription du Thibet," p. 84, mistranslated *erh-ch'a*, and made the women cover their faces with a horrible mixture of "brown sugar and boiled tea leaves"! Herodotus, IV, S. 75, speaking of the Scythians, says, "Their women make a mixture of cypress, cedar, and frankincense wood, which they pound into a paste upon a rough piece of stone, adding a little water to it. With this substance, which is of a thick consistency, they plaster their faces all over, and indeed their whole bodies. A sweet odor is thereby imparted to them, and when they take off the plaster on the day following, their skin is clean and glossy." H. W. Bellew, "Kashmir and Kashghar," p. 130, says that "the women of one part of Ladakh smear their cheeks and forehead with the juice and seeds of the ripe berry of the belladonna plant." See also Hooker, "Himalayan Journals," II, 175. Mongol women daub their faces with an unguent, and this is an ancient custom, as evidenced by Rubruk, *op. cit.*, p. 233.

2 See "Hsi-chao t'u lüeh," by Sung Yun, a former Chinese Amban at Lh'asa.

3 I must except, however, the principality of Chala (Ta-chien-lu), whose sovereign claims and exercises rule over the lamaseries in his state.

enormous, their serfs (*mi-ser*) and bondsmen (*ts'é-yo*) swarm.

To add to the embarrassment of the lay rulers of the country, the abbots of the fourteen large lamaseries in eastern Tibet are appointed by the Lh'asa authorities, and exercise a prescriptive right of high and low justice over not only their monks but their serfs and tenants. As, for the last century, the government of Lh'asa has been endeavoring by every means in its power to annex eastern Tibet, notwithstanding the violent opposition of the people of that region, we may readily conceive how disturbing to the general peace must be the presence of these independent and powerful communities, whose members are solely devoted to the advancement of the interest of mother church.[1] Nor do the lamas confine themselves to the use of peaceful means in furtherance of their policy; there is as much of the soldier about them as there was in the Templars, with whom they offer many points of resemblance. The larger lamaseries are rather fortified camps than the abodes of peace-loving Buddhist monks; every lama is well-armed, well-mounted, and always ready for the fray, whether it be to resist the local chiefs or the Chinese, or to attack a rival lamasery. Their declaration of war is unique of its kind. In times of peace lamas wear no trousers, only a long kilt called *shamta*, so when about to start on a military expedition, when they will be for days in the saddle, a nether garment becomes indispensable, and the order goes forth to

[1] No lama in eastern Tibet can have any standing among the people or in his convent unless he has been to Lh'asa and can produce the certificate delivered to all pilgrims in that city. If he has been ordained *gelong* (*i. e.*, entered the higher order of priesthood) by the Pan-ch'en Rinpoch'é of Trashil'unpo, he is sure of rapid advancement and of great popularity, but without the first-named certificate he will never be asked to read prayers or take part in any ceremony outside of his convent.

convert their shawls (*zän*) into breeches. I was assured that frequently when the weaker party learns that its enemy has thus made clear a determination to fight, it sues for peace without waiting for the attack.

There are four lamaist sects, called by the Chinese yellow, red, black, and white lamas.[1] The two first are the most numerous and influential; the red, or red-capped lamas (*Dja-mar*), are especially numerous in Dérgé, the yellow throughout the rest of the country. These sects differ on points of little importance as far as dogma or ceremonial is concerned, but the gods each sect worships are not the same. The laity do not enter into these minutiæ, but avail themselves of the services of lamas of any or all of these four sects to "beat the drum" in their houses.

There exists, moreover, in eastern Tibet a creed known as *Bön*, which represents the pre-Buddhist shamanism of the country. The *Bönbo* are usually identified by the Chinese with the Taoists, but for convenience of comparison only, because their present teachings, dress, lamaseries, etc., resemble closely those of the lamas, by whom, however, they are treated with great scorn, which does not at all prevent the common people from availing themselves of their exceptionally low charges for "beating the drum" by inviting them to their houses for religious services. These Bönbo are especially numerous in southeastern Tibet, in the Tsarong, where the French missionaries have found them much less bigoted than the Buddhist lamas.[2]

1 The Tibetan names of these sects are, respectively, Gélupa, Nyimapa, Sachyapa, and Karmapa.

2 The ordinary Tibetan will assure you that the only difference between a Bönbo and a lama is that, in walking around a sacred building or monument, the former keeps it on his left while the latter keeps it on his right. The Bönbo sacrifice living animals, especially fowls, to their gods, and this is an abomination in the eyes of lamas. The only one of the Bönbo sacred books I have read is entitled "Lu-bum karpo," and, curiously enough, the copy I bought was procured in the printing-office of a lamasery of the Gélupa sect, where

Eastern Tibet, exclusive of the nomadic tribes on its northern frontier, is divided into eighteen states, the most important of which are Dérgé, the Horba states (also called Nya rong), Lit'ang, Ba, Chala, and the lower Nya ch'u valley or Män Nya, the last being until within a few months a dependency of Lh'asa.[1] These states are ruled by hereditary chiefs whose title is either *Jyabo*, "King," or *Déba*, "Prefect or Baron." Some of them, as the Dérgé Jyabo, are independent of both China and Lh'asa; others sub-

the lama in charge told me that it was read alike by lamas of all sects as well as by Bönbo. With the exception of the substitution of terms and names peculiar to themselves, for those used by Buddhists, this work does not contain any theories or ideas antagonistic to the ordinary teachings of Buddhists; its cosmogony is purely Buddhist; the same may be said of its ethics and metaphysics. *Shen-rab* takes the place of Buddha, *Chang-ch'ub* (*Bodhi*) is *Yung-drung*, *Chang-ch'ub-sémba* (*Bodhisattwa*) becomes *Yung-drung-sémba*, *Ch'ü* (*Dharma*) is *Bön*, etc., etc. The Bön religion has been identified with Taoism, and Shen-rab with Lao-tzŭ, but without sufficient reason. Buddhism has exercised an overwhelming influence on Taoism and so has lamaism on the Bön religion, but there, I believe, the resemblance stops, for Taoism and Bön-ism undoubtedly contain non-Buddhist theories and antedate that faith in China and Tibet. Colonel Yule ("Book of Ser Marco Polo," I, 315 *et sq.*) gives about all the information accessible concerning the Bönbo, and discusses at length their identity with the Tao-shih. General Alexander Cunningham, he says (p. 318), "fully accepts this identity," but as his belief is founded on a mistranslation of Abel Rémusat in the "Fo kuo chi" (*Tao-shih* being there translated Taoist, whereas in that case it means "masters of the Truth or Dharma," *i. e.*, Buddhist priests) it cannot be accepted. As far as my observations go the rites usually performed by these Bönbo resemble those of the Lolo, Lissu, and Moso sorcerers, and it is very likely that originally this religion was the same as that of those tribes at the present day. The Bönbo are noted for their great proficiency in juggling and magic. See, also, Brian H. Hodgson, "On the Tribes of Northern Tibet," p. 80, note.

[1] For a complete list of these states, see the Appendix, *infrà*. The Chinese divide the country into thirty-three districts and seventy-nine clans (*tsu*), and speak of them as "the Hsi-fan tribes of the Yü-t'ung." The name Dérgé (in Chinese, "Tê-erh-ko-tê") is written *Sder-gi*. The Horba states are called in Tibetan *Horsé k'a nga*, "the five Horba tribes," or simply *Hor-chyok*, "Horba region." The name *Nya rong*, or "Valley of the Nya ch'u," is given it on account of the principal river of that region. Ba is the Chinese Bat'ang. The name is properly written *Hbah*. The word Bat'ang was coined by the Chinese, and is unknown to Tibetans. Chala (*Lchags-la*) is the state of which Ta-chien-lu is the capital. Män Nya (*Sman Nya*) is the Chinese Chan-tui. Its people are called *Män-nya-k'a*, Hodgson's and Baber's Maniak and Menia. Yalung, a name given the Nya ch'u by the Chinese, is only *Nya lung*, "the valley of the Nya."

mit to the supremacy of China, and receive patents of investiture from the Emperor; others, again, nominally recognize China as their suzerain so as to enjoy the valuable privilege of sending tribute to Ch'eng-tu and Peking, which secures to them the right to trade under extraordinarily favorable circumstances.[1]

Succession to the chieftainship is usually assured to the eldest son not a lama, and, in case of there being no children, it may be given to an adopted child or to the nearest relative, brother or nephew. In the principality of Po-mo (or So-mo), in the northeastern section of the country and conterminous with Sung-p'an, the government is in the hands of a woman, whether accidentally or permanently I could not learn.

Each chief appoints a certain number of civil and military officers to assist him in the government of the country, and a large proportion of them are taken from among his *Ku-ts'a*, or "body-guard," whose charges are hereditary. The highest civil officers are the *Shelngo*, or "district magistrates," each of whom administers from ten to fifteen villages, and whose term of office is three years.[2] Under each Shelngo is a military officer called *Ma-pön*. Every village is administered by a *Bésé*, whose office is hereditary in countries not ruled by Lh'asa. The Bésé are specially charged with levying taxes, arranging the ula under orders from their immediate superiors the Shelngo. They, themselves, are exempt from taxation, but receive no salaries. They are responsible for the full amount of taxes, and are held to make good any deficit, but all the real estate of persons who leave

[1] See, p. 19, what is said of the Gorkha mission to Peking.

[2] In the kingdom of Chala there are no Shelngo, but 48 *Pei-fu* (heads of hundreds) take their place. Their office is hereditary, and under them are mayors, or *Bésé*.

the country to escape paying imposts escheats to them.

Each Jyabo or Déba has a body-guard, varying in different localities from fifty-eight to twenty men, and whose members have the title of *Ku-ts'a.*[1] This office is hereditary. These officers receive no pay, but each has a grant of land in perpetuity, and they have frequently the exclusive privilege of lodging high officials and caravans passing through their towns, a source of considerable profit. From out their ranks are chosen a number of officers: (1) the *Ding-pön*, who carry the chief's orders to the Shelngo. (2) The *T'o-pön*, who watch over the chief's granaries and crops. When the granaries the chief has in each locality have been filled, the T'o-pön oblige the well-to-do inhabitants to purchase seed-grain of them. The buyers have to pay fifty per cent. interest, and moreover give the T'o-pön a present in recognition of his kindness in selling them the grain. (3) The *Ta-pön*, who look after the chief's cattle and horses. They fix the date of the harvest in their districts, after which they turn the chief's stock on the fields whether the crop is garnered or not. (4) The *Gar-pön*, or excise-men, who levy duties on all merchandise passing through their districts. Most of these offices are held for three years.[2]

There exists no written law for the administration of justice; tradition is the only code followed. Confiscation and fines are the penalties imposed for most crimes and

[1] These Ku-ts'a seem to be officers similar to the *Zeenkaubs* of the Deb Rajah of Sikkim, mentioned by Captain Samuel Turner, "Embassy to the Court of Teshoo lama," p. 8. It is written *sku-ts'ab*, literally "lieutenant, representative."

[2] In Chala, the Ku-ts'a are known as *Agia*. The Chinese call them *Ku-chung*. The Chala Jyabo has fifty-eight; the Ba Déba, fifty. Alex. Hosie, "Three Years in Western China," p. 130, says that northwest of Li-chiang Fu is a Tibetan tribe called Ku-tsung, "but the term Ku-tsung is also applied by the people of Ta-li to Tibetans generally." Probably a Chinese generalization of the term Ku-ts'a.

offenses, murder not excepted. These fines comprise, (1) a sum of money, or number of bricks of tea, determined according to the social standing of the victim in case of murder, which fine goes to the state and is called *tong-jyal* (*stong-rgyal*); (2) a fixed sum called *gé-tong* (*dgé-stong*) for the family of the victim, nominally to pay for the performance of religious ceremonies for the deceased.

Among the Horba the murderer of a man of the upper class is fined 120 bricks of tea (equivalent to Rs. 120); for the murder of a middle-class man he is fined 80 bricks, for killing a woman 40 bricks, and so on down through the social scale, the murder of a beggar, or a wandering foreigner, as my informant laughingly added, being fined only a nominal amount, 3 or 4 bricks. In case the victim is a lama, the murderer has often to pay a much larger amount, possibly 200 or 300 bricks.

The position of the Chinese government in eastern Tibet next calls for attention. North of the Dré ch'u the country is under the supervision of the Amban at Hsi-ning; south of that river, or rather south of the parallel of Jyékundo, it is under that of the governor-general of Ssŭ-ch'nan. There are no permanent military posts north of Jyékundo, but south of that point there are six: three on the highroad between Ta-chien-lu and Lh'asa, at Nya ch'u-k'a, Lit'ang, and Ba; three on the road to Jyékundo, at Tai-ling (Kata), Dawo, and Kanzé. A colonel stationed at Ta-chien-lu is the immediate superior of the officers commanding these posts, who have under them small detachments of infantry.[1] These officers have absolutely no authority over the native chiefs, their duties being

[1] None of the soldiers of any of the detachments I saw were armed. They told me that they went every year to Ta-chien-lu for bow and arrow drill, and that arms were then lent them. Most of them had some weapon of their own, usually a sword.

confined to protecting and administering the Chinese trade, reporting to Ta-chien-lu on the condition of the country, forwarding government couriers, officials, troops, funds, etc. Occasionally they are appealed to by native chiefs to arbitrate questions, but their decisions are not binding. The three stations on the Jyékundo road have been established only within the last few years, and the position of the Chinese throughout this part of the country is still extremely precarious, especially in Dérgé. T'ung-shih from Hsi-ning and Ch'eng-tu visit this region yearly to collect the "horse tax" of eight tael cents (about ten cents of our money) for each family, the only one payable by this people to the Chinese government.[1] Once in five years the chiefs under the governor-general of Ssŭ-ch'uan send a "little tribute" mission to Ch'eng-tu, and every ten years a "great tribute" mission to Peking. Unlike the Mongol chieftains, who are obliged to go in person when paying tribute, those of eastern Tibet hardly ever visit the capital, sending their stewards or some small officer in their stead.

After this long but necessary digression, we will return to Jyékundo. Ever since entering Tibet I had been in hopes of being able to reach Ch'amdo, the capital of a large independent state between K'amdo and the kingdom of Lh'asa. In 1886 I had met and become very intimate with a high Tibetan official from this state, then at Peking on business, and having spoken to him of my desire to visit Tibet he had made me promise to come to Ch'amdo, where he proffered me a hearty welcome and his assistance to continue my journey in whichever direction I chose.

Ch'amdo is only ten days distant from Jyékundo, the intervening country is inhabited by nomads, and the road

[1] See p. 191.

through it tolerably good, the only danger to be apprehended being brigands (*Chakba*), of whom there are said to be not a few. The measures taken against me by the chief of Jyékundo, forcing me to precipitate my movements, completely upset my plans. After much talk with my Chinese friends it was decided that I must leave the town at once, before the chief could return from Tendo, and push on to Kanzé as rapidly as my horses could carry me. They believed this was my only chance of seeing the country, for if I waited the Déba's return he would to a certainty compel me to return to the Ts'aidam, even if he did nothing worse. Their advice seemed sound, but how to carry it out? None of my horses were fit to undertake a fortnight's hard ride, and I was without a guide, for Dowé was to leave me here and return home. To take two of my men and the three best ponies I owned, leaving the other two men behind (to follow later if possible, or return to China by another route if prevented from taking the road after me), was the unanimous recommendation of the Chinese, and I decided to adopt it if they could secure me a guide. After a great deal of trouble, they persuaded a man from Kanzé to take me to that town for sixty rupees. I offered him double the amount if he would go to Ch'amdo, but he and the buxom woman accompanying him, and whom he introduced as his Jyékundo wife, with the apologetic remark in an undertone that his Kanzé *po-niang* was much better looking, refused my golden offer, saying he did not know the road, and that at all events three men could not venture along it. Kando was the name of this queer specimen of the Tibetan race, a wizened, blear-eyed, dirty old fellow, drunk more than half the time, but with all the cunning of the savage and a great fund of humor. His grizzly locks fell over his face and shoulders, and a big Chinese queue of silk threads, on which was strung a Chinese thumb-ring of agate, added to the beauty of his coiffure. He had been outlawed some years before in his own country, but still ventured back there now and then, for a few days at a time, to dispose of musk or gold dust. All his pride was in his horse and his gun, on both of which he bestowed endless care—when not too intoxicated. As soon as we had struck a bargain, he devoted himself to my interests, and served me faithfully and honestly to the end.

My preparations were soon made; into our saddle-bags we stuffed a few indispensable odds and ends, and on a diminutive mule belonging to old Kando we put a small bag of tsamba, a kettle, a bellows, and a little feed for the ponies. I sent one of my tents to the Hsi-ning T'ung-shih who had been so kind to me, and the other I gave to Dowé as a reward for his faithful service.

On May the 29th I said good-by to my two men and to the kind Chinese, and started on my ride to Kanzé. Our route led us at first in a southeasterly direction up the valley of the Pa-ch'i ch'u, called Momé lung-ba, at least in its upper part. After passing the Changi gomba some eight miles, the valley broadened considerably, and the distant mountains to the south rose before us to great heights. The Dawo-pato peak, which did not appear to be more than four miles from our road, was specially noticeable, deep snow extending far down its sides. We saw no villages in this valley, which is about twenty miles long, but only a few tents and two small lamaseries, the more important of which was called the Pé-ch'en gomba.[1] The face of the country remained as we had seen it north

[1] Or Pan-ch'en gomba. On A—— K——'s map it is called Shenché gomba, and Changi gomba figures as Tang gomba.

THE DREN-KOU VALLEY.

of Jyékundo, bare and bleak; in some rocky nooks a few stunted juniper trees, but no shrub or flower, no singing bird, or anything to relieve the awful stillness and dreariness of the scene.

After a miserable night during which sleet had fallen continually, we were off again by daylight; and entering the Dren-kou valley, which leads down to the Dré ch'u, the scenery changed as if by magic. A brook flowed down the glen, its banks covered with soft green grass powdered over with little white and pink flowers. On the mountain sides grew juniper and pine trees, and by the roadside were wild plum, gooseberry, honeysuckle, and other shrubs, the fragrance of their blossoms filling the air. From cavities in the tufa rock pended creepers and ferns from which the water fell in crystal drops; and we heard the cuckoo's cry echoing across the valley.

We were filled with amazement and delight; even my stolid Chinese showed their admiration for this lovely scenery by suggesting that we stop at once by the little village of Lori, and breakfast, to admire it at our ease, for we would probably soon leave this dreamland behind and reënter the desolate country we had until now been traversing. But their fears proved groundless; about two miles below Lori we came once more on the Dré ch'u, and the scenery grew even finer as we wound along the steep mountain sides some five or six hundred feet above the blue river, which went dashing by in eddying and seething masses in its narrow bed. The mountains rose several thousand feet on either hand, those on the left bank reaching to above the snow line and stretching as far as the eye could reach along the river's sinuous course. Lamaseries and villages, around which were little patches of culture, were numerous on either side of the river; and great droves of yak were grazing around the white tents of parties of tea traders, whose goods were piled up under white cotton awnings to protect them from the frequent showers of rain.

Passing through Min-kou and several other small villages we reached Tongu (altitude, 12,880 feet)[1] towards evening, and put up at an inn where we had a very large, if empty, room. Kando, the old guide, managed after much haggling to buy a very small kid, so we fared sumptuously, but here and in fact all along the road the people were much disinclined to sell us any food, saying that they had barely enough for themselves. So likewise as to horse feed—all we could buy was here and there a little hay, or some peas after entering Dérgé, north of which country this vegetable does not grow.

[1] The village is about four hundred feet above the river-bed.

The following day we reached the ferry across the Dré ch'u,[1] and stopped for the night in the ferryman's house, built in a most picturesque position on a perpendicular bluff of over two hundred feet in height overhanging the Drushi-tsa, which here empties into the Dré ch'u. Huge piles of tea carefully packed in rawhide were waiting on either side of the river for transportation, and droves of yak were continually arriving, carrying more of the same commodity. This locality, called Drenda or Dré ch'u dru-k'a (*i. e.*, "the Dré ch'u ferry"), marks the boundary between Jyékundo and the kingdom of Dérgé.

Dérgé is the richest agricultural and manufacturing district of eastern Tibet, and also the most densely peopled one, its population being estimated at eight thousand families or about thirty-two thousand souls, exclusive of lamas of whom there must be at least ten thousand. Its capital, called Dérgé dron-cher (*Sder-gi grong-k'yer*, *i. e.*, "the city of Dérgé"), is situated on the Dré ch'u some four days' journey below Drenda, from which latter place a bad road leads to it. The Nyimapa or red-capped sect of lamas predominate in this country, their greatest lamaseries being at Dérgé dron-cher and Zoch'en. The king of the country has managed to preserve his independence of China and Lh'asa, notwithstanding that the latter contrived to seize the Män Nya (Chan-tui) states to the southeast of his kingdom,[2] during the famous occupation of Dérgé by the Lh'asa general Pön-ro-pa, which commenced in 1864 and extended to 1877.[3] The present king is a man of about thirty-five, who passes much of his

1 We passed on the way thither the villages of Dondi and Drento, and the lamasery of Ch'üdé, all on the left bank of the river; also a small village on the right bank, whose name I did not learn.

2 Monseigneur Felix Biet, in a letter to me dated Feb. 26, 1890, writes that the Chan-tui has revolted against Lh'asa and killed or driven out all officials sent there from that place.

3 See E. C. Baber, *op. cit.*, 98 *et seq.*

time making retreats in lamaseries either at Lh'asa or in his own kingdom. His dislike of Chinese is very strong, and none can remain for any length of time in his capital, extraordinary taxes and imposts of every description forcing them to leave the place; hence most of the Chinese trading with this kingdom is done at Kanzé.

Dérgé is especially famous throughout Tibet for the excellence of its metal-work. The swords, guns, tea-pots, tinder-boxes, seals, bells, etc., made there command high prices wherever they are offered for sale; its saddles are also the best in eastern Tibet, where those from Lit'ang hold the second place in popular favor. I have a number of specimens of Dérgé metal-work which would be creditable to any workman, and have seen others extremely artistic in design and perfect in finish.

BRONZE CHURCH-BELL. (CAST IN DRÉGÉ DRON-CHER.)

The kingdom of Dérgé stretches north of the Dré ch'u as far as the country occupied by the Golok, and on the east it touches the Horba states;[1] to the south it is conterminous with Ba, and on the west it confines on Draya and Ch'amdo.

We recrossed the Dré ch'u in skin boats similar to that we had used on our crossing at Dré-kou; only that here two coracles were lashed together, and in one trip we and our belongings were carried over. For the next fifteen miles the valley broadened a little; villages became more numerous than before, and cultivation more extensive. Passing

1 The boundary lines of eastern Tibetan states are most difficult to define. In this special case I am not quite sure whether the districts of Zoch'en and the Yi-lung should be put down as belonging to Dérgé or not, but they certainly do *de facto*. On its eastern side Dérgé touches the Horba country, in the Rungbatsa district, the western half of which belongs to Dérgé, the eastern to Chuwo, a Horba state.

through Seupa, Ch'üdé, Drimalahuo, and a number of other villages,[1] whose names I did not learn, we came to Kawalendo, and stopped in a house on the outskirts, belonging to a miller. A brook flowed in front of his door, and wide-spreading elm-trees stretched their branches over the roof. As to his mill it was somewhat similar to those I had previously seen in use in Shan-hsi, the nether stone being put in motion by a small water-wheel directly underneath it. We could see on the other side of the river the Ch'üdé gomba. Behind it rose precipitously the tree-clad mountains, their summits lost in eternal snows. The miller, his wife, sister-in-law, and a brother — a lama at home on a visit—treated us so kindly and did so much to entertain us that I will long remember the night I passed in their house. In fact, wherever I was thrown in contact with the people I met with extraordinary kindness, and it was only when there were large numbers of lamas among them that I experienced any trouble, and even then the "black people," as the laity are called, took but little share in the disturbance.

At Kawalendo the Dré ch'u commences its great southerly bend which ends only in southeastern Tibet, and our route left the river-bank and led across the foot-hills, where the small, sharp stones covering the ground soon made several of our horses so footsore that we had to put up at a little village called Rarta, only nine miles from our starting point.[2]

While stopping near Bora to make our tea, we saw a man herding some horses, and, calling to him, asked if he would

[1] On A—— K——'s map (in Petermann's "Geographische Mittheilungen," 1885), Seupa is called Sila, Ch'üdé gomba is Dhingo gomba, and Kawalendo is Kavang. This Ch'üdé gomba is not that mentioned on p. 227, note 1.

[2] Four miles east of Kawalendo we passed the Karpo gomba, and three miles farther on the village of Bora. On A—— K——'s map the first place figures as Kaphu gomba, the second as Baga. Rarta, he calls Rara.

not sell us one. He replied that as far as he was concerned he was willing, but as his wife was not at home he could not possibly entertain any offer, however advantageous it might be. Such experiences befell us frequently, and never failed to excite the surprise of my Chinese and myself. By what means have these women gained such a complete ascendency over the men, how have they made their mastery so complete and so acceptable to a race of lawless barbarians who but unwillingly submit even to the authority of their chiefs, is a problem well worth consideration.[1] Would that Madame Blavatsky, who has conferred on us so many esoteric blessings derived from Tibet, might disclose to us this mystery! She, or one of the mahatmas, her coadjutors in the noble work of enlightening the world, who are in constant relations with Tibet, probably could easily solve this riddle, and unborn generations of oppressed womankind would bless their names.

The next day we entered the basin of a little affluent of the Dré ch'u, passing on the way six large lamaseries,[2] one of them most picturesquely situated on the summit of a precipitous hill in the center of the valley, the little river sweeping around its base. The country was well cultivated and the people busy plowing and weeding their fields, men and women working together. Their plows and hoes were of the most primitive description, the blades of the latter implements being of wood. The plows are made at or near Kanzé, and the iron plowshares are imported from Ta-chien-lu.

[1] I find in Dr. Wm. Junker's recently published "Travels in Africa," p. 132, that among certain Bega (Bedouin) tribes the wife "rules the roost, in a way which it seems difficult to reconcile with the defiant and haughty nature of those untamed nomads."

[2] One near Rarta, at the village of Nojylé (A—— K——'s Nagli), was abandoned.

We camped not far from a little village called Rigé, about half-way up the valley. The lower part of this valley is inhabited by husbandmen, and the upper part, through which we went the following day, by Drupa, or nomads. The head of it was very thinly timbered, and in the lower portion there was not a tree to be seen. The timber all through eastern Tibet is most unevenly divided and seems to be dying out in many places; the people use but little on account of the trouble of felling it, and prefer dried dung for fuel, probably because it does not require chopping, so the disappearance of the wood cannot be charged to them. Forest fires are, I was told, of but rare occurrence; I saw traces of only one in the Yi-ch'u valley, and that of no great extent.

Ascending the valley to its head by an extremely easy gradient, we crossed a low pass called Latsé kadri (altitude, 14,590 feet) and entered the valley of Shéma or Shéma t'ang, and the district of Zoch'en. Two or three little streams meet on its northeast side and, flowing through a narrow gorge, empty into the Za ch'u. Along its southwest side rises a range of high mountains of granitic formation, most of its peaks covered with perpetual snow; among them the huge white mass of the Poyushiaté ri, behind Zoch'en gomba, is by far the most imposing. This chain forms the water-shed between the Dré ch'u and the Za ch'u, and we had it in view nearly all the way to Kanzé. Shéma t'ang is inhabited only by Drupa, as is the valley of the Muri ch'u, another affluent of the Za ch'u, whose basin we entered the next day. Here stands the great Zoch'en lamasery, on the steep flank of a hill in a little "park"

STEEL AND TINDER CASE. MOUNTINGS, SILVER AND CORAL. (MADE AT DÉRGÉ DRON-CHER.)

at the foot of the great Poyushiaté ri, down whose precipitous sides tumble endless snow streams, meeting near the convent. On the edge of the little brook thus formed stand a few houses, partly of logs, partly of stone, where live some Chinese traders and a few families of natives. Over the stream are a number of little log-huts not more than ten feet square; under each of them is a horizontal water-wheel. These mills grind out only prayers, for in them are but barrels covered with rawhide, and filled with printed sheets on which are repeated myriads of times the favorite six-syllable formula, *om mani padmé hum.*

Zoch'en gomba is one of the chief lamaseries of the Nyimapa, the "red-capped" lamas of the Chinese, of whom over two thousand live here. In no other part of eastern Tibet are they so numerous as in Dérgé, their other strongholds being Sikkim, Bhutan, and Ladak.[1]

The Drupa near the convent were very numerous. I counted no less than fifty tents in two camps only a few miles apart. Taking into consideration the vast droves of yak continually passing along this road and the immense quantities of grass they devour, it is surprising that so many nomads live in proximity to it. From what I could learn, the country along the Za ch'u, to the east of my route, is thickly peopled with Drupa, but they are so exposed to forays of the Golok, who are distant only two days' ride (or about sixty miles) to the east, that many prefer to live near villages or large lamaseries,

[1] The chief lamasery of this sect is at Sakya, 100 miles northwest of Shigatsé, in Ulterior Tibet. There lives the incarnation of Ujyen Pamé (Padma sambhava), the reputed founder of the sect. Although they visit sanctuaries of the Gélnpa sect and worship the Talé lama,—an incarnation of Shenrézig,—the most saintly personage in Tibet is, according to them, the one at the Sakya gomba. The Dharma rajah of Ladak is another of their saints, and others live in Sikkim and Bhutan.

where they can find refuge in case of need, even if the grazing is not so good.

Here I was fortunate enough to exchange two of my horses for fresh ones; and the rest of the journey to Kanzé was made without changing them again. The horses in this part of the country are larger and heavier than the Mongol or Koko-nor ponies; those from Lit'ang are especially prized, good ones fetching a hundred rupees and more. The natives take great pride in them; nearly all the travelers we passed on the road were well mounted; the big red saddle-blanket, the green cloth covered saddle with red leather trimmings, the crupper frequently covered with leopard skin, and other bright bits about the harness, showed off the horses to great advantage.

Our road on leaving the Zoch'en gomba led up the course of the Muri ch'u through a narrow valley covered with brushwood and timber, to the foot of a steep but short incline to the summit of the Muri la (altitude, 15,880 feet), the only important pass between Jyékundo and Kanzé. The descent was very precipitous and stony, and showed unmistakable signs of the former presence of a glacier extending down to the little lake, Muri ts'o, some six miles beyond.[1] On the eastern side of the pass is the source of the Yi ch'u or Yi lung ch'u, a short but important tributary of the Za ch'u.

We had hardly camped on a grassy bottom near the western extremity of the little lake, when we saw riding down the valley towards us a large party of lamas driving in front of them a drove of heavily laden yak. They were returning home from a fruitful begging expedition, and the yak were loaded with flour and pottery, hides, cloth, and any and every thing they could get hold of. A

[1] This little valley in which is the lake is called Tamundo.

storm was gathering on the mountains near by, and they were hurrying to make camp, and much to our consternation they came and pitched their tents not twenty yards from us. Even old Kando showed signs of uneasiness at such close proximity to my enemies, and not unreasonably, for if they noticed anything peculiar about me or my party, they would not fail to spread it abroad wherever they went, and thus get us in trouble. Fortunately the rain began falling and I could use my felt cloak to cover my head and body without exciting suspicion. I was always less apprehensive of discovery than were my men for me: my color, a dark reddish brown by seven months of exposure without washing; with neither beard nor hair to betray me, and my eyes, my ever obnoxious blue eyes, hid behind horsehair blinkers that I never removed except at night, I believe that even my friends would have had some difficulty in recognizing me. Once only on the road I heard a man say as he rode by, "Why, there goes a *p'iling* (a foreigner)!" "No," replied his comrade; "can't you recognize eastern Mongols (*Mar sok*) when you see them?"

But it was a miserable night we passed by the Muri ts'o. Soaked by the incessant downpour, we sat wrapped in our felt cloaks, with an occasional pipe as our only solace. Now and then a lama came over and talked for a few minutes, but we did not encourage any attempt at intimacy. It was long after midnight before we could light a fire, and warm ourselves with a little tea and fill the aching void within us with some tsamba. In the morning, however, the lamas found us all apparently soundly sleeping, our heads well covered with our capes, when they came to say good-by; and we gave them a two hours' start before we followed down the valley. The rain continued dripping from the clouds; now and then snow also falling. We rode slowly on for about six miles, and then seeing some tents on the hillside we went up and asked for shelter till the morrow. The inhabitants gave us the use of a small tent in which they stored pack-saddles, and we were soon "drowning our mighty minds in tea," with which the good people kept us liberally supplied. This valley was the broadest I had yet seen, its width at the head being probably something over a mile. The side hills were not over 500 feet in height, and sloped gently up from the river; no trees were seen on them, but timber was plentiful on other hills beyond and in many of the side valleys.

The following day we continued down the valley. The only buildings in it were two small lamaseries: one facing our camp of the previous day, the other called Yanzé gomba, about three miles below it at the mouth of the Chodu ch'u, here spanned by a substantial log-bridge. A few miles below this point we passed the ruins of the former abode of the magistrate or Pönbo of this district, who now lives to the north of this valley. We did not see twenty tents in the whole length of the Yi lung. The sides of the mountain in its lower part, facing east, were well covered with spruce, cedar, juniper, and a variety of other kinds of trees, all of them much larger than any I had previously seen, many of the spruce reaching a foot and a half in diameter.

The valley as we advanced grew narrower, and at the point where we camped for the night, facing Mount Ito, it was little more than a gorge. Several large tea caravans bound for Lh'asa camped near us, the traders of that country frequenting in great numbers this route, which, though longer than that by Lit'ang and Ba, is much easier and has good grazing everywhere along it. We passed on an average 300 yak-loads of tea a day, destined for all points of the country; each yak carried two or three *gam*, each weighing 45 Chinese pounds (58 pounds), so I could not have seen much less than half a million of pounds during the ride from Jyékundo to Dawo. I was assured that this road was thronged with caravans at nearly every season of the year, and I have no reason to doubt it, as I was told at Ta-chien-lu that there never passed a day when several hundred loads of tea did not leave the town for Tibet. We constantly met Chinese traveling with these caravans, but they were hardly distinguishable from the natives, wearing the popular red turban and trying to assume the Tibetan swagger and roughness.

The valley of the Yi ch'u below the Ito ri has much of the beauty of the Dré chu, fine pine forests adding to its attractions. Suddenly it came to an end, the river entered a rocky, impassable gorge on the east, and the road, continuing in a southeasterly direction, ascended the course of a little affluent, and once more the long range of snow peaks burst into view on our right.

Crossing a low *col* marking the boundary between the Yi lung and Rungbatsa, we entered the basin of the Ribo ch'u, an affluent of the Za ch'u, into which river it empties less than a mile below Dajé gomba.

At Ribo commences the garden of this part of Tibet—the fertile valley of Rungbatsa; and villages are as thickly scattered over the country as in Switzerland. Around each grow some fine elms or other trees, and walls or hedges inclose the fields, where peas, barley, and wheat were more than a month in advance of what I had seen in Dérgé. Four or five miles before reaching Ribo I could see some thirty miles down the valley the glistening mass of Ka-lo ri, "the mountain of snows of a myriad years," all tinged with roseate hues by the setting sun.

Ribo,[1] though a very small village, is one of some importance on account of its sacred rock on a hillock in the valley covered with scarfs of every color, and with long rows of offerings arrayed around it. The village is built at the base of a high cliff, where a number of hermits (*ri-tru-ba*) have made their cells, from which they never descend; in a bag tied to a cord they haul up the offerings of the faithful, and pass their lives ecstatically thinking of the unthinkable and unknowable.

From the crest of the hill just beyond Ribo, a most exquisite view was before us. Down a broad valley, some twenty-five miles long, flowed a river glistening in the sun; on either bank were villages shaded by wide-spreading elms and willows, and lamaseries with white aud red walls and gilt spires amidst fields of the brightest green. Less than a mile from us was the big village of Rung-batsa; a little farther on was the great Dajé gomba; on our right opened another valley which led to Lagargo, and overhanging all were the snow peaks of the eastern range, and Ka-lo ri closing the valley with its huge mass.

The highroad passed close by the Dajé gomba,[2] but Kando was afraid to go by it in the daylight, as he said the lamas were the worst lot in all K'amdo, a horde of two thousand rascals from every part of Tibet. Leaving the highroad we followed a bridle path to the village of Gényi at the mouth of the gorge out of which issues the Za ch'u,[3] and put up in the house of some acquaintances of our guide.

[1] On A—— K——'s map this locality is called Riphug. This is probably the correct name, *ri p'ug* meaning "mountain cavern, or cell."

[2] A—— K——'s Dagé gomba. He gives its altitude as 10,550 feet; I made it 1000 feet higher.

[3] See note, page 261.

Kando, availing himself of being among friends, got more drunk than usual; he became maudlin, cried over me, then told me of his life at Darjeeling where he had lived two years. The *barré*, as he called the beer the P'iling used to give him, was a cherished recollection, and with the P'iling was associated in his mind their extraordinary habits, especially their fashion of riding, rising in their stirrups as if about to dive over the horse's head, their women riding with both legs on one side; the memory of this comical sight made him weep with delight.

The next morning we descended to the river, some two hundred feet below the village, which is built nearly perpendicularly above it, and were ferried across in the usual way, our horses swimming. The river was about seventy-five yards wide, clear, very swift, and deep. Considerable quantities of building logs were being floated down it; a heavy sweep at the bow, another at the stern of each raft, help to steer it through the strongest eddies, and the natives show a good deal of skill in managing these unwieldy contrivances.

We rode quickly along through numerous villages, passing on the road all sorts and conditions of people, both Chinese and Tibetans. Parties of lamas were especially numerous. Sometimes among them would be one of particular saintliness, dressed in yellow satin gown, with a gilt and varnished broad-rimmed hat, a tinkling bell on top of the crown; a lama attendant led his horse, and the people he met doffed their hats and approaching him with bended shoulders craved his blessing, when he touched the crowns of their heads with his two outstretched fingers and passed on. Some of these lamas were probably returning from a festival in a neighboring lamasery, or from reading prayers in a layman's house, for they had on their yellow hats, which, unlike those previously described, made them look as if they had stuffed their heads in the top of huge tassels whose short fringe fell down around their heads.

At the Bérim gomba the Za ch'u bends around a steep hill jutting out on the right bank. On the top of this promontory is the beautiful Nyara gomba, whose gold roof is seen from miles away. Near it on the same hill is the residence of the Bérim Déba, one of the five great chiefs of the Horba.

Four or five miles farther down we came to some cliffs covered with a thick deposit of loess. Ascending these we turned northward, going through some deep cuts, and in a little valley beyond we saw the crowded houses of the town and lamasery of Kanzé; and all over the face of another broad valley on which it opened, villages and lamaseries, and in a prominent position a Chinese temple (*Han jen ssŭ*), showing that there must be here an important settlement of that people. The lamasery is on the hillside commanding the village, the buildings crowded together and rising story above story, looking like a huge cliff-dwelling fastened on the face of the hill. The town was disappointingly small, not more than 300 houses, only three or four of which were very large, and they belonged to the two Débas who live here, the Kanzé Déba and the Mazur Déba.[1]

We found lodgings in a small, dark room in the house

[1] General J. T. Walker, "Proc. Roy. Geog. Soc." VII, in his account of A—— K——'s journey in Tibet, says (p. 73): "The famous lamasery of Kanzego, which is inhabited by 2000 lamas and surrounded by a town of 2500 houses, is so old and sacred that the people of the surrounding districts swear by its name in confirmation of their declarations." Two thousand five hundred houses suppose a population of 10,000 persons; absolutely impossible in this case. He gives its altitude as 10,200 feet; I make it 11,830 feet.

of one of the Chinese, but if the lodging was mean and dirty, the welcome was hearty, and what was better, the food they quickly set before us was abundant and tasted deliciously, though it was nothing but vermicelli with some greens and a very little hashed meat.

We had hardly swallowed our meal when we found that the street before the house was crowded with people and so was every housetop, all anxious to see the three queer-looking strangers just arrived. The lamas were especially insolent and on the rampage. I at once sent one of my men to the Chinese official stationed here, and asked him if he could not explain matters to the general satisfaction and tell the people that we were not dangerous characters. It was as much as my man could do to get back to the inn; the people pulled him about in every direction and made themselves generally disagreeable. The Ch'ien-tsung, or Lieutenant, Lu Ming-yang, took prompt measures to prevent any trouble, sending word to the Déba that I was a Hsi-ning official on my way to Ssŭ-ch'uan, and that due courtesy ought to be shown me. Before, however, the crowd could be dispersed the people broke into the inn and tried to drag us out, saying that we should not remain in town another hour. We managed to keep them off good-naturedly, laughing at their excited remarks and trying to divert their thoughts from ourselves by suggesting different purchases we were desirous of making, and by nightfall the hubbub had quieted down. The next day, however, it commenced again, though there seemed to be less animosity and more curiosity in the crowd; and by the third day of our sojourn in town we were treated nearly like any other of the Chinese. Still, had we lost our tempers the first day, we might have got into very serious trouble, for the people were not only excited over the sudden arrival of three suspicious-looking travelers without any luggage or any acknowledged purpose, but the whole population had been drinking and having a jollification for the last few days, and all heads were heated and many of the men were primed for a fight.

The day after our arrival was the 15th of the 4th moon of the Tibetan calendar,[1] a time of great rejoicing, when the people from all parts of the country assemble here for horse-racing, drinking, fighting, and flirting.

On the day after my arrival, I called on the Ch'ien-tsung, who, I was surprised to find, had his wife and children living with him. The Chinese government does not allow women to go to Tibet, hence all Chinese living there, whether officers, soldiers, or traders, have to take native wives. Many told me at Jyékundo, Kanzé, and other localities, that they greatly preferred these Man-tzŭ women to those of their native country, and that they remained in the country through devotion to them, as they could not take them back to China, where their large feet would make them a public laughing-stock.[2]

Lu was very much astonished that I had been able to

[1] Unlike most dependencies of China, Tibet has preserved its own system of reckoning time. The intercalation of months and days does not agree with that followed in China. Thus in 1889 the Tibetans had a third intercalary month; the Chinese did not. Days are divided into lucky and unlucky ones. The latter are disposed of by being dropped out; thus, if the thirteenth is unlucky, they skip it and count the fourteenth twice. As at least half the days of the year are unlucky, this must be a most confusing system.

[2] The Ssŭ-ch'uanese call all eastern Tibetans *Man-tzŭ* or *Man-chia;* the latter term is the only one acceptable to the natives, who for some reason to me unknown consider the first derogatory. The country itself is frequently spoken of as *Ts'ao-t'i,* "Steppe." Curiously enough, Tibetans often call Chinese *Manzé,* a name given to China south of the Yellow River until A. D. 1276, when the Sung dynasty was destroyed by the Mongols. The children of these mixed marriages are called by the Chinese *pan-ko ch'ien,* "half cash," and by Tibetans *Jya ma peu,* "Chinese (father), mother Tibetan," or else *Ra ma lug,* "Father goat, mother sheep." The word *Argon,* used in Jaeschke's Dictionary for these half-breeds, is understood but not used in the country.

get through the country, but he said that from this point to Dawo the people were so much worse than farther north that he could not let me pursue my journey unguarded. He would give me an escort of four men as far as Dawo, six days' journey from Kanzé, and send orders to the sergeant there to furnish me men from that place to Ta-chien-lu. I tried to get him to send me to Lit'ang, but he said he could not do so; along that road there were no saddle-horses and pack-animals, or any other ula procurable for the escort, and without an escort I could not travel. The distance to Lit'ang is little more than to Dawo, but there are no villages along the road, only Drupa, who will not furnish the ula unless paid for it. Old Kando had offered, before reaching Kanzé, to go to Lit'ang with me, and I had felt quite confident of reaching that town, but since our arrival at Kanzé he had been very badly treated by the people for having brought me there, and was afraid to have anything more to do with me. Again I had to submit to the inevitable, and prepare to go to Dawo.

Kanzé[1] is the chief city of the Horba states, locally called *Horsé k'a nga*, "the five Horba clans"; their names are Kangsar, Mazur, Bérim, Chuwo, and Chango.[2] This region is, after Dérgé, the most populous and wealthy of

[1] Written *Dkang-mdzés;* so it would be more correct to transcribe it *Kang-zé.* In the country the final *g* is not, however, heard.

[2] The Horba country is also called *Nya rong*, "The valley of the Nya ch'u," and *Hor chyok* (*p'yogs*), "The Hor region." The population of this country is estimated by Chinese authors (see "Hsi-yü k'ao ku lu," B. XVI) at about 8000 families or 35,000 souls, exclusive of lamas, of whom there are certainly between 8000 and 10,000. The district of Chango is said to be the most populous, with about 14,000 inhabitants. Bérim, the smallest state, has only 1500. In a memorial to the Emperor from the Tartar general at Cheng-t'u, and the governor-general of Ssŭ-ch'uan, published in the Peking "Gazette" of January 8, 1884, and translated on p. 253 *et seq.*, this country is spoken of as a portion of the Chien-Ch'ang circuit, a most extraordinary blunder, as this latter district is to the southeast of Ta-chien-lu some 150 to 200 miles away. The Chinese divide the Horba into seven tribes. (See

eastern Tibet. The country is ruled by five chieftains or Déba, in whose respective families the dignity is hereditary.

The people are among the best-looking I have seen in Tibet; they are smaller than those farther north and from central Tibet, and have less heavy features; aquiline noses, hazel eyes, and curly or wavy hair are not uncommon. The women especially are good-looking, and the natural

EASTERN TIBETAN WITH LIT'ANG HEAD-DRESS.

comeliness of the people is not a little increased by their bright-colored attire and gold and silver ornaments. The men clothe themselves in high-collared gowns or *chuba*

Appendix, *infrà.*) The titles of the five Horba Déba were given me as follows, by the secretary of the Chala Jyabo at Ta-chien-lu: K'ang-sar Déba, Mazur Déba, Dra-mon Déba, Bérim Déba, and Dri-tu Déba, but instead of Dra-mon and Dri-tu Déba one usually hears Chuwo and Chango Déba, titles taken from the names of their principal towns. So too the K'ang-sar Déba is called Kanzé Déba.

of violet pulo, dark red turbans, and often loose trousers of violet pulo falling over their boots. Their locks hang over their shoulders, but they also wear a large Chinese queue mostly made of silk threads, a large agate or white glass thumb-ring ornamenting it; this they twist around the head, hardly ever letting it hang down the back. In the left ear is a silver ring in which is set a turquoise or coral bead, and their swords are handsomely ornamented with *repoussé* silverwork and also set with coral. The women dress in gowns of pulo, usually woven in stripes of different colors. Their hair is left loose over the shoulders, like that of the men, or else done up in innumerable little plaits, the common fashion of the country.[1] The married women wear on the front of the head a large embossed plate of silver or gold, called *serja*, in which is set a coral bead, but if they have married Chinese they wear it on the back of the head. From the belts of both men and women hang a needle-case, a flint-and-steel box, often an eye-shade case prettily embroidered, and in some parts of the country a bag in which to carry their wooden bowls. The well-to-do people wear shirts of coarse unbleached silk of Indian manufacture, with a high red collar, and half-rupee pieces as buttons in the case of the men, and elaborate gold buckles and coral buttons mounted with gold or silver for the women.

It must not be thought that this clothing is worn by them all the time; it is their holiday costume, that which

[1] Friar Odoric, in the fourteenth century, speaking of the dress of Tibetan women, says: "The women have their hair plaited in more than one hundred tresses, and they have a couple of tusks as long as those of wild boars." See Yule's "Cathay and the Way Thither," I, 148. The tusks may be ornaments made of the musk-deer's tusks, but I saw none such in the country. Alex. Hosie, *op. cit.*, p. 124, speaking of the aboriginal women of southwest Ssŭ-ch'uan, says that their turbans were in many cases adorned with circlets of hog's tusks.

they had on while I was at Kanzé. The every-day dress is much plainer: undyed *la-wa* in summer, and sheepskin in winter, without ornament, save the sword which never leaves the man's belt, and the chatelaine of silver worn by the woman, to which are fastened her keys.

The Horba, like all of their race, are much given to the use of tobacco, especially in the form of snuff. The modes of taking it in Tibet are quite curious. Among the K'amba a small bag of rather stiff leather is used; in it the crushed leaf (usually of Sikkim or Bhutan tobacco) is put, and the bag rubbed between the hands. Then it is opened, and with the little sheath-knife which every one has hanging from the belt, the side of the bag is scraped and the finest particles of tobacco got together. In the more civilized parts of the country a circular wooden box is used; the crushed tobacco is put into the top and covered with a piece of woolen stuff, and the box is shut; when snuff is needed, they strike the box on the knee, and the tobacco is sifted through the cloth into the bottom. Both men and women take snuff, but not as much as the Mongols do. Smoking is indulged in moderately by some of the men; the Chinese pipe is the only one used. Lamas, however, never smoke, the use of tobacco, except as snuff, being prohibited inside their convents. I saw a few Tibetans smoking opium, but I do not believe that the habit has taken any hold of them, and, in fact, many persons told me that the use of this drug was unknown to them, though all the Chinese settled in the country use it continually, both eating and smoking it.

The people in the more civilized parts of eastern Tibet are not entirely devoid of some elementary education. Reading and writing is, however, about as far as they get, and even writing is an accomplishment of only a few outside of the lamaseries, although most people can read both the capital script (*wu chän*), and the cursive character (*wu méd*), the latter not without difficulties, on account of the numerous abbreviations introduced in it. At Ta-chien-lu and other large places the girls attend school as well as a few of the boys, learning to read and write letters, the polite forms of address, and some other necessary rudiments, in which arithmetic does not, however, enter.

SILVER INK-BOTTLE, PENS AND PEN-CASE.

Besides the very large religious literature extant in Tibet, there are a number of works of a semi-biographical nature, called *nam-t'ar*, histories, and translations of Chinese standard works; also books of songs and a few of pure fiction, these latter of Chinese origin and published probably by Chinese enterprise. The nam-t'ar are the favorite compositions, however, just as the historical novel is the most popular literature throughout China, and quite a numerous class of men earn their livelihood by giving readings of these books. These story-tellers afford the nearest approach the people have to theatrical representations, if we except the *Ripa* or itinerant mummers (mostly boys) who with hideous masks over their heads perform a grotesque dance to the music of their song, whose burden, as far as I could make it out, was a courting of one's expected generosity, becoming fulsome praise when one gave them anything, such expressions as

Pönbo rinpoch'é, "Most precious official," being among the mildest.[1]

There are in this country certain festivals, but of a religious character and performed by the lamas, such as the Chambé ch'ü-k'or, or "Procession of the god Chamba" (*Maitreya*) around the temples, to drive away demons, the festivities of the Lu-gon Jyabo dung-dri, or "Expulsion of the Prince of Devils," etc., which present much analogy to the medieval mystery plays. But these are not given for the amusement of the people, and form no part of their life. Horse-racing is one of their favorite pastimes, but they do not understand this amusement as we do, confining themselves rather to showing off their horses and themselves in their finest trappings, or else racing by twos or threes, but not for a purse or any reward.

Singing, a pastime of which they are very fond, is not much more agreeable to the foreign ear than is that of the Chinese or Japanese, though the Tibetans' voices are often full and sweet, and there is frequently a perceptible tune in their songs. Of musical instruments, the only ones I noticed were a double flute made of reed or bamboo, and a three-stringed banjo similar to the Chinese *san-hsien*.

Dancing is also a favorite amusement, especially in the spring of the year, when the girls go in large parties and dance on the soft green grass under the trees, the young men forming appreciative spectators. The dances I saw could hardly be called graceful; two groups formed, and while one stood still the other, to the music of their own singing, danced slowly backward and forward, swaying their bodies and taking high, slow steps. Then the

[1] Captain Turner, *op. cit.*, p. 227, mentions seeing these clowns when on his way to Trashil'unpo. The title *rinpoch'é* is used in addressing high officials; Mgr. Biet, the Bishop of Ta-chien-lu, is sometimes thus styled in writings.

other group had their turn, and so the dance went on by the hour.

I noticed but few games of chance among them. Dice they have, but they are used for divining purposes, not for gambling. A few men who had passed much of their time among the Chinese played cards, and chess is also known among them, but both are of foreign importation, and I could hear of no national games.

Among the Horba I saw more drinking than farther north; nä ch'ang and a strong spirit distilled from it called *arrak* being the only two liquors in use. The latter is imbibed either cold or warm in Chinese fashion.

Although the Tibetans are essentially a religious people, it is surprising how small a place the performance of religious ceremonies occupies in their daily life. The most pleasing ceremony I noted among them is the evening prayer, observed by nearly every one in the larger villages and towns. As night falls lamps are lit on the altars of every Buddhist temple, and a short service is chanted, while lamas seated on the porch play a rather mournful hymn on long copper horns and clarinets. This is the signal for the housewives to light bundles of aromatic juniper boughs in the ovens made for the purpose on the roofs of their homes, and as the fragrant smoke ascends to heaven they sing a hymn or litany in which the men of the house often join, the deep voices of the latter and the clear high notes of the former blending most agreeably with the distant music in the lamaseries. In the morning, juniper boughs are again burnt; there is no singing, but offerings—bowls of water, wine, milk, or butter lamps—are placed before the household gods.

It is a universal custom among this people, before eating or drinking anything, to dip the forefinger of the right hand in it and scatter a little of the contents towards the four cardinal points, reciting a short prayer the while. This and the mumbling of the mani prayer (*Om mani pémè*

EVENING DEVOTIONS IN A TIBETAN VILLAGE.

hum), or some special formula given them by a lama, as *Om, p'é, swaha*, or the like, are practically the only religious observances of the people.

They have, however, another way of showing their religious feelings, that love of mankind dear to Buddhism; this is, in multiplying for the weal of sentient creation written or sculptured copies of the mani prayer. It is no uncommon thing to pass a family established under a tent in a locality where shaly stones are abundant, every member busily occupied incising on slabs of rock the sacred formula, and building up after months, perhaps years, of labor, a "mani wall," each stone in it having the prayer sculptured on it and frequently carefully painted. I have seen these walls a hundred yards and more long, and eight or ten feet high. Others will shape the letters composing the prayer with blocks of white stone on some far-seen mountain side, giving them such huge dimensions that they can be read four or five miles away.

Small stones on which this prayer is sculptured are continually offered to one by beggars, who are paid for them by a handful of tsamba or a little tea; and a person of any respectability never dreams of refusing to buy all offered to him, placing them along the walls of his house, or else on the nearest mani wall.

The Chinese at Kanzé number some eighty men; most of them are Shen-hsi traders, the others are foot-soldiers commanded by a Ch'ien-tsung, or lieutenant. Under him are a clerk, and a T'ung-shih or interpreter. The Ch'ien-tsung receives Tls. 170 a year as salary, but as he draws pay for fifty soldiers (at the rate of Tls. 24 a year) and has only twenty he adds considerably to his meager income. This practice is a common one throughout China, and is winked at by the authorities.

The Chinese traders have a number of small grist-mills worked by mules, and grind the wheat grown in the country, deriving large profits from the sale of the flour.

They have introduced swine,[1] poultry, and a variety of vegetables (cabbages, greens, onions), but the natives care little for them, preferring tsamba and tea. The most valuable trade of this place is in musk, the price obtained being about the same as at Jyékundo (Rs. 20 to 30 a cod); this, gold dust, yak hides, lambskins, wool, deer horns, and a few furs are the chief products of the country, which are paid for by the Chinese in silks, satins, lastings, cotton

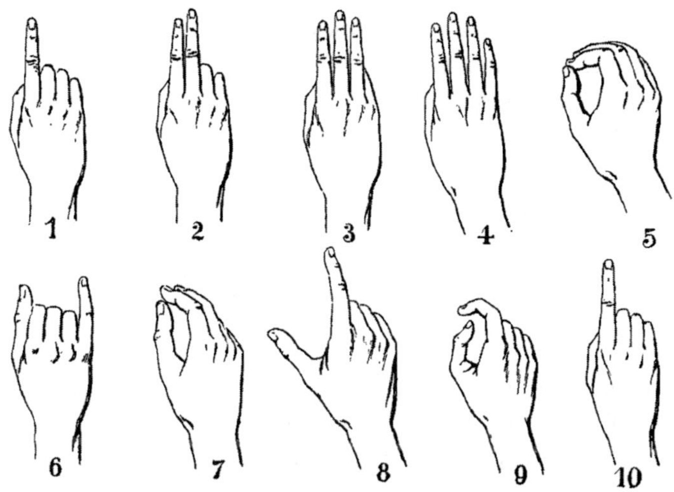

MONGOL AND CHINESE MODE OF DUMB BARGAINING.

fabrics (*lao pu*), red leather, tobacco, flour, vinegar, needles, buttons, etc., etc., much the same as in other localities of this region. Russian broadcloth, Vienna matches, American shirtings were for sale here, but their use was confined to the Chinese, the natives preferring the national pulo and products of Indian manufacture, even though much dearer.

In trading, Tibetans, in common with the Chinese, Mongols, and many other Asiatic peoples, make use of a

[1] Lamas do not eat pork, and in Mongolia (Ts'aidam) no one will touch it.

sign language or dumb bargaining. The buyer and seller take each other's right hand, well covered by the long sleeves, and having agreed upon the unit of count, rupee, ounce of silver, or brick of tea, the vendor takes hold of a certain number of the other's fingers, thus telling him the price at which he offers his goods. The other makes his offer in the same manner; and so, with many knowing winks, shakes of the head, and remarks to bystanders, the trade goes on till finally they come to an agreement. Thus, if one wants thirty-five ounces of silver for a pony, he will take hold of the other's first three fingers (three), next of his index and second finger crossed (ten), and then of all his fingers (five). The only points in which Tibetans depart from the system followed throughout China and Mongolia are in expressing figures from six to ten. Six is twice three fingers, turning the hand over on the second count; seven is four and three, eight is twice four, nine is four and five, and ten twice five—the hand always reversed when counting the second number.[1]

I have never seen a Tibetan do a multiplication, but when adding or subtracting he commonly avails himself of his prayer-beads, taking nine beads on the right side of one of the larger beads to represent units, and setting down the tens to the left of it. This mode of counting has probably come to them from seeing the Chinese use their counting boards, or *suan-pan*. They are very inexpert as to figures, and I have often seen in good manuscript 135, for example, written 100 30 5. The use of figures is mostly confined to astrological calculations, at least in that section of the country which I have visited.

[1] Cf. Cæsar Fredericke, in "Hakluyt," IX, pp. 282 and 289 (Ed. Goldsmid's edition). The "nipping of joynts" there referred to is, I believe, unknown in China and central Asia.

The Horba states, it has been said, are divided into five districts or cantons, but it would be a mistake to think that they are accurately defined regions marked with boundary stones. All the territory of one district is not conterminous: thus in the country west of Chuwo there is a village belonging to the Déba of Chango; and Dawo, to the east of Chango, is under the rule of the Kanzé Déba. My very short stay in the country did not allow me to inquire into this seemingly curious division of land.

It is only since 1883 that Chinese have been able to live in comparative peace in the Horba country. Prior to that date numbers of them were murdered, the lamas of the Chango lamasery being especially inimical. In 1883 an expectant Tao-t'ai, Ch'ing Shan by name, was sent by the Governor-General of Ssŭ-ch'uan on a mission to this country for the purpose of establishing some kind of order. He put to death two of the ringleaders in the Chango gomba, and since that time the Chinese have remained unmolested.[1] The account of the pacification of the Horba country by Ch'ing Shan would lead one to

[1] The official report concerning this mission is found in the "Peking Gazette" of Jan. 8, 1884, in a memorial to the Emperor. It reads as follows: "A Memorial from the Tartar General at Cheng-t'u Fu, and the Governor-General of Ssŭ-ch'uan, reporting the suppression of a petty war between certain tribal chieftains in the Chien-ch'ang circuit of that province [see *ante*, p. 242, note 2], the commencement of which was earlier reported to his Majesty, who was pleased to give orders for its immediate repression. A certain expectant Taot'ai, Ch'ing Shan by name, was sent with a force of three hundred aborigines to the place on news of the outbreak reaching the Memorialists, and subsequently Ting Shih-lan, the acting Taot'ai of the Ch'eng Hsien circuit, who has had much experience amongst the aborigines, was ordered to assist in effecting a settlement of the dispute. The report of these officers has now come to hand, from which the following account of the origin, development, and conclusion of the quarrel is gathered:

"In the district in question there are five aboriginal clans, viz.: the Mazur, K'angsar, Chuwo, Chango, and Bérim, who were at one time a single clan, but had separated some generations back, and the members had intermarried. The head of the Chango clan, a Déba or tribal chieftain [the text calls him *t'u-ssŭ*], of the name of Jya-mts'o tsan-chyang-chu, having no issue, the chief of the Mazur tribe

believe that it was under the absolute rule of the Chinese; however, such is not the fact, and several grains of salt must be taken with the Memorial wherever it relates to the action of the Chinese in this matter. According to what I learned from Lu Ming-yang the object of the mission was to put a stop to the turbulence of the lamas, who continually attacked the Chinese; this is not mentioned indeed, but the Memorial is historically and ethnologically interesting, nevertheless.

A day or two before my departure for Dawo, Lieutenant Lu sent a messenger ahead, bearing a circular to all the chiefs and head men along the route, announcing my com-

gave the said Jya-mts'o one of his own sons as a successor. On the death of Jya-mts'o, his adopted son, whose name was Wän ch'é, assumed charge of the affairs of Chango, and took to wife the younger sister of the chief of K'angsar, by whom he had a son called Trashi wang-jyal. The chief of K'angsar, whose name was Konsé nundro pönso, was thus uncle of the child Trashi wang-jyal. Three years ago [*i. e.*, in 1880] he was the go-between for his nephew in the arrangement and completion of a marriage between the latter and the eldest daughter of the Chuwo Déba. This arrangement having subsequently come to the knowledge of the Mazur Déba [the lad's grandfather], he objected to it on the ground that Wän ch'é, the lad's own father, was the person to decide whom he was to marry, and he ordered the girl, with whom the marriage had already been consummated, to be sent home again. He then arranged a second marriage for his grandson, Trashi wang-jyal, with the daughter of one Ch'osé jyal. Thus ill-feeling arose between the chiefs of K'angsar and Chuwo, the insult received by the latter [by having his daughter sent back to him, after marriage with Trashi wang-jyal] so enraging him that he became a deadly enemy of the K'angsar Déba. Attempts to compromise the quarrel were made by the native administrator of Chan-tui [an official appointed from Lh'asa], who suggested that both marriages should be considered null and void, and that neither of the two girls should ever be allowed to marry again; but in spite of this arrangement the Mazur Déba insisted on the marriage with the daughter of Ch'osé jyal, and the Mazur and K'angsar tribes went to war.

"As soon as the [Chinese] authorities heard of it they went and expostulated with the combatants, when they found that the Chango and Mazur tribes had been willing to abide by the decision of the native governor of Chan-tui, but as the K'angsar tribe refused to do so they had gone to war, each side getting their kinsfolk to send them reinforcements: on the one side were the Mazur, Chango, and Män-nya [*i. e.*, Chan-tui] tribes; on the other, the K'angsar, Chuwo, and Bérim ones. Each army took up strong positions and built stockades, barriers, stone forts, and gun towers, and commenced to make war on each

ing. It was written in Chinese and Tibetan, and wrapped around an arrow, to signify that it must be forwarded from one locality to another post-haste. The Tibetan text, of which I made a copy at the time as a specimen of ula order, read as follows:

"A Chinese official from Zur (*i. e.*, Hsi-ning?), with two servants, is going down country (*i. e.*, to Ta-chien-lu) on private business. He does not require any ula. With him are four Chinese soldiers from Kanzé. These are not mounted, and will require four saddlehorses and a packhorse at each of the stations along the road.

"Issued under my seal the 15th day of the 4th moon."

other, to the serious detriment of [Chinese?] trade and almost complete stoppage of traffic.

"Now the chief of the K'angsar tribe, to whose obstinacy the war was due, was really a mere tool in the hands of his nephew Tengsé lopo, a member of the Chuwo tribe. This latter was a man of dark and dangerous ways, who had always consorted with characters of the most criminal type, and seeing in this war an opportunity of indulging his predatory propensities, it was he who prevailed upon his uncle to refuse to abide by the decision of the governor of the Chantui. In the [Chuwo] district there is a lamasery called [by the Chinese] Shou-ning ssŭ, occupied by some two thousand lamas with whom Tengsé lopo was on good terms, and who had a grudge against the Chango Déba. He accordingly prevailed upon these lamas to incite the people to surround the stockade of Chango, burn the villages, carry off the men and cattle, and proclaim him chief of the Chango tribe. These disturbances went on for three weeks, until the arrival of Ch'ing Shan with his troops; but on his calling upon the chiefs to withdraw their forces and to leave the quarrel to official arbitration they all did so. . . . Having quelled the disturbance, Ch'ing Shan sent for the three chiefs concerned, and having obtained their promise to abide by his decision, he proceeded to give his award. As both the girls had consummated marriage with Trashi wang-jyal, he considered that the proposal of the Governor of Chan-tui that they should be sent to their respective homes and never be allowed to marry again was most unreasonable; and as in his opinion the only way out of the difficulty was to marry them both to Trashi wang-jyal, he decided that they should both return to him in the respective capacities of first and second wives, the daughter of the Chuwo Déba taking precedence as she was the first to be married. This arrangement was gladly accepted by the chiefs, who entered into bonds undertaking nevermore to create disturbance.

"The Memorialists propose to close the affair by fining each of the chiefs a year's salary, and cutting off the head of Tengsé lopo who was killed in the sortie; the prisoner Kochén lopo has already been decapitated."

Before leaving, Lu asked us to dine with him, his writer, and T'ung-shih; and on the shady veranda on top of his house we enjoyed a very good dinner with much wine-drinking, and I heard many stories about his long and varied experience in Tibet. He had been stationed for three years at Lh'asa and about fifteen years in other localities in Tibet, and being an observant man had much of interest to tell about. When speaking of the wild tribes to the north of the Horba country, he assured me that men in a state of primitive savagery were found in Tibet. Some few years ago there was a forest fire on the flank of Mount Ka-lo, east of Kanzé, and the flames drove a number of wild men out of the woods. These were seen by him; they were very hairy, their language was incomprehensible to Tibetans, and they wore most primitive garments made of skins. He took them to belong to the same race as the Golok, of whom many lived in caves in a condition of profound savagery.

I left Kanzé on the 13th June. Four Chinese soldiers in half Chinese, half Tibetan costumes, mounted on prancing ponies with collars of jingling bells around their necks, formed the escort; two Tibetans wearing the high-crowned white summer hat drove some pack-ponies, and my two men and I brought up the rear, feeling very forlorn and dirty beside our gorgeous companions.

Some five or six miles east of the town the river bends sharply to the south; here at the village of Puyü-lung, about a mile and half from the river-bank, we stopped to take tea in a handsome house belonging to the Déba of Chuwo, while the horses were changed. Then crossing a low range of mountains where we saw many black tents, we entered the valley of the Tongo ch'u, and passed in front of the Jori gomba situated in a hollow near a little lakelet called the Jori ts'o. We came on the Tongo ch'u about two miles below this point, and found it a swift, clear stream about seventy-five feet wide and over three feet deep.

The little village of Chuwo, the capital of this district, is two and a half miles farther down the valley, on a steep, rocky bit of ground on the left bank of the river. A large lamasery overshadows it. The Déba's, the only imposing house, rises four stories high, the corners of the roof decorated with the peculiar black trophy called *jyal-tsän* (*rgyal-mtsán*), looking like a fat, closed umbrella, with a white band near its lower edge and two other vertical ones, forming with the first conspicuous white crosses, which always startled me, so like a missionary station did they make the houses look. A wooden bridge, closed at either end by a wicket gate, led to the village, where we found excellent quarters in the Déba's house.

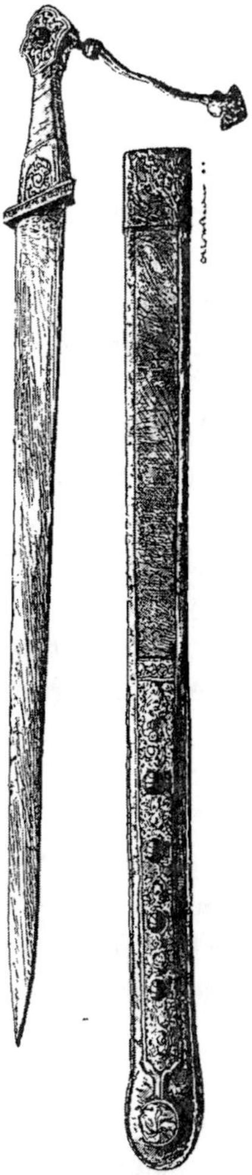

TIBETAN SWORD (FROM DÉRGÉ) — HANDLE AND SCABBARD ORNAMENTED WITH SILVER AND CORAL.

Nearly all the villagers were busily occupied molding little cones of clay called *ts'a-ts'a*, which are later on put as offerings in some ch'ürten, of which there are endless numbers all over the country. The occasion seemed quite a jollification, the people laughing and joking and vying with each other to turn out as many ts'a-ts'a as they could, and lamas seated under a tent reading prayers and superintending the work. The hillside was already covered with these little mud pies, but shortly after our arrival a violent rain-storm came sweeping down the valley, and soon their day's work melted away. Let us hope that as the work was done to acquire merit, their labor will not be counted them as naught by the judge of the dead when he comes to weigh their good deeds against their bad.

During the journey from Kanzé to Dawo I enjoyed all the comforts afforded officials traveling in this country. We put up at nights in the houses of the chiefs or in others set aside for the accommodation of officials traveling, to which reference has been previously made (p. 196), and every morning fresh horses were in readiness for the day's journey. Sometimes there was a delay in securing these latter, as the people insisted that they had all their stock grazing in remote localities. The head-man would come into our room and make his excuses, and generally my escort would squeeze a rupee or two out of him; but there was never any loud or angry talk, the whole thing was arranged in the most amicable manner, the head-man listening, with his palms joined respectfully before him, and only saying *La so, la so*, "Yes, yes," to all the Chinamen's remarks.

At Chuwo were a certain number of Chinese traders; in fact, from Kanzé eastward we found some of these people, mostly Ssŭ-ch'uanese, in every town and village we came to. Many of them had become thoroughly Tibetanized, in manners, in dress, and moreover in religion. Even Lu Ming-yang at Kanzé conformed to the local religious observances — using a rosary, burning juniper boughs, dipping his finger in his wine or tea cup before drinking and scattering a little around him, and others elsewhere mentioned.

Leaving Chuwo our road led down the valley of the Tongo ch'u, which in many places flowed in a narrow bed worn deep down in the rock, the mountains rising on either side some 1800 feet, those on the right bank finely wooded. Villages were numerous; peas, wheat, and barley were growing in the fields, and flowering shrubs hung over the path. Had it not been for the droves of yak, laden with tea, and the strange-looking people, I could have imagined myself in some Swiss valley.

After a most agreeable ride of twenty miles we came to Rantro, where all the houses, save the one in which we stopped, had been burnt down in the disturbance of a few years ago, referred to in a preceding note. Rain fell several times during the day and in torrents towards nightfall, and there was not a day passed during the remainder of my journey to Ta-chien-lu without a downpour lasting frequently the better part of the day.

A little above the town of Chango, ten miles below Rantro, the Tongo ch'u empties into the Nya ch'u. We had stopped before reaching this point, to take our noonday meal, and, as we were eating, a number of lama pilgrims came up to beg a little tea and tsamba from us. They were Amdowa from Kumbum, and two of them were old acquaintances of my Chinese. They said that they were on their way to Lh'asa, and had come by way of Kuei-tê and Lh'abrang gomba. They had been three months on the road, and hoped to reach their destination in about four months more. They were going to Dérgé dron-cher, and thence viâ Draya and Ch'amdo, along the usual high-road. They told me that this roundabout route was frequently taken, as over it two or three men could travel in safety, while over the *chang lam* (*i. e.*, across the T'saidam and over the Burhan bota pass to Nag chu-k'a) a large party was an absolute necessity, on accouut of the Golok.

The great Chaugo gomba is built on the top of the hills, overlooking the Nya ch'u; the town is on the steep hillside below. Some two thousand Gélupa lamas inhabit the gomba, and are held to be a bad lot by all who know them. The village contains about seventy-five houses, the two largest, in fact the only large ones, belonging to the Déba. The vicinity of China commenced here to make itself unpleasantly known by the vile odors, and filthy streets where pigs wallowed, and by other tokens of Chinese civilization. Vegetables were plentiful, and so were eggs, but no meat, save pork, was to be had. Most of the natives eat their tsamba without the addition of even a little butter in their tea, an unpalatable mess, and evincing a most inexplicable taste, for they prefer it to the vegetable diet of the Chinese, which should recommend itself, one would think, as being more varied and having at least some flavor. Potatoes have become known in this country within the present century, probably through the medium of the French missionaries, but they are not a popular food, and are used only by the poorest people.[1]

The Chinese population of Chango is said to be over a hundred, and the half-breeds are very numerous, but hardly distinguishable from the Tibetans in features, and

[1] Warren Hastings directed Mr. Bogle to plant some potatoes at every halting-place on his journey to Trashil'unpo, in order that a valuable new product might be introduced into Bhutan. See Markham's "Tibet," p. 19. Captain S. Turner, "Embassy to Court of Teshoo lama," p. 140, remarks that potatoes in Bhutan were called after Mr. Bogle, but they had not been a success at Punakka, the capital of Bhutan. In western Ssŭ-ch'uan they form one of the most valued crops. They are known by a variety of names in Tibet. In K'amdo they are called *lu-seu* or *dro-ma;* in western Tibet, *a-lu;* in central Tibet, *a-nya, dro-ma, yung-ma, chyi-wa, chyi-u,* or *jya dro. Dro-ma* (*gro-ma*) originally means "grain, corn." *Jya dro* means "Chinese corn."

not at all in dress and manners. No Chinese troops are stationed here, the locality having been until recently too dangerous for them, as one of my escort candidly admitted.

The steward of the Déba came in the evening and said it would be impossible to supply the post-horses before morning of the second day, and so we had to resign ourselves to pass a whole day amidst the myriads of fleas and other vermin with which the *kung-kuan* swarmed. To add to my vexation, some one, looking at my traps, let my saddle-bag fall and broke my aneroid and boiling-point thermometer, thus simplifying my work for the remainder of the journey.

The Nya ch'u flows out of the mountains to the north of Chango a broad river, quite as wide and swifter than the Za ch'u above Kanzé, and the only muddy stream I saw in Tibet.[1] On leaving Chango we followed the bank of the river for thirteen miles through a well-cultivated

[1] It will be noticed that the name I give this river does not agree with our previous information concerning the country, for heretofore this name was given to the river which flows by Kanzé. I was assured, however, that it was the Za ch'u, and that the Nya ch'u passed by Chango and Dawo, giving its name to the main river farther south. Though the testimony was unanimous it does not yet convince me, for then the Za ch'u valley is called Nya rong, "Nya valley," and there are places along its course in which the word *Nya* appears. However, the name Nya rong may properly be applied to the basin of the Nya ch'u in which is the Za ch'u. On A—— K——'s map the Nya ch'u is called Tao (Dawo) ch'u, a mistake as will be seen hereafter, and it is not given its real importance. The best Chinese authorities ("Shui tao t'i k'ang," VIII, 16) also disagree with my informants. The Kanzé River is their Ya lung chiang; the Chango River, the Tsa (*i. e.*, Za) ch'u. I give, however, the names as I heard them. A—— K—— does not mention Chango, but gives a Dango (*sic*) gomba and uses the same name for the whole district, but there can be no doubt that his ear served him badly in transcribing this name and nearly every other he heard along his route. In "Report on the Trans-Himalayan Explorations during 1865-67," p. xxvi, I find it stated: "From Chango city, in the Kham territory, an enormous quantity of musk perfume is brought to Lh'asa, which eventually finds its way to Europe through Nepal." General J. T. Walker, in the article Tibet, in ninth edition of the "Encyclopædia Britannica," also calls this town Dango.

country, dotted with small villages of from six to twelve houses. Caravans of tea were still quite as numerous as north of Kanzé, and travelers of all sorts were continually passing by. Crossing to the other bank at the village of Kara ch'u (the Chinese call it Kala chung), the road for a few miles diverged from the river, which here makes a little bend southward, and crossing some hills followed the Jasa ch'u till it ran into the Nya ch'u, not far below. From about this point this river flows in a gorge between splendidly timbered mountains rising several thousand feet above its bed, and reminding one of the scenery along the Fraser River, in British Columbia. Chinese wood-choppers were busily engaged felling timber, and floating it down to Dawo or other points farther south. The road is cut in the steep face of the mountains, several hundred feet above the river, through rocks mostly of granite and shale.

After stopping for the night in a little village called Taja,[1] we once more descended to the bottom of the valley; and after a pleasant ride of twelve miles, in an opening in the valley we saw the gilt spires of the Nin-chung gomba and the roofs of Dawo rising beyond it. We rode rapidly past the lamasery, attracting fortunately no notice, and into the town, where we found a fine, large, airy room prepared for us by one of the escort who had ridden ahead. A small stream flows through the middle of the village, and the Chinese have put up a number of grist-mills over it. The town also boasts of a blacksmith and various other mechanics, some of whom make very pretty copper bottles in which to heat wine.

1 The Chinese call it Ta-chai. It is probably A—— K——'s Dathok. *Ta-chai* means possibly "Great gorge, or narrows," an appropriate name for this place.

We nearly had a repetition of the scenes previously enacted at Kanzé, a mob of lamas and natives trying to break into the house shortly after our arrival, and for a moment things looked very serious, as swords were drawn and one man was severely cut on the arm by one of my soldiers, but this shedding of blood refreshed and cooled them, and all the trouble stopped shortly after. I was by this time quite accustomed to such scenes, and since no violence was done me I could placidly look on, if not with enjoyment, at least with no fear of the ultimate end of the "bobbery."

Dawo is sometimes called Jésenyi, and this latter name is probably its original appellation. The Nin-chung (or Nying-ch'ung) gomba, with over one thousand lamas, forms the western portion of the town, the rest of which contains about eight hundred inhabitants, of whom over a hundred are Chinese. The houses are mostly two-story, and built of logs, nicely squared and dovetailed, the general style being much more Chinese than Tibetan; furthermore, in most of the houses the notched log steps are replaced by easy staircases. The language spoken here is a wonderful mixture of Tibetan and Chinese, with difficulty understood by people from Kanzé, not so much on account of local expressions as from the very peculiar accent and intonations. The people readily understand the Lh'asa dialect, or that form of this official language spoken in eastern Tibet, so we did not experience much difficulty in carrying on conversation with them.[1]

[1] Curiously enough, the name Dawo does not figure on A—— K——'s map; he mentions only the Nichong (*sic*) gomba. General Walker, *loc. cit.*, speaks of Tao and Dao, giving these names apparently as those of two separate localities. In 1719 during the great Chinese expedition to Tibet a fortified camp was established at Dawo, and its ruins are still visible not far from the town. This point's strategic importance is great, commanding two roads to the Chinese frontier at Ta-chien-lu, also a road to

We were obliged to wait two days at Dawo, as the Sergeant (*Pa-tsung*) who commanded the little Chinese guard here was rusticating some distance away and could not get back till the morrow. We found the village terribly foul and excessively hot; at 4 P. M., in the shade the thermometer stood at 74°. The flies and vermin were indescribably thick and voracious, and, though we were able to get some fairly good meals, we did not enjoy our forced repose, and pined for the road.

The Pa-tsung was a clever young fellow and very obliging. He said there were two roads from Dawo to Ta-chien-lu, and asked me which I had rather take. The more traveled one led over the Jéto pass, the other rougher one went by Tai-ling and the valley of the Ché ch'u. This was a most agreeable piece of news, for it enabled me to branch off from the route followed by A— K—, which I had been going over since I left Jyékundo, and to study a perfectly new section of country. So my answer was not long in coming, and I announced my determination to follow the "northern road," as the latter is called.

My new acquaintance begged me not to hurry my departure but to wait for two or three days, as he was desirous of giving me a dinner, and Dawo, he claimed, was an excellent place to *flâner* in, or, to use his picturesque Ssŭ-ch'uanese expression, *hao shua.* The Ssŭ-ch'uan people's greatest happiness is to *shua*, "to loaf"; they are continually suggesting the advisability of indulging in this recre-

Chan-tui, and one to Kanzé and the north. Dawo cannot be less than 10,800 feet above sea level, as Nya ch'u-k'a, 80 to 90 miles south of it, is, according to Captain Gill, 9222 feet. Chango is 11,670 feet above sea level, and the Nya ch'u at that point is 300 feet lower than the town, or 11,370 feet. Dawo is 44 miles below Chango, and from the rapidity of the current of the river I think a fall of 20 feet to the mile would not be deemed excessive. For these reasons I have estimated the altitude of the town at 10,500 feet above sea level.

ation, and no pretext is too futile for them to reach their end. But I resisted all the allurements the Pa-tsung could hold out to me, and firmly declared that I could *šhua* only at Ta-chien-lu, now distant but a week's journey. So guides and a pack-animal to take me as far as Tai-ling were promised for the morrow. Having bidden fare-well to the good fellows who had brought me from Kanzé, and to the Pa-tsung, who waited on me in full uniform some distance outside of the village, we started off again.

The Nya ch'u bends southward at Dawo, receiving the Dawo ch'u, which comes down from the snow-capped mountains some miles to the east and southeast of the town. Up the course of the latter our route led, the ground as far as Olosu (seven miles) rough and stony, but after passing that village the country became of exceeding beauty, the mountains clothed to their summits with fine timber. Still the incessant rain which kept falling marred the pleasurable ride, and we were glad to reach Koja, a little village of four or five houses near the river-bank. Here I noticed for the first time in Tibet goitres on several of the women, and hence to Ta-chien-lu they were a common disfigurement of the people, especially the women.[1]

From Koja to the head of the Dawo ch'u the valley was uninhabited; the forest growth covered the bottom of it, the soil was soaked by the continuous rains, and ferns and creepers nearly hid the rocks and fallen trees. The ascent was imperceptible, and the *col* which led into the valley of the Ro ch'u is not entitled to the name of pass, nor has it

[1] Dr. Saunders, in Turner's "Embassy to the Court of the Teshoo lama," p. 408, remarks that while goitre is common in Bhutan, it is unknown in Tibet. He says it is very common on the coast of Sumatra, and, I may add, on the plains of north China.

any particular name in the country. It marks, however, the boundary line between the Horba states and the little principality of Kata.

Here again we had one of those sudden changes from luxuriant vegetation to barren waste, from agricultural to pastoral life. The upper part of the valley of the Ro ch'u[1] was over a mile broad, its general direction southeast, and numerous families of Drupa with small herds of yak and sheep were scattered over its face. Ten miles down the valley we came to the little village of Tsonya, half-way up the side of the hills bordering the left bank of the river.

We might have reached Kata the same day, as it was only twelve miles off, but I was suffering from a violent attack of quinsy which prevented me taking any food. It had so reduced my strength in the last few days, that I was nearly worn out, and it was exhausting work to continue my survey. The diet of tea and tsamba, to which I had been condemned for the previous four months, just kept enough strength in me, if I did not miss a meal, to enable me to accomplish my work, but one could not store up any on such innutritious food. I dreaded being laid up on the road, for I felt my strength rapidly leaving me; as it was, I could not get on my horse without the assistance of both of my men.

The next day, passing over the hills beyond Tsonya, we entered the basin of the Kata ch'u, and after a couple of miles' ride came to a little plain some three miles in diameter, into which opened a number of valleys, near the mouth of each of which was a little village. In the center of the plain the golden spires of a lamasery shone through a grove of trees; and near by, within the earthen walls

[1] This little stream receives the Kata ch'u, when south of Kata; and then, taking a southerly course, empties, I think, into the Nya ch'u, near Nya ch'u-k'a, probably.

of an old retrenched camp, I saw the tiled roofs of the Chinese village of Tai-ling. The village is composed of about a hundred houses, arranged along two narrow and dirty streets on the southern side of the old camp, built, like that near Dawo, in 1719.[1] A diminutive Yamen and a little official temple are the only monuments of this unprepossessing place, and a Pa-tsung rules over its destinies. The native population lives in the adjacent villages, Tai-ling being a strictly Chinese place, at least so far as the male population is concerned, for the women are naturally Tibetans, but a Chinesefied lot, with little of the gay, free manners of their countrywomen farther west. Tai-ling marks approximately the eastern limit of Tibet in this direction, for though that country extends really as far as Ta-chien-lu it is not inhabited by any considerable number of natives east of this point. Either the Chinese have displaced them, or else the country is too warm and damp in the Girong (as the section in the basin of the Ché ch'u is called) for Tibetans; at all events few are to be seen in it.

The sergeant called on me and begged me to *shua* a few days while he got ready two of his men to guide me to Ta-chien-lu, but the dirty and dingy hole, some eight feet square, in which I was quartered was hardly comfortable enough to keep me in the place, and so the following morning, everything having been arranged, I left the town.

Ascending a short vale along which grew a few trees we found ourselves again amidst a semi-tropical vegetation. In a deep valley at our feet, stretching from south to north, a foaming torrent was flowing northward,

[1] The Kata lamasery, known to the Chinese as Hui-yüan miao, was built in 1723. The eleventh Talé lama, Kädru jya-t'so, was born in 1837 near this place.

emptying probably not many miles to our east into the T'ung ho.[1] On the eastern side of this valley rose precipitous mountains, the summits of several of them deep in snow; and at its head was the huge, rugged mass of the Ja-ra ri, with deep beds of snow and ice extending several thousand feet down its steep flanks. A dense foliage covered the valley and the slopes, and silvery moss hung in garlands from the trees, which looked like venerated images festooned with white k'atag. Up this way our road led us past several camps of Chinese wood-choppers, and then across a shoulder of the great mountain. Over its vertical face fall two or three streams, fed by the melting snows, into basins at its foot, giving this noble summit its Chinese name of Hai-tzŭ shan, "The lake mountain."[2] From one of these lakes issues the Ché ch'u, which at Ta-chien-lu meets the Dar ch'u, the two giving to that town, situated at their confluence (*do* in Tibetan) its name of Dar-ché do (*Dar Hché mdo*), which the Chinese have distorted into Ta-chien-lu.

The Ja-ra ri[3] is composed of a cluster of three peaks, and must reach an absolute altitude of about 16,500 feet; its southern continuation forms the Jeto la, over which

[1] The Chin-ch'uan River.

[2] Captain Gill saw this mountain from the summit of Ka-ji la, when on his way to Bat'ang. He speaks of it as follows: "The view when we reached the summit was superb. Looking back in the direction from which we had come, range after range of mountains lay at our feet, culminating at last in the most magnificent snowy heights, one of which raised its head about four thousand or five thousand feet above its neighbors. It was a magnificent peak, and at this distance looked almost perpendicular. Its name in Tibetan is Ja-ra (King of Mountains), and I never saw one that better deserved the name. Never before had I seen such a magnificent range of snowy mountains as here lay stretched before me, and it was with difficulty I could tear myself away from the sight." "River of Golden Sands," II, p. 133.

[3] This name cannot have the meaning given it by Captain Gill. It appears to me to mean, "Horn of China," marking from afar where China commences; or else it is *Chala ri*, "mountain of Ta-chien-lu."

passes the southern route to Ta-chien-lu. Along its eastern flank are the Ché ch'u and the road we were to follow; the country bears the name of Girong. Hot springs, much used by the natives, are found, I was told, on its northern flank. We saw numbers of the beautiful silver pheasant (*ma chi* in Chinese) running through the brush as we ascended its side. The valley of the Ché ch'u is narrow and stony, and the descent sharp all the way to Ta-chien-lu. The river grows with extraordinary rapidity from a streamlet to a roaring torrent, in which rocks are tumbled about like corks. Every few hundred yards we had to ford some small stream tumbling down into the Ché ch'u, and adding its waters to the flood, and by the time we had reached Hsin tien, five miles from the head of the valley, that river was fifty feet wide.

Hsin tien, or "New inn," is the name of a cluster of Chinese farm-houses recently put up in this valley, the outpost of Chinese advance in this direction. The sole room of the so-called inn was taken up by a party of carpenters, brickmakers, and other mechanics bound up-country, by the innkeeper, his family, and his pigs, but we found a little corner in which to settle ourselves and pass an uncomfortable night.

On the morrow we set off early, with the pleasurable anticipation of reaching Ta-chien-lu before night. A few miles below Hsin tien, mountain-bamboo began to show itself, and strawberries were growing along the roadside. We saw but one very small Tibetan village, a little below which was a Chinese one where were hot springs, in which I enjoyed the first bath I had had since the previous December, at Lin-t'ung, near Hsi-an Fu. The few Tibetans we met on the road had lost in this close proximity to China their naturally free, independent air, and showed their submissiveness by alighting from their horses, on sight of my two ragged Chinese soldiers, and doffing their hats as they passed.

Towards three o'clock my conductors pointed out a steep mountain, slightly tipped with snow, and said that at its foot was Ta-chien-lu; and a little later on, after crossing a substantial wooden bridge, the city walls, and the north gate, shaded by wide-spreading trees, came in view. Riding past the little Catholic school (Collège St. Joseph), just outside the gate, we finally made our entry into the town, wended our way through its narrow, crowded streets, across the Dar ch'u, to an inn in a busy street, and there put up for the night; and a huge sigh of relief escaped from my two Chinese and myself when we realized that we could rest at our ease, without fear of truculent lamas, with plenty of food, and a good roof over our heads.

As soon as I arrived, I sent one of my men to the bishop, Monseigneur Félix Biet, telling him of my arrival and of my desire to call on him as soon as convenient. His steward soon after appeared and said that I could rent a house belonging to one of the Kuts'a of the Tibetan king, a large, quiet, clean, and comfortable place, near the bishop's home, where Gill, Baber, Szechenyi, and other European travelers had stopped, and where I would have all the comforts procurable. Here I took up my abode the next day, making a call on the bishop in the meanwhile. The pleasure of once more seeing Europeans I cannot describe, but it can readily be conceived by those who have had to associate for any length of time solely with Asiatics. The cordiality of my reception by the kind bishop, and Fathers Dejean, Mussot, and Soulié, has left a memory I can better feel than express.

They could hardly believe me when I told them that I had crossed the Dérgé and the Nya rong with only two men, a country they had been endeavoring ineffectually to enter for over twenty years; and their praise I shall always treasure as my greatest reward, coming from men than whom none living know better the hardships and dangers of Tibetan travel.

SILVER SHIRT-CLASP (CHINESE MAKE). WORN BY NATIVE WOMEN OF TA-CHIEN-LU.

VI

TA-CHIEN-LU (DARCHÉDO)—ITS COMMERCE. NOTES ON THE GOVERNMENT, COMMERCE, SYSTEM OF TAXATION, POPULATION, FOREIGN RELATIONS, ETC., OF TIBET

I FOUND myself so comfortably installed in Yang lama's house in Ta-chien-lu, that I made up my mind to wait there the arrival of the two men I had been obliged to leave behind at Jyékundo. But even if the place had been less comfortable I should have staid there to enjoy the society of the good bishop and the fathers of his mission, to whom I shall ever feel under a debt of deep gratitude for the kindness they showed me and the information they so freely gave to me about the country where they had lived and suffered for so many years. Monseigneur Biet has been in Tibet for twenty-six years, and though still a comparatively young man, is broken down by the many hardships he has had to endure. The history of the work of this mission has been written by the brother of Abbé Desgodins, and to that I must refer those whom the subject interests,[1] only adding a few lines concerning the last persecution to which the faithful priests have been subjected.

The principal station of the mission, since the destruction of Bonga in the Tsarong, was Yérkalo on the Lantsang chiang, to the south of Gartok. Here a fine church,

[1] "Le Thibet d'après la Correspondance des Missionnaires," par C. H. Desgodins. Paris: 1885. 1 vol. 8°.

a seminary, a bishop's house, and other costly buildings had been erected, and a considerable stretch of land had been cultivated. The bishop was rejoicing in the completion of his work, when in 1887 a general uprising, instigated by the lamas, took place. Yérkalo was soon a mass of smoldering ruins, and from every other station on Tibetan soil the priests were driven away and forced to seek refuge at Ta-chien-lu. At Bat'ang the lamas took from the grave the bones of Father Brieux, killed in 1881, filled their place with ordure, and made a drinking-cup of his skull. The native Christians who remained were not allowed to cultivate their fields by the lamas, and have been reduced to beggary. Since then Mgr. Biet has been obliged to support them from the meager funds at his disposal, but none of the fathers have been able to reënter the country beyond Tung Olo, a little village two days west of Ta-chien-lu. The bishop has appealed in vain to the Chinese authorities of Ssŭ-ch'uan, and to the French minister at Peking. He can neither obtain indemnification for the losses the mission has sustained, nor promise of reinstatement even in those stations situated

EASTERN TIBETAN (CHRISTIAN).

on territory under the direct rule of China (as in Yérkalo). The fact is that ever since the miserably managed "state of reprisals" which existed between France and China in 1884–85 foreign prestige in the interior has fallen lower than at any period since the Anglo-French expedition in 1861. Everywhere, in Shen-hsi, Kan-su, Ssŭ-ch'uan, I heard it said that the officials had changed entirely of late in their manners towards foreigners; nearly all of them showed such marked hostility and arrogance that their conduct could be explained only on the supposition that they were acting under orders from Peking. Every foreigner living in the interior of China is kept under constant surveillance; his daily doings are fully reported to the local officials, his every act pried into, his servants suborned or maltreated, and no occasion is ever lost to snub or humiliate him publicly. In some parts of Ssŭ-ch'uan the missionaries have been in the last year or two so constantly and maliciously tormented by the officials, that when I was passing through Chia-ting Fu the bishop was about to recall them and put Chinese priests in their places. More than one old white-headed father told me that there had been more real liberty for them in the old days before the "opening" of the country than in the last few years, and I can readily believe it.

Ta-chien-lu[1] is the most westerly sub-prefecture (*T'ing*) in the province of Ssŭ-ch'uan, and is also the capital of the Tibetan prince, or king (*jyabo*), of Chala, or Ming-

[1] The Chinese say, in explanation of the name, that it was here that Wu Hou of the Han dynasty (A. D. 221-263), when on his expedition to the south, sent Kuo-ta to establish a forge (*lu*) to make arrow-heads (*ta chien*), but the name is really, as stated previously (p. 268), a Tibetan one. Tibetans frequently abbreviate it and call it *Do*, as *Do mara dro-gi-ré*, "I am going down to Dar-chédo." In like manner, Chinese call it *Lu*. The river between Ta-chien-lu and Wa-ssŭ k'ou is also called Do ch'u in Tibetan, and Lu ho in Chinese; its full name is Ta-chien-lu ho.

cheng, as it is called in Chinese. The Dar ch'u passes through the town and is spanned by two bridges. The valley above and below the city is closed by crenelated walls in which are three gates known as the northern, eastern, and southern. The buildings are mostly in the Chinese style of architecture, but many of them retain some of the peculiar features of Tibetan houses, chiefly the two stories and the flat roofs. The population, which I roughly estimated at between 6000 and 8000, is, as might be expected, very mixed, the trade of the place bringing there Chinese from Shen-hsi, Yun-nan, and other remoter provinces, besides large numbers of Tibetans and aborigines from every part of the western border. This floating population, which I have not counted in my estimate, is quite considerable, and is greatly increased by the tea-porters, bringing brick tea from Ya-chou and other localities, of whom at least four hundred come or go daily. There are also eight lamaseries, two of each of the four sects mentioned on page 217, in which dwell probably one thousand inmates, besides a certain number of Bönbo priests who do not, however, inhabit convents, and are hence called *ao-gomba*, or "lay lamas." Ten thousand would therefore appear to be a fair figure for the usual population of this town.

An army commissary (*Chün-liang-fu*) administers this sub-prefecture, besides forwarding all the money, supplies, etc., necessary to the Chinese garrisons in Tibet.[1] The post was a highly lucrative one on account of the large sums levied as duties on tea, so that this officer made some $40,000 a year. But of late a deputy (*Wei-yüan*)

[1] The Taot'ai of Ya-chou supplies the funds for the garrisons in Tibet. This town used in old times to be the frontier station. The commissaries at Lit'ang, Bat'ang, Ch'amdo, Larégo, and Lh'asa are subordinate to the Chün-liang-fu of Ta-chien-lu.

has been sent here by the governor-general of the province, to superintend the levying of likin dues, and the Ta-chien-lu commissary is no longer able to feather his nest as comfortably as of yore.

The chief military officer of the place is a colonel styled Ch'in-ning Hsieh, Commander of the Fu-ho battalion (*ying*), from which are taken the various detachments stationed in eastern Tibet. He is supposed to have some two hundred men with him at Ta-chien-lu, but I do not think that, as a matter of fact, he has a hundred.

WOMAN'S CORAL SHIRT-BUTTON (LIT'ANG).

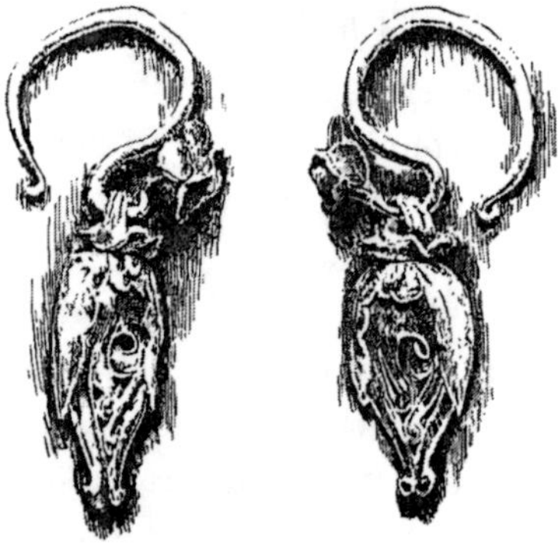

SILVER EAR-RINGS (CHINESE MAKE) WORN BY NATIVE WOMEN OF THE CHIN CH'UAN.

Prior to 1700, Ta-chien-lu and the country east of it for nearly a hundred miles was not occupied by the Chinese and was under the rule of the King of Chala, but since that date this tract has been annexed to China, though the natives have been allowed to retain their tribal organization. The native prince still resides at Ta-chien-lu, and is one of the most powerful chiefs of eastern Tibet, for among them he alone demands and obtains obedience from the lamas dwelling in his principality. He has the right to levy duties on all goods taken west of the city by Chinese or natives, and exercises exclusive control over all his people, native culprits arrested by the Chinese being turned over to him or his officers for punishment.

To the west, the state of Chala confines on the Mänya

(*Chan-tui*), and Lit'ang, and the prince has had much difficulty of late years in resisting the encroachments of the Lh'asa people, who have annexed the former country. The alliances he has made by the marriage of his daughters to the powerful chiefs of Dérgé and Lit'ang have, however, greatly strengthened his power and prestige.[1]

On the western frontier of his state, at a place called Nya ch'u-k'a, or Mä-Nya ch'u-k'a, on the river Nya, is an important station garrisoned by a few Chinese and Tibetan troops. By some this place is considered the frontier post of Tibet, for here all travelers, natives only excepted, must show their passes. The post seems to have been primarily established to arrest deserters from the Chinese forces stationed in Tibet, and this is its principal utility at the present day.

Ta-chien-lu's chief importance is as a trading center; it is the emporium between China and Tibet. Tea is the most important product exported to the latter country, from ten to thirteen millions of pounds being brought to this town annually for the Tibetan market. This tea is brought from Ya-chou and neighboring localities by porters, who are paid two-tenths of an ounce of silver for each *pao* weighing from eighteen to twenty-three pounds. On arriving at the eastern gate of the city they pass through the likin office, where a duty of Tl. 0. 8 is charged for every five *pao* (or one *t'ao*) of Ya-chou, Yün-chin Hsien, or Tien-chu'an Chou tea, that from Ch'üng Chou paying one mace more. The tea is next taken to the packing-houses owned by the great Ya-chou tea firms in the city, and each *pao* is divided into four separate packages or bricks, called in Tibetan *parka*,

1 The organization of the native government has been examined at p. 218 *et seq.* Much additional matter will be found in E. C. Baber's charming "Travels and Researches in Western China," previously referred to.

and made up into cases of nine bricks and securely sewn in rawhide; then it is ready for exportation to Tibet, two cases or *gam* making an ordinary yak-load.[1] On leaving Ta-chien-lu for Tibet a further duty of two tael cents is levied by the native ruler of Chala on every four bricks when exported by Chinese, and of one tael cent when exported by Tibetans.

I cannot do better than to quote here from a pamphlet written by Father Desgodins on the subject of the Tibetan tea trade.[2]

"All the tea bricks prepared for the Tibetan market are not of the same quality; but, according to the maturity of leaves, to the more or less perfect fermentation, to the color, to the proportion of leaves or of wood to the weight, are divided into five standards. There are besides some dozen loads of fine tea, also packed into bricks, to be sent as presents from the Emperor to the Dalai lama, or to be used by the Chinese officials and some few amongst the native gentry. This fine tea is never an article of trade.[3]

"The first standard is called *Shih chang chin* by the natives, and *Go-mang chu-pa* by the Tibetans. These tea bricks do got contain any tea wood, but only the best fermented leaves of a dark brown (not black) color. A light sprinkling of fine tea is generally added on both ends of each brick. As it is better flavored, and as a less quantity is required, it is the tea preferred as drink by those who can afford to buy it. Each brick weighs generally five and a half English pounds, and is sold at

[1] Four *parka* form a *kodru*, three kodru make a *gam*, and two gam a *jyab* or load. The average weight of a gam is forty-five lbs.

[2] "A Tea Trade with Thibet." Published in 1883 by the Bengal Secretariat. I have slightly altered the transcription of Tibetan and Chinese names. The notes are mine.

[3] It is called by the Chinese *Chin yü ch'a* or *Hsi ch'a*, and by Tibetans, *drä dong* (*hbras dong*).

R. 1.4 at Ta-chien-lu, Rs. 2 at Bat'ang, Rs. 3 out of the highroad, Rs. 3.8 in the districts of Tsarong and Zayul, adjoining upper Assam, from Rs. 3 to Rs. 4 at Lh'asa, according to the supply in market.[1]

"The second standard is called *Guié-tsé kioo-pa* by the Tibetans. This brick is nearly of the same size and weight as the first standard, but the quality is much inferior on account of the leaves being of yellow or greenish color. As the fermentation has been less perfect, the tea is worse flavored, and a larger quantity is required for the same decoction. Unscrupulous merchants sometimes try to sell it as *Go-mang chu-pa* to unwary customers, or to mix some bricks of it with the first quality. The second standard brick is sold at Re. 1 at Ta-chien-lu, Rs. 2 at Bat'ang, Rs. 3 out of the highroad as far as Tsarong and Zayul, Rs. 3.4 at Lh'asa.[2]

"The third standard brick is called *Jyä-pa* by the Tibetans, and *Pa chang chin* by the Chinese. Each brick weighs two and a half English pounds, and is sold for ten annas at Ta-chien-lu, Re. 1 at Bat'ang, Rs. 1½ to Rs. 2 out of the highroad at Tsarong and Zayul, Rs. 2 to Rs. 2½ at Lh'asa. Inferior in quality to No. 1, but superior to No. 2, this tea, made of leaves with a few tops of small branches, well fermented and of a dark yellow color, is by far the most generally used in Tibet, not only as a beverage, but especially as a staple of trade, and as the current money of traders. Men bargain by stipulating so many bricks or packets (of four bricks) of tea. They say, 'This sword has cost three bricks; this horse is worth twenty packets,' and so on. The wages of workmen and servants

[1] The Chinese name of this tea means "Ten sheets of gold," from there being ten bits of gold foil on each brick. The Tibetan name means "Imperial No. 10." I paid Re. 1 for it at Ta-chien-lu.

[2] I am unable to explain the name the author gives it; it seems to be a

are paid in so many bricks of tea, etc. When bricks or packets of tea are mentioned as money, it is always the third standard, or *Jyă-pa*, which is understood; then the bricks are not weighed, but counted. If it is agreed that tea be weighed, and not counted, then the fifth standard is understood to be the medium of exchange.[1]

"The fourth and fifth standards are both called *Jong-ma;* so there are two kinds of *Jong-ma* tea. The first quality or fourth standard, which is made up of half of leaves and half of branches or wood mixed together, is of little use either as a beverage or as an exchange token. It will be enough to say that one brick weighs five English pounds, and is sold for Re. 1 at Ta-chien-lu.

"The fifth standard, or second quality of *Jong-ma*, is made almost exclusively with the wood of the prunings mixed with a few leaves. Sometimes there are no leaves at all. For that reason it is called *Shing ja* (wood tea) by the Tibetans. Each brick weighs nearly five English pounds, is sold at twelve annas six pies at Ta-chien-lu, Re. 1 at Bat'ang, Rs. 1½ to Rs. 2 out of the highroad, Rs. 2 to Rs. 2½ at Lh'asa. This tea, after being pounded in a mortar, is drunk; and is used as current money, as above stated, because it is heavier than No. 3, though inferior in quality."[2]

I was told by the likin officials at Ta-chien-lu that the amount annually levied by them on tea brought into the city was between Tls. 110,000 and Tls. 120,000. Supposing that all tea pays Tl. 0.8 a hundredweight (or *t'ao*),

hybrid term. I have also heard it called *Gadän chamba.*

[1] The Chinese name means "Eight sheets of gold"; the Tibetan, "Number eight." When I was at Ta-chien-lu the price was Tl. 0. 2.4 (1 rupee = Tl. 0. 3.2).

[2] It is nearly universally used in eastern Tibet. I have heard the fourth standard tea called *Goka.* Ch'iung Chou tea, exported *viâ* Sung-p'an, is *Shing ja.* It is made into *pao* weighing from fifty to sixty catties. Ch'iung Chou is two days northeast of Ya-chou.

we find that about thirteen and a half millions of pounds are imported yearly.[1]

Besides the tea entering Tibet by this route there is a considerable amount, possibly a million of pounds, taken in *via* Sung-p'an, and probably the same quantity from Li-chiang Fu and Ta-li Fu *via* A-tun-tzŭ and southeastern Tibet.

Incidentally the amount of tea imported into Tibet may throw some light on the vexed question of the population of that country. Five pounds of *Shing ja* a month is not a large allowance for a Tibetan or Mongol: so, taking thirteen millions of pounds as the average yearly consumption of tea in Tibet, we find that at the above rate it would supply little more than two millions of people, a figure arrived at by slightly more rigorous methods later on (p. 296). However, notwithstanding the large amount of tea imported, it is no uncommon thing to find people reduced to using roasted barley or peas, chips of wood, willow leaves, etc., anything in fact which will impart a little color and taste to their drink, as a substitute for tea.[2]

Exclusive of tea, the following are among the principal exports from Ta-chien-lu to Tibet: Cottons, silks, satins,

[1] Father Desgodins, in the pamphlet quoted above, gives it as his opinion that 2,666,640 lbs. of tea, worth Rs. 5,99,994, pass through this town annually on the way to Tibet. E. C. Baber, *op. cit.*, p. 186, estimates the amount at 9,915,233 lbs., and Alex. Hosie, "Parliamentary Papers, China No. 2" (1884), p. 15, gives the value of the Chinese tea trade with Tibet at Tls. 800,000, or about $1,000,000.

[2] There grows on the mountains along the western border of Ssŭ-ch'uan a wild variety of tea, called *Pai ch'a*, "white tea," or *Hsüeh ch'a*, "snow tea." It is used by the Tibetans as a refreshing and cooling drink.

While on the subject of tea I must mention that I have repeatedly asked Tibetans who had been to Darjeeling if they liked Indian tea. They all thought it greatly inferior to the Chinese, too heady, and not fit to be used as a habitual beverage. They said the same of the Hu-nan brick tea which I had brought from Kan-su; though far superior to the Ya-chou tea they positively disliked it, said that it gave them headaches, and was too astringent.

gold brocades (*chinkobs*),[1] k'atag from Ch'eng-tu, tobacco, red leather, chinaware, sugar, furs, gun-barrels, hardware, drugs, and a variety of other articles which we may for convenience class as "notions."

Central and Ulterior Tibet send to Ta-chien-lu pulo, tirma,[2] yak hides, lambskins, lynx, fox, and leopard skins, musk, gold, coral beads, pearls, and other precious stones, saffron (from Kashmir), incense sticks, rugs, dried fruit, tincal, medicines (principally deer horns), dried fruits, soap (from India), a variety of coarse unbleached silken fabric (from Assam?), brown sugar cakes (*puram*), etc. The total value of these goods is far below that of the tea bought here by Tibetans, who pay in Indian rupees for much the larger part of their purchases.[3] Prior to the recent troubles between India and Tibet the quantity of rupees brought to Ta-chien-lu was so great that eight forges were kept going melting them into ingots, in which shape, and under the designation of *chiu pa*, "nine eight (fine)," this silver is in use all over western Ssŭ-ch'uan.[4]

After tea, the most valuable trade of this town is in musk. Some conception of its magnitude may be had from the

1 This word, also pronounced *kinkob*, is derived from the Chinese *chin* (or *kin*), "gold," and *cha* (or *ka*), "to twist, to weave in," gold threads being woven in among the silk ones. Chinese chinkobs are not as much prized as Indian, but they are much cheaper, hence in demand.

2 A very fine woolen stuff, woven only in short pieces and used by wealthy lamas to make scarfs. In this connection it is of interest to note that not far from Lh'asa there is a village where is kept a flock of sheep from whose wool tirma is made for the exclusive use of the Talé lama. The village has to contribute this tirma free of charge and is exempted from all other taxation. This reminds us of the Carmelite convent in Italy where were kept sheep from whose wool the papal pallium was woven.

3 General J. T. Walker shows that the exports from Tibet into India greatly exceed in value her imports from that country. Thus in 1882-83 this difference amounted to £34,125, and the Tibetan trade with Nepal is not known. This money must go to Ta-chien-lu. See "Encyclopædia Britannica," IXth edition; article, Tibet.

4 Rupees exchange for 460 cash or Tl. 0.3.2 of silver. Gold sells for Tls. 19 an ounce, or Tls. 19.5 if rupee silver is given.

fact that the agent of one foreign firm of Shanghai purchases over $150,000 worth annually. Nearly all the musk before it is brought to Ta-chien-lu is adulterated by the

GOLD ORNAMENTS FROM LH'ASA (NEPALESE WORK).
1. SHIRT-CLASP, SET WITH TURQUOISES AND CORAL. 2. CHARM-BOX, SET WITH TURQUOISES. 3. RING, SET WITH TURQUOISES.

Tibetans with blood, liver, etc., so that of one cod they make four or five.[1] The usual test to ascertain its purity is running a thread rubbed with garlic through the cod; if no odor remains the perfume is held to be sufficiently pure.

Rhubarb is also an important branch of trade at Ta-chien-lu, but the supply greatly exceeds the demand. At Yérkalo and in the Tsarong hundreds of tons could be

[1] Concerning musk and its adulterations Cæsar Fredericke says: "There is a certaine beast in Tartaria, which is wilde and as big as a wolfe, which beast they take alive and beat him to death with small staves yt his blood may be spread through his whole body, then they cut it in pieces and take out all the bones, and beat the flesh with the blood in a mortar very small, and dry it, and make purses to put it in of the skin, and these be the cods of muske." And Hakluyt, the editor, adds: "This muske the Jewes doe counterfeit and take out halfe the good muske and beat the flesh of an asse and put in the room of it." Hakluyt, Goldsmid's edition, IX, 288. François Pyrard repeats this story in his travels. Hakluyt Soc. Edit., II, Part II, p. 359.

Musk pays 25 cash a cod as likin at entry, and 3 mace a catty as *shui ch'ien*.

bought annually at a nominal price. On the hills around Ta-chien-lu it grows abundantly, but the natives, so as to be able to dispose of it rapidly, dry it by artificial heat and thus injure its quality. The price usually paid for it in town is Tls. 1.5 a picul; the sun-dried sort fetches as high as Tls. 3.[1]

The Tibetan traders of each locality are organized into companies or guilds, and keep agents or vakils stationed at Ta-chien-lu, who make all purchases for them and dispose of their goods. These are called *tson-pön*[2] or *kar-pön*, and, as at Tankar, are the responsible representatives of the merchants who appoint them. The size and importance of their caravans is very great; thus while I was stopping there I saw one leave for Shigatsé in which were over 3000 pack-animals, mostly mules, and I was assured that not a day passed without a hundred or two hundred yak-loads of goods leaving the town for Tibet.

A considerable portion of the trade of Ta-chien-lu is in the hands of Shen-hsi men, but the most enterprising traders hereabout and in the Tsarong, Zayul, etc., come from Li-chiang Fu in Yun-nan, and are known as *Yun-nan ko*, or "Yun-nan guests." The Tsarong, a rich and populous country along the Lan-tsang chiang, inhabited principally by the Lissus, is their principal field of operations, and they realize large profits from the unsophisticated

1 On the old Russian rhubarb trade at Kiakhta, see Klaproth, "Mémoires relatives à l'Asie," p. 72. William de Rubruk was, I believe, one of the first Europeans to use this root medicinally. It was given him at Karakorum by an Armenian monk, and it nearly killed him, for, thinking it was holy water, he drank two cupfuls of the infusion. See "Itinerarium," p. 323. Both Chinese and Tibetans attribute the giddiness and sickness felt by travelers when crossing some of the high passes in Tibet, as the Jeto la, at certain seasons of the year, to the violent odor of the rhubarb plants which there cover the mountain side. See "Hsi t'sang t'u k'ao," II, 17.

2 This word is also used by Tibetans when addressing Chinese, where the latter would use the expression chang-kuei-ti, "boss," the French "patron."

natives. Mgr. Biet told me that they had opposed, tooth and nail, the establishment of missionaries in that country on the score that the natives were unaware of the real value of the products of their soil, and unacquainted with weights and measures, but that if the missionaries got a foothold among them they would teach them so much that profitable trade would be destroyed.[1]

While speaking of the Tsarong it is proper to note that slavery exists there in a more aggravated form than in any other portion of Tibet. While now and then a poor Tibetan pilgrim, on his way through the Tsarong to the Doké la, or to some other famous sanctuary, may become indebted to some one for the amount of his board or the like, and be obliged to work out by four or five years

[1] The Tibetan trade centered at Li-chiang Fu in northwest Yun-nan, near the right bank of the Yang-tzŭ chiang, is of great intrinsic value; the products of the fertile regions of the Tsarong and Zayul (coming *via* Wei-ssŭ and A-tun-tzŭ), gold, musk, honey, lac, wool, timber, etc., are disposed of in that town, and large quantities of goods from Lh'asa are brought there directly. Perhaps the most valuable product of the Tsarong is logs dug out of the ground and used to make coffins for wealthy Chinese. Mgr. Biet in a letter to the author, dated February 26, 1890, writes concerning them: "Les arbres précieux enfouis dans le sol au Tsarong, à Bonga, sous les vieilles forêts du Thibet et du Yunnan, sont le cèdre, bois incorruptible que l'on trouve à des profondeurs variant de 20 à 40 mètres. Chaque cèdre retiré de ces profondeurs vaut de 200 à 300 taels; on en fait des cercueils pour les riches mandarins; on les expédie aussi pour le palais de l'Empereur à Pekin. Les Chinois, qui ne sont pas forts en botanique, lui donnent differents noms selon le pays; ici [at Shapa, near the Lu-ting ch'iao], ils le nomment *hiang-cha mou* ou *hiang-cha chou*. Le cèdre en plein air, qui d'ailleurs est rare dans les forêts, n'est pas estimé. C'est le cèdre enfoui devenu très dur et incorruptible qui est recherché; celui-là est très foncé en couleur, et très riche en marbrures." *Hiang-cha* means "fragrant pine."

S. W. Williams, in his Chinese-English Dictionary, s. v. *sha*, says that *sha mu* is "a species of pine from Ngan-hwui," and *sha t'ang* "a valuable timber tree brought from Tibet, whose soft, berry-shaped fruit tastes like a plum." See E. C. Baber, in "Proc. Roy. Geog. Soc.," V, 674. This same author, in "Travels and Researches in Western China," p. 75, gives *tchu si* as the Sifan (of Tzu-ta-ti) name of "buried pine." This word is most likely Tibetan *ch'u shing*, literally "water log." It is possibly the *Cedrus deodara* so common on the southern slopes of the Himalayas. It is also found in the Ch'ien-chang. See Alex. Hosie, "Three Years in Western China," p. 114.

of labor his little indebtedness, he at least eventually gains freedom; but such is not the case with most of the slaves in the Tsarong, who are taken from among the Lissus and other non-Tibetan tribes inhabiting the country. When one of these is in debt to a Tibetan and unable to meet the demands of his creditor, he becomes his "life servant" (*ts'é yo*). The master has the right to sell, kill, or otherwise dispose of him; he is given a wife, or a share in a woman, and all the children born to him are slaves. Even if he should be able to get together enough to pay off his debt, the master may refuse it and count his labor as only a set-off for the interest of the sum due. The missionaries have bought and freed a number of these *ts'é yo*, but usually they have been able to buy only slave children; this class of persons have formed the nucleus of several of their little Christian communities.

While at Ta-chien-lu I learnt some further details concerning the Tibetan customs relating to the disposal of the dead. No funeral services take place before the crops have been gathered, except in the case of very poor people, whose corpses are thrown into the streams at once after death. All those bodies which are to be disposed of by cremation or by being fed to birds or dogs are put in wicker baskets, well salted, and kept until the time of the funeral. In the case of the bodies of rich laymen which have been cremated, the ashes are sometimes collected in a box and a *do-bong* built over it, but generally they are left on the spot where the cremation took place. When the body is to be devoured by dogs and birds of prey the usual method is to lay the naked corpse on the ground, fastening it by a rope tied to a stake so that it cannot be dragged about. But there is another more *recherché* and desirable mode sometimes followed, as was done some years ago with the body of the "living Buddha" at Lit'ang. This was carried out of the lamasery on a stretcher which was followed by the abbot and his 3500 monks. Many of the latter (probably *ri-tru-ba*, or ascetics) had human jaw-bones fastened to their left arms, and skull-bowls hanging from their sides. The procession marched slowly to the top of a hill outside the town; the corpse was laid on the ground, and the abbot took his seat on a stone near-by. Then some lamas stripped the flesh off the body, commencing with the arms, and handed the pieces to the abbot. These he held at arm's length in the air, when vultures, which were sailing around in expectation of the feast, swooped down and snatched them from his hand. In this manner all but the bones were disposed of; then these were pounded into a pulp, and the abbot mixed this with tsamba in his eating-bowl, and fed the balls thus made to the birds, reserving for his own private delectation the last ball of the unsavory mess.[1] With this the ceremony was at an end. This form of obsequies, known as "celestial interment," is the most esteemed.[2]

One of the first questions I asked Mgr. Biet was concerning the mysterious Indian traveler who in 1882 had

[1] Among many resemblances between Tibetan and Korean Buddhism it is of interest to note that the bodies of Korean Buddhist monks are burned and that the ashes mixed with rice-flour are fed to birds.

[2] This and the other modes of disposing of the dead obtaining in Tibet may naturally have arisen among a semi-nomadic people, in a cold, rocky country, where burial of the dead would be attended with much difficulty. The reason for the preference given to the "celestial interment" is, I believe, found in the lamaist theory of the "intermediate state" (*bar-do*) between death and regeneration, which it is most desirable to shorten. Its length depends on the time requisite for the complete dissolution of the body, which here means its digestion by the birds, dogs, or fishes. So by feeding it to birds the period of *bar-do* is reduced to a minimum; dogs come next, and

reached Ta-chien-lu, coming from the Ts'aidam by the same route I had recently followed, and who had made an excellent survey of the country. To the outer world he is known only as Pundit A—— K——, or Krishna, and the greater part of the results of his wonderful four years' journey, in which he crossed Tibet from north to south, and from east to west, has been carefully pigeonholed by the Indian government, the method always followed by it where the work of any of the native explorers attached to the Great Trigonometrical Survey is concerned. If any British explorer had done one-third of what Nain Singh, lama Urjyen jyats'o, Sarat Chandra Das, or Kishen Singh (*alias* A—— K——), accomplished, medals and decorations, lucrative offices and professional promotion, freedom of cities, and every form of lionizing would have been his; as for those native explorers a small pecuniary reward and obscurity are all to which they can look forward.

A—— K—— reached Ta-chien-lu on the 9th of February, 1882, in a penniless condition, after traveling from Sa Chou in the capacity of mule-driver with a Tibetan trader. For days he hung around the door of the bishop's house, afraid to disclose his identity, lest the Tibetans should learn his true character. Finally he gained admission to Mgr. Biet, and told his story. He was most anxious to return to India through China, but the bishop dissuaded him, advised him to try and reach Assam

nibbling fishes last in the line of professional resurrectionists. In the case of some of the highest lamas, as the Talé lama, or Pan-ch'en Rinpoch'é, the body is mummified in the dry air of the country, wrapped in silks and satins, and placed in a monument.

Mortuary services are held by the lamas at the houses of the deceased, to propitiate the judge in hell (*Shinjé jyabo*), who weighs in his balance the good and evil deeds of the dead. The length of these services is regulated by that of the purse of the deceased's relatives: one hundred days for the richest; forty-nine or twenty-one for well-to-do persons; seven, three, or one day for the poor.

through the Zayul, and gave him money to help him on. He was a very clever young fellow, a native of Kumaon in British Tibet. During the greater part of his journey he had passed himself off as a peddler, carrying his sextant, aneroid, etc., in a roll of pulo. His survey, as far as I was able to control it, is wonderfully accurate. Unfortunately the names on his map had been so badly transcribed that they were absolutely unrecognizable by any of the people of the country. This is the more to be regretted as probably the fault does not lie with Kishen Singh, whose native language is Tibetan, but with those who transcribed his notes.

In a preceding chapter I have attempted to give an idea of the political and social organization of K'amdo or eastern Tibet. A few notes on the form of government existing in the kingdom of Lh'asa find place here:

In 1751, the Chinese army having quelled a rebellion in Tibet fomented by the king, Jyur-mé nam-jyal, the Emperor abolished the royal dignity and put the government in the hands of a council of ministers (*Ka-lön*), over which presided a lama, popularly known as "King of Tibet." This was made an elective office, the incumbent to be chosen in turn from one of the three great lamaseries of Drébung, Gadän, or Séra. To insure an uninterrupted succession, two lamas were chosen, one to reign as viceroy of the Talé lama, the other to live in a cloister (*réchu gomba*) surrounded with all the pomp of royalty, awaiting the death of the first-mentioned so as to succeed him; until this time came he was cut off absolutely from the outer world. This mode of selecting the *Peu-gi jyabo*, or "King of Tibet," has been retained to the present day, and I was assured that these elections are often the cause of great rioting among the lamas of the convents interested in the question, and have several times ended in serious loss of life. Usually the Chinese Amban intervenes, and puts a stop to the quarrel by giving his *placet* (subject to the final sanction of the Emperor) to the candidate whose party pays him the largest sum of money.[1]

Subordinate to the Peu-gi jyabo, but acting in conjunction with him, are the four ministers or Ka-lön (also called *Shapé*), chosen from among the most influential or wealthy laymen. Their appointments are also subject to the approval of the Emperor of China.[2]

Furthermore, as a means of preventing the office of Talé lama and of other incarnations falling into the hands of a powerful family, possibly inimical to China, the Emperor Ch'ien-lung instituted the system of the "golden vase" (*sér-gi bum-ba*), by which lots are drawn by all the candidates for such dignities, the name of the successful one being submitted to the Emperor, who, if it meets his approval, issues a patent of investiture.[3]

1 The "king of Tibet" is usually called Chyidrung Hutuketu (*p'yi-blon*, "Minister of Foreign Affairs") in Chinese documents, to which title is frequently added that of "President of the Treasury." He is furthermore called in Tibetan *Jyats'a* (*rgyal-ts'ab*), or "Viceroy," a word not to be confounded with the Mongol *Dsassak*, though frequently transcribed like it. *Cf.* what is related in the Appendix, p. 382, about the two queens of the old Tibetan country called by the Chinese Tung Nü kuo.

2 This organization of the Ka-lön dates only from 1792. See "Hsi-yü k'ao-ku-lu," Book VI, 14. For further details see "Tibet, a geographical, ethnographical and historical sketch," by W. W. Rockhill, in Journal Roy. Asiatic Soc., 1891.

3 See "Hsi-yü k'ao-ku-lu," Book VI, p. 14. The following Memorial addressed in 1879 by the Amban at Lh'asa to the Emperor is of interest. It refers to the enthronement of the present Talé lama. Sung Kuei, the Amban, memorializes the throne, as follows: "The Chyidrung Hutuketu, the President of the Treasury, has respectfully represented that, in reverent conformity with existing regulations, the reëmbodiment of the Talé lama should be enthroned at the age of four years. The reëmbodiment of the thirteenth generation of the Talé lama having now attained the age of four years, and being possessed of extraordinary spiritual gifts and intelligence that have aroused the most eager hopes and expectations of the clergy and laity, the spirits have now

It is only since 1793 that the Chinese Amban in Tibet has taken an active part in the administration of the country. The colonial office of Peking (*Li-fan-yüan*) has the general superintendence of Tibetan affairs, but it is the governor-general of Ssŭ-ch'uan who is the immediate superior of the Amban. To him the Amban reports his actions; of him he asks instructions, even sends him copies of his despatches to Peking. The regulations of the colonial office[1] contain the following rules for the guidance of the Amban in his relations with the native authorities:

"He is to consult with the Talé lama or the Pan-ch'en Rinpoch'é on a footing of perfect equality on all local questions brought before them. All officials from the rank of Ka-lön down, and all ecclesiastics holding offices, must submit to him for his decision all questions of whatever nature they be. He must watch over the condition of the frontier defenses, inspect the different garrisons, control the finances, and direct Tibet's relations with peoples living outside its border. Whenever vacancies occur among the Ka-lön, or Sha-dso-pa (treasury assistants), a report is to be made to the Amban, who, in conjunction with the Talé lama, will select suitable persons to fill the

been reverently appealed to in a special manner [this oracle is the Na-ch'ung ch'ü-jong], and the gods have been solemnly invoked [with a view to selecting a date for the ceremony] by genuine and earnest divination. The result has shown that the only superlatively auspicious date is the 13th of July, and it is accordingly proposed to go forth on that day to meet the reëmbodiment of the Talé lama and bring him to Mount Potala for enthronement, that the hopes of all may be fulfilled. . . . The memorialist would humbly observe that the matter of the enthronement of the Talé lama, being regarded throughout Tibet as an auspicious and glorious rite, it is necessary that extra care and attention be shown."

In another memorial the Amban says that on the 14th of June he sent "civil and military officers with soldiers, etc., to take charge of the Imperial gifts (to the Talé lama). They were placed under a yellow canopy and sent to the Zamatog temple at Joshag (at the foot of Mount Potala), where they will be received by the reëmbodiment as he kneels upon his knees and prostrates himself with his face turned towards the Imperial Palace in thanks for the Heavenly bounty."

1 "Li-fan-yüan tse-li," Books 61–62.

offices. These positions cannot be held by relatives of the Talé lama.

"The money in the Tibetan treasury for the pay of native troops is to be used only for that purpose under instructions from the Amban; and, even in relations with foreign nations, the Talé lama must do nothing without his sanction. The relations of the Gorkhas of Nepal with Tibet are under the supervision of the Amban. When this people bring products of their country to the Talé lama and the Pan-ch'en Rinpoch'é, return presents are necessary, and the Amban must decide as to their nature"; and so for all foreign tribes (the British not excepted).

Further on we read that "although the Ka-lön are the ministers of state of the Talé lama, they may not hold direct intercourse with the tribes outside the frontier. Should these tribes have occasion to write to the Ka-lön, the latter must forward the letters to the Amban, and he, acting in concert with the Talé lama, will prepare answers, but the Ka-lön must not answer them directly. Should letters be exchanged surreptitiously between the Ka-lön and tribes beyond the frontiers, the Amban will remove them from office at once."

The same authoritative work supplies us with some interesting details of the revenues and expenses of the Lh'asa government: "The Tibetan people have to pay annually to their government a certain amount, *per capita*, of grain, cloth, incense sticks, cotton cloth, salt, butter, cheese, dressed mutton, tea, etc. In view, however, of the frequent remoteness of their habitations and the difficulty of transporting goods, they are allowed to pay the equivalent in money. Any family owning cattle or sheep may pay as tax one silver coin (or *tranka*) a year for every two head of cattle, or ten head of sheep. The people can also give, whenever and in such amounts as they choose, money or goods as voluntary gifts to the state.

"Exclusive of the products of the country paid in to the government as taxes, the annual revenue in money amounts to probably 127,000 ounces of silver (about $177,800). All products and money received as taxes are stored away in the treasury in the Jo k'ang (in Lh'asa) and are under the control of three Sha-dso-pa (treasurers). As to the cloth, incense, and money, received as fines, as well as the various donations and the half of the estates, both real and personal, of deceased persons, they are placed in the chief treasury under the care of two other Sha-dso-pa. The Talé lama draws from these two treasuries for governmental and other expenses.

TAMDRIN. (GILT BRONZE. MADE AT LH'ASA.)

"The annual expenses of the Lh'asa government may be estimated as follows: In the first moon of the year the lamas of Potala, as well as all those from the various temples and lamaseries of Lh'asa, and from all Anterior and Ulterior Tibet, amounting to several myriads,[1] assemble in the Jo k'ang to read the sacred books for twenty days. In the second moon there is another gathering at the Jo k'ang, for the same purpose, which lasts eight days.[2] For these two celebrations some 70,900 ounces of silver (about $100,000) are used in giving the assembled lamas money, k'atag, butter, tea, tsamba, etc. Besides this,

1 At Lh'asa alone there are over 32,000 lamas.

2 This festival is called *Sung ch'ü*.

the daily religious services of the year at Lh'asa absorb some 39,200 ounces of silver (say $55,000) for supplying the officiating lamas with butter, tea, and various presents. Finally, 24,400 ounces of silver ($34,160) are required yearly for providing the lamas of Potala with food and other necessaries, and for the purchase of objects to be given as return presents to persons making offerings to the Talé lama.

"It thus appears that the expenditures are greater than the receipts. Moreover, there are the lamas of the great lamaseries of Séra, Gadän, Drébung, etc., who have to be provided for.

"When the harvest has been abundant, voluntary gifts to government are very numerous, and there is a surplus. Now in the chief treasury there is a minor or special treasury over which is a Sha-dso-pa, and every year, if there is a balance left over in the chief treasury, it is put away in this minor one. The Sha-dso-pa, having general supervision over all expenditures and receipts, make, in conjunction with the Ka-lön, reports to the Amban on the condition of the treasuries.

"Concerning moneys necessary for governmental expenses, to be withdrawn from the chief treasury, the Amban must examine, in conjunction with the Chyidrung Hutuketu (*i. e.*, the King of Tibet), into the nature of the expenses and resources. Any malversation must be at once reported by the Chyidrung Hutuketu to the Amban, whose duty it is to investigate the matter and inflict the prescribed penalty.

"As regards the people of Ulterior Tibet, they pay into the chief treasury (of their province) taxes in grain and money, but the larger portion is paid in kind. Taking into account both the products and money received, the annual receipts are about 66,900 ounces of silver (about $94,000). Formerly, voluntary gifts so increased the sum that there was annually a surplus, but since the Gorkha war (1794) the regular revenues, together with the voluntary gifts, about balance the expenditures. The Amban, acting in conjunction with the Chyidrung Hutuketu, must carefully examine the budget of Ulterior Tibet so that it always balances."

The authority of the Emperor's representative extends even to ecclesiastical appointments, for we learn from the same work that "When there occurs a vacancy among the K'anpo lamas, or abbots of the large lamaseries, the Talé lama informs the Amban of the fact, and they, having consulted with the Hutuketu under whose supervision the lamasery where the vacancy has occurred is placed, choose a new incumbent, to whom a seal of office and a patent of investiture are given, and who thereafter resides in the lamasery.

"When vacancies occur among the K'anpo of minor lamaseries, the Talé lama fills them as he sees fit."

I cannot enter here into a complete discussion of our sources of information concerning the population of Central and Ulterior Tibet. Recent writers estimate it at from four to six millions,[1] but these figures are certainly mere guesses. The latest general census of the country of which I have any knowledge was made by the Chinese in 1737; partial enumerations have been made since then, and wherever I have been able to compare the figures thus obtained with those supplied us by recent travelers I have found the former in excess of the latter. The census of 1737 fixes the population of the kingdom

[1] See C. H. Desgodins, "Le Thibet," p. 241, and "Encyclopædia Britannica," ninth edition; article, Tibet.

of Lh'asa, or Anterior and Ulterior Tibet, at 852,162 laity, and 316,200 lamas. It is highly probable that a large portion of the nomads were not counted, but this would not make a difference of 50,000, so it would seem that in the middle of last century the total population of Central Tibet did not exceed a million and a half.[1] What can have been the rate of increase of the population in the past 150 years, is the next question to inquire into. The steady increase in the number of lamas, the polyandrous marriages and general promiscuity in the relations of the sexes, the fearful and frequent ravages of small-pox, the enslaved state of a large portion of the people in the most fertile parts of the country, and other causes too numerous to mention, tend to prove that the increase has been undoubtedly of the smallest, and we positively know that in many localities there has been a notable decrease. I am thus led to believe that even the estimate of 4,000,000 by Father Desgodins is largely in excess of the truth, and that the total population of all Tibet (inclusive of Lahul, Sikkim, etc.), the Koko-nor, and K'amdo (the non-Tibetan tribes living in the southern part of the country, in the Tsarong, Zayul, Poyul, etc., excluded), will not much exceed 3,500,000 souls, of which about 2,000,000 inhabit the kingdom of Lh'asa.

I remained at Ta-chien-lu until the 10th of July awaiting the arrival of the men I had left behind at Jyékundo, but, getting no news of them, I finally made up my mind to leave for Ya-chou Fu. They reached Ta-chien-lu a few days after my departure, yet were unable to catch up with me, and I came home without ever seeing them again; but from a letter received since my return to the

[1] Nari k'a sum, or northwest Tibet, is inhabited mostly by nomads, so its population is certainly small.

United States I have learned of some of their adventures, and they prove how well my Chinese friends at Jyékundo advised me when they said to push on without delay. It will be remembered that shortly after my arrival at Jyékundo the chief of that locality went to Tendo to concert with other chiefs as to the best way to treat me. On his return he found that I had left, so he sent out men with orders to stop me dead or alive, and had my men seized, heavily chained, and locked up. After the lapse of twelve days, my friend Fu T'ung-shih fortunately arrived, and with much trouble had them finally released, given a guide, and started down the road I had followed.

Some two or three days below Jyékundo the lamas of a convent seized them, and, forcing them to abandon their horses and luggage, carried them off to the lamasery, where they were again imprisoned. This time they bought their freedom by paying a considerable sum of money, but when they got back to their camp they found that two of their horses had been killed by wolves. They pushed on, however, and after sundry other adventures reached Kanzé, where they were most kindly received by Lieutenant Lu, who sent them on, after a few days' rest, to Ta-chien-lu. Considering what those Chinese had to suffer from the lamas, one can imagine how pleasant these would have made it for me if they had laid hands on me. The old K'amba in Mar-jya-kou had said with truth: "Your only chance to get through K'amdo is to travel without losing a minute on the way."

VII

TA-CHIEN-LU, YA-CHOU, CH'UNG-CH'ING, I-CH'ANG, SHANGHAI

ON July 10 I left Ta-chien-lu, comfortably seated in a roomy sedan-chair, borne rapidly along by four coolies. Our first day's march took us to Wa-ssŭ-k'ou, where the Ta-chien-lu River (Do ch'u) empties into the T'ung,[1] the road running down a narrow rocky gorge, the mountains rising perpendicularly on either side to a height of several thousand feet. Here and there, huge masses of rock detached from the cliffs had been precipitated into the stream below, which broke in a mass of foam and spray over them as it dashed in a succession of cascades down the rapid descent. At short distances the stream was spanned by rope-bridges. A stout bamboo rope was anchored with heavy rocks on either side of the stream; a piece of bamboo about eighteen inches long, from which depended a sling used as a seat, and a small hand-line to drag oneself along by, completed one of these primitive contrivances, which are in common use all along the Tibetan border-land.

This "highroad" is practicable for only foot-travelers and pack-animals, but even the sure-footed mule cannot travel such trails with ease or rapidity; few are seen, and I experienced much difficulty in getting my horse along.[2]

[1] This river is also called Ta-tu ho, or Mo shui.

[2] Between Ta-chien-lu and Ya-chou I saw not more than thirty pack animals, and no saddle ones.

Between Ta-chien-lu and Wa-ssŭ-k'ou, a distance of about eighteen miles, there is a rapid but steady descent of over three thousand feet. Wherever possible the soil is cultivated, Indian corn being the principal crop. Fine walnut-trees, willows, and poplars grow in profusion on the south side of the valley; and in the innumerable tea-houses and inns which border the way coolies were resting, their heavy loads propped up on the long, low benches lining the walls. Most of them were carrying tea from Ya-chou, or the neighboring towns, to Ta-chien-lu, a distance of about one hundred and fifty miles, which they make in seventeen or eighteen days. They were of all ages, and I was surprised to notice quite a number of women among them.

The average load is nine packages (*pao*) of tea, or 190 to 200 pounds, but I saw several men who had seventeen packages (over 300 pounds), and, strangely enough, these men did not appear to be the most muscular; in fact, I was told that there was a great knack in carrying these heavy loads so that the weight should press equally along the back.[1] The parcels of tea are placed evenly, one above the other, the upper ones projecting so as to come slightly over the porter's head; they are held tightly together by little bamboo stakes and coir ropes. A sling, also made of coir, holds the load on his back; and a string is fastened to the top of it, by means of which he balances it. A short, strong wooden crutch is used by all porters to assist them along the steep mountain roads, and to put under their loads when they want to rest without taking them off their backs. I never saw any of these Ya-chou tea coolies using wooden frameworks

[1] Kirkpatrick, "Account of the Kingdom of Nepaul," p. 373, says that the hill-porters of that country carry 230 to 305 pounds over rough mountain roads.

to fasten their loads on, although I find that Cooper and Baber say they do. When carrying other kinds of goods, iron or cotton, flour or wine, they have framework sup-

ALONG THE T'UNG HO. TEA PORTERS ON THE ROAD TO TA-CHIEN-LU.

ports for the loads, like those used in Switzerland, and I have even seen them carrying old men or women in this way. These coolies are credited with feats of strength, or dexterity, which simply seem incredible. One of them carried an iron safe weighing over four hundred pounds to Ta-chien-lu for Monseigneur Biet; it is true that he died shortly after from the effects of this journey. Women frequently carry seven or eight packages of tea, and I have seen children of six or seven with a package, or a package and a half, trudging along behind their parents.

The regular pay for tea coolies is two mace (about twenty-five cents) a package, irrespective of weight, from Ya-chou to Ta-chien-lu. They live on maize cakes and vegetables, with now and then a little pork. The greater part of them smoke opium, and do not appear to be at all the worse for it. I saw but few with varicose veins, or showing in any marked manner that this severe labor was injurious to their general health. Nor are these men employed in this trade all the year; nearly all of them are peasants, who resort to it only as a means of gaining a livelihood when there is nothing to be done on their little farms, or when these are so small that their women can manage them. Some idea of the number of these porters on the road between Ta-chien-lu and Ya-chou may be formed from the fact that between Wa-ssŭ-k'ou and Lu-ting ch'iao (about fifteen miles) I counted 481 carrying tea, and there were perhaps 40 or 50 more loaded with sundry other goods, flour, wines, etc.; and along the whole route they were quite as numerous. I was told that at nearly any time of the year the road was as crowded as when I traveled over it.

Wa-ssŭ-k'ou is prettily situated amidst fields of paddy and of maize, and is surrounded with wide-spreading walnut-trees; and a few miles below this place I saw a profusion of peach-trees with fine large fruit on them.

The T'ung River comes from the north, and drains

the Chin ch'uan, a country which I referred to previously, and which is celebrated in Chinese history as the scene of one of the most brilliant and difficult campaigns of the Emperor Ch'ien-lung against the Tibetan mountaineers who inhabit it. At Wa-ssŭ-k'ou the T'ung is about seventy yards wide, not very deep, but swift and muddy. No marks along its banks indicate that the water ever reaches a very great height. In fact, the idea that the great and sudden freshets which occur in western China are caused by the melting of the snow on the mountains of eastern Tibet, or by the great rainfall in that country, is an entirely erroneous one. The freshets there are due to the violent and nearly continuous rains which fall in the mountainous regions east of Tibet—in northern and western Ssŭ-ch'uan — during the late spring and summer.

From Wa-ssŭ-k'ou the road lay along the right bank of the T'ung, on the steep mountain sides, in places 600 to 800 feet above the river, and in parts so narrow that two loaded coolies could not pass each other. The path was roughly paved with flagstones, and, taking it altogether, was a fairly good one. In many places traveling along it presents considerable danger, for rocks and small stones are continually falling from the hillsides, and after any heavy rain land-slides are of frequent occurrence. Thus, at a village a couple of miles above Lu-ting ch'iao, I found three or four feet of mud in the houses, brought down by a short but violent rain on the previous day. The mistaken removal of all timber and brushwood from the mountain sides is the cause of these accidents.

The Lu-ting ch'iao is one of the most famous suspension-bridges in China. It was built in 1701, is about 370 feet long and 10 feet broad, and is the only one which crosses the T'ung River, here also known as the Lu shui.

The bridge consists of nine chains of inch iron, the links five inches long. On either side are two other chains bound to the lower ones by light iron rods, forming a very imperfect guard. Upon the lower chains are narrow planks, not even fastened down, and over this frail roadway men and animals continually cross. At either end of the bridge are an archway, a gate, and a small guard-house. The chains of the bridge are attached to large windlasses under these archways, and can be tightened whenever necessary, so that the bridge is nearly horizontal. The vibration felt in crossing it is quite strong, and if a good wind is blowing through the gorge one might well feel nervous if one had to venture across, but I believe that when the wind causes the bridge to swing too much the gates at the ends are closed. Cooper's story that the bridge is shut every day from noon to 4 P. M., on account of a terrific wind which daily sweeps down the gorge,[1] is not to be implicitly accepted. Nor can his statement that there are probably eight thousand inhabitants in the villages at either end of the bridge be credited, unless things have changed very much since his time. There are certainly not over one thousand inhabitants, soldiers included, in these two villages.

A couple of miles below the bridge, on the right bank of the river, is a small Christian community called Sha-pa. I left my chair and servant at Lu-ting ch'iao, and walked down to pass the night with Father Mussot. Around the vicarage is a fine vegetable garden, and I noticed in it pomelo and lemon trees laden with fruit, but I was told that it never matured.[2]

1 T. T. Cooper, "Travels of a Pioneer of Commerce," p. 197.

2 Although pomelo and bananas do not ripen in Ssŭ-ch'uan, lichees come to great perfection. Not far to the west of Ch'ung-ch'ing there is an orchard of lichee-trees whose fruit is sent to the Emperor at Peking. I

From Lu-ting ch'iao we followed the left bank of the river for about fifteen miles, the path running along the mountain sides, several hundred feet above the stream, till we reached Leng-ch'i, a lively and dirty market-town.

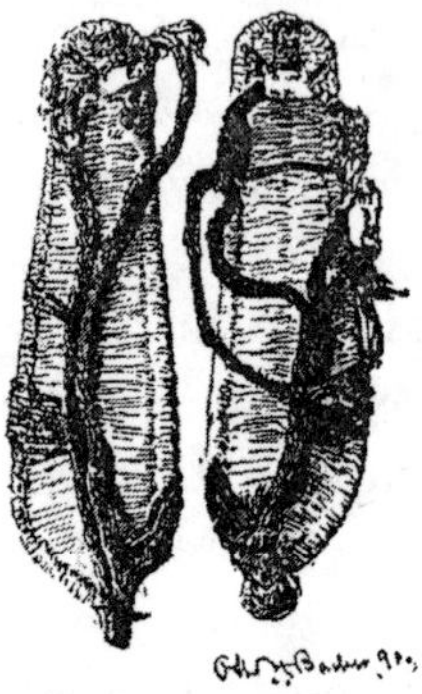

SSŬ-CH'UAN STRAW SANDALS.

About a mile and a half beyond it we left the valley of the T'ung, and ascended another, leading east, as far as the village of Hua-lin-p'ing. At the mouth of this valley is a small village called T'u-ssŭ; I suppose that it is here the native chief (*T'u-ssŭ*) of Leng-pien resides.[1] Below Lu-ting, mulberry-trees are numerous, and the fields are planted with Indian corn and sorghum, and beans between the rows; near Hua-lin-p'ing I noticed a good deal of hemp. For the last three or four miles before reaching the latter place, the road was very steep but fairly good, and tea-houses were so numerous along it that one could rest whenever the least tired. Excellent peaches and apricots were for sale everywhere, and in the inns I got capital vermicelli (*kua mien*), so I fared sumptuously. The peaches from Lu-ting ch'iao were the finest I ate in China, and compared favorably with our own.

A few miles above Hua-lin-p'ing we reached by an extremely steep ascent, more properly by a long flight of irregular steps, the top of the Fei-yüeh ling,[2] where the road passes through double gateways, between which

never heard of lichees being sold in any locality in Ssŭ-ch'uan, but the Bishop at Ch'ung-ch'ing vouched for the imperial lichee-grove.

1 The Leng-pien and Shen-pien aborigines are now undistinguishable from the Chinese. In the last century their country formed a part of the principality of Ming-cheng (or Chala). The Shen-pien people may not be of Tibetan stock, but Chinese writers say that those of Leng-pien are.

2 Baber gives its altitude as 9410 feet; Gill, 9022 feet.

is a guard-house. This mountain is also frequently called Ch'ia-tzŭ shan, and Gill speaks of it as the Wu-yai ling. As we were slowly ascending the mountain, I saw a ho-shang coming down. In his hand was a small stool on which were fastened two little metal vases with joss-sticks burning in them; at every two steps he put this altar on the ground and made a full-length prostration before it, being careful to do so facing westward. He was on his way to Lh'asa, and proposed to cover the whole distance thither, making a prostration every two steps. He had come from P'u-to shan (in the Chusan Archipelago near Ning-po), and had been seven years traveling thus far; but he was very cheerful, and said he hoped to reach Lh'asa in two or three years more. He carried with him letters from the abbots of different convents where he had stopped to rest his wearied limbs, attesting the truth of his story, and recommending him to the charity of travelers. He was a good-natured, lively fellow,[1] and this hard work did not appear to have been at all injurious to him, for he was fat and ruddy, but I felt sorry for him all the same.

The descent on the eastern side of the mountain is more precipitous and longer than that on the western, and much more fatiguing, as the path is roughly paved with granite boulders, and it is slow and fatiguing work, jumping down from one to the other. The mountain sides were thickly covered with scrub and a great variety of ferns and flowering plants, and looked very lovely in the bright sunshine. From the top of the pass I could see Ni-t'ou about fifteen miles down the valley. Although the Fei-yüeh pass is high and rugged, it is not quite as bad as Chinese itineraries make it out to be. One of

[1] See frontispiece.

them[1] describes it as follows: "This mountain is exceedingly precipitous; everywhere on it wonderful masses of crags and boulders strike the traveler's gaze. The whole year it is covered with ice and snow, and clouds hang perpetually over it. The road at its base seems to lead over piled-up clouds,"—not a bad simile for a path over granite boulders.

At Fu-lung ssŭ, a little village three miles below the pass, the hillsides are cultivated, and among other crops I noticed buckwheat. We reached Ni-t'ou in the afternoon of July 13, and found it a good-sized, lively town, with excellent inns, numerous and well-supplied shops. The innkeeper came in, shortly after my arrival, to have a bit of gossip, and told me, among other things, that the prettiest girl of the place had just been sold to a man as his concubine for Tls. 50, a wonderfully good price. Twenty taels is a very fair price for a girl, and at Shih-chia ch'iao (near Ya-chou) I saw a merchant of Ta-chien-lu taking home with him a very handsome one whom he had bought for that price.

The Ssŭ-ch'uanese are very much given to selling their superfluous girls, and numbers are exported annually from Ch'ung-ch'ing for places down the river, for Hankow, Shanghai, and other large cities. On my way down from Hankow to Shanghai I saw a man on board the steamer, who had eleven girls he had bought in Ch'ung-ch'ing for prices ranging from Tls. 7 to 11 apiece. These slaves are usually bought when very young, eight to ten years, and brought up with care by the owner's family, being treated exactly as his own children, and generally

[1] "Wei-ts'ang t'u chih," Bk. I. Cooper, *op. cit.*, p. 178, gives a very highly colored description of the dangers he experienced in crossing this mountain.

receive a good education. When they have learnt all the accomplishments expected of girls, they are sold to be the second wives (*ch'ieh*) of any men who may purchase them. The trade has absolutely nothing cruel or inhuman in it; the children are reared in much greater comfort than if left in their homes, and their after-lives are quite as happy and respected as they could fairly expect.

At Ni-t'ou we left the valley, which we had followed from the top of the Fei-yüeh ling, and continued in a due easterly direction over a series of mountains, the last and highest being the Seng-nei kuan. We reached Ch'ing-ch'i Hsien just as a violent rain commenced falling. Although the town is very small, the inns are capital, and I did not feel at all sorry when, waking the next morning, I found it still raining in torrents and I had to order a halt for the day. The fame of Ch'ing-ch'i rests on its being the windiest place in western Ssŭ-ch'uan. "Ch'ing-ch'i wind, Yung-ching drought, Ya-chou rain" (*Ch'ing feng, Yung kan, Ya shui*), say the people, referring to the climatic peculiarities of the three principal localities in this neighborhood.

Between Ni-t'ou and Ch'ing-ch'i I saw numbers of water buffaloes, which are not met with farther west. The ordinary domestic cattle are small, but extremely well-shaped; in color, solid dark-red, running into black around the eyes, at the pasterns and the nose, with fine, soft coats, small ears, and thin tails. I was surprised to see as many of them as I did, for they are not used as pack or draught animals, and the Chinese hardly ever eat their flesh. The ordinary food of the Ssŭ-ch'uanese consists of maize bread, bean curd (*t'ou-fu*), rice, vegetables, and a little boiled pork.

From Ch'ing-ch'i Hsien a rapid ascent by a large number of zigzags brought us after three hours to the top of the Hsiang-ling shan.[1] The view from the summit would doubtless have been very fine, had not clouds filled the valleys on all sides and hid the landscape from us. My coolies insisted, nevertheless, that we were in good luck, for in nine cases out of ten, they said, it poured rain there, or else the fog was so dense that one could hardly find the way over the mountain. On the west side the slopes were rather bare, a little scrub here and there the only foliage to be seen. On the east side the descent was steep and the path very bad, paved with rough stones which the incessant rains of the last few days had made extremely slippery. It was cut in the steep mountain side, and so narrow that the chair could hardly be carried along it. In many places it crossed over little gullies on a single rotten plank, and here we had endless trouble getting Yi Hsien-sheng's horse along. Lower down we crossed the torrent which rushed through the gorge over huge masses of rock, on like primitive bridges, and it was only after much labor that we got the horse to Huang-ni P'u.[2] The vegetation as we descended became more and more rank and varied, till it assumed a truly semi-tropical luxuriance; at Huang-ni P'u I first saw tea shrubs and banana plants. This gorge is usually called Mu-kung-nai (pronounced *né*), and is the upper course of the Ta ho or Yung-ching River which empties into the Ya ho near Ya-chou Fu. The road was thronged with travelers, among them a number of coolies carrying wild silk, and coming from around Yüeh-hsi, at which place and at Hou-tao, T'ien-wau, Tzŭ-ta-ti, etc., it is very abundant.

[1] Cooper's Yang-Nin mountains. [2] Cooper's Quan yin foo.

During the day we crossed several small iron-chain suspension-bridges, and a short distance below Huang-ni P'u I saw spanning the river a fine one made of four round iron bars about 1½ inches in diameter. It was about a hundred and fifty feet long, and a remarkably fine and unique piece of work; how the bars were put in place puzzled me greatly.

Some five miles below Huang-ni P'u the valley broadened considerably; all the lowlands were taken up by paddy-fields, while the uplands were planted with Indian corn and beans, with tea-shrubs scattered here and there.

Yung-ching Hsien is, after Ch'ing-ch'i, the smallest prefectural town I have seen in China, but it is a lively place and an important tea-packing center, the value of this trade being nearly as great as that of the same in Ya-chou itself. In all the cottages by the way, tea leaves and twigs were piled up in huge heaps, or drying in the sun, and looking less like tea than anything one can imagine. At Yung-ching we crossed the river in a ferry-boat, and, after following it down on the left bank for a few miles, recrossed it and continued through the valley to Shih-chia ch'iao, where we put up in an excellent inn belonging to a member of the Shih family. My host, Mr. Shih, told me that it was customary for all the men in his family to take the degree of B. A., and that his son, whom I could hear conning over his books in the garret, was preparing to go up for his examination as *hs'iu-ts'ai.* This, in a little village lost in the mountains of western Ssŭ-ch'uan!

At Shih-chia ch'iao we left the valley of the Ta ho, and ascended a little side cañon which brought us after a few miles to the top of the Fei-lung-kuan. Down-hill again and the valley broadened, and I saw before me the walls of

Ya-chou Fu. Shortly before arriving at the city we passed under a beautiful *pai-lou* of red sandstone, nearly as fine as some I had seen in Shan-hsi, standing in front of a temple dedicated to Wu Hou. The western part of the city is built on the last declivity before reaching the Ya River, but the greater part of it is on the level.

As we entered Ya-chou I saw a line of coolies carrying the luggage of the Gorkha (Nepalese) mission to Ta-chien-lu, the same I had met the previous December at T'ung-kuan. They were expected in Ta-chien-lu in about a month, when they would take another good rest before starting for Lh'asa. There was no need to impress on them the Tibetan formula, *Kalé p'eb*, "Go slowly"; they seemed to have mastered all the intricacies of the *piano e sano* mode of traveling.

Through the kindness of Père Piault, the curé of Ya-chou, I was enabled to visit one of the large tea-packing establishments, in which, however, only the better qualities of brick tea were treated. The process, like all Chinese industrial methods, is simple in the extreme. The leaves, which have been in the first place allowed to ferment and have afterward been slightly fired, are sorted and steamed, after which they are packed in long bamboo baskets, sprinkled with rice-water, and put inside a wooden mold; they are next pressed into the baskets with a heavy iron-shod rammer, then dried over the fire and closed up. The packages are now ready for transportation to Ta-chien-lu. None of this brick tea can be bought at Ya-chou, or, indeed, at any locality east of Ta-chien-lu; but the native sun-dried *mao-pien* tea is used everywhere. The establishment I visited sold between 30,000 and 40,000 packages (each nominally of eighteen catties), a year, and there are about ten more firms in the city whose business ranges from 10,000 to 30,000 packages each. Most of these establishments (*ch'a-fang*) are owned by Shen-hsi people, and the profits realized are very considerable. The best brick tea is sold for Tls. 2 a *pao* at Ya-chou, or about Rs. 6. 8.[1]

The city of Ya-chou, though not very large, is quite an attractive place, and its broad, clean, well-paved streets, its good-natured, active people make a pleasing impression on the mind, but the constant dripping of rain is a little depressing. Rain had been falling in such quantity, prior to my arrival, that the authorities had had recourse to the most drastic measure known to them for putting an end to the deluge: they had closed the north gate of the city. This I was assured, was infallible; the rain could not continue falling when this gate was closed, and every one was convinced that fine weather would soon prevail.[2]

The day after my arrival at Ya-chou I hired a raft to take me down to Chia-ting Fu, at the confluence of the Fu and the T'ung rivers, for 2500 cash. The raft used is about thirty feet long and six feet wide, and made of two sets of bamboo poles, the forward one bent up into a rather sharp bow. Two or three men at the bow propel it with long oars, and it is steered with a long sweep; a mat awning covers the middle part. It is, on the whole, a safe, rapid, but wet conveyance. As it is impossible to cook anything on board, or even to sleep there, it is not to be recommended for ascending the river.

The swift current carried us rapidly along through a country of great natural beauty. On either side the

1 This I was told by the manager, but I think he exaggerated, as will appear from what I have said, p. 279, of the price of tea at Ta-chien-lu.

2 To stop a drought it is only necessary to close the southern gate.

red sandstone of the low hills cropped out here and there amidst the vivid greens of the luxuriant vegetation which covered the soil, while in the background rose the dark, cloud-capped mass of the mountains we had just crossed, between Ya-chou and Ta-chien-lu. The lowlands along the river were covered with paddy-fields; near every little white cottage a bunch of tall bamboo waved its long graceful plumes, and down innumerable gorges rushed, in

RAFT ON THE YA HO. (MT. O-MI IN BACKGROUND.)

a mass of silvery foam, torrents falling over the red cliffs into the river below. The long-leaved banana plant and "white-wax tree" each lent its distinctive color to the scene, which was of extreme beauty.

Some fifteen miles down, we swept through a sandstone gorge about two miles long, where the scenery was most gorgeous, beautiful hanging-plants and creepers growing from out the crevices in the red rocks, over which fell two torrents in a dazzling mist shimmering in the sunlight, making even my unemotional Hsien-sheng enthusiastic. Below these gorges the scenery became less attractive, but still very beautiful. The river was covered with rafts, the only crafts which can navigate its rocky, eddying course; and, though they cannot be upset and accidents are rare, yet the shaking and spinning about one gets aboard one of them in going through the whirlpools and over the sunken rocks which everywhere obstruct the stream, make the journey quite an exciting one, so when we reached Mu-ch'in-k'ai, I was glad to land and get a good night's rest in an inn.

The next day towards 10 A. M. I saw, some thirty miles away to the southwest, rising out of the plain, the rugged outline of the famous sacred mount O-mi, and a mile or two ahead of us on the left bank the walls of Chia-ting.

This town is at the confluence of the Fu with the T'ung and the Ya ho; and, like Sui Fu and Ch'ung-ch'ing, it is built on a rather high ledge of sandstone. The walls of red sandstone over which hang long creepers, looking like some old ivy-covered English ruin, and the thatched houses outside the city, in groves of bamboo and banana, contribute to make it a very picturesque locality. The city itself is not very large but is an important industrial center, silk and medicines being the principal branches of its trade; however, I was assured that the silk trade had suffered very much of late years, through the establishment of numerous additional likin barriers around the city, and that there were not half as many looms working at present as there used to be.

Here I hired a *wu-pan* (a small boat about thirty feet long) and a crew of three men, and left for Ch'ung-ch'ing. I paid 11,000 cash for the boat, the lowder supplying us with rice, fuel, etc.; and promising furthermore to get me to my destination in less than three days. Facing the city to the east is a high sandstone cliff, on the top of which stands a fine Buddhist temple. The face of the rock has been sculptured into innumerable bas-relief figures of the Buddha, and one part of it, where the rock has a cylindrical shape, has been roughly cut to represent a colossal image or head of the god. The temple is called the Ta Fo ssŭ, "Big Buddha Temple."

We dropped rapidly down the swollen Min, passing numbers of government salt-junks and other craft laden with various goods. The country along either side of the river is thickly populated, the largest and most lively commercial places not being the prefectural cities, apparently, but market towns and villages. The crops were slightly different from what we had found farther west; maize had now completely disappeared, and its place was taken by sugar-cane, kao-liang (sorghum), rice, and beans. Before night we reached the village of Chuo-ch'i, on the right bank, some twenty-five miles from Sui Fu.

The next morning we swept past Sui Fu and entered the Yang-tzŭ, or Ta-kuan ho, as it is generally called in these parts. From here to Ch'ung-ch'ing the river has been frequently traveled by foreigners, and has been so minutely described by Captain Blakiston that I cannot add anything of interest to what has already been said of it. Below Sui Fu we passed a number of large towns, but as we stopped at none I could form no idea of their relative importance. A little below Na-ch'i Hsien, at Ming-ai-t'ou, several ledges of sandstone stretch nearly across the river, and these constitute the only serious obstacle to navigation between Ch'ung-ch'ing and Sui Fu. Below this point the river makes a bend south before reaching Lu Chou, and we passed Nan-tien-p'a, a place famous for its iron-works, where the telegraph line to Yün-nan crosses the river. Here are turned out cast-iron evaporating pans used in the salt-works, some of enormous size; one cast here weighed, I was told, 1200 catties (1600 pounds). Lu Chou (a *chih-li Chou* or independent department) is a most important market for lumber, brought here principally from the Ho-chiang district. The city had been partially destroyed by fire a short time before I passed there, and looked most miserable; I trust it will rise from its ruins more beautiful and less smelly than when I saw it.

The following day we reached Chiang-ching Hsien, and on the morning of July 25 stopped before the T'ai-ping gate of Ch'ung-ch'ing, having come a distance of about three hundred and fifty miles in less than forty hours, propelled simply by the force of the current.

At Ch'ung-ch'ing I was received with the greatest kindness by H. B. M.'s Consular Agent, Mr. Henry Cockburn, in whose pretty cottage outside the city I passed ten most enjoyable days, which I shall always remember with the greatest pleasure. The whole day and greater part of the night were not sufficient for us to spin our interminable yarns, and if the river had continued at high-water mark I should have prolonged my stay with him for a month or so without a pang. Fortunately for Cockburn, the waters of the Chia-ling ho and of the Yang-tzŭ, which had been exceptionally high during the first part of my stay, fell sufficiently for me to start for I-ch'ang on the afternoon of August 4, in a *wu-pan* similar to that which had brought me from Chia-ting.

The trip down the swollen river was a most enjoyable one, with just enough of danger in it to give it zest. The swift, eddying current swept us along at a great rate, and the boatmen had nothing else to do than to keep the little craft out of the whirlpools which in many places nearly covered the surface of the river for miles in succession. The mountains on either side sloped rapidly upward, but everywhere the soil was planted with rice, sugar-cane, beans, etc., while trees, many of them bastard banyans, shaded the innumerable cottages and villages by which we swiftly ran. Now and then we passed heavily laden junks being slowly tracked up-river by a hundred or so of bare, sturdy boatmen, swinging their arms and singing as they tramped along. But there were comparatively few boats on the river, as navigation at that season of the year is attended with not a little danger for cargo boats. In fact, several of my kind friends at Ch'ung-ch'ing had strongly advised me not to try it, but, if I did, to be sure to land at the rapids and take to the boat again only at their lower end, as accidents were of daily occurrence.

On the third day out we came to Kuei-chou Fu, the frontier town of Ssŭ-ch'uan, about two hundred and ninety miles beyond Ch'ung-ch'ing; and a little below the town we entered the Wu-shan gorges. The river here dashes through a rift in the mountains, which tower above it a thousand feet, in many places overhanging the water. A road was being cut in the rock in this most difficult and dangerous place, and if it cannot assist trackers in hauling boats up the river, it will at all events be of great service to those who have to travel along the bank, and save them a long detour. Here the skill of the helmsman came in evidence, as with unerring precision he steered our cockle-shell from side to side so as to escape the eddies and whirlpools, which would have thrown us on some of the jagged rocks that we now and then saw jutting out of the muddy waters. Once a whirlpool caught us, and we were spun around so rapidly that,

MENDICANT TAOIST MONK.

dazed and sick, we sat crouching in the bottom of the boat till the men saw the whirlpool receding, when with a great shout they bent to the oars, and safely got us out. Fortunately the boat had got across the vortex, for had only its bow reached it we should have been swamped without a doubt. I laughed a little at the fear shown by the boatmen. "Like you, I laughed," remarked one of them, "the first time I came down the river, but years of work on it have taught me better, and I now venture on it only with fear, and because it is my sole means of livelihood."

We passed heavily laden boats working their way up-stream, amidst apparently insurmountable difficulties, the trackers now straining every muscle, now slacking up, as a man seated near the bow directed them by beating, slowly or fast, on a drum held between his knees. Every little while a man, especially appointed for that work, would calmly leap into the river, or clamber on to some precipitous rock, and clear the tow-line which had got foul. In this way the junks are got up to Ch'ung-ch'ing in from thirty to forty days from I-ch'ang.

Farther down we saw other junks preparing with much firing of crackers and burning of joss-paper to make the ascent, and near by were two or three life-boats, or "red boats" as they are called from their color, with crews always ready for an emergency. Below each of the rapids is a "red boat station," kept up by private subscription. The services they render, and the number of lives they save, are very considerable.

And so we floated rapidly on, stopping at night at some town or village, to buy food and get rest. Between the different gorges (of which there were five principal ones), the country was always very beautiful. Now and then some little valley opened on the river, and we could see pine-clad hills stretching far away, while villages, nearly hid in foliage, occupied every level bit of land; many were built even against the steep face of the hills overhanging the river. Occasionally I saw a wreck of some unfortunate boat, or some less unlucky one beached, its crew busily occupied removing its cargo, or repairing its battered hull.

As I sped swiftly down, I thought of the much vexed question of steam navigation on this part of the Yang-tzŭ, about which so much has been said and so little done, and my faith in the views of those who have so emphatically asserted its feasibility was severely shaken. The Wu-shan rapids appeared to be at least as formidable as the Lachine rapids of the St. Lawrence, and I should think that if steam navigation up the one has proved impracticable it will be found the same up the other. It took me ninety-six hours to come from Ch'ung-ch'ing to I-ch'ang, a distance of about four hundred and fifteen miles, out of which only fifty-seven were spent in floating down the river, an average speed of seven miles an hour—in many places we must have gone much faster, probably not less than ten or eleven miles. I should think it would be a difficult task to build any small steamboat capable of stemming such a current; for small and of light draft the boat must be.

At I-ch'ang, which I reached on August 8, my boat journey was at an end; and here also, as far as my readers are concerned, ceases the interest in my wanderings in the Chinese Empire. After a week most agreeably spent with Henry Fraser, H. B. M. Acting Consul, I left for Hankow; and a few days later I found myself once more in Shanghai, where the hearty hospitality of my friends left in my mind only like a sweet memory of the past, the tsamba, buttered tea, and other luxuries I had enjoyed in "The Land of the Lamas."

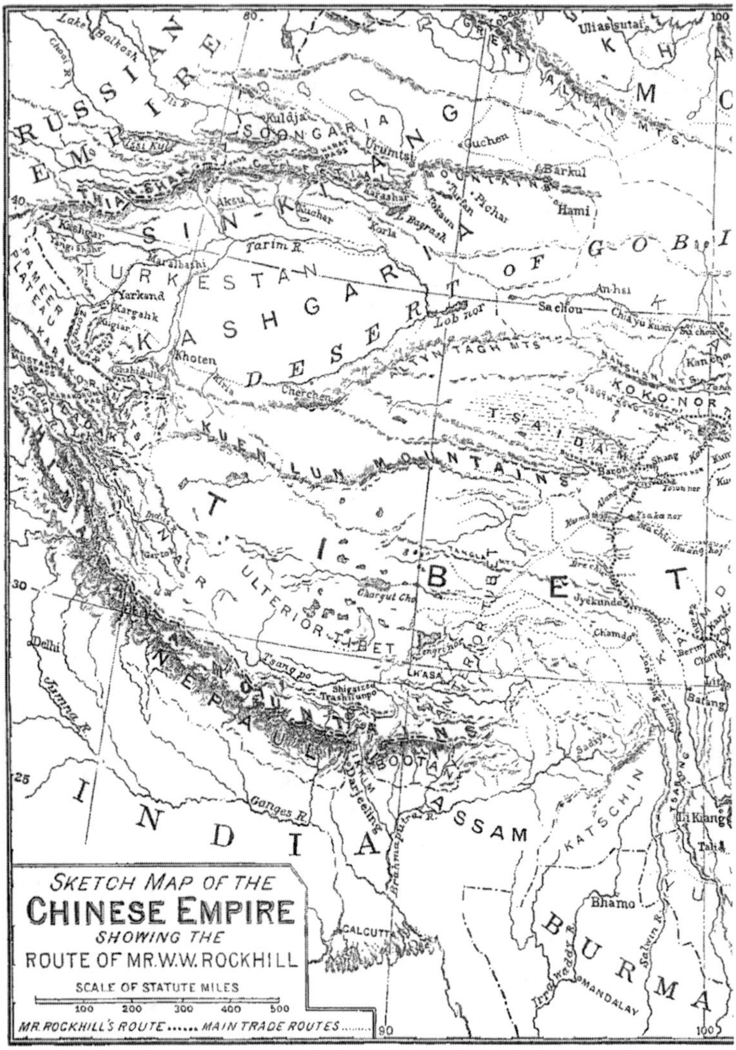

SKETCH MAP OF THE
CHINESE EMPIRE
SHOWING THE
ROUTE OF MR. W. W. ROCKHILL

SCALE OF STATUTE MILES
100 200 300 400 500

MR. ROCKHILL'S ROUTE ...... MAIN TRADE ROUTES ....

Urga
MANCHURIA
RUSSIAN EMPIRE
Vladivostok
Kirin
Mukden
SHING-KING
SHAMO
YELLOW SEA
COREA BAY
GULF OF PE-CHI-LI
Port Arthur
Seoul
Che-fu
Tientsin
PEKING
CHIH-LI
Pao-ting
Tai-yuan
Ping yang
ORDOS TRIBES
Ting yüan
Ning hsia
Lan chou
Hsi-an
Tung-kuan
Kai-feng
Chi-nan
Nanking
Shanghai
CHUSAN ARCHIPELAGO
Hang chou
Ning-po
Han-kou
I-chang
Sung-p'an
Ch'eng-tu
Chung King
Kia-ting
Tung ting Lake
Chang-sha
Nan-chang
Fu-chou
Amoy
Swatow
Canton
Macao
HONG KONG I.
Victoria
TALWAN
FORMOSA I.
Kuei-yang
Kuei-lin
Yün-nan
Hanoi
TON-KING
KUANG-HSI
KUANG-TUNG
CHIH-CHIANG
CHINA SEA
JAPAN SEA
Greenwich
JACOBWELLS N.Y.

SUPPLEMENTARY NOTES AND TABLES

SUPPLEMENTARY NOTES AND TABLES

I

FOREIGN TRIBES OF KAN-SU[1]

In the District of Ho Chou (southwest of Lan-chou Fu)

1. SA-LA.—According to the annals of the Ming dynasty (*Ming shih*), composed of a large number of clans of Hsi-ch'iang, settled between the Ho (*i. e.*, Yellow River), the Huang (*i. e.*, Hsi-ning River), T'ao Chou and Min Chou.
2. CHEN-CHU T'U-FAN or FAN-MIN.
3. CHA-TS'ANG FAN-MIN or T'U-FAN.
4. HO-FU HUI (Mohammedan) FAN-MIN, like the Salar in outward appearance.

In the District of Ti-tao Chou (south-southwest of Lan-chou Fu).

5. FAN-MIN of Ts'an-tsa and Kao-shan.

In the District of T'ao Chou (in Kung-ch'ang Prefecture).

6. CHO-NI-TO and other clans, originally Wild Fan, from the Western regions (*Hsi-yü*), numbering 475 in all.[2]
7. TI-CHI-PA and other independent clans, thirty-seven in number, paying no tribute as Black Fan-tzŭ outside the border.
8. TSO-LA and other Fan clans, fifty-nine in all, originally T'u-Fan outside the border, reclaimed in the third year of Ming Hung-wu (A. D. 1370).
9. CHU-SUN and other clans of Fan-tzŭ, eleven in all. The Ku, Lu, and Pu clans are Fan; the Yang, Ting, and Ko are inside T'u-fan. Organized in the Hung-wu period (A. D. 1368–1399).
10. LIU-SHAO CH'UNG-KU-ERH, independent (*Sheng*) Fan tribes of outside the border.

In the District of Min Chou (in Kung-ch'ang Prefecture).

11. WA-SHE-PING Fan, forty-five clans, all belonging to the Ma tribe.
12. T'U-JEN (Aborigines), or T'u-fan of MOU-CH'IA-SHAN P'U, inhabiting forty villages (*p'u*).

[1] Taken from the "Huang Ch'ing chih-kung-t'u," Bk. V.
[2] All the above settled in Kan-su in the early Ming period.

13. T'U-JEN (Aborigines), formerly T'u-fan of *Hsü-erh-chuang*, inhabiting eleven *p'u*.
14. FAN-MIN of Ma-lien-ch'uan of T'u-fan descent.[1]

In the Chuang-lang Sub-prefecture (T'ing), (in Liang-chou Prefecture).

15. HSIEH-ERH-SU, and other clans of Fan-min, eight in all, inhabiting tents.
16. MAO-T'A-LA, T'u-min.
17. HUA-TS'ANG and SHANG-CH'A-ERH-TI Fan-min, twenty clans; like the Koko-nor Fan-tzŭ, they yearly pay a money tribute. They are also called *Hsi-Fan*, which is the real name of these tribes.

In the Wu-wei Prefecture (Liang-chou Prefecture).

18. The western TO-PA, three clans of Fan-min belonging to the Ch'ing hai. Pay a yearly horse tribute of seventeen head.[2]

In the Ku-lang Prefecture (Liang-chou Prefecture).

19. A-LO and other Fan-min clans, eight in all, originally Koko-nor Hsi-fan. Pay a yearly horse tribute of eleven head.

In the Yung-chang Prefecture (Liang-chou Prefecture).

20. YÜAN-TAN and other Fan-min clans, five in all, generic name Hsi-fan. Comprise fifty Hundreds. In olden times they grazed on the Huang-liang shan, south of Yung-chang Hsien. Yearly tribute of six horses.

In the Hsi-ning Prefecture.

21. TUNG-KOU and other Fan-min clans, eight in all, of Hsi-Ch'iang descent. Live seventy *li* from Hsi-ning Hsien.
22. CH'AN-T'OU. Originally from the western regions (*Hsi yü*). First came to Hsi-ning in the Ming Hung-wu period to trade, and after that established themselves there. They live at Hsin-tseng P'u,[3] forty *li* from the city.
23. TO-PA. Fan-min. Related to the people of Great Tibet (*Hsi-Ts'ang*).
24. Aborigines (T'U-MIN) descendants of Hsi-Fan.

[1] On the Ma-lien River. See p. 27, note 3. [2] One head for every Hundred.
[3] Probably the Hsin-chen or ch'eng, referred to on p. 97.

In the Nien-po Prefecture (in Hsi-ning Prefecture).

25. TUNG-KOU,[1] T'u-min, descendants of Li Ko-yung of the Shato Turks in the T'ang period.
26. TA-TZŬ (Mongols), WAN, etc., twenty clans of Fan-min; belonged originally to the Ki-pen Mongols. In the Yüan period their ancestor, To-erh-chi Shih-chieh, was Secretary (*Tso-cheng*) of Kan-su.
27. NAN-SHAN ("South Mountain") Fan-min of Ch'ü-yün-ssŭ. This lamasery was built (according to the "Ming shih") in the Hung-wu period by the lama Sa-la chao chiang-han-tung no-pu in the Nan ch'uan of the Nien-po prefecture.
28. PA-YANG JUNG (Bayan rong) Fan-min; belong to the Ch'ing hai (Koko-nor).

In the Military District (Wei) of Ta-t'ung (north of Hsi-ning).

29. HSING-MA, etc., Fan-min, six clans; belong to the Koko-nor. Each Dsassak is called Hei-Fan.[2] They are pastoral tribes; hence, also, Sheng Fan (*i. e.* "Wild Fan").

In the Military District (T'ing) of Kuei-tê (south of Hsi-ning).

30. FAN-MIN, twenty-five clans (*tsu*). Belonged in old times to Hsi-chi'ang; formerly attached administratively to the Koko-nor. Have black tents, but cultivate the soil.

In the Prefecture of Kan Chou (Kan-liang Circuit).

31. BLACK FAN (*Hei-Fan*), commonly called Hei-jen ("black people");[3] belong to the lamas of Tibet. Have been living, for generations back, in the mountains south of Kan Chou, but take tribute to Lh'asa.

In the District of Kao-t'ai (Su-Chou Prefecture).

32. HUANG FAN ("Yellow Fan"), two clans, called the *Cha-shih-tun* and *So-nan-shih-tien*; formerly Koko-nor tribes.
33. HEI FAN ("Black Fan"); belong to the lamas of Tibet. Their chief lives in the Sa-erh-pa valley. Pay a yearly tribute of two head of horses.

1 *Cf.* the name *Dungans*, given to the Mohammedan rebels of Kan-su, which may possibly be derived from Tung-kou. See Bretschneider, "Not. of Med. Geog. of Central Asia," p. 125.

2 I do not understand this; there is possibly a misprint.

3 All the laity is called by this name in Mongol countries.

In the District of Wen Hsien (*Chieh Department*).

34. FAN-MIN of Lien-ch'in-shu, a tribe of eastern Tibetan (*Miao-Man*) descent; not like the Fan on the west border (of the province). They live to the south of the district. Their dwellings are on high slopes, and on mountains.

II

ORIGIN OF THE PRAYER, "OM MANI PADMÉ HŪM"

THE Buddhist magic formula *om mani padmé hūm* occupies such an important place in the every-day worship of the people of Tibet, so much time and money are expended by them in reproducing on stone and paper the six syllables composing it, that it deserves more than a passing mention.

Although the six-syllable prayer (*vidyā shadaksharī*, it is called in Sanskrit) is not found in early Buddhist writings, it is probably coeval with the rise of the cult of Avalokiteshwara, which we know to have been popular as early as the fourth century of our era. It is therefore possible, as is in fact claimed by native historians, that it was introduced into Tibet by the first missionaries who visited that country in the seventh century, but, for the time being, we have not sufficient evidence to settle the question definitely.

The earliest mention I have found of it by any European writer dates from the second half of the thirteenth century. Willelm de Rubruk, speaking of the Buddhist monks at Karakorum, says: "Habent etiam quocumque vadunt semper in manibus quamdam testam c. vel ducentorum nucleorum, sicut nos portamus pater-noster, et dicunt semper hec verba, *on man baccam*,[1] hoc est, *Deus, tu nosti*, secundum quod quidam eorum interpretatus est michi, et totiens exspectat remunerationem a Deo quotiens hoc dicendo memoratur."[2]

The explanation the friar gives of this prayer is, of course, wide of the mark, and so are nearly all those which subsequent

[1] Some MSS. have *mani hactain*, and *mani hactani*.

[2] "Itinerarium Willelmi de Rubruk. Recueil de Voyages et de Mémoires publié par la Soc. de Géog. de Paris," IV, p. 285.

writers have offered from time to time. The *mani*, as the prayer is colloquially called in Tibet, is an invocation to Avalokiteshwara, the Merciful One, whose one great self-imposed mission is the salvation of all living creatures from the miseries incident to sentient existence, in the hope that it may lead them on in the way of salvation, and that he will, hearing it, ever keep the world in mind. The continual repetition of this prayer is recommended as a means of acquiring merit, and as the only way of keeping in the road to freedom; its diffusion and reproduction by writing, printing, and engraving are held to be highly philanthropical acts.

The legendary origin of this prayer is set forth in a Tibetan work called "Mani kabum" (also pronounced Mani kambum) or "Hundred thousand precepts of the Mani."[1] This work is attributed to Srong-tsan gambo, the first Buddhist sovereign of Tibet, who lived in the seventh century of our era; but it is probable, from internal evidence, that it was written at a more recent date, in all likelihood in the fifteenth century, after the establishment of the Lh'asa pontificate. As the genesis of Avalokiteshwara and his vain efforts to save the world are intimately connected with the origin of the prayer, it is necessary to begin the history of the formula (Chap. IV) with that of the god addressed in it, which is also found in the "Mani kabum" (Chaps. II and III). The following is a translation:

(Chap. II.) "Then the Perfect Buddha, called 'Infinite Brightness (*Nang-wa t'ä-yä*), Light eternal' (*Wu-pa-mé*), having discerned that the Great Compassionate One (*T'u-jé ché*) was wise in means and filled with compassion, bethought him of using him under the appearance of a god, and the goddess Drolma under that of a goddess, in the work of redemption of the world. So Nang-wa t'ä-yä entered the state of profound abstraction called 'Redemption of the world by T'u-jé-ché,' and from his left eye came a ray of white light out of which issued the Bodhisattwa called 'the Lord looking with a glance of his eye' (*Shen-rä-zig Wang-ch'yuk*),[2] and from his right eye came a ray of blue light out of which issued the goddess Drolma. Moreover, after this apparition had been thus miraculously born for the redemption of the kings and other mighty ones of the world, he appeared from out a lotus (*Padma*), for there came (as

[1] The title of this work has frequently been translated "Hundred thousand precious commandments," but, as I have said, the word mani is used to designate the prayer whose power and efficacy this work sets forth.

[2] A literal translation of the Sanskrit *Avalokiteshwara*.

will now be related) a light out of a Lotus pond (*Ts'o padma-chan*) and he was born in the body from out a lotus in his apparitional person.

"It happened that in the western lands, in the realm called 'Lotus abode of bliss' (*Padma-chan Dé-wa-chan*), there reigned a mighty monarch, a universal king (*chakravartin rāja*), called 'the Best One' (*Zang-po ch'ok*). He ruled over the four continents, and all riches and power were his, but his consort was barren and had borne him no son, though, this excepted, he enjoyed every blessing given the righteous. Now there was a lake in that country, called 'the Lotus pond' (*Ts'o pa-mé*), and when the lotuses had bloomed on the lake and it was time for the king to make offerings to the Chief Rarity (*Kon-ch'ok*) swift messengers were sent to get flowers which they brought to the king, and he offered them to the Kon-ch'ok. It happened one day that a messenger, having come to get flowers, was filled with the greatest amazement on seeing in the pond on a lotus stem surrounded with spear-like tendrils and shield-like leaves a closed flower. He went and told this to the king, who said: 'It is certain that there is in that flower a miraculously born creature; I will go myself to see this much-to-be-revered object.' So, having called to him his queen, his ministers, and his inner and outer attendants, with boats to go on the lake, chariots, all kinds of presents, banners, flags, etc., and to the sound of a great music, carrying *akaru*, *duruka* and every other kind of sweet perfume, and many garments of *Kashika* cotton, he came to the Lotus pond. And having embarked on the pond in a boat he came to where was the flower, which opened, and in it he saw a youth of sixteen marked with all the signs and characteristics of a Buddha. A mighty glory came from out his white body, and he was in the full bloom of youth. He carried a sharp sword, and he was gorgeous with all kinds of precious jewels. He was wrapped to his middle in silk, and a deerskin hung over his shoulders. From out his mouth there came these words: 'Love of all creation.'

"Then the king and all his attendants bowed down and worshiped him, and the king, having presented him with a piece of *Kashi* cloth,[1] requested him to ascend a chariot, and, all the offerings having been made him, he went to the royal palace, where he became an object of worship. Having been born from out a

[1] We are reminded here of the Tibetan custom of offering k'atag, so frequently referred to in the body of my narrative.

lotus (*padme*) he was named 'Lotus-born' (*Pamé-lä chyé*) and also 'Lotus-heart' (*Pamé nying-po*).

"The religion-defending monarch asked his master, the Buddha Nang-wa t'ä-yä, 'What means this miracle; who is this miraculous personage?' And the Buddha replied, 'Great King, this miracle is in consequence of the universal prayer of the Buddhas, and has occurred for the weal of the whole created world. It is an apparitional manifestation from out the bosom of all Blessed Ones (*Dé-war shé-pa*)[1] of the three ages, and its name is *P'apa*[2] *Shen-rä-zig Wang-ch'yuk.* My lord, he will be a blessing to all creation.'

"After this, the king, when came the full moon, made great offerings to the Kon-ch'ok, and showed also every honor to this miraculous creature, and made him offerings without number. And the miraculous child, bearing in mind that he had come at the prayer of all the Buddhas, thought within himself what could be for the good of creatures. And with his compassionate eye he looked at all the sentient creatures in the three regions of space, and he saw in his mercifulness that all, through their wickedness, were sunk in the waters of lust, burnt with the fire of passions, wrapped in the dark folds of ignorance, held by the force of pride, blown about by the wind of envy, bound in the fetters of selfishness, plunged in the fiery pit of the miseries of regeneration. Then tears flowed from his eyes, and from the tears which fell from his left eye came out the goddess Drolma, and from those which fell from his right eye came the goddess Tronyer ('She with the angered face'). And the goddess Drolma said: 'Lord, for the sake of sentient creatures, exert your powers of omniscience (*bodhi*).' And the goddess Tronyer said: 'For the weal of sentient creatures, let not your mind become wearied.' Then they both said: 'Lord, we will be your helpmates,' and they once more vanished in his eyes.

"Now the king asked why it was that when tears fell from this miraculous child Bodhisattwa, two goddesses had come out of his eyes. The child replied: 'The tears fell because I could not bear the sight of the sufferings of all creation, and the two goddesses I have selected as helpers of the world. As for me, I must accomplish what is for the good of the infinity of sentient creatures, and I seek thy leave to do it, great king.' The king replied, 'Lord, all those who have come in like man-

[1] In Sanskrit, *Sugata*, an epithet frequently given to Buddhas.

[2] *P'apa* (hp'ags-pa) means "Venerable," and renders the Sanskrit, *Arya*.

ner (*Dé-dzin shé-pa*) [1] of the three ages have done, when in the state of Bodhisattwa, what thou now wishest to do for the weal of all creation, and afterwards have become Buddhas; so be it,' and he granted him his request.

(CHAP. III.) "So then the incarnate god, the Great Compassionate One, P'apa Shen-rä-zig, set about as follows, laboring for the welfare of all creation. The incarnate god-child prepared a great offering and worshiped all the innumerable Blessed Ones (*Déwar-shé-pa*) who abide in the ten regions of space, and, casting himself on the ground, he prayed to them in his sweet voice, which sounded like that of the cuckoo (*Kalapingka*), saying, 'What shall I do for the weal of all creatures?' Then from out the ten corners of the heavens there came voices saying, 'Lord, let thy heart be strong in love and mercy; let not despondency and weariness take hold of thee.'

"Then asked the child, 'How may I acquire the peace (*samadhi*) of love and mercy?' and at the same moment the Lord of peoples, the Buddha Nang-wa t'ä-yä, appeared in all his person merged in the state of calmness called 'Great diffused light.' And then, to initiate the greatest of the Bodhisattwas, P'apa Shen-rä-zig Wang-ch'yuk, in the way of doing good to creation, there came out of his body a glory greater than man can possibly conceive, from which emanated a great number of 'regions of bodies of perfect enjoyment' (*long-dzog-kui-djing*), in which appeared many Buddhas with bodies of perfect enjoyment (*sambhogakāya*), whence great good was done to sentient creatures. From the hearts of these bodies of perfect fruition there emanated an infinite number of 'regions of apparitional bodies' (*trul-pé kui-djing*), in which appeared many Buddhas with apparitional bodies (*nirmānakāya*). Moreover, from out the hearts of these apparitional bodies there emanated an unspeakable radiance from out of which came P'apa Shen-rä-zig Wang-ch'yuk, Tronyer-ma, Drolma, and countless numbers of sentient creatures, and the good of creation was accomplished.

"Furthermore, there came a radiance from the Buddha's body, whence emanated regions of the world as infinite in number as are the atoms composing the universe, and there were also innumerable Buddhas (*Tathāgata*), and they were a blessing to all creatures. And from the bodies of these latter Buddhas there

[1] This is the well-known Sanskrit epithet of Buddhas, *Tat'āgata.*

came unbounded lights, from each of which there emerged an India (*Dzambuling*), each with a Diamond throne (*dojé-dän*),[1] each with a barbarous snowclad country to the north of the Diamond throne, each with a king of horses Balaha, each with an eleven-faced Shen-rä-zig, each with a Drolma, and a Tronyer, in each a king Srong-tsan, a white and a blue princess.[2] And from their (*i. e.*, the Buddhas'?) bodies there came an unspeakable effulgence whence emanated the Great Compassionate One and the Six Syllables,[3] and sentient creatures without end, and they were a blessing unto them.

(CHAP. IV.) "The mightiest of all the Bodhisattwas, P'apa Shen-rä-zig Wang-ch'yuk, his mind intent on the work of saving all creatures, made an oath in the presence of the Buddha Wupamé and all the eleven times ten millions of Buddhas, saying 'In me are embodied for the work of salvation the deeds and the perfection which passeth all human understanding of all the Buddhas of the three ages. I pledge myself to bring every sentient creature to the highest and most perfect state of enlightenment. But should I so long for rest and peace as to stop in the way, may my head burst into ten pieces as would a cotton boll (*ardzaké-dog*)!'

"Then spoke the Buddha Wupamé, 'So be it, so be it, Lord. This is also the prayer of myself and the Buddhas of the three ages inhabiting the ten regions of space. Furthermore, I who am a Buddha will be thy helpmate in the work of saving all creatures.'

"Then from out the body of P'apa Shen-rä-zig Wang-ch'yuk there came six rays of light which reached to the six inhabited regions. Some rays penetrated to the abode of the gods (*Lh'a*),[4] where, for the purpose of redeeming the gods, they became the lord of gods 'Hundred Sacrifices' (*Jya-chyin*);[5] and then were heard the sacred words saying: 'Subject to the misery of the fall of the gods through the power of pleasure and carnal desires, if I have entered the abode of the gods, let there be an end to all the misery of the fall of death and regeneration!' Some rays penetrated to the abode of the fallen gods (*Lh'a-mayin*),[6] where, for the

[1] *Vadjrāsana*, the seat of the Buddha at Gaya, where he obtained omniscience.

[2] The two wives of King Srong-tsan gambo, a Chinese and a Nepalese princess.

[3] *I. e.*, the prayer *Om mani padmé hum.* This chapter is a fair sample of the jargon of Tibetan mysticism.

[4] *Deva*, celestial beings. Applied to the inhabitants of the twenty Brahmalokas and the six Devalokas.

[5] *Shatakratu*, epithet of Indra.

[6] *Asura*, Titans, and, like them, at war with the gods or Devas.

purpose of redeeming them, they became the lord of the Lh'a-mayin T'ag-zang-ris; and then were heard the sacred words saying: 'Subject to the misery of war through the might of pride and anger, if I have entered the abode of the Lh'a-mayin, let the misery of death and regeneration through the sin of waging war be ended!' And some rays penetrated to the abode of men, where, for the purpose of redeeming them, they became the lord of men, 'the Mighty One of the Shakya' (*Sachya t'upa*); and then were heard the sacred words saying: 'Held in bondage through the power of desires and lust, and subject to the misery of birth, old age, disease and death, if I have entered the abode of men, let the misery of becoming man be ended!' Some rays penetrated to the abode of brute creation, where, for the purpose of redeeming them, they became the lord of brute creation called 'Great-enduring-lion' (*Senggé rabtan*); and then were heard the sacred words saying: 'Through the power of ignorance, subject to the misery of servitude and violent death, if I have entered the abode of brute creation, may all of you, now held in the meshes of ignorance, be quickly endowed with enlightenment such as that I enjoy!' Some rays penetrated to the abode of the departed (*Yidag*)[1] where, for the purpose of redeeming them, they became the lord of the Yidag, 'Treasury of the Sky' (*Nam-k'a dzo*), and then were heard the sacred words saying: 'Bound through the might of avarice, subject to the misery of hunger and thirst, if I have entered the abode of the Yidag, let there at once be an end to hungering and thirsting, and let happiness be reached!' Some rays penetrated to hell, where, for the purpose of redeeming it, they became the lord of hell, 'King of the Law' (*Ch'ü-gi jyabo*), and then were heard the sacred words saying: 'Bound through the might of lust and subject to the misery of being killed by heat and cold, if I have truly entered hell, let the torments of hell, the agonies of being killed by heat or cold, be ended!'

"And thus the six classes of sentient creatures, who heretofore could not be freed, when arose these six Mighty Ones from out the light, and the sacred words were heard, escaped from out their abodes as out of an iron box which has been opened, and all the six realms were completely emptied of creatures.

Then the Great Compassionate One ascended to the top of

[1] *Preta*, manes, with huge bellies and narrow throats, condemned to suffer perpetual hunger and thirst, and to wander about in graveyards and near houses.

Mount Sumeru (*Rirab*), and looked with the eye of wisdom, and saw that there were as many creatures in the world as before, so a second and a third time in his mercy he emptied the divers regions of the world of all creation, but the numbers (of sufferers) decreased not, and he was filled with despondency and despair. 'Alas,' he cried, 'through the instrumentality of the Blessed One (*Sugata*) innumerable regions of conversion, innumerable heavenly realms, innumerable regions of sentient creatures have been brought into the truth. But though I have released so many creatures, yet this orb cannot be emptied even for an instant, and the redemption of sentient creatures is never accomplished! So having found my own peace and happiness, I will be with the Completely-passed-away-Buddhas.' And then he remembered his former prayer, and his head split into a hundred pieces. He cried aloud at the pain, which he could not bear: 'Alas, merciful Buddhas and Bodhisattwas, and thou Buddha Wupamé, I cry not for myself but from anguish at not having accomplished the salvation of the world!' and he wept aloud.

"Then the Buddha Wupamé gathered together all the pieces of the head of the Great Compassionate One and made them into eleven faces, and as the orb of transmigration has neither beginning nor end he made them placid faces, and though placid he made them to be as dark and angry countenances to the wayward man. Moreover, he said: 'The orb of transmigration (*k'orwa*) has neither beginning nor end, and thou mayest not take all creatures out of it.'

"Then spoke P'apa Shen-rä-zig, saying: 'Since I have not been able to remove all creatures from the orb of transmigration, may I have a thousand hands and a thousand eyes, so that the thousand hands may be as those of a thousand universal monarchs, and the thousand eyes as those of the thousand Buddhas of the cycle (*bhadrakalpa*), and by them I may serve all creatures.' And at the self-same moment he became eleven-faced, with a thousand hands, in the palms of which were a thousand eyes.

"Then spoke the Buddha Nang-wa t'ä-yä: 'Most Compassionate P'apa Shen-rä-zig Wang-ch'yuk, by the following six letters the door of birth for the six classes of created beings may be closed: *Om mani padmé hūm.* By *Om* the gate of birth among gods (*Lh'a*) is closed; by *ma* the gate of birth among Titans (*Lh'a-ma-yin*) is closed; by *ni* the gate of birth among men is closed; by *pad* the gate of birth among brute beasts is closed; by *mé* the gate of birth among *pretas* (*Yidag*) is closed, and by *hūm* the gate of birth in hell is closed. These can empty the kingdoms of the six classes of creatures. Understand it well, remember them, repeat them, impress them well upon your mind."

The six-syllable prayer is pronounced *ōm mani pémé hum* by all Tibetans; occasionally you will hear Mongols pronounce the third word *padmé*, but no one, save T. T. Cooper, ever pronounced it *omanee peminee*.[1] The repetition of this formula is the most common mode of praying met with among Mongols and Tibetans, and is spoken of as *mani-dön*. The prayer-wheel or "*mani*-wheel" (*mani k'orlo*) is another way of repeating mechanically this formula. The prayer-wheel has probably its origin in a misinterpretation of the term *dharma chakra pravarteti*, literally "to turn the wheel of the law," which properly means "to establish the supremacy of Truth."[2] The prayer-wheel consists of a cylinder in which are arranged, one on top of the other, sheets of paper, on which the formula *om mani padmé hūm* is printed in fine characters. The sheets must be wound on the axis from left to right, and the wheel, when set in motion, must revolve in the opposite way, so that the writing passes in front of the person turning the wheel in the way in which it is read, *i. e.*, from left to right. If made to revolve from right to left, it is held sacrilegious. General Cunningham[3] says that the earliest mention of the prayer-wheel is found in the "Fo kuo chi" of Fa-hsien. This, however, is an error resulting from a mistranslation in Abel Rémusat's rendering of this text. Fa-hsien does not mention the prayer-wheel at all, nor does Hsüan-chuang or any of the Chinese dynastic histories, although one would have expected this peculiar custom noticed in these minute and carefully prepared works. The practice is unquestionably old, as we find prayer-wheels, in a modified form it is true, in Japan and Korea, countries which have not received any extraneous Buddhist practices for five or six centuries at least. Cunningham (*op. cit.*, p. 375) gives a medal of Hushka (first century, A. D.) representing, according to him, a man holding a prayer-wheel in his hand. To my untutored mind the implement may be anything one chooses, consequently a prayer-wheel is not an impossibility.

[1] "Travels of a Pioneer of Commerce," p. 209.

[2] See R. C. Childers, "Pali Dictionary," s. v. *dhammacakkam*.

[3] Alex. Cunningham, "Ladak," p. 375, and Abel Rémusat, "Foe koue ki," pp. 27, 28.

III

EARLY ETHNOGRAPHY OF THE KOKO-NOR AND EASTERN TIBET

THE annals of the Sui (A. D. 581–618) and of the T'ang (A. D. 618–905) dynasties[1] contain some interesting notices on the early population of the Koko-nor and Ts'aidam, the T'u-ku-hun, and on two important tribes or nations of Eastern Tibet, the T'ang-hsiang and the Kingdom of Su-pi or Nü Kuo, "Kingdom of Women," as the Chinese always call it from its peculiar form of government. The accounts of these people contained in the "T'ang shu" are nearly reproductions of those in the older "Sui shu," but as they are clearer in a number of passages I have thought best to copy them. I have called attention in foot notes on preceding pages to the most striking resemblances between the customs, dress, etc., of the tribes of the present day and those of these older ones; I will not point them out again here.

T'U-KU-HUN

("Sui shu," Bk. 83.) "T'u-ku-hun was originally the name of the son of Shih Kuei who lived on the Pei-t'u ho of Hsi hsien in Liao-tung.[2] Shih Kuei had two sons, the elder called T'u-ku-hun, the younger Jo-lo Kuei. Shih Kuei dying, he was succeeded by Jo-lo Kuei, but some of the clans could not be made to transfer their allegiance from T'u-ku-hun, and migrated with him to the Hsi Tu-lung and established themselves to the south of Kan (Chou) and Sung (Chou, *i. e.*, Sung-p'an in northwest Ssŭ-ch'uan), and to the southwest of the T'ao ho, taking in several thousand *li* of the Pai shan and Lan shan (districts). Later on, T'u-ku-hun founded a kingdom.[3] During the Wei and Chou

1 "Sui shu," Bk. 83, and "T'ang shu," Bk. 221A. Other dynastic histories do little more than reproduce these accounts.

2 The "Pei shih," Bk. 96, says Tan-tu ho. This eastern origin of the T'u-ku-hun appears to me improbable. The account given in the "Pei shih" differs considerably from that of the "Sui shu," but only in details. The migration is said to have taken place between A. D. 265 and 313.

3 The "Pei shih" says that he left sixty sons. The eldest, called T'u-yen, was seven feet eight inches high.

dynasties (A. D. 550–581) (the chief?) was known as Ko-han-t'u-t'a-ssŭ. The capital was 50 (or 15) *li* west of the Koko-nor. It had walls; the people did not live in it, however, but went wherever there were grass and water.[1] Their officials comprised a prince, dukes, chamberlains (*Po-shih*), presidents of boards (*Shang-shu*), vice-presidents (*Lang-chung*), generals (*Chiang-ch'ün*). The prince[2] wore a black hat, the queen (or the married woman) a gold-embroidered one. Their implements, arms, and clothing were like those of China. The prince, the dukes, and many of the wealthy people among them wore broad-brimmed hats, like the Chinese straw hats in shape. The women wore a plaited skirt and a jacket; they did up their hair in plaits on which they sewed pearls (or beads) and cowries. This people had no regular system of taxation. They put a man to death for stealing horses; for all other crimes the culprit paid a fine in goods. Their customs were somewhat like those of the Tu-küeh (Turks). They wore mourning clothes (or special clothes for a funeral) until the funeral rites were at an end. Their other characteristics were covetousness and cruelty. Their country produced barley, millet, and beans. . . . They had a great many yak. There was much copper, iron, and cinnabar, also *shan-shan ch'ieh mo* (?)[3] found here."

("T'ang shu," Bk. 221A.) "The T'u-ku-hun live to the south of the mountains of Kan Chou and Sung Chou, and to the southwest of the T'ao ho.[4] . . . They live in tents and eat meat and grain. . . Their sovereign wears his hair in a knot, with a black head-covering; his consort wears an embroidered brocade gown, woven skirts with gold embroidery, and head ornaments. The men's clothes consist in a long robe, and a head-cover of light stuff, or a broad-brimmed hat.[5] The women do up their hair in little braids, and sew beads (or pearls) and cowries on them. As to their marriage customs, the rich get wives by purchase, the

1 "The country was 3000 *li* from east to west, and over 1000 *li* from north to south," adds the "Pei shih."

2 The "Pei shih" calls him *Kua-lü*, probably a word of their language.

3 The "Pei shih" adds "mules and nautilus shells (*ying-wu*). It also says of them that "like the Turks, the brother married his deceased brother's wife, the son his deceased father's wife." The "Annals of the Anterior Han" (*Ch'ien Han shu*, Bk. 94) attributes this custom also to the Hsiung-nu (Turks), who justified it by their abhorrence of mixing families and their desire to keep the family stem untainted.

4 Southwest Kan-su, approximately the territory occupied at present by the South Koko-nor Panak'a and the Golok.

5 A broad-brimmed hat is the peculiar head-covering of the K'amba and the Koko-nor people of the present day.

poor steal theirs. When the father dies his wife is married by his son; the brother marries the wife of his deceased brother. They wear mourning until the funeral is over, when they put on again their every-day dress. The country is very cold, fit only for barley, beans, millet, and greens (*wu-ching*)."

T'ANG-HSIANG

("Sui shu," Bk. 83.)[1] "The T'ang-hsiang are descendants of the San-miao. They comprise the Tang-chang, Pai-lang, etc., and are (collectively) known as the Monkey tribes (*Mi hou*).[2] They border to the east on Lin and T'ao Chou, and to the west (north ?) on P'ing. To the west they constitute a barrier against the Yeh Hu. From north to south their country is several thousand *li* in breadth. They live in mountain gorges and each cognomen constitutes a separate clan, the large ones containing over 5000 horsemen, the small ones over 1000. They weave yak and goat hair and sheep's wool, and make tents. Their clothes consist of a fur-lined cloth robe and a felt jacket ornamented outside. They are all warriors, but do not know how to use a sword scientifically. They have at present regular troops which they bring together. They have no *ula*, and object to taxes. They move about from place to place, tending their herds of yak, sheep, and swine, of all of which they eat. They do not till the soil. As to their customs they are given to lechery and obscenity to an extent unknown even among any other savage race. They keep account of the seasons of the year by means of reeds. Every three years they have a great gathering, when they sacrifice oxen and sheep to heaven. When people of eighty or over die, the relatives do not mourn, for they say that those had reached the end of their allotted time, but if a young person dies they cry and lament, saying that it is a great wrong. They have banjos (*p'i-pa*), flutes, and they use bits of bamboo to mark the measure."

("T'ang Shu," Bk. 221.) "The T'ang-hsiang form a portion of the Hsi Ch'iang tribes of the Han period. Since the time of the

1 Cf. "Pei Shih," Bk. 96; but it contains no new matter.

2 The legend translated in Supplementary Note VI may possibly explain the origin of this name of "Monkey tribes."

Wei and Chou dynasties (A. D. 535–581), they have greatly spread, embracing in their territory, Mi, Tang, Chang, and Teng. Their country is the *Hsi-chih* of antiquity. To the east they border on Sung Chou,[1] to the west on the Yeh Hu, to the south on the Ch'un-sang, Mi-sang and other Ch'iang (Tibetan) tribes, and to the north on the T'u-ku-hun. They live in secluded, rugged valleys, many of them three thousand *li* from any other tribe. A tribe is divided into little clans. A large one comprises a myriad horsemen, a small one several thousand. It is impossible to give the names of all these clans, but we may mention among them the Hsi-feng clan, the Fei-t'ing clan, the Wang-li clan, the P'o-ch'ao clan, the Yeh-tzŭ clan, the Fang-tang clan, the Mi-ch'in clan, and the T'o-pa clan. The T'o-pa is the most important one.[2]

"They have no houses, but with the hair of their yak and the wool of their sheep they weave stuff out of which they make tents, whose location they change according to the season of the year. They are all fighting men but ignorant of military art; at present they have regular levies. They reach to excessive old age, many of them exceeding an hundred years. They are much given to robbing and plundering, and consider it most commendable; they covet everything they see. Their hair is matted, their faces filthy, and their feet bare. They live on roots and game. Men and women wear long skin gowns, or of coarse woolen stuff with a nappy surface. Their domestic animals comprise yak, horses, asses, and sheep, which they eat. They do not till the soil. The country is cold; in the 5th moon the grass sprouts, in the 8th moon there is frost. They have no written characters, but record the years by means of little reeds. Once every three years they assemble together and worship heaven by sacrificing oxen and sheep. They get barley from neighboring countries; from it they make a fermented drink. A son may marry his deceased father's or uncle's wives (or wife); a younger brother, his deceased brother's wife, but he may not marry a person of the same cognomen as himself. When an old person dies the children and grandchildren do not weep, but if a young person dies they say that it is a great wrong and they lament over him."

[1] Sung-p'an in northwest Ssŭ-ch'uan.

[2] From this clan descended the founders of the Hsi Hsia or Tangut dynasty in the 10th century A. D.

NÜ KUO (KINGDOM OF WOMEN)

("Sui shu," Bk. 83.) "The Kingdom of Women is south of the Tsung-ling mountains.[1] In this country the sovereign is a woman; her family name is Su-pi. . . . The queen's husband is called Chin-tsu,[2] but he has nothing to do with the government of the state. The men of this country fight its wars. The capital is on a mountain, and is five or six *li* square. There are ten thousand families (in the kingdom). The sovereign lives in a nine-storied house, and has several hundred female attendants. Every fifth day there is a council of state. There is also a "little queen" (*hsiao Nü-wang*), the two together ruling the kingdom. As to its customs, the women hold in light esteem their husbands, nor are they jealous. Both men and women paint their faces with different colored clays; every day or so they change (the color). All the people arrange (or cover) their hair. They wear rawhide boots. They have a system of taxation, but on no fixed basis. The climate is very cold, and they live by the chase. The country produces *tou-shih*,[3] cinnabar, musk, yak, fast horses (*tsun ma*), striped horses (*shu ma*), and salt,[4] in great abundance, which they carry to India and make great profit by the trade. They have often waged war with Hindustan and the T'ang-hsiang. When their queen dies they collect a large sum in gold coins, and then seek in the clan of the deceased for two women of ability, one to be queen, the other to be the 'little queen.'

"When a wealthy person dies they remove the skin of the body and put the flesh and bones mixed with gold dust in a vase and bury it. After a year they put (the remains together with) the skin in an iron vase and bury it.

"They usually address their prayers to devils (*Asura*, *O-hsiu-lo*) and to the gods. At New Year's they sacrifice men or monkeys, and then go into the mountains and pray until a bird like a hen pheasant comes and perches on the diviner's hand. He splits open the bird's crop and examines it. If there is grain in it the

1 From the text of the "T'ang shu" we learn that by this is to be understood that the Nü kuo embraced all northern Tibet.

2 Meaning "gold gathered together." Cf. the account of the "T'ang shu," which says that the family name was *Suvarna gotra*, a Sanskrit name meaning "Golden family."

3 A kind of copper ore containing gold.

4 Probably by salt "borax" must be understood. Tincal is still exported from Tibet to India.

year will be fruitful, but if it only contains sand and gravel there will be calamities. This is called 'bird divination.'

"In the 6th year of Sui K'ai-huang (A. D. 586) this country sent tribute to court; since then it has discontinued doing so."

("T'ang Shu," Bk. 122.) "The Eastern Kingdom of Women (*Tung Nü kuo*), also called Su-fa-la-na chü-chü-lo,[1] is a division of the Ch'iang. There is also in the far west (*Hsi hai*) a country ruled by women, so this is called the eastern one. To the east it borders on the T'u-fan, the T'ang-hsiang and Mao chou. To the west it touches the San-po ho (Yaru tsang-po). To the north it is conterminous with Yü-tien,[2] and to the southeast with Ya chou (in Ssŭ-ch'uan), the Lo-nu Man-tzŭ and the Pai-lang savages. From east to west it is a nine days' journey, from north to south twenty days'. It has eighty towns, and is ruled over by a woman who resides in the K'ang-yen valley, a narrow, precipitous gorge around which flows the Jo River in a southerly direction. There are over 40,000 families and 10,000 soldiers. The sovereign is styled *Pin chin*, and the officials, called *Kao-pa-li*, are like our *Tsai-hsiang* (ministers of state). They depute men to perform all outside duties, and these are thence known as 'women's deputies' (*ling nü kuan*). From the interior (of the palace) the men receive and transmit the orders.

"The sovereign has near her person several hundred women, and once every five days there is a council of state. When the sovereign dies the people pay in several myriad of gold coins, and select from the royal clan two clever women (one to reign), the other as assistant sovereign to succeed her in case of death. If the one who dies is a maiden, the other, a married woman, succeeds her, so that there is no possibility of the dynasty becoming extinct, or of a revolution.

"They inhabit houses: that of the sovereign is nine stories high, those of the people six. The sovereign wears a black (or blue) plaited skirt of a rough texture, with a black (or blue) robe with sleeves trailing on the ground, and in winter a lambskin gown ornamented with embroideries. She wears her hair done

[1] For Sanskrit, *Suvarna gotra*, "Golden family."

[2] *I. e.*, Khoten, also called Ho-tien in Chinese.

up in little plaits, also ear-rings, and on her feet a kind of leather boot known (in China) as *so-i.*

"The women do not esteem highly the men, and rich ones have always men-servants who arrange their hair and paint their faces with black clay (*t'u*). The men do also the fighting and till the soil. The sons take the family name of their mother. The country is cold, and only suitable for barley. Their domestic animals comprise sheep and horses. Gold is found here. Their customs resemble closely those of Hindustan. Our 11th moon is their first. To divine they go in the 10th moon into the mountains and scatter grain about and call a flock of birds. Suddenly there comes a bird like a pheasant. The diviner splits it open and examines it. If (its crop) contains grain the coming year will be fruitful, but if there is none the year will bring calamities. This is called 'bird divination.'

"They wear mourning for three years, not changing their clothes and not washing. When a man of wealth dies, they remove the skin from the body and put it aside; the flesh and bones they place in an earthen vase, mixed with gold dust, and this they carefully bury. When the sovereign is buried several tens of persons follow the dead into the tomb."

IV

DIVINATION BY SHOULDER-BLADES SCAPULAMANCY OR OMOPLATOSCOPY

THE following, taken from G. Klemm's "Allgemeine Culturgeschichte der Menschheit," III, pp. 200, 201, who himself quotes from Pallas's "Nachrichten," II, p. 350, agrees exactly with what information I have been able to obtain on the subject, it being only necessary to remark that the interpretation of the cracks in the bone varies according to the object in view or the undertaking in hand, and is not confined to the words given in the text.

Fig. 1 represents the upper side of the right shoulder-blade. It shows:

(*a*) *Amin chalga*, "the road of life," the line of business with the impediments and events which can take place in it, as follows:

(*b*) *Booduk*, a special impediment or misfortune, (*c*) death of a Prince, (*d*) of a Saissan, (*e*) of a commoner, (*f*) of a servant.

(*g*) *Mangna bair*, prompt good luck.

(*h*) Tardy good luck.

(*i*) *Mangna-aschida*, very tardy but enduring good luck.

(*k*) *Chudurga*, "saddle crupper," impediment and delay.

(*l*) *Denggna daissun*, line of war and the chase; when the cracks meet on the ridge or stop on either side of it, it shows that the parties will meet or not, that the chase will be either good or bad.

(*m*) *Zalma*, "loop," the death of a sick person, or recovery of lost cattle.

(*n*) *Chaissan*, "kettle," the joint cavity, plenty or poverty according to the marks in it.

Fig. 2 represents the under side of a shoulder-blade, on which there are fewer cracks to note; they show:

(*oo*) *Tsehetkurin chalga*, malevolent spirits, working of evil.

(*pp*) *Tenggrien chalga*, assistance of good spirits.

(*q*) *Sanggi*, news, which, when the crack is single, will come late; when it forms a cross, will come soon.

The other shoulder-blade (Fig. 3) shows cracks and alterations concerning a sick person. They are:

(1) *Amin chalga*, the road of life.

(2) *Jerrien sam chalga* or *ollon chalga*, roads leading to life.

(3) *Dallain-daissun*, signs of the attack.

(4) *Aschida*, duration of good luck and of life.

(5) *Setkirin obo*, signs of evil spirits, standing near the living.

(6) *Boodok*, or signs opposing these evil spirits.

(7) *Chal-bajar*, prompt recovery of patient.

(8) Portent of protracted suffering which will not prove fatal.

(9) *Tenggrien alliga*, good spirits' crack.

I find the following interesting account of the method of divining by sheep shoulder-blades in William of Rubruk's "Itinerarium," p. 318 (Edit. Soc. de Géog. de Paris): "Et dum ingrediemur (domum Mangucam) exibat quidam famulus exportaus ossa scapularum arietum, combusta usque ad nigredinem carbonum, super quo miratus sum valde quid hoc sibi vellet. De quo cum postea inquisivissem, intellexi quod nichil facit in toto mundo quin primo consulat iu ossibus illis, unde nec per-

Fig. 2

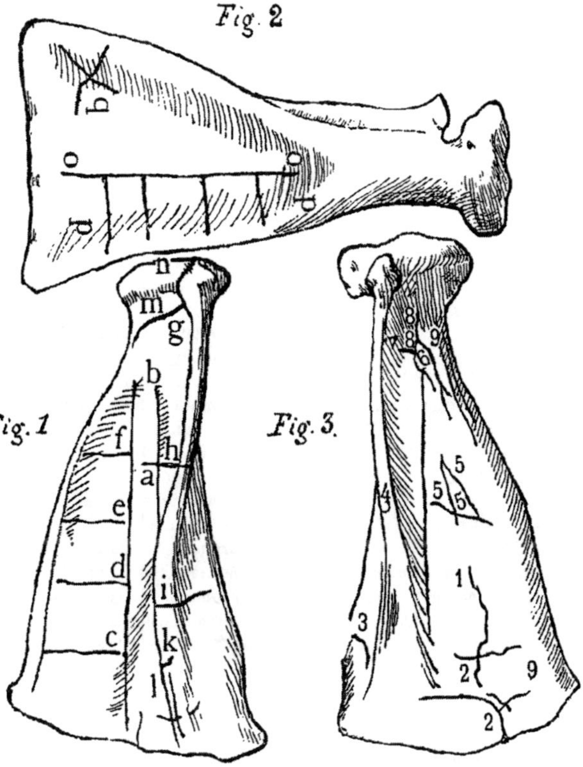

Fig. 1

Fig. 3.

mittit hominem ingredi domum suam, primo consulat os illud. Quod genus divinationis ita fit: quando vult aliquid facere, facit sibi afferri tria de ossibus illis nondum combustis, et tenens ea cogitat de illo facto de quo vult consulere, utrum faciet vel non; et tunc tradit famulo ossa ad comburendum. Et sunt due parvule domus, juxta domum in qua jacet, in quibus comburuntur ossa illa, et queruntur diligenter cotidie per totam herbergiam. Combustis ergo illis usque ad nigredinem, referuntur ei, et tunc ipse inspicit si ossa fixa fuerint ad calorem ignis recte per longum. Tunc via aperta est quod ipse debeat facere. Si autem crepata fuerint ossa ex transverso, vel pecie rotunde exilierunt, tunc non facit. Semper enim finditur ipsum os in igne, vel quedam tela que est extensa desuper. Et si de tribus unum recte findatur, ipse facit."

V

POLITICAL GEOGRAPHY OF EASTERN TIBET

(List given me by the Secretary of the Chag-la jyal-bo at Ta-chien-lu.)

1. Nang-ch'en-wa Sbring-pa......pronounced Dring-pa.
2. Lchags-la.....................pronounced Chag-la.
3. K'ro-skyab....................pronounced Tro-jyab.
4. Hbah..........................pronounced Ba (Bat'ang).
5. Li-t'ang......................pronounced Lit'ang.
6. Sder-gi.......................pronounced Dérgé.
7. K'ang-gsar....................pronounced Kang-sar.
8. Ma-zur........................pronounced Ma-zur.
9. Brag-mon......................pronounced Dra-mon.
10. Hbé-rim......................pronounced Bé-rim.
11. Gri-htu......................pronounced Dri-tu.
12. Hgo-zi.......................pronounced Go-zi.
13. Po-mo........................pronounced Po-mo.
14. Lchog-rtsi...................pronounced Chog-tsi.
15. Nying-hgag...................pronounced Nying-ga.
16. Smi-li.......................pronounced Mi-li.
17. Brag-sting...................pronounced Dra-ting.
18. Lo-dgu and Ba-bam............pronounced Lo-gu and Ba-bam.

No. 1 is frequently called Mupin (or ping).

No. 2 is the district under the rule of the native king residing at Ta-chien-lu, and is called by the Chinese Ming-cheng-ssŭ.

Nos. 7, 8, 9, 10, and 11 are called collectively *Hor-sé k'a nga*, "the Five Clans of the Horba," the whole region being also frequently called *Hor chyok* (*p'yogs*), "the Horba district."[1]

Nos. 12, 14, and 15 occupy the upper course of the T'ung River, called Chin ch'uan.

No. 13 is frequently called So-mo. It is situated near Sung-p'an T'ing, and is at present ruled by a woman.

[1] Conf. E. C. Baber, *op. cit.*, p. 95.

No. 16 is situated to the west of the Ta-chien-lu country, and is governed by a lama.

Nos. 17 and 18 are to the north of the Chin ch'uan, between it and Sung-p'an.[1]

Another list was furnished me by a lama who had lived at Ta-chien-lu for some years. In it Ba, Li-t'ang, and Dérgé are omitted. It agrees closely with the list which Baber gives, but is fuller than his. I give the two in parallel columns. The second column is Baber's; the numbers in parentheses refer to the first list given above:

(1) Drumba	Djum-ba.
Jya-k'a	Djia-k'a.
(12) Wo-jé	Wo-jé or Go-jé.
Tsen-la and Raten	Tsen-la and Rap-ten.
Tam-ba	Tam-ba.
(13) Sa-ma	So-mung.
(14) Cho-tsé	Djiu-tse or Djiu-tzŭ.
(15) Zun-ga	Zur-ga.
(3) Tru-jyab	Tchro-shiop.
Pa-ti-pa wang	Pa-wang.
(17) Tra-ti	Tchra-tin.
Gi-shé-ts'a	Ge-shie.
(18) Leur-go	"
(16) Me-li	"
(2) Ja-la	"
Jyé-dam	"
(7) Kon-ser	"
(8) Ma-zer	"

The general name of *Nya-rong jyä-k'a chu-bjyä*, or "the Eighteen Tribes of the Nya-rong," sometimes shortened to Jyä-k'a chu-jyä, is given to the tribes mentioned in this list, Nya-rong being the name of the upper basin of the Nya-ch'u and its affluents. The tribes inhabiting along the lower course of the Nya ch'u are called Män-nya-k'a or "inhabitants of the lower Nya ch'u," and are the Maniak of Hodgson, the Mènia of Baber.

So much for the native divisions of the country. For those whom the subject interests, I append two lists taken from Chinese works, both published about fifty years ago, the first called "Hsi-yü k'ao ku-lu," the second the "Sheng-wu chi." These lists

[1] The Mä-nya country, or Chan-tui, is omitted, as it formed from 1864 until 1889 part of the kingdom of Lh'asa.

are interesting, moreover, as giving the boundaries of each district, the population, the amount of taxes due the Imperial government, the Chinese rank of the native chiefs, and, in some cases, their head village. The list given in the "Sheng-wu chi" comprises probably places occupied by non-Tibetan tribes, but as I am not able to determine all of these I have concluded to give it as it stands. Shen-pien and Leng-pien are in Ssŭ-ch'uan, in the Ya-chou Fu district, Shen-pien being conterminous with Ch'ing-ch'i Hsien, and Leng-pien with T'ien-chüan; but both of them have native chiefs (*T'u-ssŭ*). The people of these two tribes are at present undistinguishable in dress from the Chinese, but they speak a Tibetan patois.[1]

The "Hsi-yü k'ao ku-lu" distinguishes thirty-three tribes, which it calls "the thirty-three Yü-t'ung[2] Hsi-fan Tribes." The "Sheng-wu chi" gives fifty-one, about half of which are identical with those of the first list.

1 See Yule's "Marco Polo," second edition, II, p. 37, and his note in Gill's "River of Golden Sands," II, 77.

2 Baber, *op. cit.*, p. 54, says that Yü-t'ung is a tribe of the T'ung valley, a little above Wa-ssŭ-k'ou. It certainly is not in the accompanying list, although it generally has not so broad a meaning.

THIRTY-THREE YÜ-T'UNG HSI-FAN TRIBES.

Names.	Boundaries.	Capitals.	Population (by families, *hu*, of five persons).	Chiefs.	Taxes (in taels).
1. Shen-pien	E. Ching-ch'i Hsien S. Ta-tien-ma t'u-ssŭ W. Ming cheng ssŭ N. Leng-pien	Shen-pien	122	Ch'ang-kuan-ssŭ.	55
2. Leng-pien	E. T'ien-ch'uan S. Shen-pien W. Tsan-li t'u-ssŭ N. Mu-ping ssŭ	Leng ch'i	275	Ch'ang-kuan-ssŭ.	41
3. Ming-cheng (*Chagla*)	E. Leng-pien S. Chien-chang t'ing W. Li-t'ang ssŭ N. Sun-k'o tsung	Ta-chien-lu	6,591	Hsüan-wei-shih-ssŭ.	Not stated.
4. Cho-ssŭ-chia	E. Ts'a-ku t'ing S. Ta chin-ch'uan W. Ko-shih-tsa N. Wa-shu mu-ch'üeh-ya	Cho-ssŭ chia	9,000	An-fu-shih-ssŭ	2.6.9
5. Tan-tung Ko-shih-tsa.	E. Ta chin-ch'uan S. Ming-cheng W. Kan-mu N. Hor Chango	Tan-tung	830	An-fu-shih-ssŭ	2.6.9

THIRTY-THREE YÜ-T'UNG HSI-FAN TRIBES—*Continued*.

Names.	Boundaries.	Capitals.	Population (by families, *hu*, of five persons).	Chiefs.	Taxes (in taels).
6. Pa-ti (*Pati pawang*)	E. Hsiao chin-ch'uan S. Ming-cheng W. Ko-shih-tsa N. Ta chiu-ch'uan	Pa-waug	850	An-fu-shih-ssŭ	2.6.9
7. La-kun	E. Ming-cheng S. Li-t'ang W. Lower Chan-tui N. Ming-cheng	La-kun	970	An-fu-shih-ssŭ	Not stated.
8. Li-t'ang (*Lit'ang*)	E. Ming-cheng S. Ba-t'ang W. Wa-shu N. Chan-tui	Li-t'aug	5,322	Hsüan-fu-shih-ssŭ	450.0.0
9. Ba-t'ang (*Ba*)	E. Li-t'ang S. Lh'asa W. Sang-ang-pang N. Chamuto	Ba-t'ang	3,063	Hsüan-fu-shih-ssŭ	1,895.4.8
10. Tê-ko-tê (*Dérgé*)	E. Upper Chan-tui S. Chamuto W. Upper Na-to N. Lin-tsung	....	7,977	Hsüan-wei-shih-ssŭ	280.0.0

THIRTY-THREE YÜ-T'UNG HSI-FAN TRIBES—*Continued*

Names.	Boundaries.	Capitals.	Population (by families, *hu*, of five persons).	Chiefs.	Taxes (in taels).
11. Wa-shu Ch'ung-hsi	E. Ming-cheng S. Li-t'ang W. Li-t'ang N. Chan-tui	....	308	Ch'ang-kuan-ssŭ	26.0.0
12. Wa-shu Mao-ya	E. Li-t'ang S. Yang-la W. Lamaya N. Dérgé	....	371	Ch'ang-kuan-ssŭ	36.0.0
13. Wa-shu Shan-t'eng	E. Li-t'ang S. Jo-ts'o W. Ba-t'ang N. Ch'un-ta	....	243	Ch'ang-kuan-ssŭ	12.0.0
14. Wa-shu Ssŭ-ta	E. Keng-p'ing S. Lower Chan-tui W. Hor K'ang-sar N. Hor Chuwo	....	250	Ch'ang-kuan-ssŭ	7.5.0
15. Wa-shu Keng-p'ing	E. Ko-shih-tsa S. Chang-t'an W. Bérim N. Ko-chi	....	300	Ch'ang-kuan-ssŭ	10.0.0

THIRTY-THREE YÜ-T'UNG HSI-FAN TRIBES—*Continued*

Names.	Boundaries.	Capitals.	Population (by families, *hu*, of five persons).	Chiefs.	Taxes (in taels).
16. Wa-shu Yü-k'o	E. Ko-shih-tsa S. Hor Kung-sa W. Wa-shu Ssŭ-ta N. Ch'o-ssŭ-chia		640	An-fu-shih-ssŭ	24.0.0
17. Huo-erh Chuwo (*Hor Chuwo*)	E. Keng-p'iug S. Upper Chan-tui W. Kan-Ma-ch'ü (*Mazur*) N. Tung-k'o	Chuwo	1,660	An-fu-shih-ssŭ	92.0.0
18. Huo-erh Chang-ku (*Chango*)	E. Tung-p'ing S. Lower Chan-tui W. Hor Kangsar N. Hor Chuwo	Chango	3,320	An-fu-shih-ssŭ	182.0.0
19. Huo-erh K'ung-sa (*Kangsar*)	E. Chuwo S. Wa-shu Chung-hsi W. Bérim N. Ko-chi		923	An-fu-shih-ssŭ	70.0.0
20. Huo-erh Kan-kung Ma-ch'ü (*Kanzé Mazur*)	E. Ming-cheng S. Yü-k'o W. T'u-ken man-tieh N. Sung-p'an t'ing		665	An-fu-shih-ssŭ	57.0.0

THIRTY-THREE YÜ-T'UNG HSI-FAN TRIBES—*Continued*

Names.	Boundaries.	Capitals.	Population (by families, *hu*, of five persons).	Chiefs.	Taxes (in taels).
21. Huo-erh Pai-li (*Bérim*)	E. Ma-chu (*Mazur*) S. Wa-shu W. Lin-tsung N. Sung-p'an t'ing	Bérim	315	Ch'ang-kuan-ssŭ	18.0.0
22. Huo-erh Tsa	E. Tung-k'o S. Dérgé W. Lin-tsung N. Sung-p'an t'ing	......	711	An-fu-shih-ssŭ	40.0.0
23. Huo-erh Tnug-k'o	E. Ssŭ-ta S. Kangsar W. Hor Tsa N. Sung-p'an t'ing	......	348	An-fu-shih-ssŭ (A lama appointed from Hsi-ning.)	25.0.0
24. Upper Chan-tui	E. Hor Chango S. Maoya W. Dérgé N. Hor Mazur	......	422	Ch'ang-kuan ssŭ	16.0.0
25. Middle Chan-tui	E. Ming-cheng S. Lower Chan-tui W. Upper Chan-tui N. Na-lin chung	......	200	Ch'ang-kuan ssŭ	Not stated.

THIRTY-THREE YÜ-T'UNG HSI-FAN TRIBES—*Continued*

Names.	Boundaries.	Capitals.	Population (by families, *hu*, of five persons).	Chiefs.	Taxes (in taels).
26. Lower Chan-tui	E. Ming-cheng S. La-kun W. Jo-sang-ni N. Hor	....	340	An-fu-shih-ssŭ	Not stated.
27. Ch'un-ko	E. Lin-tsung S. Upper Na-to W. Hsi-ning N. Hsi-ning	....	588	An-fu-shih-ssŭ	46.0.0
28. Yü-na-t'u	E. Ch'a ch'ü (*Mazur?*) S. Lower Chan-tui W. Upper Chan-tui N. Na-lin-chung	....	206	Ch'ien-hu	8.0.0
29. Meng-ko-chieh (*Jyékundo*)	E. Hor tsa S. Hsi-ning[1] W. Hsi-ning[2] N. Hsi-ning[3]	....	304	Ch'aug-kuan-ssŭ	23.0.0

[1] Seventy *li* from the Dré-ch'u. [2] Two hundred and eighty *li* from Chao-wu. [3] At the Hara-ussu (Dré ch'u). (Notes of the Chinese author.)

THIRTY-THREE YÜ-T'UNG HSI-FAN TRIBES—*Continued*

Names.	Boundaries.	Capitals.	Population (by families, *hu*, of five persons).	Chiefs.	Taxes (in taels).
30. Lin-tsung	E. Hor Tsa S. Dérgé W. Ch'un-k'o N. Meng-ko-chieh	......	1,096	An-fu-shih-ssŭ	64.0.0
31. Upper Na-to	E. Ch'un-k'o S. Chamuto (*Ch'amdo*) W. Chamuto N. Na-chi	......	650	An-fu-shih-ssŭ	16.0.0
32. Sa-tun-t'u	E. Hor Chango S. Wa-shu Maoya W. Dérgé N. Hor Mazur	......	50	Ch'ien-hu	16.0.0
33. Wa-shu Mao-mao	E. Hor Chango S. Wa-shu Maoya W. Dérgé N. Hor Mazur	......	100	Po-hu	8.0.0
Grand Total	......	......	49,010	......	Tls. 3,526.0.5

FAN TRIBES WITHIN THE JURISDICTION OF SSŬ-CH'UAN

(List taken from "Sheng-wu chi")

N. B.—Numbers in parentheses refer to preceding list.

HSÜAN-FU-SHIH.

1. Chiung-pu.
2. Lit'ang (8).
3. Bat'ang (9).

AN-FU-SHIH.

4. Chang-ning.
5. Wu-li.
6. Wa-ssŭ.
7. So-mo.
8. Kua-pieh.
9. Mu-li.
10. Tan-tung ko-shih-ch'a (5).
11. Pa-li (6).
12. Ch'o-ch'i chia (4).
13. La-kun (7).
14. Wa-shu Yü-k'o (16).
15. Chu-wo (17).
16. Hor Chang-ku (18).
17. Hor Kung-sa (19).
18. Hor Cha-li (22).
19. Hor Lin-tsung (30).
20. Hor Kan-tzŭ (20).
21. Ma-shu (20).
22. Tung-k'o (23).
23. Chun-k'o (27).
24. Lower Chan-tui (26).
25. Upper Na-to (31).

CH'ANG-KUAN SSŬ.

26. Ching-chou.
27. Lung-chou.
28. Yo-hsi.
29. Sung-kang.
30. Cho-k'o-chi.
31. Wei-lung chou.
32. P'u-chi chou.
33. Chang chou.
34. Shen-pien (1).
35. Leng-pien (2).
36. Wa-shu Chung-hsi (11).
37. Wa-shu Mao-ya (12).
38. Wa-shu Ch'ü-t'eng (13).
39. Wa-shu T'a-ssŭ (Ssŭ-t'a) (14).
40. Wa-shu Keng-ping (15).
41. Hor Na-lin chung.
42. Hor Pa-li (21).
43. Ch'un-ko-kao-ji.
44. Upper Chan-tui (24).
45. Middle Chan-tui (25).
46. Meng-ko-chieh (29).
47. Ni-ch'i.
48. Ping-i.
49. Shu ch'uan.
50. Chiu-hsing.

FU CH'ANG-KUAN SSŬ.

51. Ma-la.

It is to be noticed that Dérgé and Ming-cheng (Chag-la or Ta-chien-lu) do not figure in this list, in which also the Horba country is divided into nine districts.

The six Wa-shu tribes, or districts, are subordinate to Lit'ang.

VI

ORIGIN OF THE TIBETAN PEOPLE, AS TOLD IN THE "MANI KAMBUM," CHAPTER XXXIV

(Translation.)

Om mani padmé hum.

Then the greatest of all the Bodhisattwas, P'apa Shenräzig Wang-ch'yuk, came to the Realm-of happiness (*Déwa-chan*), and the Buddha Nangwa t'ä-yä (*Amitayus*) spoke to him, saying: "Merciful Bodhisattwa, the Buddha Sachya t'upa (*Shakyamuni*) did not convert the Realm of snow (*i. e.*, Tibet), he did not set his foot upon it, did not illumine it with the light of his word, did not show it his bounty. It is for thee to gather together the low-lived creatures of the Abode of snow and bring them into a fit state for receiving the holy truth."

So then the Bodhisattwa P'apa Shenräzig Wang-ch'yuk repaired to the many-jeweled dwelling on the top of Mount Potala,[1] and looked at the living creatures inhabiting the Abode of snow, and saw that they in their ignorance of the religion of the Buddha were plunged in darkness like the black darkness of night; they were like the snow which falls on the surface of a lake and which can rise no more and must keep on going downward, for they were ever getting lower in the evil way. And he saw how there was no freedom for them; they moved as it were in a tightly closed iron coffer.

Then he caused a ray of bright light to come out of the palm of his right hand, and from out it appeared the king of the monkeys, the Bodhisattwa Hilumandju. Bethinking him of making mankind in the Abode of snow, he asked the monkey-king, "Wilt thou be able to give thyself to deep meditation in that snowy realm of the north?" "I will," he replied. Then he bound him by the oath of the five highest duties, and expounded to him the deep and far-reaching doctrine, after which the monkey transported himself by supernatural means to the Abode of snow, and, sitting down on a rock, was soon plunged in profound abstraction.

1 At Lh'asa, where now lives his incarnation, the Talé lama. This hill is also called Marpori, "Red hill." This god's favorite abodes are Pu-t'o shan, in the Chusan archipelago; Adams Peak, in Ceylon; Potala, near the mouth of the Indus, and Lh'asa.

Now at that time Peu-yul (*i. e.*, Tibet) was divided into nine regions. The first three, called *Rinpoch'é od-gi ling* ("the jeweled light region"), reaching to the highest peaks of slate and ice, were held by elephants and deer. The *Ru-dzi sog-pé ling* ("the region of the four horns") comprised the three middle zones of rocks and alps, and was held by rock-ogres (*drasinpo*) and monkeys. The *Ma-jya od ling* ("the peacock-light region"), comprising the three lowest zones of forests and valleys, was occupied by ogres (*sinpo*). So it was that the very name of man was unknown in that land.

Some time after the advent of Hilumandju, it happened on a day that a rock-ogress, burning with lust, took the semblance of a she-monkey and went near unto the monkey-king, lost in profoundest meditation, and endeavored by every kind of blandishment and lascivious gesture to excite his passions, but though for seven days she thus bedeviled him she could not arouse him from his abstraction.

So she thought within herself that perhaps her failure was due to the ugliness of her face and form; so she transformed herself into a lovely woman, gorgeously arrayed in jewels, and with bare bosom, and again she tried to arouse his passions. Then the monkey-king stole a glance at her out of the corner of his eye, and she, seeing her opportunity, moved near him and said, "Be mine." "I am a follower of P'apa Shenräzig," he replied, "and I may not be yours."

Then spoke the rock-ogress, saying: "Alas, monkey-king, I love thee passionately. Listen to me: my destiny has made me what I am, an ogress, but I pine for thee with all the force of love, and I would clasp thee in these arms. If thou refusest to be my husband I will call together all the ogres of the realm, and daily we will kill creatures by the tens of thousands, and nightly we will devour them by the thousands. And the ogresses will bear young, and they will be many; and this Abode of snow will be the kingdom of ogres, and they will devour the world. If death overtakes me while in this mind, my punishment will be to fall into the depth of hell. But thou, sin cannot overtake thee, shielded with the power of deep abstraction; fear not, lest it gradually forsake thee. Think of me kindly and spare me, that the voice of love be not changed to that of lamentation."

Then the monkey Bodhisattwa's heart was moved with commiseration as he considered the ogress, and he thought, "If I, in ignorance of possible consequences, take unto myself a wife, my powers of meditation may become impaired. On the other hand, if I do not take this woman as my wife, and she dies, great will be my sin!" So he resolved to go and question the Bodhisattwa, the knowing P'apa Shenräzig, and, having transported himself by his power of magic to the dwelling on Mount Potala, he did obeisance to the knowing Shenräzig, and thus addressed him: "Alas, Lord of creatures, Merciful One, I am thy disciple (*gényen*), and my strength lies in my power of deep meditation, but an ogress of the devil's race, with mind filled with lechery, has assailed me, and my power of abstract meditation is about to depart. What shall I do to preserve my power of meditation? Merciful One, instruct me, I beseech thee. The ogress has said: 'Thou must be my husband; if thou wilt not, I will fling away my life, and it will be counted unto thee as sin.' Tell me, is it proper, or not, that I take her to me as a wife?"

"Highly proper," replied P'apa Shenräzig, "though it may not be that thou and thy wife become human beings; in the days to come, when thy children's children have multiplied in the Abode of snow, they will become human beings, and the Holy Truth will be diffused among them and it will be mighty in the land."

Then the Lady Drolma (*Jo-mo Drolma*) added, "When men kind shall have multiplied (in Tibet), they will be pillars of religion."

"So be it (*Laso*)," he made answer. Then the monkey Bodhisattwa, fearing lest the rock-ogress should destroy herself, departed in all haste for the Abode of snow, and as soon as he arrived he took her unto him as his wife. When the space of nine months had elapsed she bore him six sons, who participated of the nature of the six classes of sentient creatures subject to birth and death. As their father was a monkey, so their bodies were covered with hair, and as their mother was a rock-ogress, so they had tails;[1] their faces were reddish and they were most unsightly. From the mortal gods, one had gentleness and patience; from the mortal (lit., subject to birth and death) Asuras (*lh'a-mayin*), one of them derived angry passions and quarrelsomeness. One of them had in part great lusts, and love of worldly riches, which qualities he owed to mortal man. One of them owed to hell's mortal fiends, hate, and anger, and great hardiness. One partook of the mortal Préta's (*yidag*) characteristics in being deformed,

[1] The text says "no tails" (*mjug-ma méd-pa*), but the context does not bear out this reading, and a little farther on we find that "their tawny tails disappeared" (*mjug-ma skya-wa bdzin-du song*).

from his cravings for food (lit., bad stomach), and his avariciousness. One partook of mortal brute beasts in not being able to distinguish right from wrong, and in having neither comprehension nor cleverness. When born they were ruddy-faced, had a taste for flesh and blood, and hair covered their heads and bodies, and, moreover, they knew how to speak.

Now when the little ones and their mother, the rock-ogress, became ahungered and in want of food, their father, the monkey Bodhisattwa, took them to a forest in the south, called "The Peacock woods," where there were monkeys for them to live with. And they lived with the female monkeys. After the space of a year the father visited them to see how they fared, and he saw that they had increased by five hundred, and their offspring were neither monkeys nor yet men, and they were exposed to the rain and the sun's rays in summer and to the snow and the wind of winter, and they had neither food nor raiment. Then the monkey Bodhisattwa, their sire and grandsire, was filled with anguish, and the five hundred young monkeys came to him, holding out beseechingly their helpless hands, exclaiming: "Father, what shall we eat? with what shall we clothe ourselves?"

And the monkey, when he saw this the great distress of his progeny and that there was neither food nor clothing for them, was afflicted, and filled with compassion. They had already devoured all the edible fruits, etc., but he got fruits and other things and brought them to them; but hardly had they eaten them, than they were racked with pain, and all the hair on their bodies fell off, the briars pricked their hands and feet,[1] and their tails shriveled up and disappeared. Then the old monkey in anguish and dire distress bethought him, "Why am I in such sorrow and misery? and these young monkeys, why has this befallen them? and the rock-ogress, my wife, why has this come to her, when there is the prophecy of the Knowing One Shenräzig and of the Jomo Drolma? Alas, it is doubtless on account of my former wickedness. The Venerable One cannot have been mistaken in his forecast. It is not right for me to be angered and disturbed in mind; I will question the Venerable One, himself."

So by magical means he repaired to the palace on Mount Potala, and, having done obeisance to the Venerable One, he

[1] That is, as I understand the text, briars could prick their hands and feet, which were no longer protected by a covering of hair.

stood before him, and spoke as follows: "If I, moved only through compassion and regardless of the poison leaf of passion, have unwittingly brought myself into the prison of the Devil, and have beguiled the woman into the toils of the Evil One, my children and grandchildren into the orb of Māra, and we have all sunk in the mire of lust and are weighed down under a mountain of misery; if we have become wrapped in the smoke of the misery of sin and struck down by the plague of evil deeds; if I myself have been seized with the disease of misery, it is only I who have brought us into the world of transmigration, and have been caught in the net of dark ignorance; protect my (sinless) children and grandchildren. What has happened to me has been at the word of the Venerable One, and I shall without a doubt fall hereafter into hell. But be merciful to me, I beseech thee. Knowing One, I and the rock-ogress, our children and children's children, have moreover nothing to sustain life on, and I have sought thee in deep anguish to know what to do."

Then spoke P'apa Shenräzig Wang-ch'yuk, saying: "Pen-yul, the Abode of snow, was in utter darkness and in the power of creatures not human, and was not within the sphere of my conversion; but these (thy descendants) have become men, and thou hast, in bringing this transformation about, opened to them the gate to heaven and redemption. Doubt me not, be single-hearted and despair not, for these thy children and grandchildren have finally become men, and will some day enter the fold of my redeemed. Thou hast done no evil, but only made them take a step in the road towards freedom; it is well. Think not to be in anguish, for these thy progeny shall be provided with both worldly goods and spiritual goods. These thy progeny shall be of two kinds: some of them shall be of their grandsire's race, and have great faith and kind-heartedness, great understanding and application, they shall delight in the subtilities of religion and ever thirst after virtue, they shall have broad understanding and Bodhisattwa great-mindedness; some shall be of the mother's race, and shall delight in killing and will like flesh and blood, they will be fond of trade and lucre, strong in body and mind, given to unrighteousness, liking to hear of others' shortcomings, cruel, prying,[1] butchering animals, and eating meat.

[1] I have translated by these two words the following phrase, *rkang lag-gis hdug mi ts'ugs-pa, mig mi-la lta mi ts'ugs pa*, which appears to mean, literally translated, "hurting man with hands and feet, looking at men with the eye and hurting them," but my interpretation is conjectural.

"And the food portions of thy descendants are these seven varieties of seed"; and he gave him barley, wheat, beans, pease, *soba* (thick-shelled barley), etc., saying unto him, "carry these to the Abode of snow, and these seeds shall fructify and increase. Moreover, to satisfy the longing after riches, which they derive from the rock-ogress thy wife, here are handfuls of precious dust, gold, silver, copper, iron, etc.; scatter them in the Abode of snow, and they shall become treasures in the earth and shall be found in mines, and after a season these thy progeny, become men, shall subsist by this precious gold, silver, etc., and after a time they shall open these precious mines." [1]

And he spat in the direction of the Abode of snow, saying: "After a while there shall arise in the land an incarnate Bodhisattwa, who will be a defender of religion, a man exalted above all others." [2]

Then the monkey Bodhisattwa transported himself to the Abode of snow, where he sowed the seed in a part of the land well suited for the purpose, level and warm, and with every qualification. And after that the monkey Bodhisattwa had gathered together in the summer the monkey children in the Peacock woods, the autumn came after the sowing of the seeds, and it was time to look after them, and they were all ripe and fit to eat. Then he called the monkey children and instructed them, saying: "These P'apa Shenräzig has given you as your food portion; cultivate them; let this be your work. This is the first labor in the land, but later on there shall be treasures found in Tibet, and they will be in mines; these the Bodhisattwa Shenräzig Waug-ch'yuk has also given you." And they acquired worldly goods, after which for the first time they became bound together by religion. [3]

The narrative goes on to state that Shenräzig caused a ray of light to issue out of the palm of his right hand, and from out it came a youth with all the signs and characteristics of a Buddha, who came among the people of Tibet, described as still being

[1] This is in conformity with the Tibetan idea that minerals grow, that large nuggets are the seeds of which the smaller ones are the fruit as it were.

[2] An allusion to Srong-tsan gambo, the king of Tibet, in whose reign Buddhism is said to have been introduced into Tibet, and who is the reputed author of this work. He reigned from A. D. 636 to 698.

[3] According to East Indian legends given by the Chinese pilgrim Hsüan Chuang, which show some analogy with those here given, the people of Ceylon descended from a lion, who took to wife a daughter of a king of southern India. See "Vie et Voyages de Hiouen-Thsang, trad. par Stan. Julien," I, p. 194.

something between men and monkeys, "with curtailed hind parts and hairy bodies"; and he taught them the profit arising from observing the ten cardinal virtues (*pāramitā*), etc., and they believed him, and the first seeds of the Buddhist faith were sown in Peu-lung-ba (Tibet).

VII

NOTES ON THE LANGUAGE OF EASTERN TIBET

IN the following note I have endeavored to present some of the peculiarities of the pronunciation of the Koko-nor Tibetans, to which I have added a syllabary giving the pronunciation at Lh'asa, Bat'ang, and the Ts'aroug, the first being the modern standard of excellence. The pronunciation of the Koko-nor Tibetans is harsher than that in any other section of the country with which I am acquainted, and presents a number of peculiarities which I must leave to philologists to explain. Its vocabulary and phraseology do not differ essentially from those of Lh'asa, nor, for that matter, of any of the other dialects spoken in K'amdo. There are, of course, in each a large number of local expressions, of patois words, many of Chinese, or Turki, some of unknown origin, but so slight are these peculiarities that a native of Lh'asa can master them in a very short time. Prof. Terrien de Lacouperie, speaking of the tribes of eastern Tibet, says: "In the east, near the borders of China, are the numerous tribes called Gyarung or Chen-tui; their language has been studied by Hodgson, who has pointed out its remarkable similarity of structure to that of the Tagals of the Philippines."[1] However this may be, the Mänyak'a from the Chan-tui, like the people of Bat'ang, Ta-chien-lu, Kanzé, and Jyékundo, speak Tibetan; and the educated ones among them endeavor to pronounce as much like the Lh'asa people as they possibly can.

I regret that I was unable to collect a vocabulary of the language spoken by the Golok, for, while I feel sure that it is a Tibetan dialect, I believe that in its pronunciation it is even more archaic than that of the Panak'a of the Koko-nor.

[1] "Encyclopædia Britannica," 9th edition, *s. v.* "Tibet," p. 344.

PECULIARITIES OF THE AMDOWA AND PANAK'A PRONUNCIATION

Transcription.	Meaning.	Pronunciation.	Observations.
Dus	Time	Du	Like French *du*, "of."
Ch'os	Law	Ch'ua	Lh'asa — pronounced *ch'ü*.
Dzus	Asked	Dzu.	
K'ro	Auger	Cho	Lh'asa — pronounced *tru*.
Gus	Garment	Gü.	
K'rag	Blood	Chak	Lh'asa — pronounced *tra*.
Nyid	Self	Nyit	High tone.
T'us	Heard	T'ü	Like French *tu*, "thou."
Dag-par	Purely	Dak-war.	
Legs-par	Well	Lek-war.	
P'an ch'en rin-po-ch'é	A title	Han ch'en rin-po-ché	Or *P'an*—but this is considered Mongol pronunciation.
P'ug	Cavern	Huk.	
P'ul-nas	Having given	Hul-né.	
T'eg-pa	Carriage	T'é-wa.	
Chi smos	Why speak of	Chi rmé	Lh'asa — pronounced *chi mö*.
Bu gchig	One child	Vu chik.	
Sha-stag	Only	Shartak.	
Ma mt'ong	Not seen	Mam t'ong.	
Mi ldan	Not having	Mir-dän	The first syllable pronounced like English *mere*.
Mi gyo	Unmoved	Mir-yo	" " " " "
Zak-pa	Sorrow	Zak-hua.	
Zla-wa	Moon	Da-va.	
Os	Proper	Eu.	

PECULIARITIES OF THE AMDOWA AND PANAK'A PRONUNCIATION—*Continued*

Transcription.	Meaning.	Pronunciation.	Observations.
Shig	Louse	Shiek.	
Grol	Free	Drol.	
Gtso	Chief	Rtso.	
Gdzan	Other	Rdzan.	
Gso	To cure	Rso.	
Gsum	Three	Rsùm.	
Gzugs	Figure	Rdzuk.	
Dkah	Difficult	Rka.	
Dgra	Enemy	Rja.	
Dpag	Fut. of *dpog*	Huak	Lh'asa — pronounced *pa.*
Dpal	Glory	Hual.	
Dpé	Example	Hué.	
Dper-na	For example	Huer-na.	
Dbus-nas	From the midst	Dwu-né.	
Dugos-po	Reality	Rnyö-po.	
Dkyil-hk'or	Circle	Dchyil-k'or	Lh'asa — pronounced *chi k'or.*
Dpung	Host	Hung.	
Dben	Solitude	Wen.	English *when.*
Dbyangs	Song	Ryang.	
Dbul-p'ongs-pa	Indigent	Wul-p'ong-va.	
Dbye-dzing	Being divided	Djé dzäng	Lh'asa — pronounced *jyé-dzin.*
Dmah	Low	Ma.	
Bral	Deprived of	Jal.	

PECULIARITIES OF THE AMDOWA AND PANAK'A PRONUNCIATION—*Continued*

Transcription.	Meaning.	Pronunciation.	Observations.
Bkra	Good	Ja	*Tra* is also heard.
Bkah hstsal	Spoke	Kuar-tsal.	
Bskyod	Moved	Rshyot	Or *Kyot.*
Brla	Thigh	Vla.	
Brjod	Spoke	Ryot.	
Bgyis	Made	Bjye.	
Byams-pa	The Merciful One	Chuam-pa	Or *Suam-pa.*
Brgyan-pa	Adorned	Rgyan-pa.	
Brgya-ba	The hundredth	Rgya-wa	Or *Rya-ra.*
Bzla-par	Spoken	Rdä-par.	
Bkra-shis	Good luck	Chua-shi	Lh'asa — pronounced *tra-shi.*
Bkag	Forbade	Kuak.	
Bsgral-wa	Cut	Dral-va.	
Bgegs	Hindrance	Hgek.	
Brnyan	Reward	Rnyan.	
Brtsegs	Built	Rtsek.	
Mk'as	Learned	K'ua	Lh'asa — pronounced *k'é.*
Mk'an-po	Abbot	Kuan-bo.	
Mngon	Evident	Won.	
Mt'ah-yas	Endless	Mt'a-yé	Lh'asa — pronounced *t'ä-yä.*
Mk'ah-hgro	A kind of fairy	K'ua-dru.	
Mngah	Might	Mua.	
Hdi	This	Dé.	

PECULIARITIES OF THE AMDOWA AND PANAK'A PRONUNCIATION — *Continued*

Transcription.	Meaning.	Pronunciation.	Observations.
Hk'rul	Mistaken	Chul.	
Hdi hdra vai	This kind	Dendra vi.	
Hdus-byas	Compound	Dub-ché.	
Hp'os-na	If he died	Hu-na.	
Hjog-pa	Placed	Jok-pa	Or *wa*.
Hbar	To burn	Bar.	
Hkrug-med	Peaceful	Chuk met	Lh'asa — pronounced *tru-mé*.
Hbyang	Clean	Hjyang	Also, *ayang* and *psyang*.
Mi gtsang	Unclean	Mir-tsang.	
Sdug-bsngal	Misery	Rduk-rnal.	
Legs-par	Well	Lek-war.	
Sprin p'ung	A lot of clouds	Drin p'ung.	
Baidũrya	Lapis lazuli	Betriyé	Lh'asa — pronounced *bendrya*.
Od-hpro	Light	Od-cho	Lh'asa — pronounced *wö-tro*.
Ting-nge-hdjin	Meditation	Teng-en-dzin.	
Pyak-hts'al-lo	Saluted	Shyak-ts'alo.	
Hbrug-sgra	Thunder	Druk-dra.	
Gtsug-p'ud	Tuft of hair	Tsuk-hut.	
Bkah drin ch'e	Thank you	Kua drin ch'e.	
Bkah hbum	Title of book	Kuam bum.	
Bkah hgyur	Title of book	Kuan jur.	
Bkur-sti	Homage	Kur-ti.	
Blun	Stupid	Hlun.	

PECULIARITIES OF THE AMDOWA AND PANAK'A PRONUNCIATION — *Continued*

Transcription.	Meaning.	Pronunciation.	Observations.
Ma ste	Is not	Marté.	
Shākya t'ub-pa	Shakyamuni	Shakcha t'uba	Lh'asa — pronounced *Sacha t'upa.*
Mi hjigs-pa	Not afraid	Min je-va	Like *min* in *minister.*
K'ri-stan	Seat	Chir-tan.	
Sra-brtan	Firm	Sar-tau.	
Kyang	Also	Jang	Lh'asa — pronounced *jyang.*
Hjam-dpal	Name of a god	Jam-hual.	
Hjog-pa	To place	Jok-wa.	
Hp'ags-pa	Exalted	Hp'ak-wa.	
Sku	Body	Rku.	
Skyong	Defect	Schyong.	
Sgyu-ma	Illusion	Ryü-ma.	
Sgrai	Of the voice	Dri	Or *gri.*
Sgral	To cut	Jal	Lh'asa — pronounced *dral.*
Sgrigs-te	Arranging	Drik-té.	
Sna	Nose	Rna.	
Sgrogs-pa	Comrade	Jok-wa.	
Sgo	Door	Rgo.	
Sngar	Formerly	Rnar.	
Smras-pa	Spoken	Rmä-wa.	
Skrag-pa	Frightened	Drak-hua	Lh'asa — pronounced *tra-pa.*
Slob-dpon	Teacher	Lob-huon	Lh'asa — pronounced *lopön.*
Sgoms	Meditated	Rgom.	

PECULIARITIES OF THE AMDOWA AND PANAK'A PRONUNCIATION — *Continued*

Transcription.	Meaning.	Pronunciation.	Observations.
Ltar	Like	Rtar.	
Lta	To see	Rta.	
Rta	Horse	Sta.	
Rten-hbrel	Cause and effect	Ten-brel	Lh'asa — pronounced *teundrel.*
Rgyal-wa	Victorious	Yal-va.	
Rgyal-po	Prince	Yaro.	
Rdjing-bu	Pond	Rdjing-vu.	
Rgan-po	Old	Rgan-po.	
Rdju-hprul	Witchcraft	Rdjum-chul	Lh'asa — pronounced *dju-tr'ul.*
Rgyal-mts'an	Trophy	Ryam-ts'an	Lh'asa — pronounced *jyal-ts'än.*
Rgyun	Continual	Ryun.	
Rdjogs	Finished	Rdjok.	
Ji skad	Thus	Jir-kad	Lh'asa — pronounced *ji kä.*

TIBETAN SYLLABARY, WITH PRONUNCIATION OF LH'ASA, BAT'ANG, AND THE TSARONG

Tran-scription.	Lh'asa.	Bat'ang.	Tsarong.	Tran-scription.	Lh'asa.	Bat'ang.	Tsarong.
Ka	ka	ka	ka.	k'ra	tr'a	tra	tr'a.
k'a	k'a	k'a	k'a.	gra	dra	dra	dra.
ga	ga	ga	ga.	tra	tra	tra	tra.
nga	na	nga	nga.	t'ra	t'ra	tr'a	tr'a.
cha	cha	chiă	chiă.	dra	dra	drā (soft)	dra.
ch'a	ch'a	ch'ia	ch'ia.	nra	na	sha	na.
ja	ja	ja	ja.	pra	tra	tra	tra.
nya	nya	nya	nya.	p'ra	tr'a	tr'a	tr'a.
ta	ta	ta	ta.	bra	dra	drā (soft)	dra.
t'a	t'a	t'a	t'a.	mra	ma	na	ma.
da	da	da	da.	sra	sa	sa	sa.
na	na	na	na.	h'ra	h'a	sha (soft)	h'a.
pa	pa	pa	pa.	kla	la	la	la.
p'a	p'a	p'a	p'a.	gla	la	lā	la.
ba	ba	ba	ba.	bla	la	lă	la.
ma	ma	ma	ma.	zla	da	da	da.
tsa	tsa	tsa	tsa.	rla	la	la	la.
ts'a	ts'a	ts'a	ts'a.	sla	la	la	la.
dja	dja	dja	dja.	rka	ka	ka	ka.
wa	wa	wa	wa.	rkya	chya	chya	chya.
dza	dza	dza	dza.	rga	ga	ga	ga.
za	za	za	za.	rgya	jya	jya	jya.
a	ă	ă	ă.	rnga	na	nga	nga.
ya	ya	ya	ya.	rja	ja	ja	ja.
ra	ra	ra	ra.	rnya	nya	nya	nya.
la	la	la	la.	rta	ta	ta	ta.
sha	sha	shia	shia.	rda	da	da	da.
sa	sa	sa	sa.	rna	na	na	na.
h'a	h'a	h'a	h'a.	rba	ba	ba	ba.
a	ā	ā	ā.	rma	ma	ma	ma.
kya	chă	chia	chia.	rtsa	tsa	tsa	tsa.
k'ya	ch'a	ch'ia	ch'ia.	rdza	dza	dzā	dza.
gya	jya	gyā	gya.	lka	ka	ka	ka.
pya	cha	hsia	hsia.	lga	ga	gā	ga.
p'ya	cha	hs'ia	hs'ia.	lnga	na	nga	nga.
bya	ja	hsia	hsia.	lcha	cha	chia	chia.
mya	nya	nya	nya.	lja	ja	jya	jya.
kra	tra	tra	tra.	lta	ta	ta	ta.

TIBETAN SYLLABARY, WITH PRONUNCIATION OF LH'ASA, BAT'ANG, AND THE TSARONG—*Continued*

Transcription.	Lh'asa.	Bat'ang.	Tsarong.	Transcription.	Lh'asa.	Bat'ang.	Tsarong.
lda	da	da	da.	dkra	tra	tra	tra.
lpa	pa	pa	pa.	dgah	ga	gā	ga.
lba	ba	ba	ba.	dgyah	jya	jya	jya.
lh'a	h'la	h'la	h'a.	dgra	dra	dra	dra.
ska	ka	ka	ka.	dngah	na	nga	nga.
skya	chya	chya	chya.	dpa	pa	pa	pa.
skra	tra	tra	tra.	dpya	chya	hsia	hsia.
sga	ga	ga	ga.	dpra	tra	tra	tra.
sgya	jya	jya	jya.	dbah	ba	ba	ba.
sgra	dra	dra	dra.	dbra	dra	dra	dra.
snga	na	nga	nga.	dbya	jya	ya	hsia.
snya	nya	nya	nya.	dmah	ma	ma	ma.
sta	ta	ta	ta.	dmya	nya	nya	nya.
sda	da	da	da.	btah	ta	ta	ta.
sna	na	nha	na.	bkya	cha	chya	chya.
spa	pa	pā	p'a.	bkra	tra	tra	tra.
spya	ch'ya	hsia	hsia.	bkla	la	la	la.
spra	tra	tră'	tra.	brka	ka	ka	ka.
sba	ba	ba	ba.	brkya	chya	gya	chya.
sbya	jya	hsia	hsia.	bska	ka	ka	ka.
sbra	dra	dra	dra.	bskya	chya	hsia	chya.
sma	ma	mh'a	ma.	bskra	tra	tra	tra.
smya	nya	nh'a	nya.	bgah	ga	ga	ga.
smra	ma	mh'a	ma.	bgya	jya	jyā	jyā.
stsa	tsa	tsa	tsa.	bgra	dra	dra	dra.
gchah	cha	chia	chia.	brga	ga	ga	ga.
gnyah	nya	nya	nya.	brgya	jya	jyā	jya.
gtah	ta	ta	ta.	bsga	ga	ga	ga.
gdah	da	dā	da.	bsgya	jya	jyā	jya.
gnah	na	nă	na.	bsgra	dra	dra	dra.
gtsah	tsa	tsa	tsa.	brnga	na	nga	nga.
gdzah	dza	dza	dza.	bsnga	na	nh'a	nga.
gzah	za	za	za.	bchah	cha	chiă	chiă.
gyah	ya	ya	ya.	brja	ja	jyă	jyă.
gshah	sha	ha	shia.	brnya	nya	nyă	nyă.
gsah	sa	sa	sa.	bska	ka	ka	ka.
dkah	ka	ka	ka.	brah	ra	ra	ra.
dkya	chya	chya	chya.	brtah	ta	ta	ta.

TIBETAN SYLLABARY, WITH PRONUNCIATION OF LH'ASA, BAT'ANG, AND THE TSARONG — *Continued*

Transcription.	Lh'asa.	Bat'ang.	Tsarong.	Transcription.	Lh'asa.	Bat'ang.	Tsarong.
blta .	ta....	ta......	ta.	mch'ah	ch'a..	ch'ia ...	ch'ia.
bsta..	ta.. .	ta......	ta.	mjah.	ja....	nja.. ..	ja.
bngah	na ...	nga	nga.	mnyah	nya ..	nya	nya.
bdah .	da ...	d'a. ...	da.	mt'ah	t'a ...	t'a	t'a.
brda	da ...	da	da.	mdah	da ...	nda	da.
blda	da ...	da	da.	mnah	na ...	na	na.
bsda	da ...	da	da.	mts'ah	ts'a ..	ts'a	ts'a.
bsna .	na ...	na ..	na.	mdjah	dja.	dja.....	dza.
brna .	na ...	na	na.	hk'ah	k'a...	k'a.....	k'a.
btsah.	tsa...	tsa	tsa.	hk'ya	ch'ya.	ch'ya...	ch'ya.
brtsa .	tsa...	tsa.....	tsa.	hk'ra .	tra ...	tra.....	tra.
bstsa.	tsa...	tsa or sa	tsa.	hgah .	ga . .	ga	ga.
brdja.	dja...	dja...	za.	hgya .	gya ..	gya	gya.
bdzah	dza ..	dza	dza.	hgra .	dra ..	dra	tra.
bzah .	za ...	za	za.	hch'ah	ch'a..	ch'a....	ch'a.
bzla..	da ..	da	da.	hjah	ja....	nja ..	ja.
brla..	la....	la......	la.	ht'ah .	t'a ...	t'a	t'a.
bshah	sha ..	ha	shia.	hdah .	da ...	nda	da.
bsah .	sa....	sa......	sa.	hdra	dra ..	dra	dra.
bsra	sa ...	sa......	sa.	hp'ya.	p'a...	p'a.....	p'a.
bsla..	la....	lh'a	da.	hp'ya	ch'a..	hsia....	hsia.
mk'ah	k'a...	k'a.....	k'a.	hp'ra .	tr'a ..	t'ra	tr'a.
mk'ya	ch'ya.	ch'ya...	ch'ya.	hbah .	ba ...	ba	ba.
mk'ra	tr'a ..	tr'a	tr'a.	hbya .	ja ...	hsia....	hsia.
mga..	ga ...	nga	ga.	hbra	dra ..	dra	dra.
mgya	gya ..	gya	gya.	hts'ah	ts'a ..	ts'a	ts'a.
mgra.	dra ..	dra	dra.	hdja	dja ..	dja ...	dja.
mngah	na ...	nga	nga.				

VIII

ITINERARY, AND BAROMETRIC OBSERVATIONS

In the following table will be found my itinerary, with observed aneroid measures and deduced altitudes. From Peking to the water-shed between the basin of the Yellow River and the Dré ch'u (reached May 17, 1889), I have taken Peking as my lower station, using, in calculating the barometric pressure and temperature, the tables published by H. Fritsche in H. Wild's "Repertorium für Meteorologie," Bd. V, pp. 25 and 35. From the summit of Mt. Rawa to Ta-chien-lu I have taken Ch'ung-ch'ing (Ssŭ-ch'uan) as my lower station, using the tables prepared by E. C. Baber in his "Archæological Researches in Western China," p. 145.

I claim no great exactitude for the deduced altitudes; such was absolutely impossible under the circumstances, but considering the roughness of my work the results compare fairly well with those obtained by previous travelers wherever our routes have crossed. It will be noticed that the altitudes I have obtained are all about $\frac{1}{10}$ higher than those of Pundit A—K—. The constant difference arises probably from our methods of calculating; had I simply deduced the altitude from the reading of the aneroid without using a lower station or applying corrections for temperature (the method followed in his case, I believe), our observations would be found to agree closely.[1]

I repeatedly made observations for altitude by boiling-point thermometer, and have applied the corrections thus supplied to my aneroid readings.

In the column of remarks I have put down altitudes given by Colonel Prjevalsky, A—K—, Lieutenant Kreitner, and Colonel Mark Bell.

[1] A comparison of heights calculated by Captain Wm. Gill with those of A—K— between Ta-chien-lu and Nyach'u-k'a, shows differences ranging from 400 to 800 feet.

ITINERARY, AND CALCULATION OF ALTITUDES

Date.	Place.	Distance (in miles).	Corr. Bar.	Ther.	Bar. at L. S.	Ther. at L. S.	Deduced Altitude (in feet).	Remarks.
1888.	Peking							Alt. 123 ft. (Fritsche, 37 m. 50.)
Dec. 19	Pao-ting Fu	111½	29.40	28.0	30.21	28.0	823	Probably 200 feet too high.
" 20	Fang hsün ch'iao	20	29.25	33.0	30.21	28.0	785	Probably 50 feet too low.
" 20	Ching feng tien	21½	29.05	34.0	30.21	28.0	1150	
" 21	" "	......	29.25	......	30.22	......	975	N. B.—For localities where correction for temperature has not been made, multiply by $\frac{1}{12}$ the altitude given.
" 21	Fu-cheng-i	43⅓	28.85	......	30.22	......	1335	
" 22	Huo-lu Hsien	33⅓	28.90	......	30.22	......	1289	
" 22	Pass W. of town	8⅓	28.40	......	30.22	......	745	
" 22	Yü shui	8⅓	28.65	32.0	30.22	28.0	1509	
" 23	Pei t'ien men (Gate in Great Wall)	......	26.85	......	30.22	......	3212	
" 23	Huai shui P'u	22	26.70	......	30.22	......	3358	
" 23	Pass	8⅓	25.75	......	30.22	......	4305	
" 23	Hsi chiao P'u	16½	26.75	......	30.22	......	3309	
" 24	Ch'ang-ch'ing-i	23⅓	25.75	......	30.22	......	4305	
" 24	T'u-hsü ling (Pass)	......	25.25	......	30.22	......	4817	
" 24	Huang men	48	25.95	......	30.22	......	4103	
" 25	Shih lieh	25	25.70	......	30.22	......	4356	
" 25	Ming tien	15	26.75	23.0	30.22	28.0	3259	
" 26	T'ai-yüan Fu	17	26.80	31.0	30.22	28.0	3240	Col. Mark Bell, 2260 feet.
" 27	Pei ko chen	17	26.80	......	30.23	......	3270	
	Carried forward	438½						

ITINERARY, AND CALCULATION OF ALTITUDES—*Continued*

Date.	Place.	Distance (in miles).	Corr. Bar.	Ther.	Bar. at L. S.	Ther. at L. S.	Deduced Altitude (in feet).	Remarks.
1888.	Brought forward	438½						
Dec. 27	Kao hua	17	26.80	.....	30.23	.....	3318	
" 28	Hung shan ts'un	28⅓	27.05	.....	30.23	.....	3058	
" 28	Chang-lan ch'eng	16	26.95	.....	30.23	.....	3124	
" 29	Liang t'u	31½	26.95	.....	30.23	.....	3124	
" 29	Ling shih Hsien	10	26.95	.....	30.23	.....	3124	
" 30	Han Hou ling (Pass)	6½	25.90	.....	30.23	.....	4162	
" 30	Lao ch'ang wan	18	25.95	.....	30.23	.....	4112	
" 30	Huo Chou	15	27.45	.....	30.23	.....	2643	
" 31	Chao ch'eng Hsien	20	27.95	.....	30.23	.....	2272	
" 31	Han-lo Hsien	10	28.05	.....	30.23	.....	2078	
" 31	T'ien hsing	10	28.20	.....	30.23	.....	1939	
1889.								
Jan. 1	Chao ch'ü ch'eng	23⅓	28.30	.....	30.24	.....	1846	
" 1	Kao Hsien	20	28.30	.....	30.24	.....	1846	
" 2	Nieh kou	17⅓	28.25	.....	30.24	.....	1902	
" 2	Wen hsi Hsien	20	28.35	.....	30.24	.....	1809	
" 3	Chiang-ch'ün miao	23	28.45	.....	30.24	.....	1717	
" 3	Liu-t'u ch'eng	17	28.60	.....	30.24	.....	1580	
" 4	Yü chih	31½	28.80	.....	30.24	.....	1399	
	Carried forward	773						

ITINERARY, AND CALCULATION OF ALTITUDES—*Continued*

Date.	Place.	Distance (in miles).	Corr. Bar.	Ther.	Bar. at L. S.	Ther. at L. S.	Deduced Altitude (in feet).	Remarks.
1889.	Brought forward	773						
Jan. 5	Hai yang ch'eng	15	28.85	......	30.24	......	1353	
" 5	Bank of Yellow River	17	28.90	......	30.24	......	1307	
" 5	T'ung kuan	1	28.85	......	30.24	......	1353	Col. Bell, 1560 feet.
" 6	Hsi yüeh miao	11½	28.75	......	30.24	......	1443	
" 6	Hua Hsien	25	28.95	......	30.24	......	1262	Probably 200 feet too low.
" 6	Wei-nan Hsien	17½	28.85	......	30.24	......	1353	
" 7	Lin kou	13	28.65	......	30.25	......	1542	
" 7	Lin t'ung Hsien	26	28.35	......	30.25	......	1817	
" 8	Hsi-an Fu	17	28.35	37.0	30.25	24.0	1809	Bell, 1700 feet.
" 10	Hsien-yang Hsien	17½	28.00	......	30.25	......	2142	
" 11	Li chüan Hsien	23	27.45	......	30.25	......	2660	
" 11	T'ieh Fo ssŭ	15	26.45	......	30.25	......	3630	
" 12	Yung shou Hsien	17	25.15	......	30.25	......	4947	
" 12	Col N. of Yung shou	4	24.95	......	30.25	......	5125	
" 12	Ta yü	9	26.25	30.0	30.25	24.0	3786	
" 13	Ping Chou	10	26.95	30.0	30.25	24.0	3141	Bell, 2620 feet.
" 13	T'ing k'ou	17	27.00	30.0	30.25	24.0	3092	
" 14	Chang-wu Hsien	13	25.80	30.0	30.26	24.0	4289	
" 14	Yao-tien (Kan-su)	10	25.50	30.0	30.26	24.0	4595	
	Carried forward	1051½						

ITINERARY, AND CALCULATION OF ALTITUDES—*Continued*

Date.	Place.	Distance (in miles).	Corr. Bar.	Ther.	Bar. at L. S.	Ther. at L. S.	Deduced Altitude (in feet).	Remarks.
1889.	Brought forward	1051½						
Jan. 14	Kao ch'ia niao	10	25.25	17.0	30.26	24.0	4726	
" 14	Ching Chou	16⅓	26.35	......	30.26	......	3738	
" 15	Hua-tê shuang	20	26.10	23.0	30.26	24.0	3918	
" 15	Ssŭ-shih li P'u	20	25.35	44.0	30.26	24.0	4769	
" 16	Ping-liang Fu	13⅓	25.55	24.0	30.26	24.0	4464	Bell, 4700 feet.
" 16	Hao tien	23⅓	24.40	......	30.26	......	5750	
" 17	Wa t'ing kuan	8	23.75	......	30.26	......	6452	Bell, 6000. Kreitner, 5702.
" 17	Wu sh'eng P'u	5	23.05	......	30.26	......	7234	
" 17	Summit of Liu p'an shan	5	21.25	......	30.26	......	9358	Bell, 8700. Kreitner, 8550.
" 17	Lung-tê Hsien	5	23.05	22.0	30.26	24.0	7092	
" 18	Ching-ning Chou	30	24.30	......	30.26	......	5885	
" 18	Kao ch'ia P'u	17	24.20	28.0	30.26	24.0	5852	
" 19	Ch'ing chia i	13½	23.25	......	30.26	......	7008	
" 19	Pass west of town	6	23.00	......	30.26	......	7290	
" 19	T'ai-ping tien	3	23.40	......	30.26	......	6840	
" 19	Ch'ang-ch'eng P'u	15	23.80	26.0	30.26	24.0	6399	
" 20	Hui-ning Hsien	7	23.90	......	30.26	......	6288	
" 21	Hsi k'ung-i	20	23.90	......	30.26	......	6288	
" 21	An-t'ing Hsien	20	23.55	......	30.26	......	6673	
	Carried forward	1309						

ITINERARY, AND CALCULATION OF ALTITUDES—*Continued*

Date.	Place.	Distance (in miles).	Corr. Bar.	Ther.	Bar. at L. S.	Ther. at L. S.	Deduced Altitude (in feet).	Remarks.
1889.	Brought forward	1309						
Jan. 21	Ts'an k'ou	17	23.75	.....	30.26	......	6452	
" 22	Pass west of town	10	22.50	......	30.26	......	7865	
" 22	Kan ts'ao tien	13	23.60	......	30.26	.....	6618	
" 22	Ch'eng kou i	13	24.05	36.0	30.26	24.0	6097	
" 23	Tung kuan P'u	23	24.60	33.0	30.25	24.0	5476	
" 24	Lan Chou Fu	5	24.60	32.0	30.25	24.0	5476[1]	Bell has 5500.
Feb. 3	Hsin ch'eng	23	24.65	27.0	30.23	29.0	5506	
" 4	Mouth of Hsi-ning ho	6	24.55	33.0	30.23	29.0	5648	
5	Ho-tui tzŭ	17	24.20	28.0	30.23	29.0	5948	
" 7	Hsiang-t'ang (mouth of Ta-t'ung ho)	30	23.75	26.0	30.22	29.0	6417	
" 8	Nien-po Hsien	32	23.25	37.0	30.21	29.0	6980	
" 8	Ch'ang ch'i ts'ai	15	23.00	29.0	30.21	29.0	7209	Obs. on 9th gives average of 7115.
" 9	Hsi-ning Fu	22⅓	22.70	29.0	30.21	29.0	7540[2]	Kreitner, 7559.
10	Summit of range south of city	2	22.00	22.0	30.21	29.0	8317	
" 10	Summit of range east of Lusar	17	21.10	39.0	30.21	29.0	9541	
" 10	Lusar (Kumbum)	⅓	21.15	39.0	30.21	29.0	9468[3]	
" 24	Serkok gomba (Kuo-mang-ssŭ)	52	21.10	25.0	30.13	29.0	9278	
March 4	Chen hai P'u	13½	22.00	32.0	30.09	41.0	8376	Distance counted from Lusar.
	Carried forward	1620⅙						

[1] An average of 14 observations made from Jan. 24 to Feb. 3 gives 5416 feet as the altitude of this city. [2] Average of 8 observations in February, 7676 feet. [3] Average of 57 observations from February 10 to March 23, 1889, gives 9285 feet.

ITINERARY, AND CALCULATION OF ALTITUDES—*Continued*

Date	Place.	Distance (in miles).	Corr. Bar.	Ther.	Bar. at L. S.	Ther. at L. S.	Deduced Altitude (in feet).	Remarks.
1889.	Brought forward	1620⅙						
Mar. 5	Tankar (Tan-ka-erh)	17½	21.30	41.0	30.08	41.0	9,320[1]	
" 25	Gomba soba	13	20.80	30.0	29.96	41.0	9,727	Average with obs. of 26th, 9,495 ft.
" 26	Hsi-ning ho	25	20.35	38.0	29.96	41.0	10,385	Average with obs. of 27th, 10,254 ft.
" 27	Water-shed of Koko-nor	25½	19.15	58.0	29.95	41.0	12,248	
" 27	Rongwa gu	6½	19.80	18.0	29.95	41.0	10,864	Aver. with obs. of 28th, 29th, 11,023.
" 29	Hargi t'ang	15½	19.75	33.0	29.94	41.0	11,113	Aver. with obs. of 30th, 10,960.[2]
" 30	Dré ch'u	17½	19.60	43.0	29.94	41.0	11,437	Aver. with obs. of 31st, 11,251.
" 31	Chou ch'u	9	19.55	58.0	29.93	41.0	11,400	
" 31	Hata	7½	19.30	44.0	29.93	41.0	11,495	Average with obs. April 1st, 11,473.
Apr. 1	Plateau west of Hata	7	18.85	41.0	29.92	56.0	12,524	
" 1	Ch'u-jya gi	23	19.45	33.0	29.92	56.0	11,675	Average with obs. Ap. 2d, 11,550. Buha gol 30 to 40 feet lower.
" 2	Kundu lung	15½	18.90	38.0	29.92	56.0	12,524	Average with obs. Ap. 3d, 12,329.
" 3	Pass over Dagar té ch'en	6	18.30	28.0	29.91	56.0	13,243	Prjevalsky, for Pass a few miles east, 13,500.
" 3	Dorung charu	6	19.45	35.0	29.91	56.0	11,690	
" 4	Tsahan-nor	3⅓	19.55	30.0	29.91	56.0	11,503	
" 4	Dulan kuo	12	19.80	40.0	29.90	56.0	11,283[3]	Prjevalsky, 10,600.
" 8	Dulan (or Hulan)-nor	15	20.15	58.0	29.88	56.0	11,108	Probably 200 feet too high.
" 9	South of Dabesun-nor	3	20.35	40.0	29.87	56.0	10,505	
	Carried forward	1848						

[1] Average of 14 observations from March 5 to 25, gives 9389 feet. [2] No perceptible difference of level with Lake Koko-nor. Prjevalsky has for Koko-nor 10,000, 10,495, 10,547, and 10,700. Kreitner has 10,934. [3] Average of 8 obs. from April 4 to 8, gave 11,108 feet.

ITINERARY, AND CALCULATION OF ALTITUDES—*Continued*

Date.	Place.	Distance (in miles).	Corr. Bar.	Ther.	Bar. at L. S.	Ther. at L. S.	Deduced Altitude (in feet).	Remarks.
1889.	Brought forward	1848						
April 9	Head of Kashu osu	12	19.60	60.0	29.87	56.0	11,326	
" 9	Talun turgen (Tsatsa gol)	14	20.20	37.0	29.87	56.0	10,660	Average with obs. April 10, 10,482. Prjevalsky, 9,700.
10	Sulim bomen (Tsatsa gol)	5	20.35	72.0	29.87	56.0	10,862	Average with obs. April 11, 10,419.
" 11	Ergetsu (Tsatsa gol)	15	20.45	81.0	29.86	56.0	10,803	Average with obs. April 12, 10,357.
" 12	Camp in Dsün	18	20.65	48.0	29.86	56.0	10,185	Average with obs. April 13, 10,084.
" 13	Tsuhu	16½	20.70	45.0	29.85	56.0	10,067	Average with obs. April 14, 9,904.
" 15	Village of Baron Ts'aidam	19½	20.85	32.0	29.84	56.0	9,739	Average with obs. April 16, 9,880.
" 16	Shang (Village)	32	20.25	41.0	29.84	56.0	10,611	Average with 16 obs. April 16 to 24, 10,493 feet.
" 24	Yohuré gol (Upper Bayan gol)	28	19.50	35.0	29.79	56.0	11,512	Average with obs. April 25, 11,439.
" 25	Amyé kor (Pass)	27	16.15	20.0	29.78	56.0	16,222	
" 25	Camp south of Pass	2	16.60	35.0	29.78	56.0	15,831	Average with obs. April 26, 15,786.
" 26	Tseldum gol	18½	17.05	33.0	29.77	56.0	15,071	Tosun-nor 500 feet lower.
" 27	Confluence Yohuré and Alang gol	21	18.25	50.0	29.77	56.0	13,502	Average with obs. April 28, 13,325.
" 28	Alang gol (mouth of Yuktu gol)	30	17.95	35.0	29.76	56.0	13,712	Average with obs. April 29, 13,517.
" 29	Alang nor	11	17.80	59.0	29.75	56.0	14,286	Probably 300 feet too high.
" 29	Nomoran k'utul (Pass)	14	16.10	28.0	29.75	56.0	16,521	Prjevalsky has 16,100.
" 30	North side of Pass	2	17.10	30.0	29.75	56.0	14,944	
	Carried forward	2133½						

ITINERARY, AND CALCULATION OF ALTITUDES — *Continued*

Date.	Place.	Distance (in miles.)	Corr. Bar.	Ther.	Bar. at L. S.	Ther. at L. S.	Deduced Altitude (in feet.)	Remarks.
1889.	Brought forward	2133½						
May 1	Narim (Baron dsassak)	13½	18.90	52.0	29.75	67.0	12,554	Av. 10 obs. May 1st to 5th, 12,354.
" 5	Iké gol	13	19.00	36.0	29.72	67.0	12,304	
" 6	Hato gol	7	18.25	36.0	29.72	67.0	13,287	Average with obs. May 7th, 13,209.
" 7	Hato k'utul (Pass)	6½	17.00	34.0	29.71	67.0	15,290	
" 7	Yuktu ulan bulak	17	17.85	29.0	29.71	67.0	13,906	Prjevalsky for Yamtu ulan bulak, 10 miles west, has 13,400.
" 8	Bordza kéra k'utul (Pass)	20	16.80	35.0	29.71	67.0	15,646	
" 8	Dsatsu hosho	14	17.15	28.0	29.71	67.0	14,925	
" 9	Camp 200 ft. above Karma t'ang	18	17.40	40.0	29.70	67.0	14,619	Av. with obs. April 10th, 14,487.
" 10	Tsulmé tsarang k'utul (Pass)	12	16.90	45.0	29.70	67.0	15,639	
" 11	Tsulmé t'aug	9	17.20	25.0	29.69	67.0	14,828	Av. 4 obs. April 10th, 12th, 14,972.
" 12	Pass to Lamatolha	5½	16.95	42.0	29.69	67.0	15,602	
" 12	Dojong valley	14	17.00	30.0	29.69	67.0	15,208	Av. with obs. April 13th, 15,147.
" 13	Pass	7	16.95	42.0	29.68	67.0	15,473	
" 13	Rajong valley	9	17.20	32.0	29.68	67.0	14,881	Av. with obs. April 14th, 14,806.
" 14	South of Rajong	11	17.20	34.0	29.67	67.0	14,935	
" 16	North side of Rawa (Pass)	12	16.80	18.0	29.66	67.0	15,369	
" 17	Rawa la (Pass)	½	16.55	20.0	29.01	70.0	15,509	Ch'ung-ch'ing as lower station.
" 17	Mar jya kou	9½	17.80	42.0	29.01	70.0	13,750	
	Carried forward	2332						

ITINERARY, AND CALCULATION OF ALTITUDES—*Continued*

Date.	Place.	Distance (in miles).	Corr. Bar.	Ther.	Bar. at L. S.	Ther. at L. S.	Deduced Altitude (in feet).	Remarks.
1889.	Brought forward	2332						
May 18	Ser jong	4	17.85	41.0	28.95	73.0	14,180	Av. 5 obs. May 18th, 20th, 13,881.
" 20	Lh'a dang la (Pass)	9	17.30	52.0	29.01	70.0	15,220	
" 20	Ta kou	9	18.35	48.0	28.95	73.0	13,498	Av. with obs. May 21st, 13,259.
" 21	Oyo la (Pass)	10	16.70	56.0	28.90	76.0	15,673	
" 21	South side of Pass	1	17.75	41.0	28.95	73.0	14,335	
" 22	Rungo la (Pass)	7	16.95	54.0	29.01	70.0	15,820	
" 22	Bank of Dré ch'u (UpperYang-tzŭ)	5	18.75	43.0	28.90	73.0	13,002	Average with obs. May 23d, 12,746. Camp 100 feet above river.[1]
" 23	Yonyik valley	6	18.15	42.0	28.95	73.0	13,721	
" 24	Yonyik la (Pass)	3	16.40	35.0	29.01	70.0	16,308	
" 24	Tagluug la (Pass)	1	16.25	43.0	29.01	70.0	16,659	
" 24	Ranyik valley	9	17.95	40.0	28.95	73.0	13,998	Av. with obs. May 25th, 13,869.
" 25	Nyi ch'en la (Pass)	4½	16.55	50.0	29.01	70.0	16,453	
" 25	Jyékundo	9	18.75	55.0	28.95	73.0	12,999	Average 8 obs., May 25th–29th, 12,941. A— K— has 11,800.
" 29	Head of Momé valley	24	17.45	45.0	28.90	75.0	14,283	
" 30	Trugu	16	18.80	54.0	28.95	73.0	12,901	Av. with obs. May 31st, 12,880. Village 400 feet above Dré ch'u.
	Carried forward	2449½						

[1] Prjevalsky gives altitude of river, about 30 miles west of this place, as 13,100; and A— K— has 11,990 as height at Tuden gomba (Chudé gomba?), some 30 miles below it.

ITINERARY, AND CALCULATION OF ALTITUDES—*Continued*

Date.	Place.	Distance (in miles).	Corr. Bar.	Ther.	Bar. at L. S.	Ther. at L. S.	Deduced Altitude (in feet).	Remarks.
1889.	Brought forward	2449½						
May 31	Drenda (Ferry over Dré ch'u)	11½	19.40	52.0	28.95	73.0	12,000	Average with obs. June 1, 11,763.[1] House 300 feet above river.
June 1	Kawalendo	18½	19.75	54.0	28.91	77.0	11,531	Average with obs. June 2, 11,461. Village 200 ft. above Dré ch'u.
" 2	Rarta	9	18.50	54.0	28.91	77.0	13,363	
" 3	Rigé	17	18.65	51.0	28.84	80.0	13,079	
" 4	Latsé kadri (Pass)	11	17.75	60.0	28.84	80.0	14,596	
" 4	Shéma t'ang	5	18.20	45.0	28.84	80.0	13,672	Average with obs. June 5, 13,463.
" 5	Pass into Muri ch'u valley	7½	18.45	52.0	28.93	75.0	12,881	
" 6	Zoch'en gomba	5	18.60	39.0	28.93	75.0	13,026	Probably 300 feet too high.
" 6	Muri la (Pass)	10	17.00	65.0	28.84	80.0	15,880	
" 7	Muri ts'o (Lake)	4½	18.20	35.0	28.93	75.0	13,572	
" 8	Yi ch'u valley	5	18.55	39.0	28.93	75.0	13,000	
" 9	Yi ch'u valley (facing Ito ri)	17	19.00	39.0	28.93	75.0	12,339	
" 10	Gényi (on Za ch'u)	20	19.45	52.0	28.93	75.0	11,930	Village 300 feet above river.
" 11	Kanzé	16	19.55	54.0	28.93	75.0	11,711	Average with obs. June 11 to 13, 11,830. A— K— has 10,200.
" 13	Chuwo	25	19.35	61.0	28.91	77.0	12,197	
" 14	Rantro	15	19.85	60.0	28.91	77.0	11,453	Village on bank of river.
" 16	Chango	17	19.30	60.0	28.93	75.0	11,171	Town 300 feet above river.
	Carried forward	2663½						

[1] A—K—has for Seupa, about 5 miles below the ferry, 10,890 feet.

ITINERARY, AND CALCULATION OF ALTITUDES — *Continued*

Date.	Place.	Distance (in miles).	Corr. Bar.	Ther.	Bar. at L. S.	Ther. at L. S.	Deduced Altitude (in feet).	Remarks.
1889.	Brought forward	2663½						
June 17	Ta chai	32½						
" 18	Dawo (Jésenyi)	12					10,500	Estimated.
" 20	Koja	16						
" 21	Tsonya	18½						
" 22	Kata (Tai-ling)	12						
" 23	Hsin tien	28						
" 24	Ta-chien-lu	30					8,480	E. C. Baber.
July 10	Wa-ssŭ k'ou	15					4,933	Capt. Wm. Gill.
" 11	Lu-ting ch'iao (Bridge)	16					4,515	E. C. Baber.
" 12	Hua-lin-p'ing	17½					7,073	E. C. Baber.
" 13	Fei-yüeh ling (Pass)	17½					9,410	E. C. Baber.
" 13	Ni-t'ou	12½					5,090	E. C. Baber.
" 14	Ch'ing-ch'i Hsien	22					5,478	Capt. Wm. Gill.
" 16	Kuan-yin P'u	15½					3,725	Capt. Wm. Gill.
" 17	She ch'ia P'u	16½					2,190	Capt. Wm. Gill.
" 18	Ya-chou Fu	16					1,671	Capt. Wm. Gill.
" 20	Mu chin kai	16						
" 21	Chia-ting Fu	70						
" 22	Chuo ch'i	87						
	Carried forward	3134						

ITINERARY, AND CALCULATION OF ALTITUDES — *Continued*

Date.	Place.	Distance (in miles).	Corr. Bar.	Ther.	Bar. at L. S.	Ther. at L. S.	Deduced Altitude (in feet).	Remarks.
1869.	Brought forward	3134						
July 23	Sui Fu	35						
" 23	Lu Chou	60						
" 24	Chiang-ching Hsien	75						
" 25	Ch'ung-ch'ing Fu	30	.....	.....	.....	.....	845	E. C. Baber.
Aug. 4	Lo chi	45½	.....	.....	.....	.....	.....	Distance estimated by Capt. Gill.
" 5	Chung Chou	118½	.....	.....	.....	.....	.....	Distance estimated by Capt. Gill.
" 6	Kuei Chou	126	.....	.....	.....	.....	.....	Distance estimated by Capt. Gill.
" 7	West of Ta-tung rapids	95	.....	.....	.....	.....	.....	Distance estimated by Capt. Gill.
" 8	I-ch'ang	30	.....	.....	.....	.....	.....	Distance estimated by Capt. Gill.
" 16	Han-k'ou	350						
" 20	Shang-hai	600						
	Total	4699						

INDEX

GENERAL INDEX

(N. B.— Words in parentheses supply alternative names.)

I

J

L

M

N

O

P

Q

R

T

U

V

W

Y